# Abu Dhabi
## street atlas

The **Complete A to Z** Street Atlas

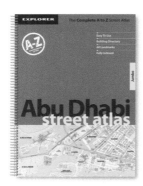

**Abu Dhabi Street Atlas** 1st Edition   ISBN 13 - 978-9948-441-20-5

**Explorer Publishing & Distribution**
PO Box 34275, Dubai, United Arab Emirates
**Phone** (+971 4) 340 8805 **Fax** (+971 4) 340 8806
**Email** info@explorerpublishing.com
**Web** www.explorerpublishing.com

# Contents

## Welcome...

... to the most significant advancement in Abu Dhabi navigation since the compass. The staff at Explorer have worked non-stop for over six months to bring you the most complete, most up-to-date street and building atlas ever. Along with 122 pages of detailed maps, there is an easy-to-use index categorised by streets & roads and places & buildings. There is also a categorised directory that lists the venues you most use, such as restaurants, hospitals and malls. If you know the name of your destination, chances are it's listed in the index and marked on the map. Happy navigating.

The Explorer Team

**For more information about Explorer Products see the back section.**
Explorer has long provided Abu Dhabi residents with the best maps and guidebooks available. From the Mini Guides and Residents' Guides to the popular Mini Map series, Explorer Publishing has Abu Dhabi covered.

### Introduction

| | |
|---|---|
| Emergency Rooms & Police Stations | IV |
| Driving In Abu Dhabi | VIII |
| Main Roads & Area Names | X |
| Customising Explorer Products | XII |

### Quick Reference Directory

| | |
|---|---|
| Embassies & Consulates | VI |
| Hospitals | VI |
| Hotels | VI |
| Restaurants & Nightlife | VI |
| Shopping Malls | VII |
| Universities & Higher Education | VII |

### Maps

| | | |
|---|---|---|
| Maps 1-39 | Detailed City Maps | 1 |
| Maps 40-61 | Surrounding Area Maps | 40 |

### Index

| | |
|---|---|
| Street & Road Index | 62 |
| Place & Building Index | 66 |

**EXPLORER**

Of course, Abu Dhabi is developing at a fearsome rate, and new projects are popping up all the time. If you notice that a road has closed, a track has opened, or another development is rising from the sands, let Explorer know by logging on to www.explorerpublishing.com or email us at maps@explorerpublishing.com

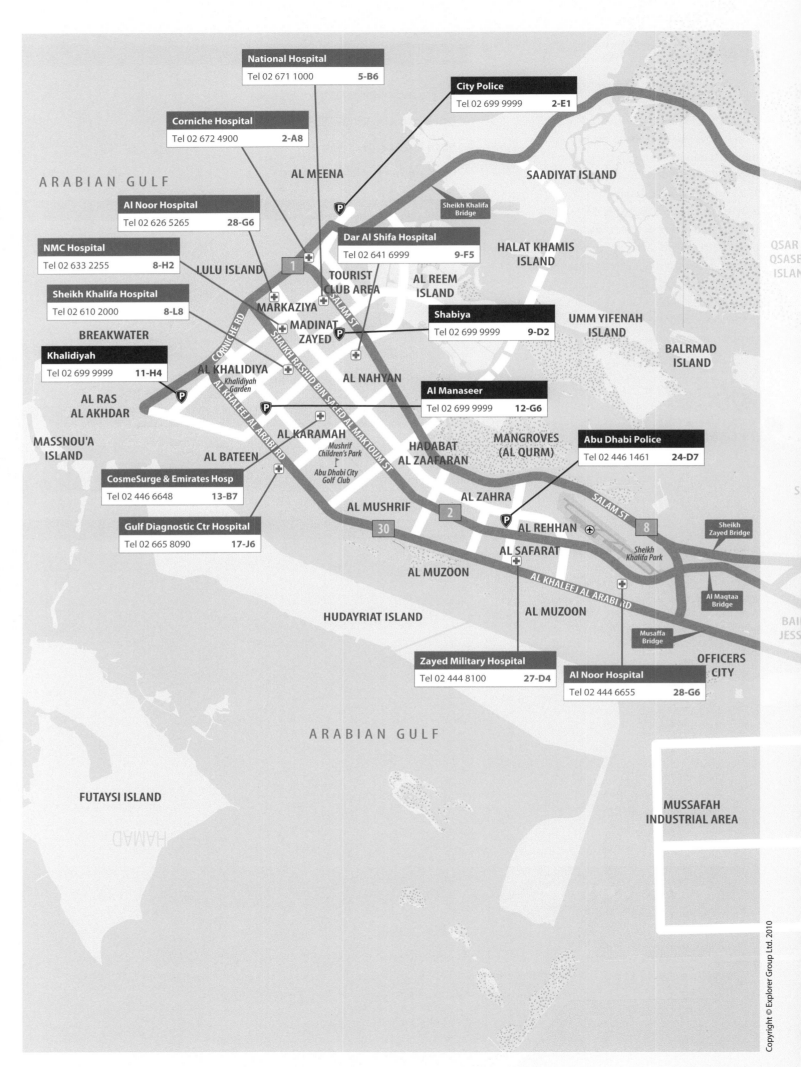

**National Hospital**
Tel 02 671 1000      **5-B6**

**City Police**
Tel 02 699 9999      **2-E1**

**Corniche Hospital**
Tel 02 672 4900      **2-A8**

ARABIAN GULF

AL MEENA

SAADIYAT ISLAND

Sheikh Khalifa Bridge

**Al Noor Hospital**
Tel 02 626 5265      **28-G6**

**Dar Al Shifa Hospital**
Tel 02 641 6999      **9-F5**

HALAT KHAMIS ISLAND

QSAR QSASE ISLAN

**NMC Hospital**
Tel 02 633 2255      **8-H2**

LULU ISLAND

TOURIST CLUB AREA

AL REEM ISLAND

UMM YIFENAH ISLAND

**Sheikh Khalifa Hospital**
Tel 02 610 2000      **8-L8**

MARKAZIYA

**Shabiya**
Tel 02 699 9999      **9-D2**

BALRMAD ISLAND

BREAKWATER

MADINAT ZAYED

**Khalidiyah**
Tel 02 699 9999      **11-H4**

AL KHALIDIYA

Khalidiyah Garden

AL NAHYAN

AL RAS AL AKHDAR

**Al Manaseer**
Tel 02 699 9999      **12-G6**

MASSNOU'A ISLAND

AL KARAMAH

Mushrif Children's Park

Abu Dhabi City Golf Club

HADABAT AL ZAAFARAN

MANGROVES (AL QURM)

**Abu Dhabi Police**
Tel 02 446 1461      **24-D7**

AL BATEEN

**CosmeSurge & Emirates Hosp**
Tel 02 446 6648      **13-B7**

AL MUSHRIF

AL ZAHRA

SALAM ST

**Gulf Diagnostic Ctr Hospital**
Tel 02 665 8090      **17-J6**

30

2

AL REHHAN

Sheikh Zayed Bridge

Sheikh Khalifa Park

8

AL SAFARAT

AL MUZOON

Al Maqtaa Bridge

HUDAYRIAT ISLAND

AL KHALEEJ AL ARABI RD

AL MUZOON

BAI JESS

Musaffa Bridge

OFFICERS CITY

**Zayed Military Hospital**
Tel 02 444 8100      **27-D4**

**Al Noor Hospital**
Tel 02 444 6655      **28-G6**

ARABIAN GULF

FUTAYSI ISLAND

HAMAD

MUSSAFAH INDUSTRIAL AREA

CORNICHE RD

SHAIKH RASHID BIN SAEED AL MAKTOUM ST

AL KHALEEJ AL ARABI RD

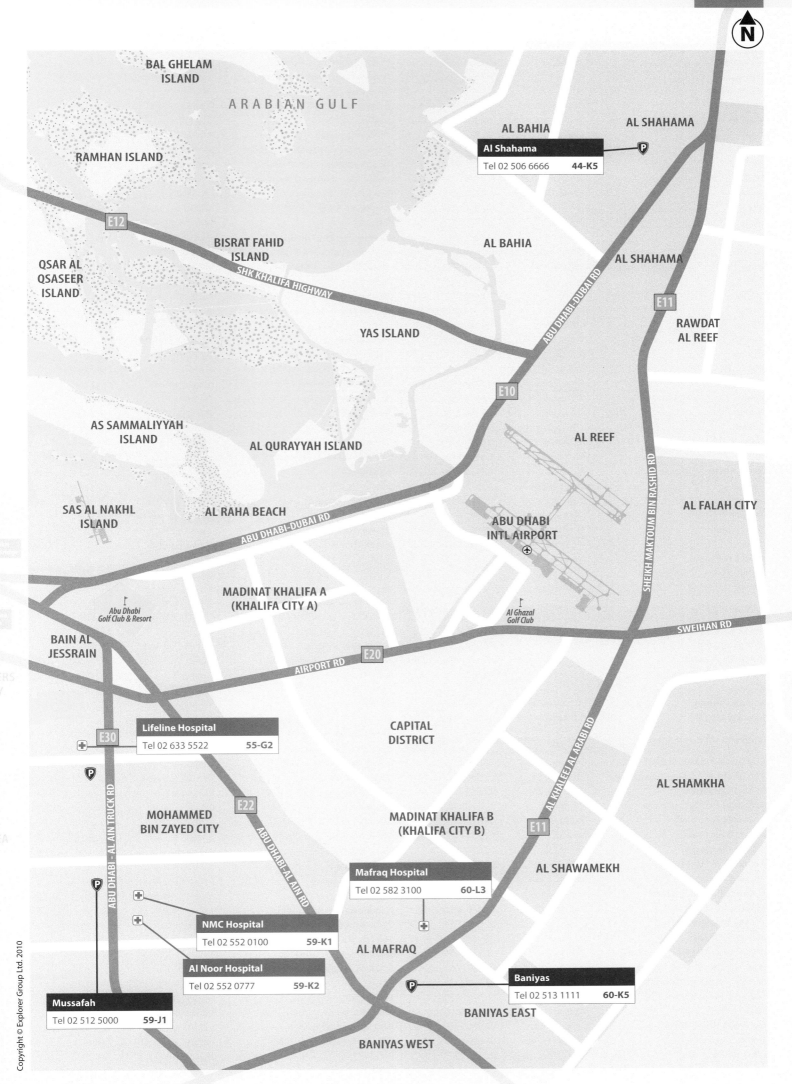

N

ARABIAN GULF

BAL GHELAM ISLAND

RAMHAN ISLAND

E12

QSAR AL QSASEER ISLAND

BISRAT FAHID ISLAND

SHK KHALIFA HIGHWAY

AL BAHIA

AL SHAHAMA

**Al Shahama**
Tel 02 506 6666      **44-K5**

AL BAHIA

AL SHAHAMA

ABU DHABI-DUBAI RD

E11

RAWDAT AL REEF

YAS ISLAND

E10

AS SAMMALIYYAH ISLAND

AL QURAYYAH ISLAND

AL REEF

SHEIKH MAKTOUM BIN RASHID RD

AL FALAH CITY

SAS AL NAKHL ISLAND

AL RAHA BEACH

ABU DHABI-DUBAI RD

ABU DHABI INTL AIRPORT

MADINAT KHALIFA A (KHALIFA CITY A)

Abu Dhabi Golf Club & Resort

Al Ghazal Golf Club

SWEIHAN RD

BAIN AL JESSRAIN

E30

AIRPORT RD      E20

CAPITAL DISTRICT

AL KHALEEJ AL ARABI RD

AL SHAMKHA

**Lifeline Hospital**
Tel 02 633 5522      **55-G2**

ABU DHABI - AL AIN TRUCK RD

MOHAMMED BIN ZAYED CITY

E22

ABU DHABI-AL AIN RD

MADINAT KHALIFA B (KHALIFA CITY B)

E11

AL SHAWAMEKH

**Mafraq Hospital**
Tel 02 582 3100      **60-L3**

**NMC Hospital**
Tel 02 552 0100      **59-K1**

AL MAFRAQ

**Al Noor Hospital**
Tel 02 552 0777      **59-K2**

**Mussafah**
Tel 02 512 5000      **59-J1**

**Baniyas**
Tel 02 513 1111      **60-K5**

BANIYAS EAST

BANIYAS WEST

Copyright © Explorer Group Ltd. 2010

Abu Dhabi **Street** Atlas

## Embassies & Consulates

| | | | |
|---|---|---|---|
| Australia | Al Manhal | 02 634 6100 | 8-G4 |
| Bahrain | Al Bateen | 02 665 7500 | 12-B8 |
| Bangladesh | Al Karamah | 02 446 5100 | 12-M8 |
| Belgium | Markaziya East | 02 631 9449 | 4-K6 |
| Canada | Tourist Club Area | 02 694 0300 | 5-G4 |
| China | Al Mushrif | 02 443 4276 | 22-A1 |
| Egypt | Al Safarat | 02 444 5566 | 27-H2 |
| Finland | Markaziya East | 02 632 8927 | 4-K6 |
| France | Al Karamah | 02 443 5100 | 17-L1 |
| Germany | Tourist Club Area | 02 644 6693 | 5-G3 |
| Greece | Al Matar | 02 665 4847 | 24-L2 |
| India | Al Safarat | 02 449 2700 | 27-F2 |
| Iran | Al Safarat | 02 444 7618 | 27-J4 |
| Italy | Al Karamah | 02 331 4167 | 12-L8 |
| Italy | Al Karamah | 02 443 5622 | 12-L8 |
| Japan | Al Karamah | 02 443 5696 | 12-L8 |
| Jordan | Al Safarat | 02 444 7100 | 27-E1 |
| Kenya | Al Bateen | 02 666 6300 | 12-E4 |
| Korea | Al Mushrif | 02 443 5337 | 18-H7 |
| Kuwait | Al Mushrif | 02 447 7146 | 23-C6 |
| Lebanon | Al Safarat | 02 449 2100 | 27-E2 |
| Malaysia | Hadabat Al Zaafaran | 02 448 2775 | 19-D2 |
| The Netherlands | Al Karamah | 02 632 1920 | 12-K8 |
| Oman | Al Mushrif | 02 446 3333 | 18-J7 |
| Pakistan | Al Safarat | 02 444 7800 | 27-E3 |
| Poland | Al Karamah | 02 446 5200 | 13-B7 |
| Qatar | Al Safarat | 02 449 3300 | 27-D3 |
| Russia | Markaziya East | 02 672 1797 | 4-M3 |
| Saudi Arabia | Al Safarat | 02 444 5700 | 27-G2 |
| Spain | Markaziya East | 02 626 9544 | 4-K6 |
| Sri Lanka | Madinat Zayed | 02 631 6444 | 4-M7 |
| Sweden | Madinat Zayed | 02 621 0162 | 4-K8 |
| Switzerland | Al Bateen | 02 627 4636 | 12-E6 |
| Syria | Al Safarat | 02 444 8768 | 27-J3 |
| United Kingdom | Markaziya West | 02 610 1100 | 8-D2 |
| United States Of America | Al Safarat | 02 414 2200 | 27-F3 |
| Yemen | Al Safarat | 02 444 8457 | 27-E1 |

## Hospitals

### Main Government Hospitals

| | | | |
|---|---|---|---|
| Al Mafraq Hospital | Mahawi | 02 582 3100 | 60-L3 |
| Corniche Hospital | Tourist Club Area | 02 672 4900 | 2-A8 |
| Sheikh Khalifa Medical City | Al Manhal | 02 610 2000 | 8-L8 |

### Main Private Hospitals

| | | | |
|---|---|---|---|
| Al Noor Hospital | Mohd Bin Zayed City | 02 626 5265 | 59-K2 |
| National Hospital | Al Baladia | 02 671 1000 | 5-B6 |

## Hotels

| | | | |
|---|---|---|---|
| Abu Dhabi Airport Hotel | AUH Intl Airport | 02 575 7377 | 53-D1 |
| Abu Dhabi Plaza Hotel Apartments | Markaziya East | 02 634 7577 | 4-M6 |
| Al Ain Palace Hotel | Markaziya East | 02 679 4777 | 4-K2 |
| Al Baheya Hotel Apartment | Al Bateen | 02 678 0008 | 16-H1 |
| Al Diar Capital Hotel | Tourist Club Area | 02 678 7700 | 2-C7 |
| Al Diar Dana Hotel | Tourist Club Area | 02 645 6000 | 5-E3 |
| Al Diar Mina Hotel | Tourist Club Area | 02 678 1000 | 5-A1 |
| Al Diar Palm Suites Hotel | Al Dhafrah | 02 642 0900 | 9-A5 |
| Al Diar Regency Hotel | Tourist Club Area | 02 676 5000 | 5-A1 |
| Al Hamra Plaza Residence | Al Baladia | 02 672 5000 | 5-A6 |
| Al Maha Arjaan | Markaziya East | 02 610 6666 | 4-L5 |
| Al Raha Beach Hotel | Al Raha | 02 508 0555 | 50-D7 |
| Aloft Abu Dhabi | Al Safarat | 02 406 4700 | 27-J5 |
| Armed Forces Officer's Club & Hotel | Officers Club | 02 441 5900 | 34-A7 |
| Beach Rotana Hotel & Towers | Tourist Club Area | 02 697 9000 | 5-G4 |
| Cassells Ghantoot Hotel & Resort | Markaziya East | 02 506 8888 | 4-G8 |
| City Seasons Al Hamra Hotel | Al Baladia | 02 678 8000 | 5-A6 |
| Cristal Hotel | Madinat Zayed | 02 652 0000 | 8-K1 |
| The Eclipse Boutique Suites | Markaziya East | 02 626 8800 | 4-G6 |
| Emirates Palace | Al Ras Al Akhdar | 02 690 9000 | 10-L5 |
| Emirates Plaza Hotel | Tourist Club Area | 02 672 2000 | 2-C8 |
| Fairmont Bab Al Bahr | Bain Al Jessrain | 02 654 3333 | 29-J8 |
| Fortune Hotel Apartments | Tourist Club Area | 02 645 0666 | 5-E4 |
| Garden View Hotel Apartments | Markaziya East | 02 622 8484 | 4-J5 |
| Gava Hotel | Al Dhafrah | 02 642 5667 | 9-F5 |
| Grand Continental Flamingo Hotel | Markaziya East | 02 626 2200 | 4-L5 |
| Hilton Abu Dhabi | Al Khubeirah | 02 681 1900 | 11-D5 |
| Hilton Baynunah | Markaziya West | 02 632 7777 | 8-C2 |
| Howard Johnson Diplomat Hotel | Markaziya East | 02 671 0000 | 4-L3 |
| InterContinental Abu Dhabi | Al Bateen | 02 666 6888 | 11-D8 |
| International Rotana Inn | Tourist Club Area | 02 677 9900 | 5-B2 |
| Ivory Hotel Apartment | Tourist Club Area | 02 644 7644 | 5-D4 |
| Kingsgate Hotel | Tourist Club Area | 02 499 5000 | 5-E6 |
| L'Arabia | Mohd Bin Zayed City | 02 553 3532 | 55-L3 |
| Le Meridien Abu Dhabi | Tourist Club Area | 02 644 6666 | 5-F2 |
| Le Royal Méridien Abu Dhabi | Markaziya East | 02 674 2020 | 4-L3 |
| Marina Al Bateen Resort | Al Bateen | 02 665 0144 | 16-H4 |
| Millennium Hotel | Markaziya East | 02 342 3333 | 4-K4 |
| Novotel Centre Hotel | Markaziya East | 02 633 3555 | 4-J7 |
| One To One Hotel – The Village | Al Nahyan | 02 495 2000 | 9-J6 |
| Oryx Hotel | Al Khalidiya | 02 681 0001 | 11-K1 |
| Park Rotana | Al Matar | 02 657 3333 | 29-A3 |
| Rainbow Hotel Apartment | Markaziya East | 02 632 6333 | 4-K7 |
| Ramada Abu Dhabi Mafraq Hotel | Mahawi | 02 582 2666 | 60-M3 |
| Ramee Garden Hotel Apartments | Markaziya East | 02 647 4000 | 4-J5 |
| Ramee Guestline Hotel Apartments 1 | Tourist Club Area | 02 674 7000 | 5-C1 |
| Royal Regency Hotel Apartment | Markaziya East | 02 626 6566 | 4-H7 |
| Saba Hotel | Tourist Club Area | 02 644 8333 | 5-F5 |
| Sahara Hotel Apartments | Al Dhafrah | 02 631 9000 | 8-M7 |
| Shangri-La Hotel, Qaryat Al Beri | Bain Al Jessrain | 02 509 8888 | 34-J4 |
| Shangri-La Residences | Bain Al Jessrain | 02 509 8888 | 34-J2 |
| Sheraton Abu Dhabi Hotel & Resort | Tourist Club Area | 02 677 3333 | 4-M1 |
| Sheraton Khalidiya Hotel | Markaziya West | 02 666 6220 | 8-C6 |
| Traders Hotel | Bain Al Jessrain | 02 510 8888 | 34-K1 |
| The Yas Hotel | Yas Island | 02 656 0000 | 50-K2 |
| Zakher Hotel | Markaziya East | 02 627 5300 | 4-L4 |

## Restaurants & Nightlife

### American

| | | | |
|---|---|---|---|
| 49er's The Gold Rush (Al Diar Dana Hotel) | Tourist Club Area | 02 645 6000 | 5-E3 |
| Rock Bottom Café (Al Diar Capital Hotel) | Tourist Club Area | 02 678 7700 | 2-C7 |

### Arabic/Lebanese

| | | | |
|---|---|---|---|
| Al Birkeh (Le Meridien Abu Dhabi) | Tourist Club Area | 02 644 6666 | 5-F2 |
| Ashiyana (Emirates Plaza Hotel) | Tourist Club Area | 02 672 2000 | 2-C8 |
| Atayeb (The Yas Hotel) | Yas Island | 02 656 0000 | 50-K2 |
| La Maison Du Café Najjar (Abu Dhabi Mall) | Tourist Club Area | 02 645 4858 | 5-G3 |
| Mawal (Hilton Abu Dhabi) | Al Khubeirah | 02 681 1900 | 11-D5 |

### Bars, Pubs & Nightclubs

| | | | |
|---|---|---|---|
| 49er's The Gold Rush (Al Diar Dana Hotel) | Tourist Club Area | 02 645 6000 | 5-E3 |
| Black Pearl (Al Raha Beach Hotel) | Al Raha | 02 508 0492 | 50-D7 |
| Bravo Tapas Bar (Sheraton) | Tourist Club Area | 02 677 3333 | 4-M1 |
| Captain's Arms (Le Meridien Abu Dhabi) | Tourist Club Area | 02 644 6666 | 5-F2 |
| The Cellar (Howard Johnson Diplomat Hotel) | Markaziya East | 02 671 0000 | 4-L3 |
| Chameleon (Fairmont Bab Al Bahr) | Bain Al Jessrain | 02 654 3333 | 29-J8 |
| Cinnabar (Hilton Abu Dhabi) | Al Khubeirah | 02 681 1900 | 11-D5 |
| Cloud Nine (Sheraton Abu Dhabi Hotel & Resort) | Tourist Club Area | 02 677 3333 | 4-M1 |
| Dock Side Pool Bar (Marina Al Bateen Resort) | Al Bateen | 02 055 8644 | 16-H4 |
| Escape Lounge (Hilton Abu Dhabi) | Al Khubeirah | 02 692 4247 | 11-D5 |
| G Club (Le Meridien Abu Dhabi) | Tourist Club Area | 02 644 6666 | 5-F2 |
| Havana Club (Emirates Palace) | Al Ras Al Akhdar | 02 690 8021 | 10-L5 |
| Hemingway's (Hilton Abu Dhabi) | Al Khubeirah | 02 681 1900 | 11-D5 |
| Illusions (Le Royal Méridien Abu Dhabi) | Markaziya East | 02 674 2020 | 4-L3 |
| The Jazz Bar & Dining (Hilton Abu Dhabi) | Al Khubeirah | 02 681 1900 | 11-D5 |
| Jhankar (Emirates Plaza Hotel) | Tourist Club Area | 02 672 2000 | 2-C8 |
| L.A.B. – Lounge At The Beach Bar (Beach Rotana Hotel & Towers) | Tourist Club Area | 02 644 3000 | 5-G4 |
| Left Bank (Souk Qaryat Al Beri) | Bain Al Jessrain | 02 558 1680 | 34-J3 |
| Mood Indigo (Novotel Centre Hotel) | Markaziya East | 02 633 3555 | 4-J7 |
| NRG Sports Café (Le Meridien Abu Dhabi) | Tourist Club Area | 02 644 6666 | 5-F2 |
| Opus Bar (Le Meridien Abu Dhabi) | Tourist Club Area | 02 644 6666 | 5-F2 |
| PJ O'Reilly's (Le Royal Méridien Abu Dhabi) | Markaziya East | 02 674 2020 | 4-L3 |

| | | | |
|---|---|---|---|
| **Red Lion** (International Rotana Inn) | Tourist Club Area | 02 677 9900 | 5-B2 |
| **Regent's Court** (Al Diar Regency Hotel) | Tourist Club Area | 02 676 5000 | 5-A1 |
| **Rock Bottom Café** (Al Diar Capital Hotel) | Tourist Club Area | 02 678 7700 | 2-C7 |
| **Rush** (The Yas Hotel) | Yas Island | 02 656 0000 | 50-K2 |
| **SAX** (Le Royal Méridien Abu Dhabi) | Markaziya East | 02 674 2020 | 4-L3 |
| **Scorpio** (International Rotana Inn) | Tourist Club Area | 02 677 9900 | 5-B2 |
| **Sharazad** (Emirates Plaza Hotel) | Tourist Club Area | 02 672 2000 | 2-C8 |
| **Tavern** (Sheraton Abu Dhabi Hotel & Resort) | Tourist Club Area | 02 677 3333 | 4-M1 |
| **Vintage Lounge** (Emirates Plaza Hotel) | Tourist Club Area | 02 672 2000 | 2-C8 |

### Brazilian
**Chamas Brazilian Churrascaria**

| | | | |
|---|---|---|---|
| (InterContinental Abu Dhabi) | Al Bateen | 02 666 6888 | 11-D8 |

### Cafes & Coffee Shops

| | | | |
|---|---|---|---|
| **Al Naba'a Lounge** (Fairmont Bab Al Bahr) | Bain Al Jessrain | 02 654 3333 | 29-J8 |
| **City Café** (Al Maha Arjaan) | Markaziya East | 02 610 6666 | 4-L5 |
| **La Maison Du Café Najjar** (Abu Dhabi Mall) | Tourist Club Area | 02 645 4858 | 5-G3 |
| **Latitude** (The Yas Hotel) | Yas Island | 02 656 0000 | 50-K2 |
| **Longitude** (The Yas Hotel) | Yas Island | 02 656 0000 | 50-K2 |
| **Yas Lounge** (The Yas Hotel) | Yas Island | 02 656 0000 | 50-K2 |

### Chinese

| | | | |
|---|---|---|---|
| **Grand Shanghai** (International Rotana Inn) | Tourist Club Area | 02 677 9900 | 5-B2 |
| **Noodle Box** (The Yas Hotel) | Yas Island | 02 656 0000 | 50-K2 |
| **The Noodle House** (Al Wahda Mall) | Al Nahyan | 02 443 7391 | 13-B1 |
| **Restaurant China** (Novotel Centre Hotel) | Markaziya East | 02 633 3555 | 4-J7 |
| **Shang Palace** (Shangri-La, Qaryat Al Beri) | Bain Al Jessrain | 02 509 8888 | 34-J4 |

### Dinner Cruises

| | | | |
|---|---|---|---|
| **Shuja Yacht** (Le Royal Méridien Abu Dhabi) | Markaziya East | 02 674 2020 | 4-L3 |

### Far Eastern

| | | | |
|---|---|---|---|
| **Wasabi** (Al Diar Mina Hotel) | Tourist Club Area | 02 678 1000 | 5-A1 |

### French

| | | | |
|---|---|---|---|
| **Bord Eau** (Shangri-La Hotel, Qaryat Al Beri) | Bain Al Jessrain | 02 509 8888 | 34-J4 |
| **La Brasserie** (Le Meridien Abu Dhabi) | Tourist Club Area | 02 645 5566 | 5-F2 |
| **Le Beaujolais** (Novotel Centre Hotel) | Markaziya East | 02 633 3555 | 4-J7 |
| **Le Bistrot** (Le Meridien Abu Dhabi) | Tourist Club Area | 02 644 6666 | 5-F2 |

### German

| | | | |
|---|---|---|---|
| **Brauhaus** (Beach Rotana Hotel & Towers) | Tourist Club Area | 02 644 3000 | 5-G4 |

### Indian

| | | | |
|---|---|---|---|
| **Angar** (The Yas Hotel) | Yas Island | 02 656 0000 | 50-K2 |
| **Bukharah** (Al Diar Regency Hotel) | Tourist Club Area | 02 676 5000 | 5-A1 |
| **Casa Goa** (Zakher Hotel) | Markaziya East | 02 627 4400 | 4-L4 |
| **Indigo** (Beach Rotana Hotel & Towers) | Tourist Club Area | 02 697 9334 | 5-G4 |
| **Southern Comfort** (Howard Johnson Diplomat) | Markaziya East | 02 671 0000 | 4-L3 |
| **Zari Zardozi** (Al Raha Mall) | Al Raha | 02 556 5188 | 50-E7 |

### International

| | | | |
|---|---|---|---|
| **Al Fanar** (Le Royal Méridien Abu Dhabi) | Markaziya East | 02 674 2020 | 4-L3 |
| **Bay View** (Beach Rotana Hotel & Towers) | Tourist Club Area | 02 644 3000 | 5-G4 |
| **Café 37** (Abu Dhabi Golf Club) | Madinat Khalifa A | 02 558 8990 | 31-B5 |
| **Elements** (Fairmont Bab Al Bahr) | Bain Al Jessrain | 02 654 3333 | 29-J8 |
| **Flavours** (Sheraton Abu Dhabi Hotel & Resort) | Tourist Club Area | 02 677 3333 | 4-M1 |
| **La Veranda** (Sheraton Khalidiya Hotel) | Markaziya West | 02 666 6220 | 8-C6 |
| **Le Vendôme Brasserie** (Emirates Palace) | Al Ras Al Akhdar | 02 690 9000 | 10-L5 |
| **L'Opera Brasserie** (Le Royal Méridien) | Markaziya East | 02 674 2020 | 4-L3 |
| **The Palm** (Al Diar Capital Hotel) | Tourist Club Area | 02 678 7700 | 2-C7 |
| **Rosebuds** (Beach Rotana Hotel & Towers) | Tourist Club Area | 02 644 3000 | 5-G4 |
| **Sevilla** (Al Raha Beach Hotel) | Al Raha | 02 508 0555 | 50-D7 |
| **Sofra Bld** (Shangri-La Hotel, Qaryat Al Beri) | Bain Al Jessrain | 02 509 8888 | 34-J4 |
| **Vasco's** (Hilton Abu Dhabi) | Al Khubeirah | 02 681 1900 | 11-D5 |
| **The Village Club** (One To One Hotel) | Al Nahyan | 02 495 2000 | 9-J6 |
| **The Yacht Club** (InterContinental Abu Dhabi) | Al Bateen | 02 666 6888 | 11-D8 |

### Italian

| | | | |
|---|---|---|---|
| **Amalfi** (Le Royal Méridien Abu Dhabi) | Markaziya East | 02 674 2020 | 4-L3 |
| **Amici** (The Yas Hotel) | Yas Island | 02 656 0000 | 50-K2 |
| **BiCE** (Hilton Abu Dhabi) | Al Khubeirah | 02 681 1900 | 11-D5 |
| **Boccaccio** (InterContinental Abu Dhabi) | Al Bateen | 02 666 6888 | 11-D8 |
| **Ciro's Pomodoro** (Al Diar Capital Hotel) | Tourist Club Area | 02 678 7700 | 2-C7 |
| **Frankie's** (Fairmont Bab Al Bahr) | Bain Al Jessrain | 02 654 3333 | 29-J8 |
| **La Mamma** (Sheraton Abu Dhabi Hotel & Resort) | Tourist Club Area | 02 677 3333 | 4-M1 |
| **Mezzaluna** (Emirates Palace) | Al Ras Al Akhdar | 02 690 7070 | 10-L5 |
| **Pappagallo** (Le Meridien Abu Dhabi) | Tourist Club Area | 02 644 6666 | 5-F2 |
| **Peppino** (Grand Continental Flamingo Hotel) | Markaziya East | 02 626 2200 | 4-L5 |

| | | | |
|---|---|---|---|
| **Prego's** (Beach Rotana Hotel & Towers) | Tourist Club Area | 02 644 3000 | 5-G4 |
| **Riviera** (Marina Al Bateen Resort) | Al Bateen | 02 665 0144 | 16-H4 |

### Japanese

| | | | |
|---|---|---|---|
| **Benihana** (Beach Rotana Hotel & Towers) | Tourist Club Area | 02 644 3000 | 5-G4 |
| **Kazu** (The Yas Hotel) | Yas Island | 02 656 0000 | 50-K2 |
| **Soba** (Le Royal Méridien Abu Dhabi) | Markaziya East | 02 674 2020 | 4-L3 |
| **Sushi Bar** (Abu Dhabi Golf Club) | Madinat Khalifa A | 02 558 8990 | 31-B5 |
| **Wasabi** (Al Diar Mina Hotel) | Tourist Club Area | 02 678 1000 | 5-A1 |
| **Zen** (Al Ain Palace Hotel) | Markaziya East | 02 679 4777 | 4-K2 |

### Latin American

| | | | |
|---|---|---|---|
| **Hemingway's** (Hilton Abu Dhabi) | Al Khubeirah | 02 681 1900 | 11-D5 |

### Mediterranean

| | | | |
|---|---|---|---|
| **Casa Verde** (Abu Dhabi Golf Club) | Madinat Khalifa A | 02 558 8990 | 31-B5 |
| **La Terrazza** (Hilton Abu Dhabi) | Al Khubeirah | 02 681 1900 | 11-D5 |
| **The Olive Tree** (Howard Johnson Diplomat) | Markaziya East | 02 671 0000 | 4-L3 |
| **Pearls & Caviar** (Shangri-La, Qaryat Al Beri) | Bain Al Jessrain | 02 509 8777 | 34-J4 |

### Mexican

| | | | |
|---|---|---|---|
| **El Sombrero** (Sheraton Abu Dhabi Hotel & Resort) | Tourist Club Area | 02 677 3333 | 4-M1 |

### Mongolian

| | | | |
|---|---|---|---|
| **Coconut Bay** (Hilton Abu Dhabi) | Al Khubeirah | 02 681 1900 | 11-D5 |

### Pizzerias

| | | | |
|---|---|---|---|
| **Boccaccio** (InterContinental Abu Dhabi) | Al Bateen | 02 666 6888 | 11-D8 |
| **Figaro's Pizza** (Marina Mall) | Breakwater | 02 681 3300 | 7-A5 |
| **Il Forno** (Abu Dhabi Mall) | Tourist Club Area | 02 644 7511 | 5-G3 |
| **La Mamma** (Sheraton Abu Dhabi Hotel & Resort) | Tourist Club Area | 02 677 3333 | 4-M1 |
| **Pizzeria Italiana** (Al Diar Mina Hotel) | Tourist Club Area | 02 678 1000 | 5-A1 |

### Polynesian

| | | | |
|---|---|---|---|
| **Trader Vic's** (Beach Rotana Hotel & Towers) | Tourist Club Area | 02 644 3000 | 5-G4 |
| **Wakataua Terrace** (Le Meridien Abu Dhabi) | Tourist Club Area | 02 644 6666 | 5-F2 |

### Seafood

| | | | |
|---|---|---|---|
| **FINZ** (Beach Rotana Hotel & Towers) | Tourist Club Area | 02 644 3000 | 5-G4 |
| **Fishmarket** (InterContinental Abu Dhabi) | Al Bateen | 02 666 6888 | 11-D8 |
| **Il Paradiso** (Sheraton Abu Dhabi Hotel & Resort) | Tourist Club Area | 02 677 3333 | 4-M1 |
| **Oceans** (Le Royal Méridien Abu Dhabi) | Markaziya East | 02 674 2020 | 4-L3 |
| **Sayad** (Emirates Palace) | Al Ras Al Akhdar | 02 690 9000 | 10-L5 |

### Spanish

| | | | |
|---|---|---|---|
| **Bravo Tapas Bar** (Sheraton) | Tourist Club Area | 02 677 3333 | 4-M1 |

### Steakhouses

| | | | |
|---|---|---|---|
| **18Oz** (One To One Hotel – The Village) | Al Nahyan | 02 495 2000 | 9-J6 |
| **The Meat Co** (Souk Qaryat Al Beri) | Bain Al Jessrain | 02 558 1713 | 34-J3 |
| **Rodeo Grill** (Beach Rotana Hotel & Towers) | Tourist Club Area | 02 644 3000 | 5-G4 |

### Thai

| | | | |
|---|---|---|---|
| **Royal Orchid** (Hilton Abu Dhabi) | Al Khubeirah | 02 681 3883 | 11-D5 |
| **Talay** (Le Meridien Abu Dhabi) | Tourist Club Area | 02 644 6666 | 5-F2 |
| **Taste Of Thailand** (Al Ain Palace Hotel) | Markaziya East | 02 679 4777 | 4-K2 |

### Vietnamese

| | | | |
|---|---|---|---|
| **Hoi An** (Shangri-La Hotel, Qaryat Al Beri) | Bain Al Jessrain | 02 509 8888 | 34-J4 |

## Shopping Malls

| | | | |
|---|---|---|---|
| **Abu Dhabi Mall** | Tourist Club Area | 02 645 4858 | 5-G3 |
| **Al Muhairy Centre** | Al Manhal | 02 632 2228 | 8-G3 |
| **Al Raha Mall** | Al Raha | 02 556 2229 | 50-E7 |
| **Al Wahda Mall** | Al Nahyan | 02 443 7000 | 13-B1 |
| **Dana Plaza** | Al Khalidiya | 02 665 1333 | 8-A7 |
| **Delma Mall** | Markaziya East | 050 132 8776 | 59-H2 |
| **Hamdan Centre** | Markaziya East | 02 632 8555 | 4-J7 |
| **Khalidiyah Mall** | Al Manhal | 02 635 4000 | 8-D8 |
| **Madinat Zayed Shopping Centre & Gold Centre** | Madinat Zayed | 02 631 8555 | 8-K1 |
| **Marina Mall** | Breakwater | 02 681 8300 | 7-B5 |
| **Mina Centre** | Al Meena | 02 673 4848 | 40-J8 |
| **Rotana Mall** | Al Khalidiya | 02 681 4433 | 11-M1 |
| **Souk Qaryat Al Beri** | Bain Al Jessrain | 02 509 8888 | 34-J3 |

## Universities & Higher Education

| | | | |
|---|---|---|---|
| **Abu Dhabi University** | Capital District | 02 5015555 | 56-C4 |
| **Higher College of Technology** | Madinat Khalifa A | 02 445 1514 | 52-H2 |
| **New York University** | Markaziya West | 02 406 9677 | 8-E1 |
| **Paris-Sorbonne University Abu Dhabi** | Sas Al Nakhl | 02 509 0555 | 29-M6 |
| **Zayed University** | Al Nahyan | 02 445 3300 | 13-E4 |

# A to Z of Abu Dhabi Driving

**The general standard of driving in Abu Dhabi is not good. Drivers often seem completely unaware of other cars and drive too fast, too close, swerve erratically, pull out suddenly and drift mindlessly across lanes. The most important advice for drivers is to stay alert. However, standards are improving, and the following A to Z of hints and tips should set you on the right path.**

## Accidents

All accidents must be reported to the police. If it is serious, dial 999 for emergency help. For minor collisions that do not require emergency services to attend, call the police in the relevant emirate (999 in Abu Dhabi).

If there is only minor damage, and the vehicles are blocking traffic, they can be moved to the side of the road. Be warned that there is no clear definition of what constitutes 'minor damage' and you can also be fined for illegally moving your vehicle after an accident. The police control room will be able to give you guidance when you phone to report the incident.

If there is any doubt as to who is at fault, or if there is an injury (however slight), do not move the cars. If you do, the police may hold you liable should anything then happen to that person. Once the police arrive, they will assess the accident and apportion blame on site. It can be an unscientific process, and there's no right of reply if you disagree. You should calmly, politely and firmly give your account of events. This may be a good chance to try your Arabic pleasantries.

The police will provide a copy of the accident report. Submit this to your insurance company to get the vehicle repaired. A pink report means you are considered at fault, and green means you are the innocent party.

The number of accidents rockets during the holy month of Ramadan, as many drivers are tired and hungry, and in a rush to get home in the late afternoon and evening. Also beware of animals (typically camels) crossing more remote roads.

## Better Driving

### Keep The Hard Shoulder Clear

NEVER drive along the hard shoulder.  Not only is it very dangerous, it is also ILLEGAL.

### Keep Right

ALWAYS move over as far right as possible, as soon as it is safe to do so.

### Keep Your Distance

NEVER drive too close to the vehicle in front. Always leave at least a three second gap between you and the next vehicle.

### Box Junctions

NEVER enter a box junction until your exit is clear.

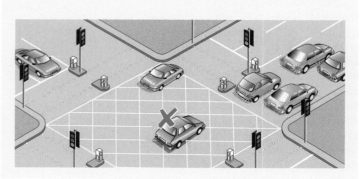

## Blood Money

As the law currently stands, the family of a pedestrian killed in a road accident is entitled to Dhs.200,000 diya (blood) money. This is usually paid by the insurance company, unless the driver was under the influence of alcohol. Blood money is not automatically due if the victim was walking across a road not intended for use by pedestrians.

## Breakdowns

In the event of a breakdown, pull your car over to a safe spot until help arrives. It's best to keep water in your car at all times in case you have to wait longer than expected.

## Children

Children under 10 years old are no longer allowed to sit in the front of a car.

## Further Information

For complete information on safety and road rules, check out the Safe Driving Handbook available from the Emirates Motor Sports Federation, or the Abu Dhabi Police website (www.adpolice.gov.ae).

## Insurance

All motor vehicles must be insured in Abu Dhabi. Car insurance is linked to the car, not the driver. If you let someone drive your car and they get in a wreck, you are technically still responsible for whatever charges your insurance company issues.

## Mobiles

Using handheld mobile phones while driving was banned in 2007. This is still widely ignored, but pull over or use a hands-free set to ensure you avoid a fine.

## Petrol Stations

Petrol stations in Abu Dhabi are run by the Abu Dhabi National Oil Company (ADNOC). On the island, petrol stations are mostly tucked away and difficult to find, although they are often signposted. Most offer extra services, such as a car wash, snacks and a convenience store. Many have a 'cash only' policy.

## Radio

Avoid a traffic jam by tuning in to any of the following FM radio channels: Al Arabiya (98.9), Al Khallejiya (100.9), Dubai 92 (92), The Coast (103.2), Dubai Eye (103.8), Channel 4 (104.8), Emirates 1 (100.5 or 104.1) and Emirates 2 (99.3 or 98.5). The BBC World Service can be picked up on 90.3 in Abu Dhabi and 87.9 in Dubai.

## Road Rules

In the UAE, you drive on the right hand side of the road. Abu Dhabi has its own police force, and rules vary slightly between there and the other emirates. For finer details about road rules, have a look at the Abu Dhabi police website (www.adpolice.gov.ae).

## Saaed

Saaed, a private company half-owned by Abu Dhabi Police, responds to most minor traffic accidents in which there are no injuries, and uses hand-held electronic devices to prepare reports, including diagrams of crash scenes, to help determine fault. The information is sent to insurance companies and is made available to motorists on the website (www.saaed.ae). The company can fine motorists Dhs.500 if they are found at fault for accidents, but there are no fines in cases where no driver is determined to have been at fault. All fines are paid to Abu Dhabi Police in the same way other violations are paid.

## Seatbelts

It is mandatory to wear seatbelts in the front seats.

## Speed Limits

Speed limits are usually 60kph to 80kph around town, and 100kph to 120kph on major highways. The speed limit is clearly indicated on road signs. Speeding fines begin at Dhs.400 for being up to 10kph over the limit. Parking fines start at Dhs.100. Both come with black points. You can also be fined Dhs.50 on the spot for being caught driving without your licence. Fixed and movable radar traps catch the unwary. In most cases you won't know you've received a fine until you check on the police website or renew your vehicle registration.

## Swearing

Rude gestures, like extending your middle digit, can lead to prison, as can giving other drivers an earfull of abuse.

## Violations

To report a traffic violation, call the Traffic Police's toll free hotline (02 446 2462). The Abu Dhabi Police website (www.adpolice.gov.ae) has details of traffic violations and contact numbers.

## Zero Tolerance

Police exercise a strict zero tolerance policy on drinking and driving. If you have had anything to drink, you should not get behind the wheel. If you have an accident, whether responsible or not, and fail a blood-alcohol test you will probably be held in custody until trial and are then likely to face prison. In addition, your insurance is automatically void. Police have increased the number of random drink-driving checks. Be aware that alcohol may still be in your system from the night before.

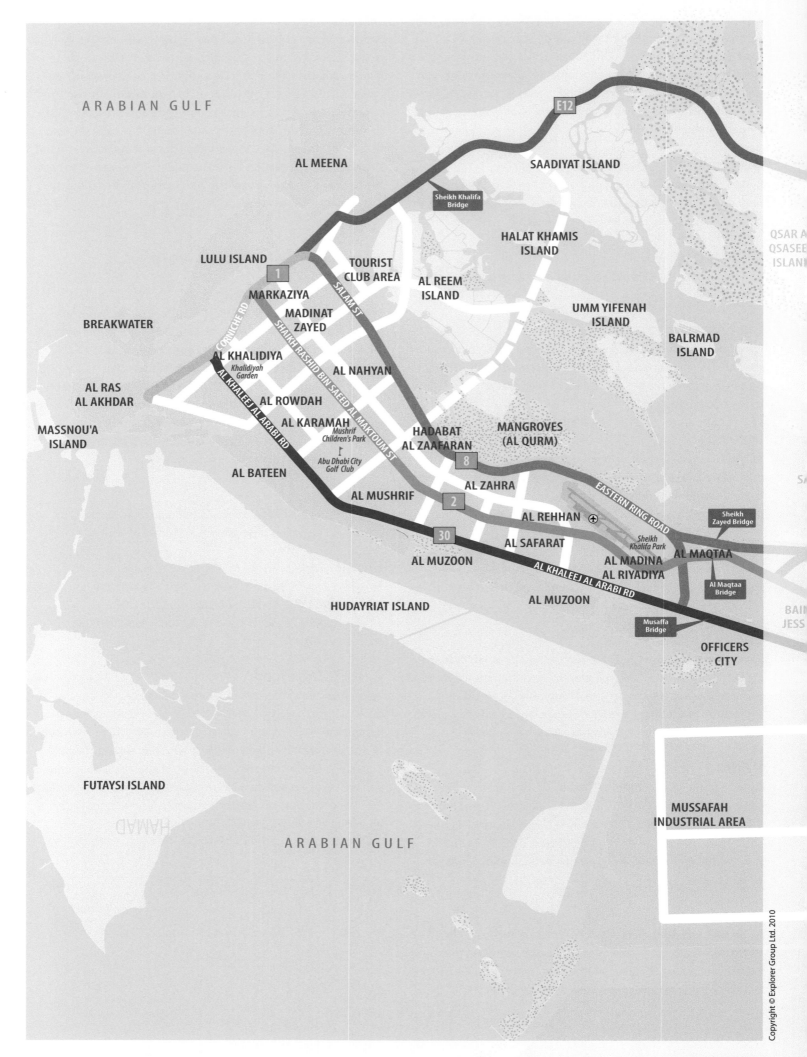

ARABIAN GULF

AL MEENA

SAADIYAT ISLAND

E12

Sheikh Khalifa Bridge

HALAT KHAMIS ISLAND

LULU ISLAND

1

TOURIST CLUB AREA

AL REEM ISLAND

UMM YIFENAH ISLAND

QSAR A QSASEE ISLAN

MARKAZIYA

BREAKWATER

MADINAT ZAYED

SALAM ST

BALRMAD ISLAND

CORNICHE RD

AL KHALIDIYA

Khalidiyah Garden

AL NAHYAN

SHAIKH RASHID BIN SAEED AL MAKTOUM ST

AL RAS AL AKHDAR

AL KHALEEJ AL ARABI RD

AL ROWDAH

MASSNOU'A ISLAND

AL KARAMAH

Mushrif Children's Park

Abu Dhabi City Golf Club

HADABAT AL ZAAFARAN

MANGROVES (AL QURM)

8

AL BATEEN

AL ZAHRA

EASTERN RING ROAD

Sheikh Zayed Bridge

AL MUSHRIF

2

AL REHHAN

Sheikh Khalifa Park

AL MAQTAA

30

AL SAFARAT

AL MADINA AL RIYADIYA

Al Maqtaa Bridge

AL MUZOON

AL MADINA AL RIYADIYA

BAIN JESS

AL KHALEEJ AL ARABI RD

Musaffa Bridge

HUDAYRIAT ISLAND

AL MUZOON

OFFICERS CITY

FUTAYSI ISLAND

HAMAD

MUSSAFAH INDUSTRIAL AREA

ARABIAN GULF

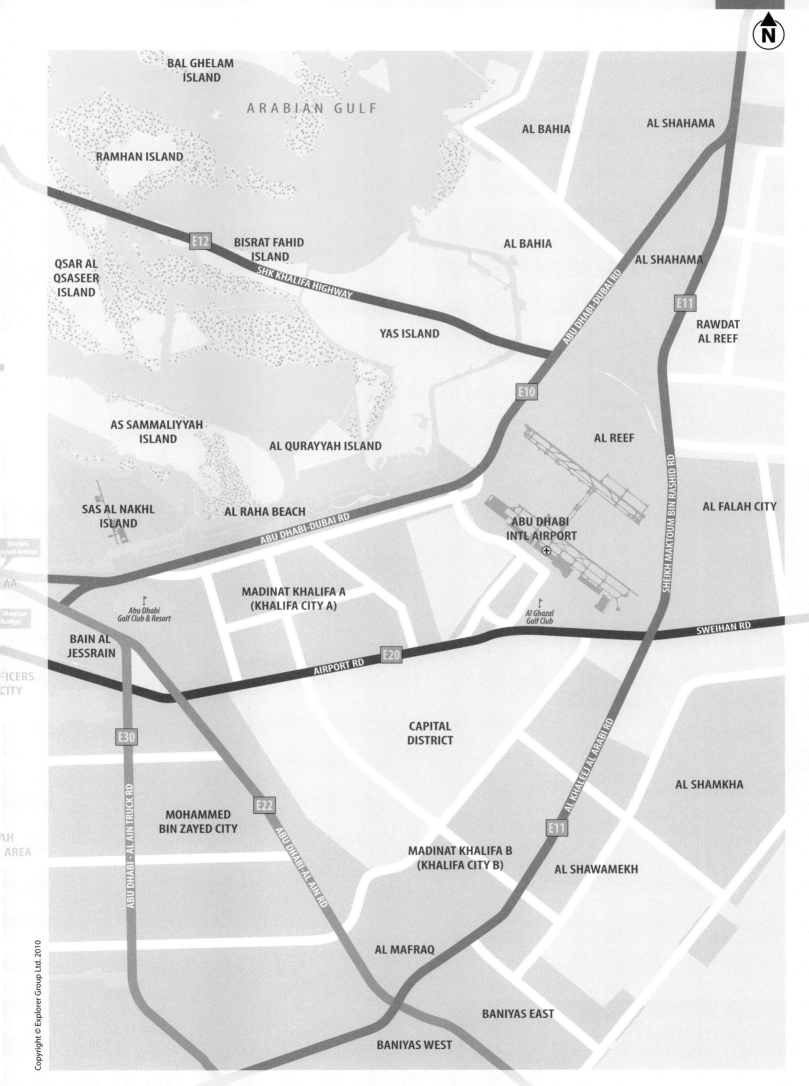

## Product Customisation

Explorer products can be customised and used as corporate gifts, orientation packs for new staff, or promotional giveaways. Clients can add a new cover designed to meet their branding guidelines, or add a new cover image. Copy and contact details can be added to the back cover, advertisements placed inside, pages inserted, changes made to the colour scheme, a welcome message added, and new locations (with contact details) placed on maps.

Regular Explorer cover

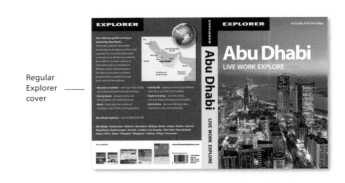

Regular Explorer cover

New cover image

New cover image

Company logo

Samples of previous customised covers

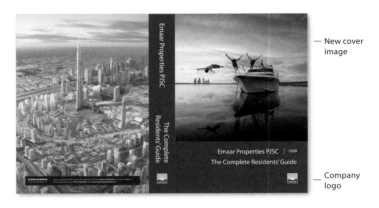

New cover image

Company logo

Regular Explorer cover

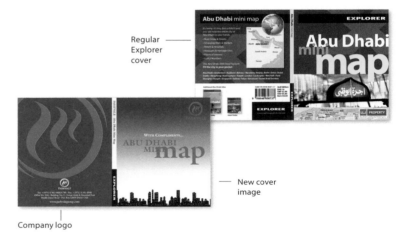

New cover image

Company logo

## 3D Maps

Explorer can also provide customised 3D maps. These act as an excellent visual guide to an area, but can also include comic touches and tiny slice-of-life details.

There are two significant advantages to using 3D maps. Firstly, their similarity to the physical world means that even the most map-phobic people can understand them, and secondly, the scope for creative flourishes is unlimited. Corporate clients may choose to include logos (a streetside billboard, a branded plane flying across the city) or examples of their business in action (smiling customers receiving their goods, staff on their way to work).

**For more information on any of these options please go to www.explorerpublishing.com**

Abu Dhabi **Street** Atlas

## Location Maps

Explorer Publishing's maps cover the whole of the UAE, and major cities in the Arabian Gulf and throughout the world.

These products are well known and relied on by people across the globe. The maps highlight local landmarks, museums, hospitals, schools, malls, markets and other areas of interest. They are also an invaluable tool for finding your way around.

If people can't find you, they can't buy your products or services. Maps for any city that Explorer has covered can be customised to help clients get to you. Explorer covers all the GCC capital cities, along with commercial hubs in Asia (Beijing, Shanghai, Hong Kong, Singapore, Sydney), North America (New York, LA, Vancouver) and Europe (London, Paris, Barcelona, Dublin, Amsterdam, Berlin).

These can be printed in any format you want, from business cards to laminated posters, or as a PDF for email.

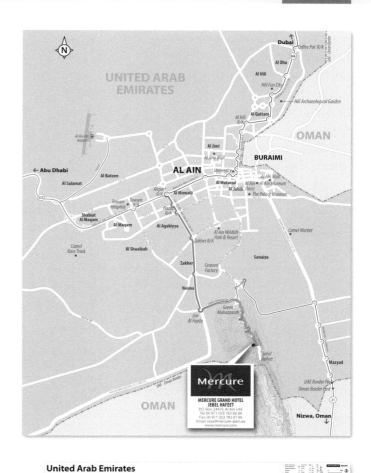

## Wall Maps

If there's a part of the planet that is particularly important to you, we can create a poster of it. Our maps cover major cities across the world, any of which can be blown up as wall maps in your chosen size. Just choose the area you're interested in, and decide if you'd like an overview or greater detail. Then, opt for landscape or portrait and pick any size you want.

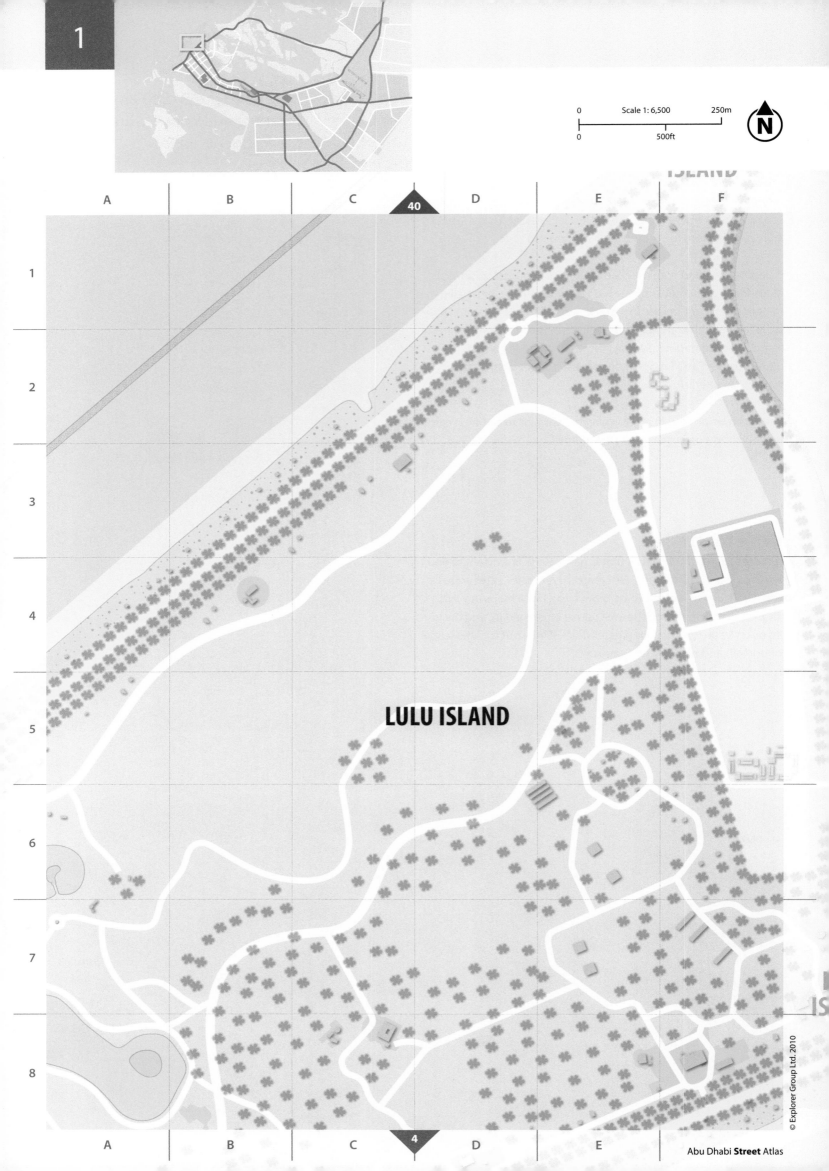

Scale 1: 6,500

0          250m

0          500ft

N

1

2

3

4

**LULU ISLAND**

5

6

7

8

© Explorer Group Ltd. 2010

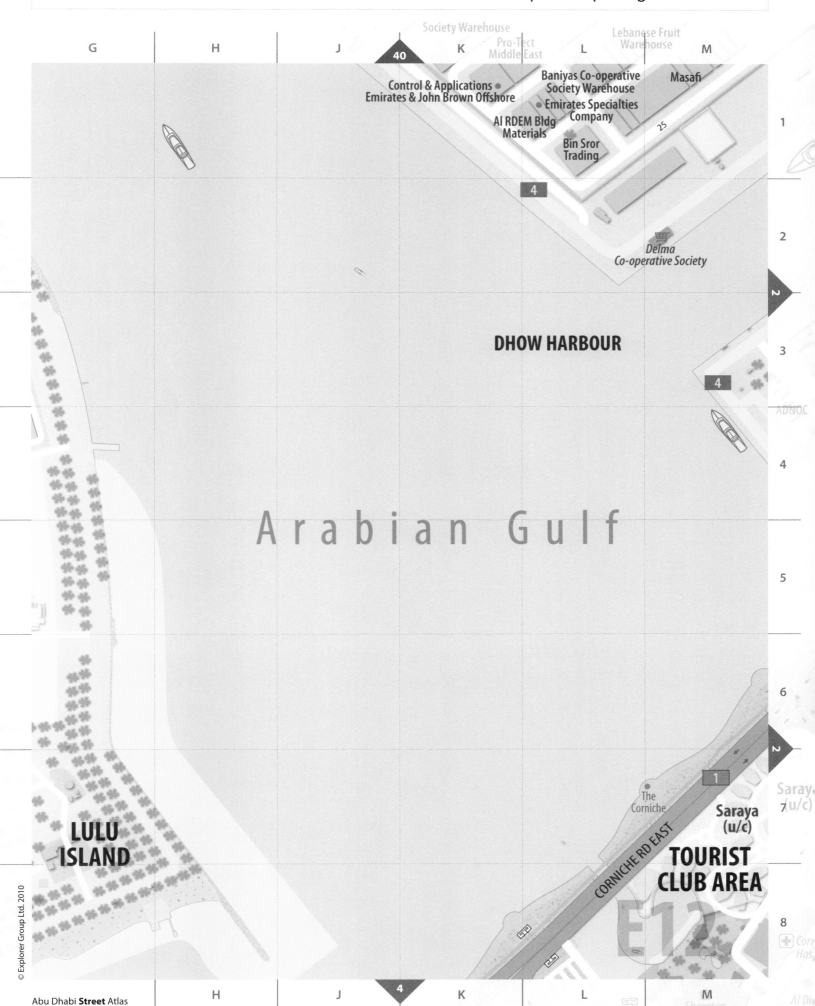

Society Warehouse

Pro-Tect
Middle East

Lebanese Fruit
Warehouse

G   H   J   40   K   L   M

Control & Applications
Emirates & John Brown Offshore

Baniyas Co-operative
Society Warehouse

Masafi

Emirates Specialties
Company

Al RDEM Bldg
Materials

25

Bin Sror
Trading

1

4

2

Delma
Co-operative Society

2

**DHOW HARBOUR**

3

4

ADNOC

4

# Arabian Gulf

5

6

2

The
Corniche

1

Saraya
7(u/c)

**LULU
ISLAND**

Saraya
(u/c)

**TOURIST
CLUB AREA**

CORNICHE RD EAST

E1

8

Cor
Ho

H   J   4   K   L   M
Sheraton

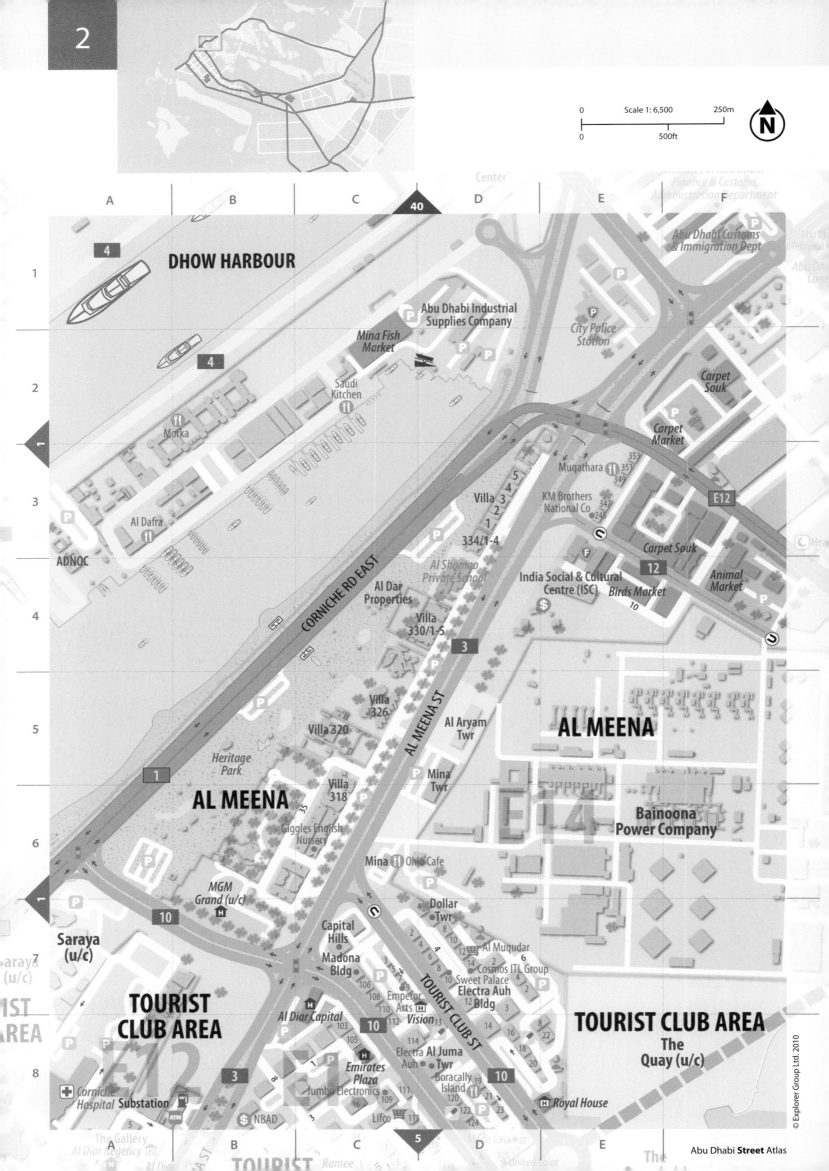

Scale 1: 6,500

0 — 250m
0 — 500ft

**N**

**A**    **B**    **C**    40    **D**    **E**    **F**

Center

Emirates of Abu Dhabi
Finance & Customs
Administration Department

Abu Dhabi Customs
& Immigration Dept

**4**

**DHOW HARBOUR**

Abu Dhabi Industrial
Supplies Company

City Police
Station

1

Mina Fish
Market

Carpet
Souk

**4**

Saudi
Kitchen

Carpet
Market

2

Morka

353
351
349

Muqathara

KM Brothers
National Co

E12

347
245

Villa 3

3

Al Dafra

5
4
2
1

Carpet Souk

ADNOC

334/1-4

12

CORNICHE RD EAST

Al Shomoo
Private School

India Social & Cultural
Centre (ISC)

Birds Market

Animal
Market

Al Dar
Properties

$

10

4

Villa
330/1-5

3

AL MEENA

Villa
326

AL MEENA ST

Al Aryam
Twr

5

Villa 320

Heritage
Park

Mina
Twr

Villa
318

**AL MEENA**

Bainoona
Power Company

Giggles English
Nursery

35

6

Mina   Ohio Cafe

MGM
Grand (u/c)

Dollar
Twr

Saraya
(u/c)

**10**

Capital
Hills

Al Muqudar

7

Madona
Bldg

Cosmos ITL Group

Sweet Palace

Electra Auh
Bldg

**TOURIST
CLUB AREA**

106

**TOURIST CLUB AREA**
The
Quay (u/c)

108

Emperor
Arts

110

Al Diar Capital

112   Vision

TOURIST CLUB ST

103

**10**

114

105

Electra   Al Juma
Auh   Twr

8

Emirates
Plaza

Boracally
Island

**10**

Corniche
Hospital   Substation

Jumbo Electronics

111

Royal House

109

NBAD

Lifco   113

The Gallery
Al Diar Regency

**5**

Ramee

**A**    **B**    **C**    **D**    **E**

Abu Dhabi **Street** Atlas

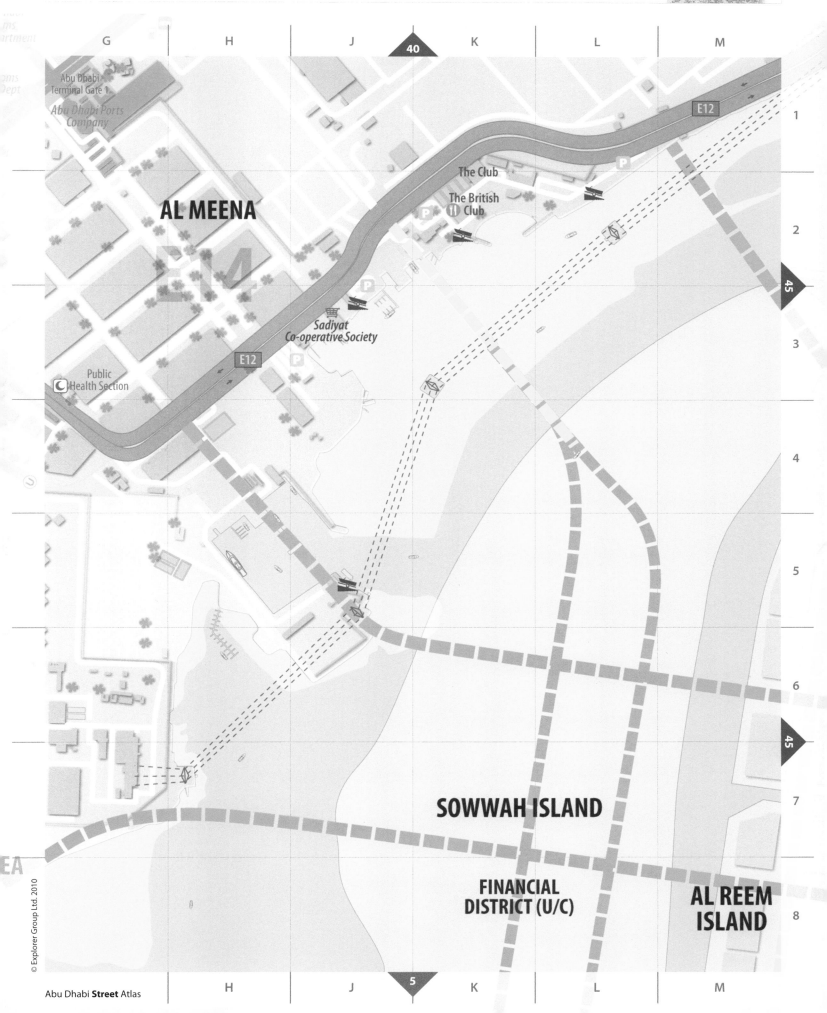

G H J **40** K L M

Abu Dhabi Terminal Gate 1

Abu Dhabi Ports Company

**AL MEENA**

E14

E12

The Club

The British Club

P

E12

Sadiyat Co-operative Society

Public Health Section

1

2

**45**

3

4

5

6

**45**

7

**SOWWAH ISLAND**

**FINANCIAL DISTRICT (U/C)**

**AL REEM ISLAND**

8

EA

H J **5** K L M

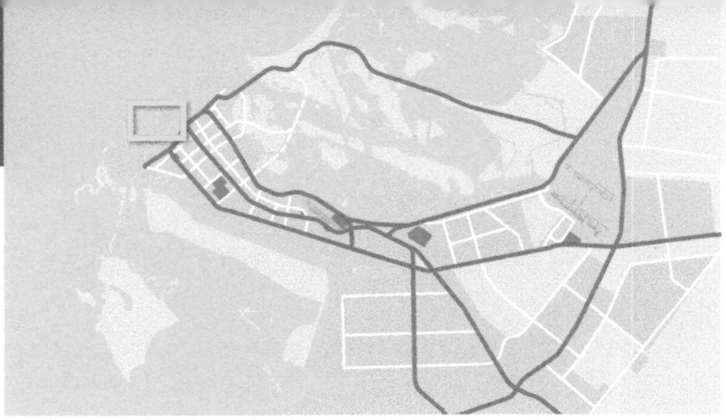

Scale 1: 6,500

0        250m

0        500ft

N

A      B      C      D      E      F

1

2

3

4

# Arabian Gulf

5

6

7

8

A      B      C      D      E

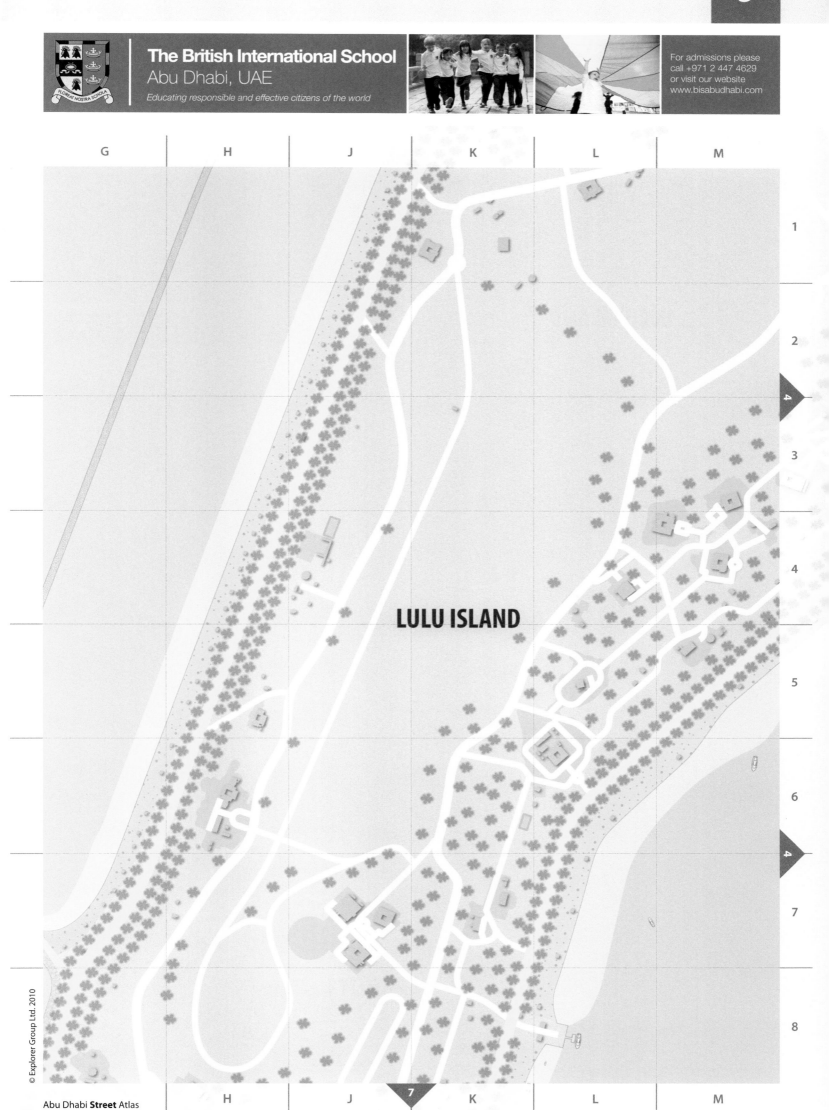

The British International School
Abu Dhabi, UAE
Educating responsible and effective citizens of the world

For admissions please
call +971 2 447 4629
or visit our website
www.bisabudhabi.com

LULU ISLAND

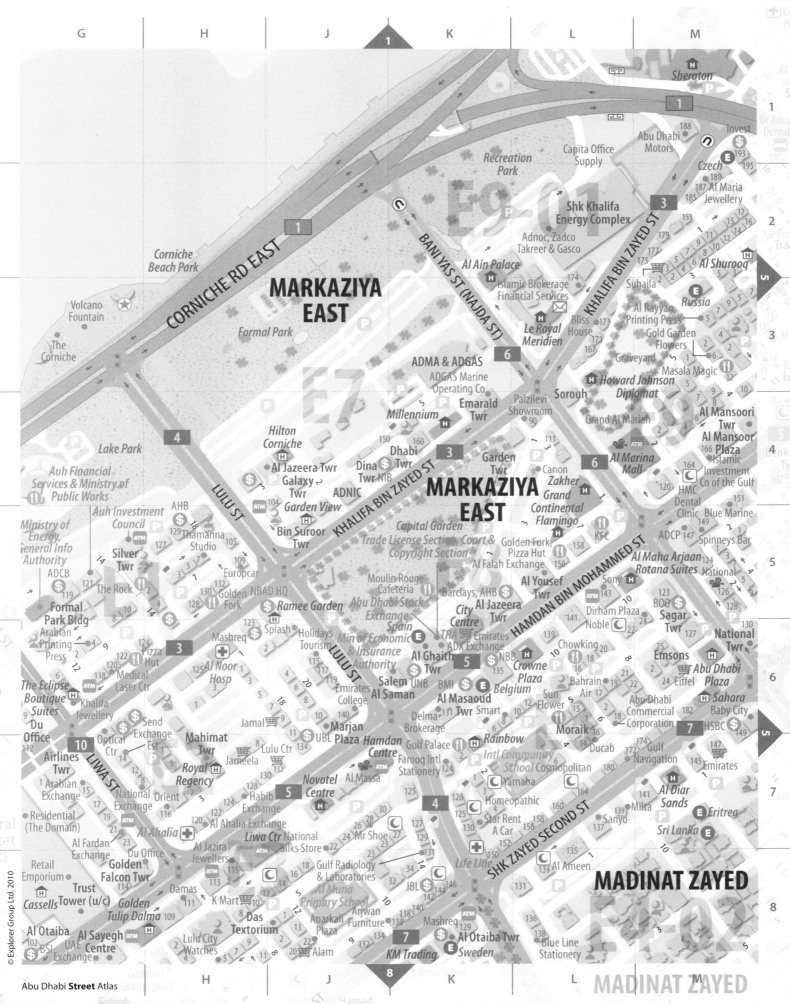

Scale 1: 6,500

0     250m
0     500ft

N

A   B   C   2   D   E   F

NBAD   Lifco   Jumbo Electronics   21   Royal House

Corniche Hospital Substation

The Gallery
Al Diar Regency
Shamyat   Al Diar Mina
Dr Adna Merih Dental Clinic
Porsche Centre Auh

**TOURIST CLUB AREA**

Ramee Guestline I
Giant Billiards Nursery
Emirates Hosp Supply
Modern Bakery
Land Mark Plaza
Morocco
Smokers Ctr
Moda Casa   27
United Color Films
Mazna Light Bldg   314

The Quay (u/c)

**TOURIST CLUB AREA**

Le Meridien

BOS
197
Marina Dental Centre
199
Lulu Centre
301
Power Garments
Transco
Elite Modern
Dr Moosa Abu Saeed Dental Clinic
Arab Udupi
Health Care Intl Ctr Clinic
Al Ain Twr
Rafa Audio
Emirates Twr   Symbol Computers
Snow White
British Dental Clinic
Xerox Emirates
Benkaram Twr
Emirates General Mkt

Al Ansari Travels
Business Ctr   Elenco
Emirates Grp
Intl Rotana Inn
Al Masraf Twr
Bel Mondo Café
Dnata Travel
My Way
KM Trading
Siddiq Gifts
Business & Technology
Ideal Curtain
Al Salam Twr
Sadiyath Twr
Sara Institute
Royal Seasons (u/c)

**HAMDAN BIN MOHAMMED ST**

Sangeetha
Bin Ghanim Twr
Planet Café
Al Kuwaisi
EMCC   Mr Jabir Jasem
Al Maraiki
Al Jaber
Khoory
Ali & Sons Co
Al Salmeen Gold Twr

Hazza Bin Zayed Mosque
Hard Rock Internet
Gulf Way Rent A Car

**SHK ZAYED SECOND ST**

Al Futtaim Engineering
Polaris Automobile
Continental Tyres   Arzanah Twr
Ivory
Al Basma Studio
NBAD

African & Eastern
Oasis Ctr   Pizza Hut
KFC
Dar Al Shifa Medical Ctr
Al Diar Dana
Osool Finance Co   Al Manzel
Colours Fashion
Lovely Studio
Slide Star Real Estate
Fortune   Fathima
Al Ghazal Travels
Darbar
Kia Motors

Tennis Courts

Cafe

**TOURIST CLUB ST**

Old Auh Co-operative Society
Al Baba Subway Sweets
Shk Khalifa Res Complex (B)
Al Fardan Exchange
Mandoos
United Emirates Aviation
Al Reyami Office Furniture
RAK
ADCB   Pizaa More
Exotica Emirates
Green Oasis Co
Saba
Nasar Sparks
Shams Auh   AS Diamond Palace
Abi Alfida

**MARKAZIYA EAST**

Juma Al Majid Complex

**TOURIST CLUB AREA**

Al Rostamani
Max Mart   Adams
FGB
Eldorado
Trading Enterprises Co
Galadhari Automobiles
Al Hamra Plaza Res
City Seasons Al Hamra

SHK ZAYED SECOND ST

MTS
Education Ctr
National Ind Co
UTS Store
Sahara
SIB
Al Dhafra Insurance
Global Office Twr (u/c)

Auh Co-operative Society
ADCB
Sycoms College
ADNOC National Drilling Co
Al Baheya
Zaatar Wa Zeit
Al Saqia Trd   Suzuki
National Paint Shop
German Home

UNB
NBAD
Abu Azooz Trding
DIB
FGB
Century   ADDC
Kingsgate
ADSA Cargo Ctr

**AL SALAM ST**

Abu Azooz Trding
Central Tent

First Rent A Car   Oasiss
Marroush

City Seasons Al Hamra
Micco
Spinneys
Jotun Paint Shop
Jotun Paints
Al Salah Twr

**BANI YAS ST**

National Hosp

Vision Twin Twr 2
Vision Twin Twr 1
Al Khazna Insurance Twr
Al Wathaba Twr
Emirates NBD
Al Masood Automobiles
Tilusanz More
Nahel Twr
World of Lights
Shobra
Sana Fashion

Abu Dhabi Food Control Authority
Etisalat

**AL BALADIA**

Abu Dhabi Traffic Control Centre

Abu Dhabi Municipality

Fast Rent A Car
Peugeot
HSBC
Gulf Commercial Grp
Awtar
Harley Davidson Motorcycle

Al Nadi School for Busics Education
Dept of Municipal Affairs
Dept of Economic Development

Liberty Auh Automobiles
Abu Dhabi Chess Club

A   B   C   9   D   E   F

**Abu Dhabi Street Atlas**

© Explorer Group Ltd. 2010

SOWWAH ISLAND

FINANCIAL DISTRICT (U/C)

Danik Restaurant & Bar

Party Boat

Abu Dhabi Marina

Marina Office

Dry Dock

Auh Co-operative
Dubai & ADCB
Grand Abu Dhabi

Abu Dhabi Mall
Germany
Canada
Towers at the Trade Centre

TOURIST CLUB AREA

Marina Base (u/c)

Skygardens (u/c)

Harbour Heights (u/c)

Safeer
Shk Khalifa Res Complex (A)
Beach Rotana

10   10

Abu Dhabi Airport City Terminal

Madina Printing
EIB

Future Cafe
Magic Tech
Al Maya
Oasis Printing Press
Amani
Bynuna Flower
Indonesian
Jazira
Middle East
Allied Factory Outlet

9

QASR AL BAHR

Burooj Twr (u/c)

AL REEM ISLAND

Marina Square (u/c)

Marina

Panoramic Heights (u/c)

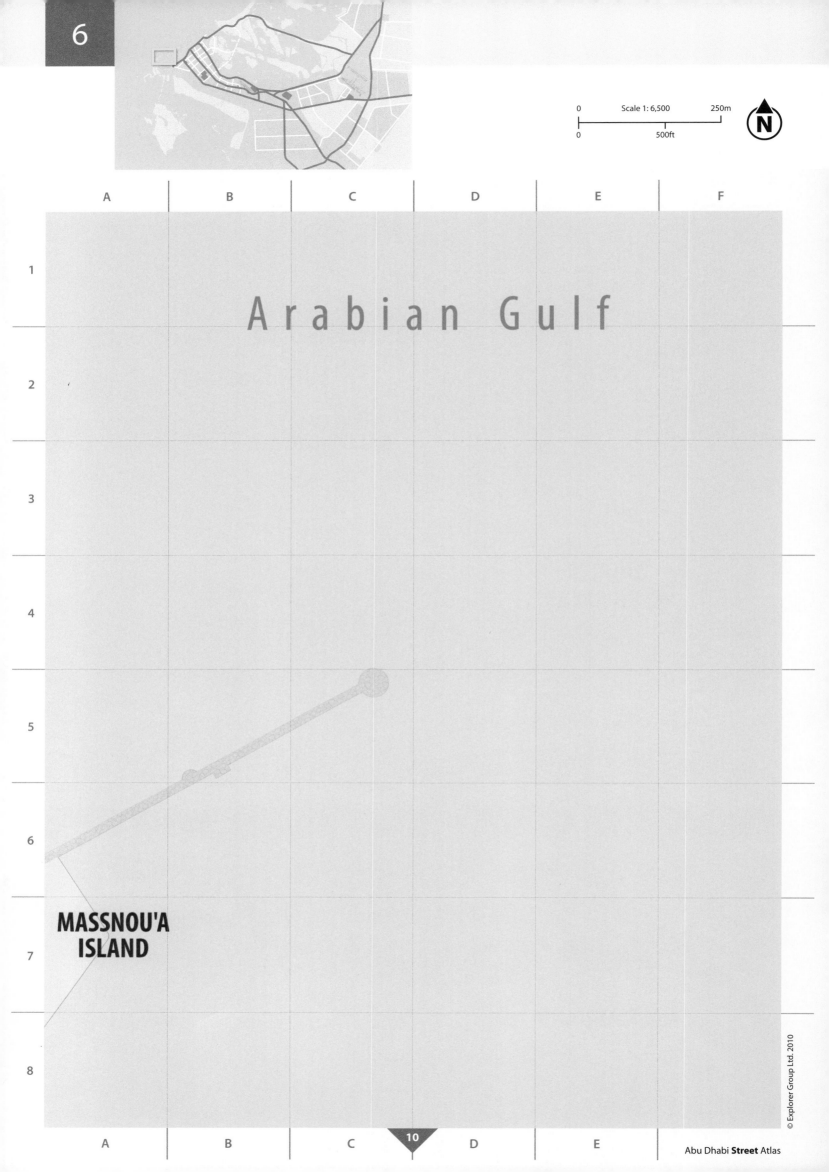

Scale 1:6,500

0        250m

0        500ft

N

A    B    C    D    E    F

# Arabian Gulf

**MASSNOU'A ISLAND**

# JASHANMAL BOOKSTORES
**Dubai:** Mall of the Emirates • Jashanmal-Wafi City • Caribou Coffee - Uptown Mirdiff, Dubai Marina Walk
The Village Mall • **Abu Dhabi:** Abu Dhabi Mall • **Sharjah:** Sahara Centre • **Bahrain:** Seef Mall • Al Aali Shopping Complex

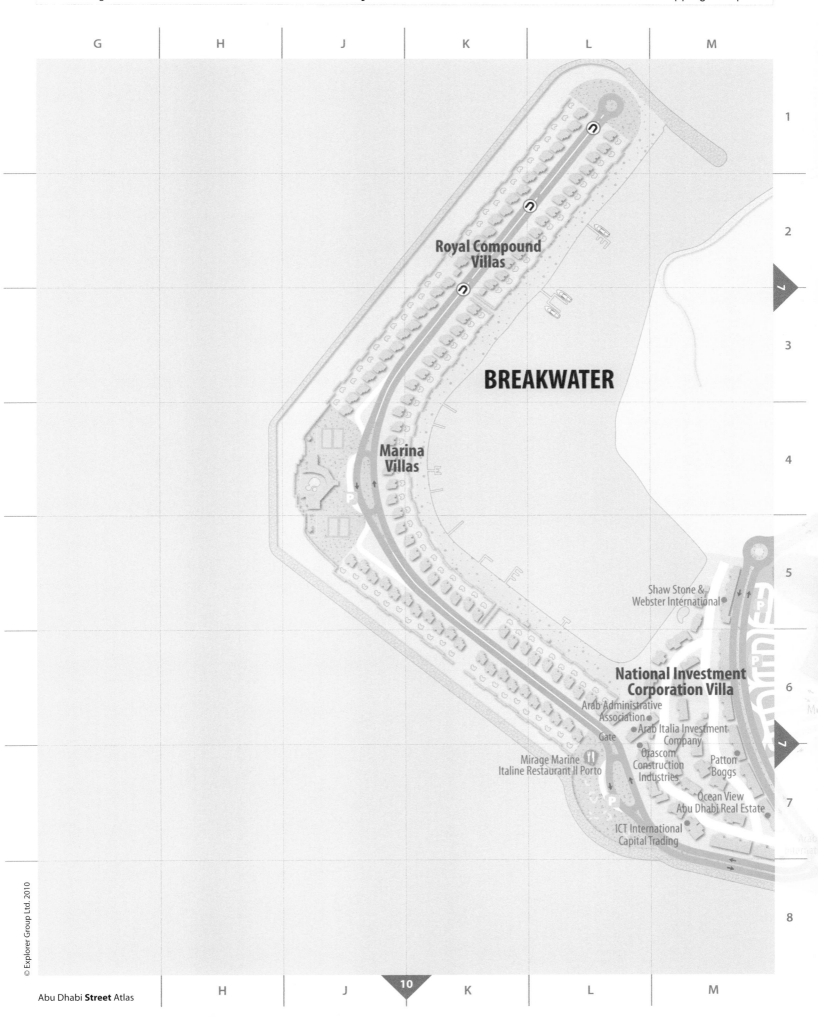

Royal Compound Villas

**BREAKWATER**

Marina Villas

Shaw Stone & Webster International

**National Investment Corporation Villa**
Arab Administrative Association
Arab Italia Investment Company
Gate
Orascom Construction Industries
Patton Boggs
Mirage Marine Italine Restaurant Il Porto
Ocean View Abu Dhabi Real Estate
ICT International Capital Trading

Scale 1:6,500

0    250m

0    500ft

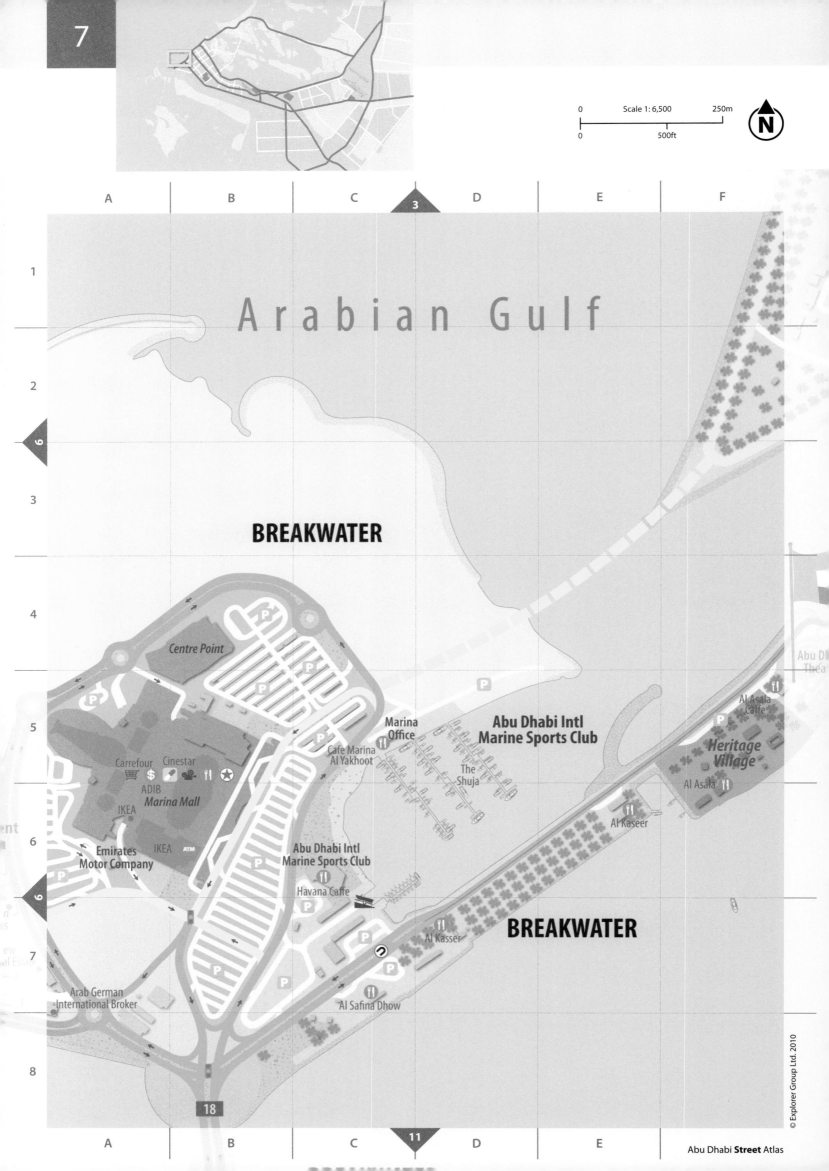

N

A    B    C    3    D    E    F

# Arabian Gulf

**BREAKWATER**

Centre Point

Marina Office

Abu Dhabi Intl Marine Sports Club

Al Asala Caffe

Cafe Marina Al Yakhoot

The Shuja

Heritage Village

Carrefour    Cinestar

ADIB    *Marina Mall*

Al Asala

IKEA

Al Kaseer

IKEA    ATM

Emirates Motor Company

Abu Dhabi Intl Marine Sports Club

Havana Caffe

Al Kasser

**BREAKWATER**

Arab German International Broker

Al Safina Dhow

18

A    B    C    11    D    E

© Explorer Group Ltd. 2010

Abu Dhabi **Street** Atlas

| | G | H | J | 3 | K | L | M | |

**LULU ISLAND**

**Arabian Gulf**

Abu Dhabi Theatre

**BREAKWATER**

Al Asala Cafe

Public Beach

Corniche Beach Park

Corniche Public Beach

Public Beach

Corniche Beach Park

West Moto

Meher Medical

Al Sawa Twr A

AL K

ADC Compo

**CORNICHE RD WEST**

Abu Dhabi For Onshore Oil Operations (ADCO)

**AL KHALIDIYA**
Environment Conservation Centre

**ADCO Compound**
Investone Financial Brokerage

Al & Sons Motors
Tameer Twrs
Lounge & Cafe

Bel Ghailam Twr

NBAD DIB 205
Venito Iranian Carpets
Binjuma
Al Suwaidi Grp

Zadco Housing

Anwa Twr B

Cafe du Roi

Al Hana Shopping Ctr

30

Al Hanyouna Twr
KFC
Areej Twr

Scale 1: 6,500

0   250m
0   500ft

N

**MARKAZIYA WEST**

Landmark Twr

Family Park

Corniche Beach Park

The Corniche

Dept of Social Service & Commercial

Hilton Baynunah

Strawberry Cafe

Arabian Palace

United Kingdom

Jearada Properties

Watch Land Abu Dhabi

Al Ghazal Rent A Car

Al Badie

Gulf Pearl

UNB

AAIB

Besco Dental Clinic

Auto Mobile & Touring Club

All Prints Book Shop

Bin Murshid Holding Bldg 2

British Council

Eduscan Nursery

Color lines Wedding Cards

Al Masraf Arab Bank Investment Foreign Trade

Iraq

Finance Dept

Al Rawafi

Bees Kingdom

**MARKAZIYA WEST**

Al Markaziyah Garden

CORNICHE RD EAST

AL NASR ST

Galaxy Electronic

Antonio

Venecia Beauty Centre

Lebanese Express

Only One

Stylee

Junana

Formula 1

Al Masood Travel

Azzam

Emco Rent A Car

Al Hosn

Advanced Rent A Car

Al Kunaiby

Al Dhaham Watches Gallery

Al Buqubai Twr

Al Jaber Jewellery

Finance House

KHALID BIN WALEED ST

AL NASR ST

Cultural Foundation

Al Hosn Fort

Al Hosn Palace

Gulf Chinese, Ansari Medical Centre

New York University

Younus Food Stuff Trading

My Campus

Golden Holidays Travels

Mohd Irfan Kaltakji

Maine Entrance

American Crescent Health Care

Platinum

Grand Store

Wear Mart

Sedar

Al Kalha Institute of Training & Judicial Studies

Al Ramla Coast

Rivoli

Gallery Art

Sea17 Shell

The University Bookshop

Khalidiya Studio

Al Sham Vedio & Gifts

Deral Dhasi Cafe

The Gate

Gardenia Internet

Jocker Sport Club

Fathima Trading & Departmental Stores

SHK ZAYED FIRST ST

Green Rent A Car

Black Cavaliero

Jumbo

Amitha

Atmosphere

Al Toufeequi

Qatar Air Ways

Emirates Flights

Western Motors

Meher Medical Ctr

Al Sawari Twr C

Al Sawari Twr B

Damac Properties

Ali & Sons Co

Super Store

Al Sawari Twr A

Grand Millennium Corniche

Gulf City

Al Kamal

Golden Fork New

Educare Ctr Villa

Sheraton Khalidiya

Elite Optical

Zarina Lingerie

KM Trading

Ghantoot Flowers

El Darawi Advertising

Royal Specialist

Seedra Fashion

Meca Quick Service Est

Happy Chocolates

**AL MANHAL**

KING KHALID BIN ABDEL AZIZ ST

**AL KHALIDIYA**

ADCO Compound

Ministry of Education Auh Educational Zone

Khalidia Centre

Al Ganadah Twr

Al Areen Twr

Al Nakheel Twr

Al Jundi Orthodontic & Dental Centre

Garden City Twr

Auh Co-operative Society

Dana Plaza

Damac Properties

CBD

Safeer Style

Al Fawari

RAK

ADIB

Choithram

Dhiyafa

Shining Twr (u/c)

Pizza Way

Al Mal

Al Iman

Al Heel Twr

Amwaj Twr

DIB

Burger King

East Light

Sinam

City Burger

Palm Oasis

Veg Mkt

Tihama

Noor Cards

Tornado Sport Cafe

Al Jazeera Printing Press

Jajan Computers

Royal Printing Rork

Queen Saba Trade

**AL MANHAL**

Agriculture Research Laboratory

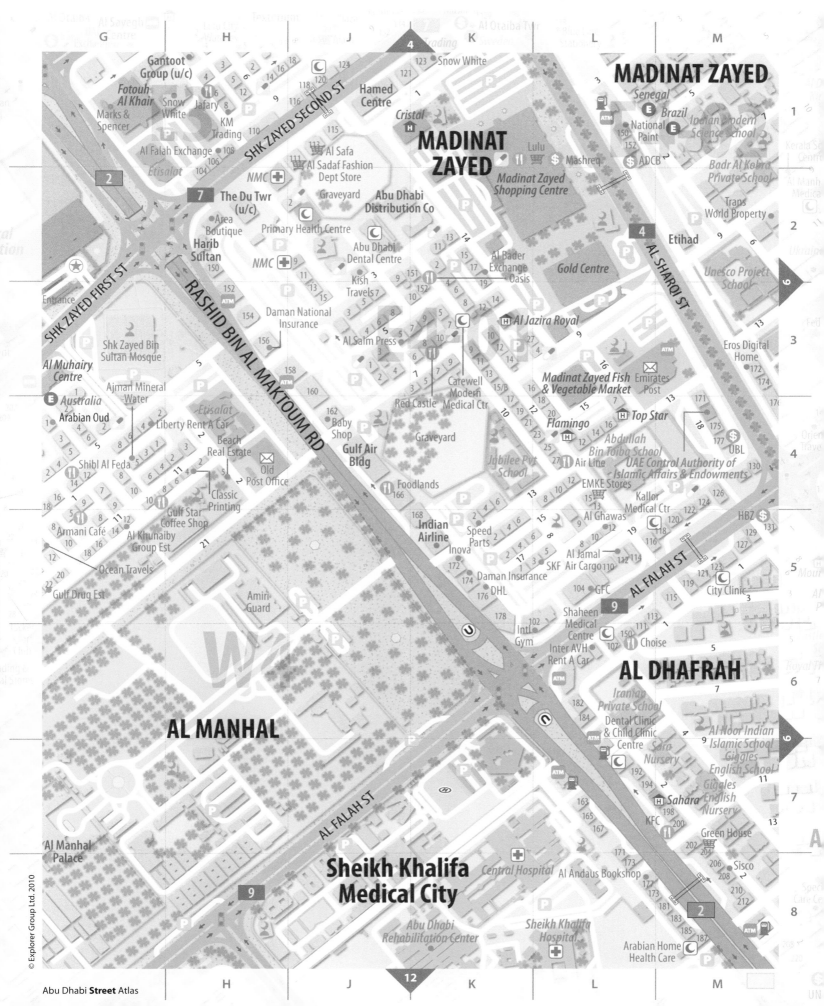

© Explorer Group Ltd. 2010

Scale 1: 6,500
0 250m
0 500ft
N

**AL BALADIA**

**MADINAT ZAYED**

**AL DHAFRAH**

**AL DHAFRAH**

**AL NAHYAN**

**AL DHAFRAH**

**AL NAHYAN**

Al Dana Private Kindergarten
Kerala Social Centre
Al Manhal Family Medical Centre
Busy Bees Nursery
Khaleej Times
National Cadet Centre (NCC)
Ukraine
J & H Emirates
Eduscan Edutainment
Home Birds of Hope Nursery
Federal Environment Agency
Al Kawsar Rent A Car
Khalifa Medical Ctr
Taha Medical Ctr
Yasmin Sweets
Orient Travels
Talent Medical Ctr
Jumbo
Elite Motors
Philippine
Emmar Future Twr 1
Blue Twr
Mourouj
Starbucks Coffee & Subway
Al Diar Palm
Symex Intl Motors
Little Flower Pvt School
Khalidiya Co-operative Society
Leens School
Leens Nursery
Cristal City Lights
Castle Private School
Royal Thai
The University Bookshop
Etisalat
Riyami Costa Coffee
VAN Yasat Pvt School
Corniche Towers
Quick Intervention Unit of Civil Defense
Sesame Street
Discount Emirates Market
Al Ahalya Medical Centre
Euro
Jotun Paints
Al Nile River
Zia
Special Care Centre
Al Ekhalis Private School
The Grand Millenium (u/c)
Lamborghini Abu Dhabi (Motors)
Deluxe Arabian Gents Tailor
Golden Motors
Abu Dhabi Taxi Stand

Baniyas Twr( u/c)
Al Mazroui Hosp
Mashreq
Gray Mackenzie & Partners (GMP)
Obeid Al Zaabi Trading
Eastern Blue
Mitsubishi Motors
Hertz Rent A Car
Jordan Stone
National Rent A Car
Golden Ticket Travels
Sudanese Social Club
Ministry of Higher Education & Scientific Research
Emirates Autism Center
Islamic International School
Abu Dhabi Womens College
Al Saqoor Model School
Islamiya English School
Lebanese Flower
The Pearl Primary School
Abu Dhabi Al Jaleel Al Faheem Primary School
Pal Group of Company
Prince Medical Ctr
Al Hawamir Seafood
Corner
Errison
Spinneys
Megawatt Electrical Trading Co
Lulu
EMKE Group
Aramex
Mashreq

Ministry of Finance
Emirates Computers
Auh Water & Electricity Company (ADWEC)
Auh Distribution Company (ADDC)
Bridge Stone Tyres
Auh Water & Electricity Company (ADWEC)
Shabiya Police Station
Gems American Academy
Al Saloom Emirates Primary School
Transco Bldg
Al Kubaisi School
Asian International School
Middle East Travels
Comassat Bldg
Dar Al Shifa Hospital
Gava
Al Baddad Intl
Mono Restaurant & Cafe
Zahrath Al Emirates Car Accessories
Deluxe Arabian Gents Tailor
Cyclone Electronics
Emirates National School for Girls
Elite Rent A Car
Al Sayadi Key
Al Masood Tyres
AMIT Intl Link
Al Asala Phones
Deluxe Mobile Phones
Granite
Kalispra
Al Taj Perfumes
Jumbo
Tasameem Real Estate
System Dvpt Division Abu Dhabi Police General Head Office Information Technology & Communication Dept

BANI YAS ST
AL FALAH ST
AL FALAH ST
BANI YAS ST
EAST RD
HAZAA BIN ZAYED THE FIRST ST
EAST RD

© Explorer Group Ltd. 2010

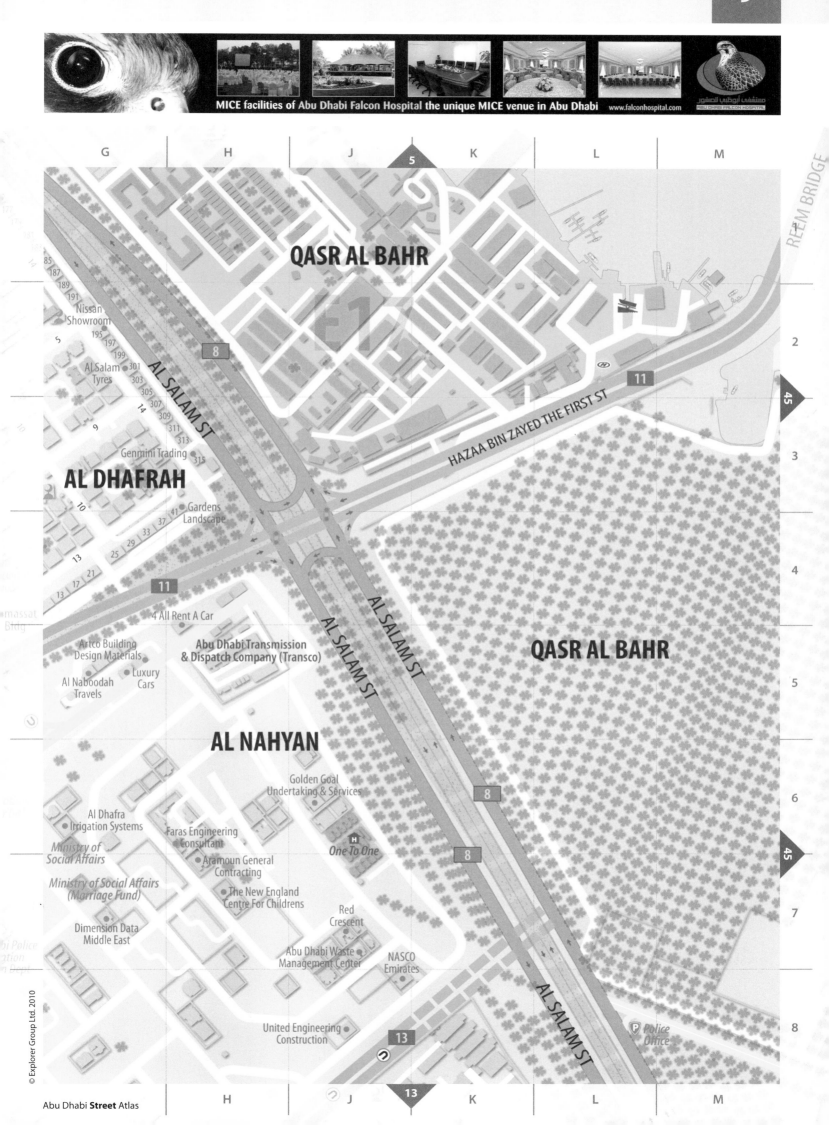

QASR AL BAHR

AL DHAFRAH

Nissan Showroom
Al Salam Tyres
Genmini Trading
Gardens Landscape

AL SALAM ST

HAZAA BIN ZAYED THE FIRST ST

4 All Rent A Car
Artco Building Design Materials
Al Naboodah Travels
Luxury Cars
Abu Dhabi Transmission & Dispatch Company (Transco)

AL NAHYAN

Al Dhafra Irrigation Systems
Ministry of Social Affairs
Ministry of Social Affairs (Marriage Fund)
Dimension Data Middle East
Faras Engineering Consultant
Aramoun General Contracting
The New England Centre For Childrens
Golden Goal Undertaking & Services
One To One
Red Crescent
Abu Dhabi Waste Management Center
NASCO Emirates
United Engineering Construction

AL SALAM ST

QASR AL BAHR

Police Office

© Explorer Group Ltd. 2010

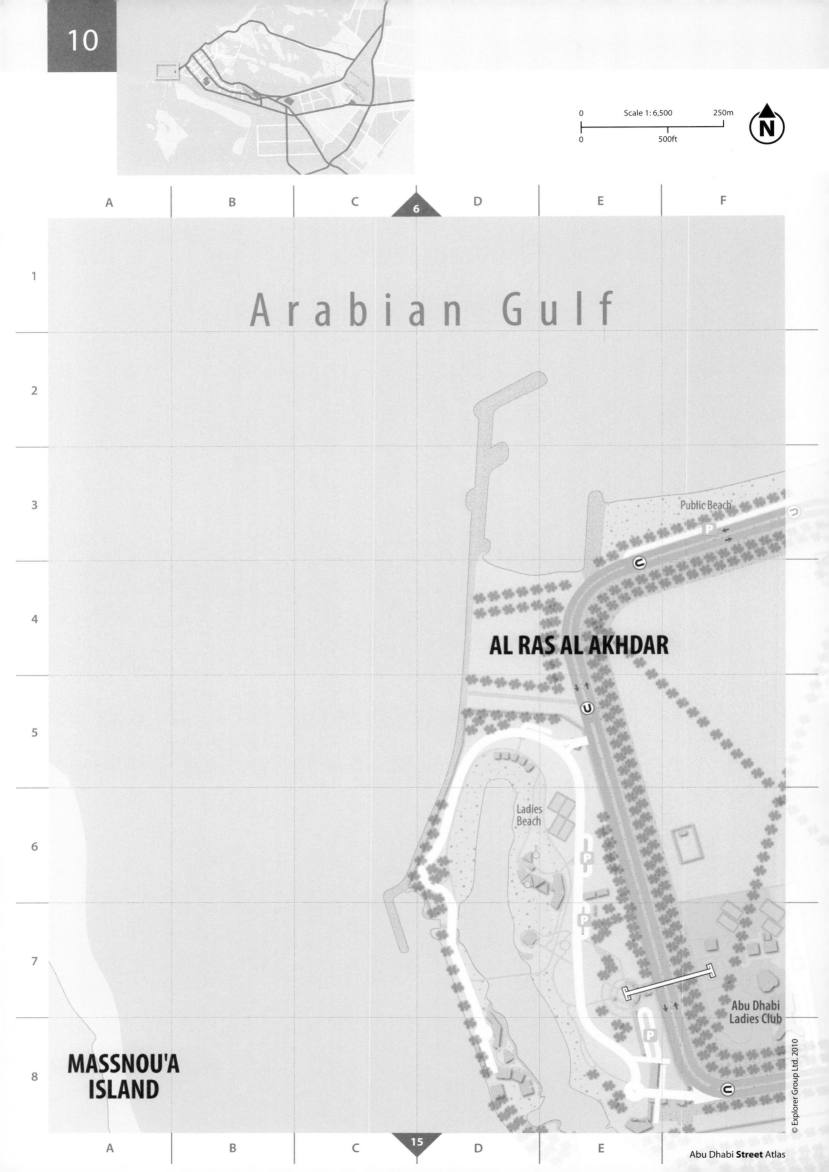

Scale 1 : 6,500

0          250m

0          500ft

N

A      B      C    6    D      E      F

# Arabian Gulf

Public Beach

## AL RAS AL AKHDAR

Ladies
Beach

Abu Dhabi
Ladies Club

## MASSNOU'A
## ISLAND

© Explorer Group Ltd. 2010

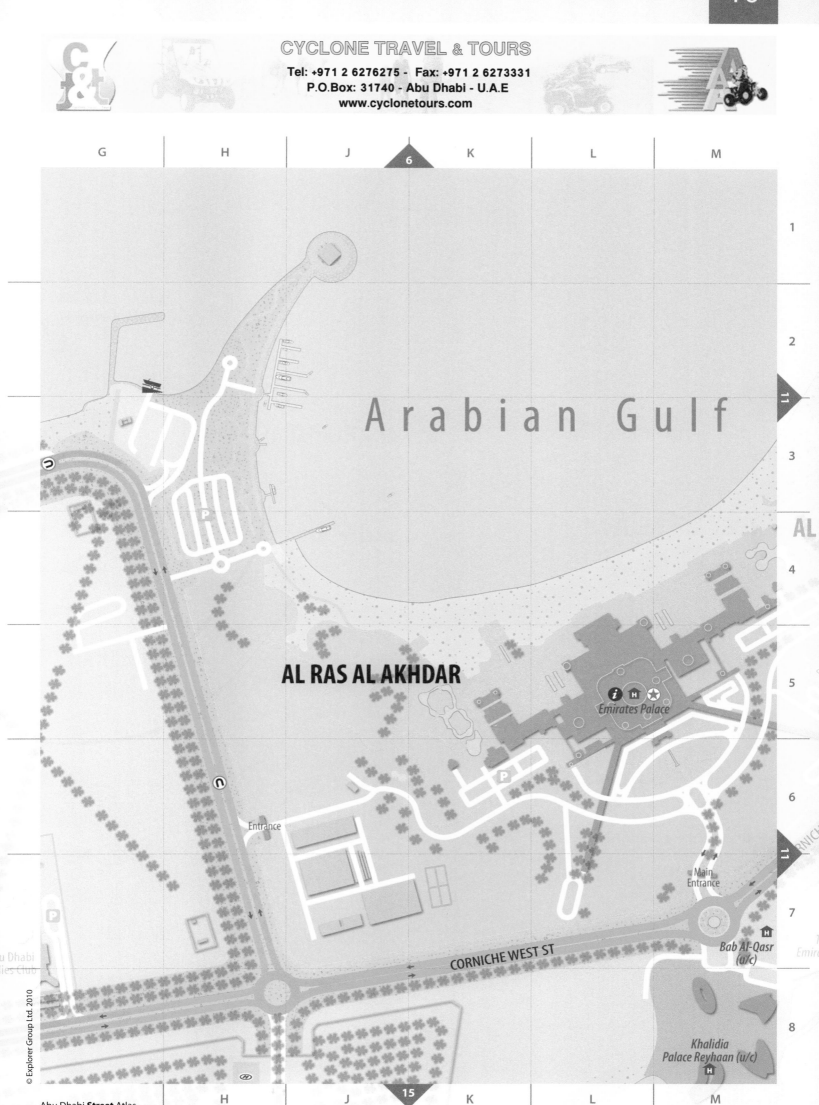

Arabian Gulf

AL RAS AL AKHDAR

Emirates Palace

Entrance

CORNICHE WEST ST

Bab Al-Qasr
(u/c)

Khalidia
Palace Reyhaan (u/c)

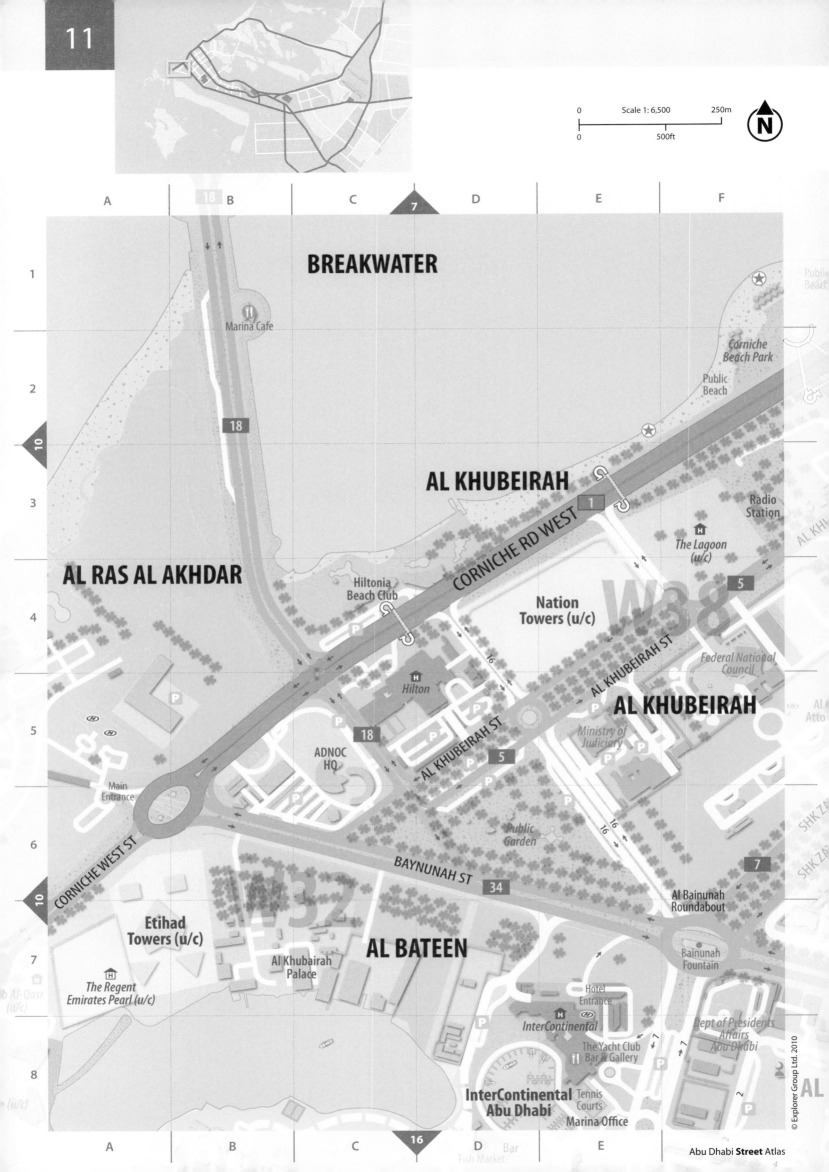

Scale 1: 6,500

0 — 250m

0 — 500ft

N

### BREAKWATER

Marina Cafe

Corniche Beach Park

Public Beach

### AL KHUBEIRAH

CORNICHE RD WEST

Radio Station

The Lagoon (u/c)

### AL RAS AL AKHDAR

Hiltonia Beach Club

Nation Towers (u/c)

Federal National Council

AL KHUBEIRAH ST

### AL KHUBEIRAH

Hilton

ADNOC HQ

AL KHUBEIRAH ST

Ministry of Judiciary

Public Garden

BAYNUNAH ST

Al Bainunah Roundabout

CORNICHE WEST ST

Etihad Towers (u/c)

Bainunah Fountain

### AL BATEEN

Al Khubairah Palace

Hotel Entrance

The Regent Emirates Pearl (u/c)

Al-Qasr (u/c)

InterContinental

The Yacht Club Bar & Gallery

Dept of Presidents Affairs Abu Dhabi

### InterContinental Abu Dhabi

Tennis Courts

Marina Office

Bar Fish Market

# The British International School
## Abu Dhabi, UAE
*Educating responsible and effective citizens of the world*

For admissions please call +971 2 447 4629 or visit our website www.bisabudhabi.com

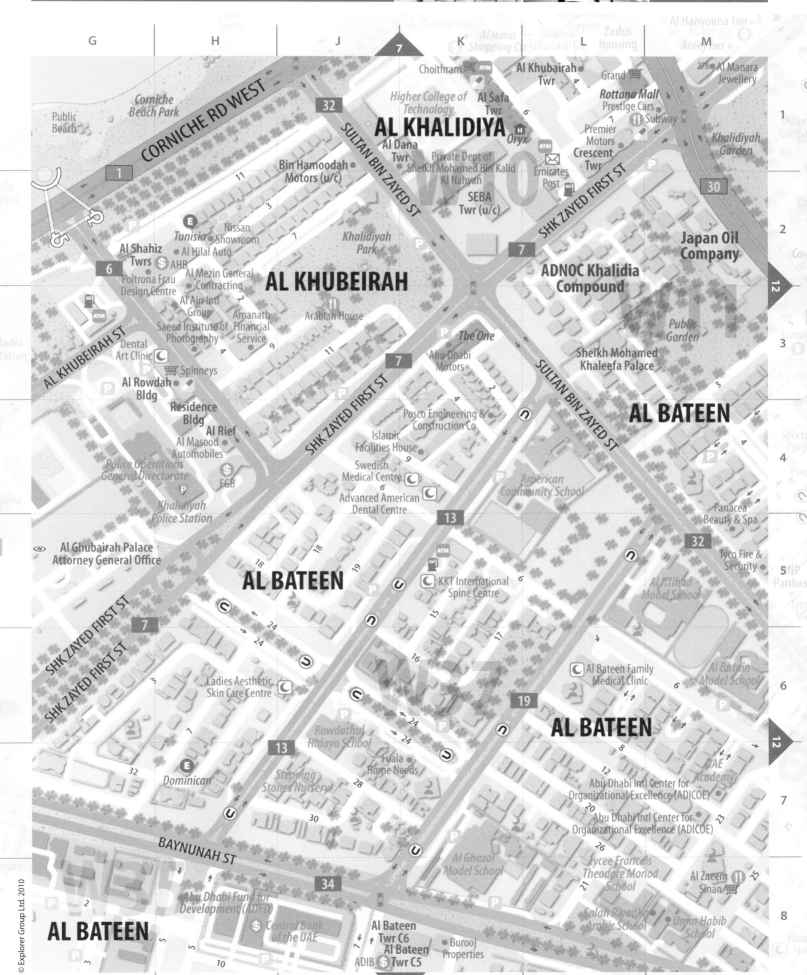

© Explorer Group Ltd. 2010

Scale 1: 6,500

0    250m
0    500ft

N

**AL MANHAL**

6 Palm Oasis
Veg Mkt
13 Royal Printing Park
Queen Saba Trade

A   B   C   D   E   F

City Burger

26

8

**AL MANHAL**

Manara Twr

Nojoom Gards

263

Thjama

Al Razi Scientific

Oxford School
Universal Computers

14
13
11

McDonalds
Dunkin Donuts

Lulu   ATM

Cine Royal

*Khalidiyah Mall*

KING KHALID BIN ABDEL AZIZ ST

**AL MANHAL**

9

Shalimar Company

Al Ameen
Rent A Car

High Class Intl
Training

Auh Centre for
Languages &
Speech Disorders

**Khalidiya
Village**

Al Khalidiya
Stationery

Khalifa Urgent
Care Centre

Sheikh Khalifa Medical City
Blood Bank Abu Dhabi

**AL MANHAL**

American Centre for
Psychiatry & Neurology

Khalidiyah Garden

**Abu Dhabi
Co-operative Society**

Amplex
Emirates

Abu Dhabi
Malayalee Samajam

Dr Ahmed Abu Sharia
Medical Centre

11

30

*Somalja*

*Gulf Horizon
My Little Angel*

*One School Rule
Respect*

Sports Care
Program

Elite Factory for
Precast & Cement Product
Holding Group

AL KHALEEJ AL ARABI ST

Dept of
Pvt Affairs

*Etisalat*

Gulf Autism
Centre

Axis Insurance
Brokers

UAE AID
Co-ordination Office

Corner Stone
Real Estate

AL FALAH ST (AL MANHAL ST)

Zayed Second
Primary School

Primary
Health Care

School Health
Administration

26

*Kenya*

**AL BATEEN**

Comma Brokerage
House
Securities

Electronic Stock
Brokerage Company

*Ayisha Ummul
Muhmineen School*

9

Majestic
Dental Centre

Hanin

*Al Thuraya
Nursery*

7

*Butterfly
Montessori
Nursery*

**AL BATEEN**

BNP
Paribas

*Al Mayaheb
Model School for Girls*

**ASAYEL**
**(Shares & Bonds)**

Al Fajer
Securities

Black Phantom

American
Gulf Medical Ctr

Al Rayan
Investment

Envitech Middle East

**AL BATEEN**

KHALIFA BIN SHAKHBOUT ST

Tyco Fire &
Security

Al Bateen
Municipality
Ctr

National Center of
Metrology &
Seismology

AL FALAH ST (AL MANHAL ST)

30

*Switzerland*

11

*Etisalat*

*Al Dhabyania
Private School*

11

Supermarket &
Departmental Stores

*Rawafeed
Private School*

*Al Amani
School*

AL KHALEEJ AL ARABI ST

Family Development
Foundation

SULTAN BIN ZAYED ST

UAE Exchange

**Al Bateen Mall**

NBAD

Emirates
Post

Cure Advanced
Diagnostic Centre

*UAE
Academy*

*Rawafeed
Private School*

ATM

Abu Dhabi
Secondary School

11

**AL BATEEN**

Gulf Travel
Training Center

**AL BATEEN**

Al Bateen
Park (u/c)

32

Future Centre for
Special Needs

*Bahrain*

17

A   B   C   D   E   F

© Explorer Group Ltd. 2010

Abu Dhabi
Rehabilitation Center

Sheikh Khalifa
Hospital

Arabian Home
Health Care

G    H    J    ▼8    K    L    M    2

# Sheikh Khalifa Medical City

9

Orient House
Development & Construction

Samsung Engineering
Construction

AL KARAMAH ST

Madhrasathul
Al Emaan Hasah

Salahuddin
School    Insead

Dept of
Service
Commerce

24

Al Jazeera
Hospital

Qaági Specialized
Hospital

Pasteur Central
Laboratories
Gava
Forwarding

11

Quality
Makers

13

## AL MANHAL

German Intl
School

Amplex
Emirates

Al Qabas Institute

White by & Bird
Engineering Consultancy

3

Nigeria

Kaya Skin Clinic

24

26

PRP Architects
International

HAZAA BIN ZAYED THE FIRST

Abu Dhabi Children's
Kindergarten

## AL KARAMAH

Al Rowdah
Clinic

Ultra Care
Medical Centre

## AL BATEEN

Abu Dhabi
Co-operative Society

Al Manaseer
Police Station

General
Head Office of
Auh Police

Mohd Bin Khalid
Secondary School

11

Abu Dhabi Intl
Private School

General Authority for
Health Service for The
Emirate of Abu Dhabi

Bateen Boys School
for Basic Education Cycle

Abu Dhabi School for
Secondary Education

Al Rawdah German
Medical Centre

First Steps
School

13

United Utilities
International

Grace
Medical Centre

Emirates Intl
Real Estate

26

Al Rayyan National
Private School

Alafaq Junior
Model School

Al Bayan Arabic
News Paper
Admiral
Foodstuff

11

AL BATEEN ST

Abu Dhabi Education
Zone (ADEZ)

## AL ROWDAH

KHALIFA BIN SHAKHBOUT ST

AL NAHYAN ST

Abu Dhabi Sewerage
Services Company (ADSSC)

MI SWACO Company

Argentina

Stepping
Stones
Nursery

11

Holland    Nigeria    Bangladesh

Hungary    Italy
Morocco
Japan

28    13

G    H    J    ▼17    K    L    M

Scale 1: 6,500

0     250m

0     500ft

N

AL NAHYAN

EAST RD

Group

Mashreq

**A**   **B**   16   **C**   9   EAST RD   Group   **E**   **F**

The Grand Millenium (u/c)

UNB

Ala Kalifa

Lulu   ADIB UBL   Bricco Cafe

Abu Tariq

Abu Dhabi Main Terminal Bus Station

Bite Rite Cafe

Al Wahda Mall

Fuala

ADCB   Football Cafe Shop

Marlin Furniture

230

232

Al Rowdah Arjan

236

238

Al Wahda Stadium (Sports Cultural Club)

Thameer Trading Est

Golden Tower Rent A Car

Dept of Social Services & Commercial

Citroen French Automobile

Italian Palace

242

Eifel Twr

Millennium Southern Fried Chicken

Abu Dhabi Junior Academy

Emirates Heritage Club

UNB

Fathima

248

250

Al Wahda Res Complex

Ups Express

2

Landmark Properties

Al Fardan

Dana Style Office Furniture

252

254

E4U Electronics

256

16

**AL NAHYAN**

18

4

Future Nursery School

12

Mr Clean Dry Cleaning

DHL

Habara House

Heris Bader Mohd Saeed Al Muraiki

13

Al Wifaq Finance Company

Akai

Akai Showroom Sada Al Ayyam

Corpo Fine SPA & Slimming Centre

Milano Furniture

Al Hidaya Kindergarten Nursery

14

Zayed University

Dream Tech Computer

Al Obaidly Ceramics

Palestine School

Ruku Al Sultan Restaurant & Grills

Galaxy Carpets

268

Casa Mobile Furniture

Auh Folklore & Theatre Society

Radiant Montessori Nursery

Al Ghadheer Specialized Medical Centre

20

18

Awafi Trading

272 274

Beauty Palace Furniture

Delmon Furniture

Police Cultural Sports Club

241

ATM

245

Al Minhaj Interiors

247

Abu Saeed Ali Khoory

276 278

280

282

Jotun Paint Shop

13

NBB Travel & Tourism

Neb Engineering Control Corporation

249

286

Gulf Palace Trading Establishment

Compressor Controls Corporation

Fast Rent A Car

Al Nayadi Dubai

Cars Rent A Car

**AL KARAMAH**

Abu Dhabi Food Control Aothority (ADFCA)

290

Mashreq

**AL NAHYAN**

Abu Dhabi Distribution Co

**Al Dhafra Compound**

Rent Dispute Settlement Committee

294

296

Public Work Dept

Canadian Medical Ctr

2

257

298

Fathima

300

Thrifty Rent A Car

Abu Dhabi Centre For Housing & Services Facilities Dept

Main Gate

ATM

Health Quest Medical Ctr

302

304

American European Medical Centre

Al Reyada Medical Ctr

Al Hosn University

Sameer Al Mahmood & Sons Furniture

306 308

Hanayen Company Middle East

Arabian House

Happy Days Garments

Faris Furniture

316

Al Sorour Bakeries

Barbanel Middle East

12

ND SatCom Middle East

13

Al Hosn University

Abu Dhabi Education Council

Al Burak

314

318

Auto Star Trading

German Rent A Car

Govt Departments Sports Association

Emirate Spanish Furnishing

320

Abu Dhabi Motor Sport Management (ADMM)

CosmeSurge & Emirates Hospital

Sheikh Sultan Bin Zayed Stadium

Pizza Hut

E

Romania

24

Poland

Al Hana

**Al Musalla**

Popeyes Chicken & Seafood

324

ADIB

Brass Light

DELMA ST

Emirates of Abu Dhabi Maritime Security Executive Committee

AL KARAMAH ST

Mashreq

**Eidgah Ground**

Al Hawai Office Furniture & Equipment

Stars For Special Abilities

EIB

Western Region Development Council

15-02

Elite Music Institute

293 295

**A**   **B**   18   **C**   **D**   **E**   **F**

24

SHK RASHID BIN SAEED AL MAKTOUM ST

DELMA ST

© Explorer Group Ltd. 2010

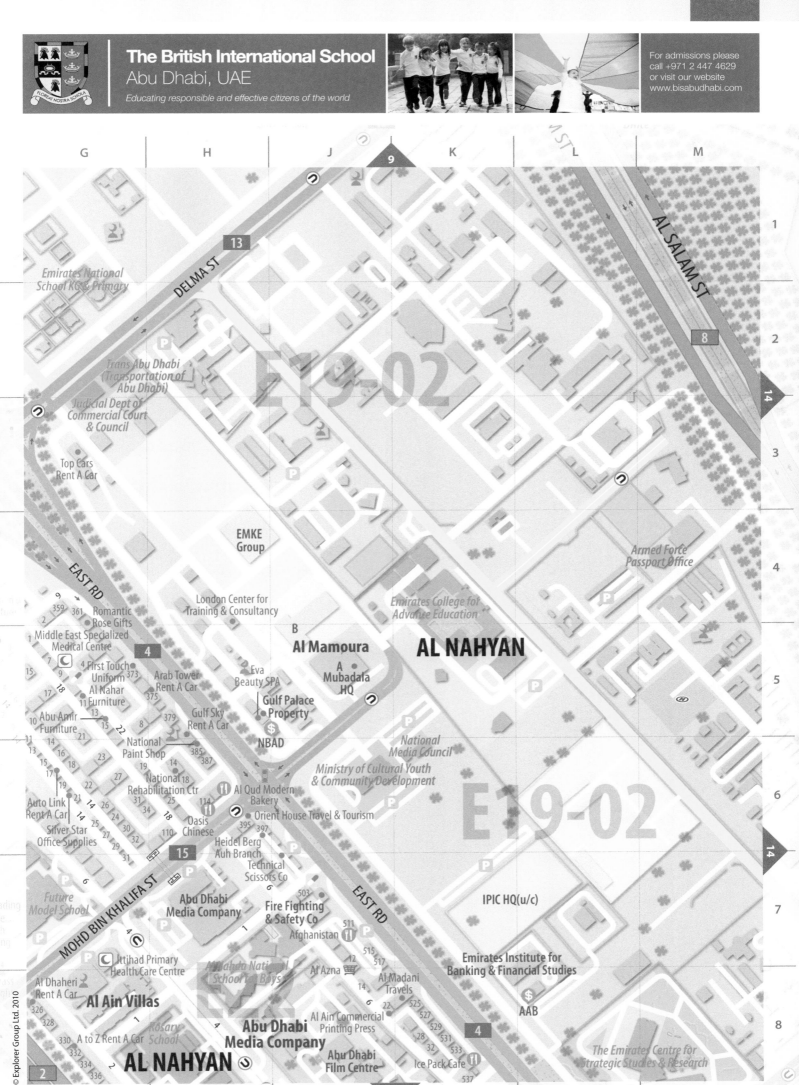

**The British International School**
Abu Dhabi, UAE
*Educating responsible and effective citizens of the world*

For admissions please
call +971 2 447 4629
or visit our website
www.bisabudhabi.com

G    H    J    9    K    L    M

1

AL SALAM ST

*Emirates National
School KG & Primary*

DELMA ST

13

E19-02

8

2

14

3

*Trans Abu Dhabi
(Transportation of
Abu Dhabi)*

*Judicial Dept of
Commercial Court
& Council*

Top Cars
Rent A Car

EMKE
Group

London Center for
Training & Consultancy

*Armed Force
Passport Office*

359 361 Romantic
Rose Gifts
Middle East Specialized
Medical Centre

B

Al Mamoura

AL NAHYAN

*Emirates College for
Advance Education*

4 First Touch
Uniform 373
Arab Tower
Rent A Car
Al Nahar
Furniture 375

Eva
Beauty SPA

A
Mubadala
HQ

Abu Amir
Furniture 13 15 22
379
Gulf Sky
Rent A Car

Gulf Palace
Property

$

NBAD

National
Paint Shop 385
387

National
Media Council

National
Rehabilitation Ctr 18
114
Al Qud Modern
Bakery

Ministry of Cultural Youth
& Community Development

E19-02

Auto Link
Rent A Car

Orient House Travel & Tourism

395 397
Oasis
Chinese 110

Silver Star
Office Supplies

15

Heidel Berg
Auh Branch
Technical
Scissors Co

14

*Future
Model School*

MOHD BIN KHALIFA ST

Abu Dhabi
Media Company

Fire Fighting
& Safety Co 503

IPIC HQ(u/c)

7

511
Afghanistan

Ittihad Primary
Health Care Centre

515
517

Emirates Institute for
Banking & Financial Studies

Al Azna

Al Madani
Travels

Al Dhaheri
Rent A Car
326

AL Ain Villas

525
527 529

AAB

$

8

328

A to Z Rent A Car
330
332
334
336

*Rosary
School*

Abu Dhabi
Media Company

Al Ain Commercial
Printing Press

Abu Dhabi
Film Centre

531
533
537

Ice Pack Cafe

*The Emirates Centre for
Strategic Studies & Research*

2

AL NAHYAN

H

J

18

K

L

M

Abu Dhabi

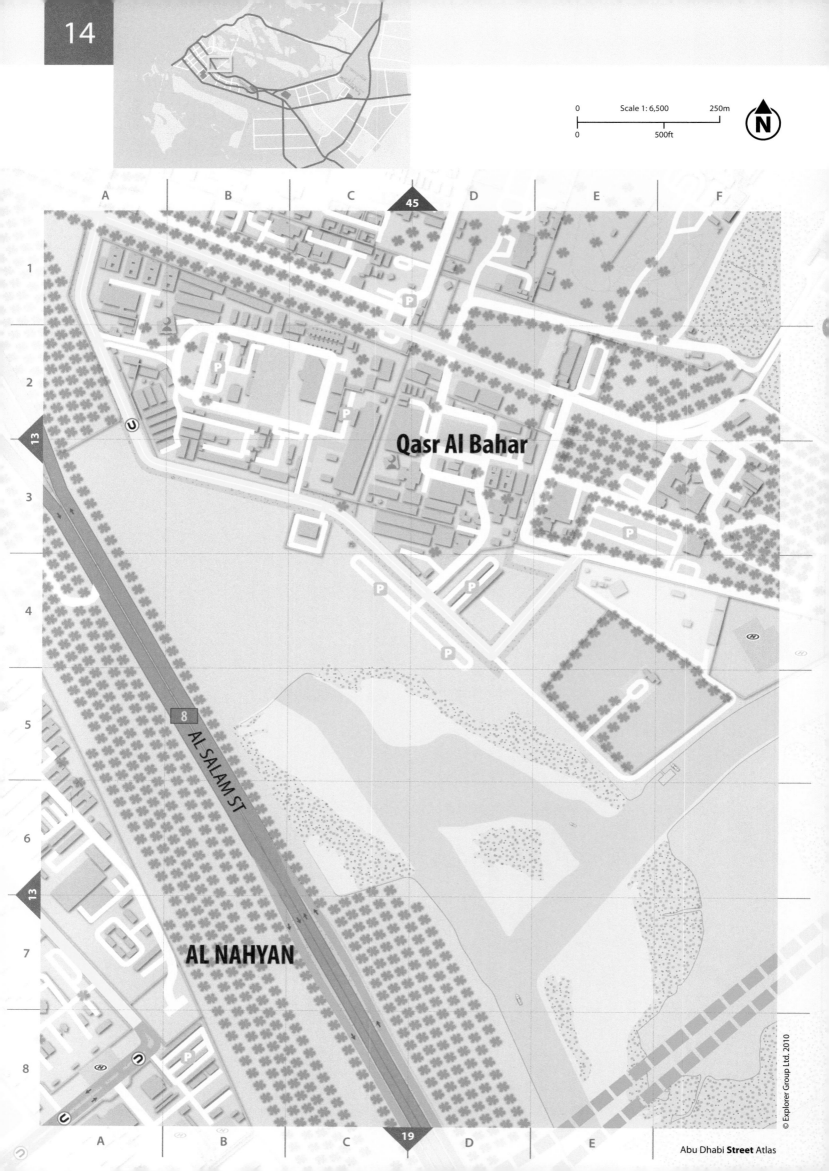

Scale 1: 6,500

0 — 250m
0 — 500ft

N

A  B  C  45  D  E  F

1

2

13

3

**Qasr Al Bahar**

4

5

8

AL SALAM ST

6

13

7

**AL NAHYAN**

8

A  B  C  19  D  E

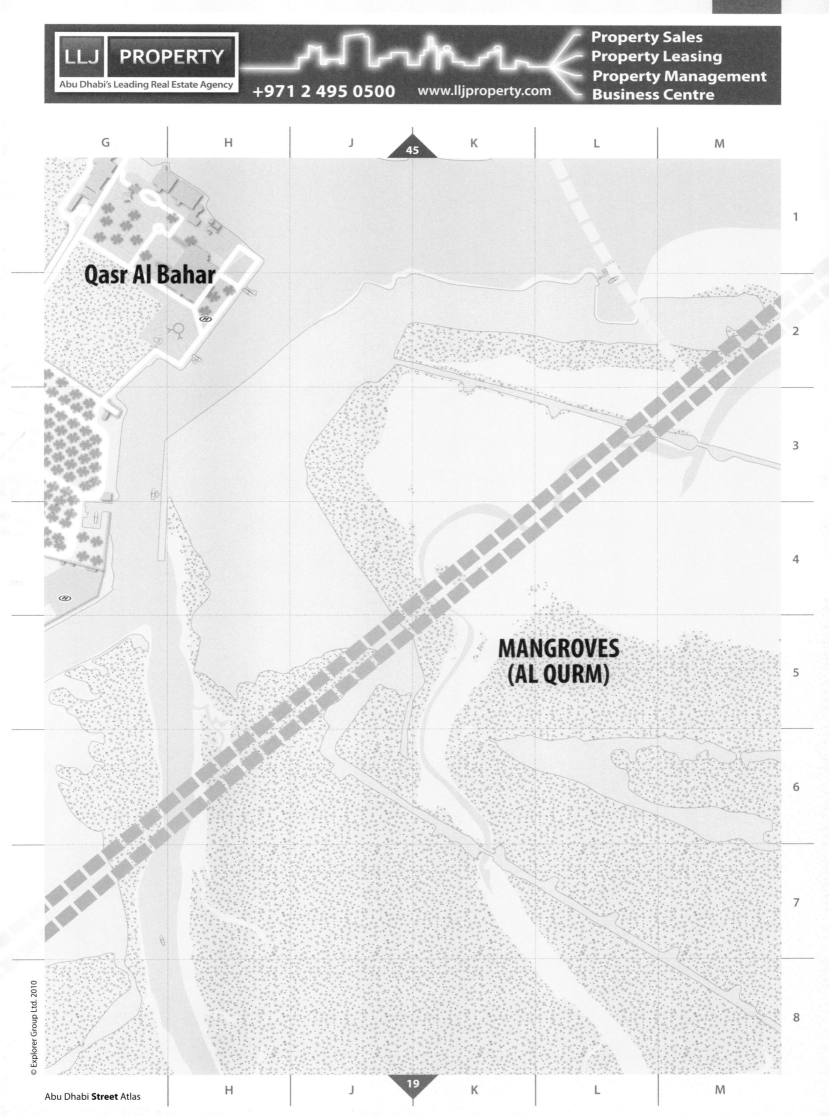

Qasr Al Bahar

MANGROVES
(AL QURM)

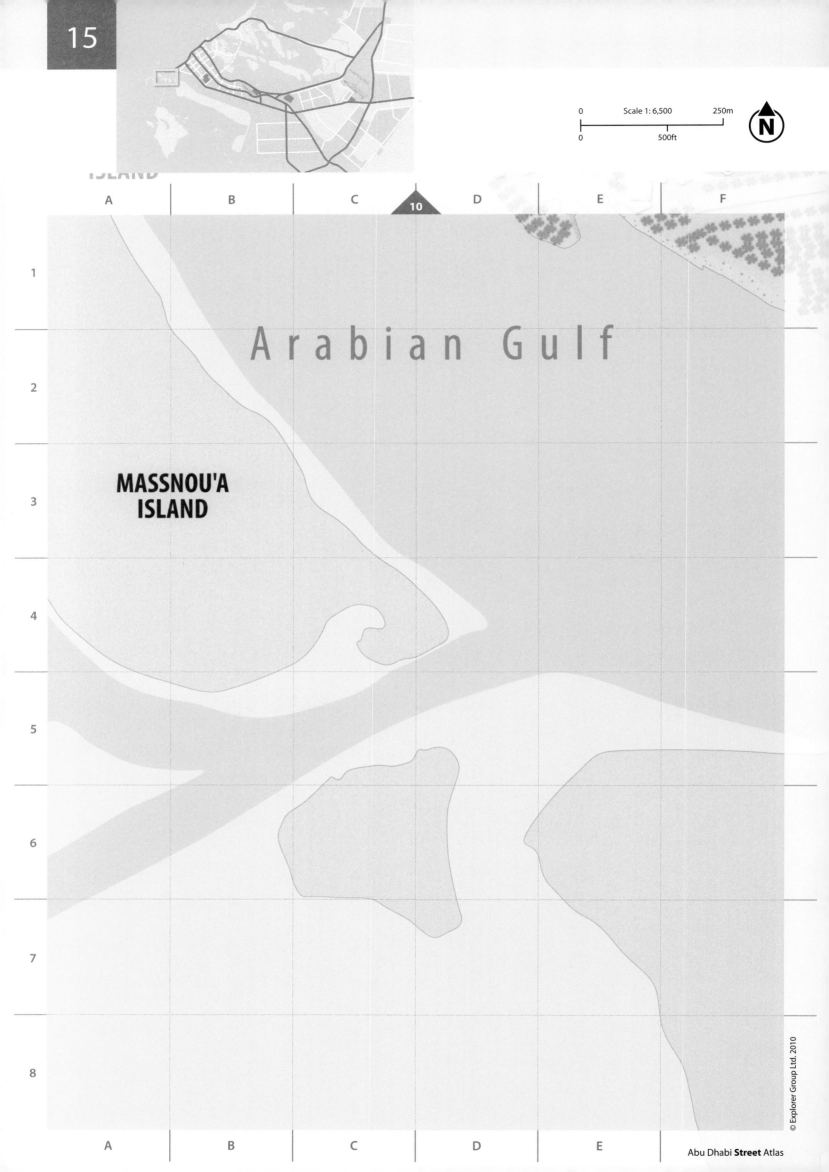

ISLAND

A    B    C    10    D    E    F

1

Arabian Gulf

2

MASSNOU'A
ISLAND

3

4

5

6

7

8

A    B    C    D    E

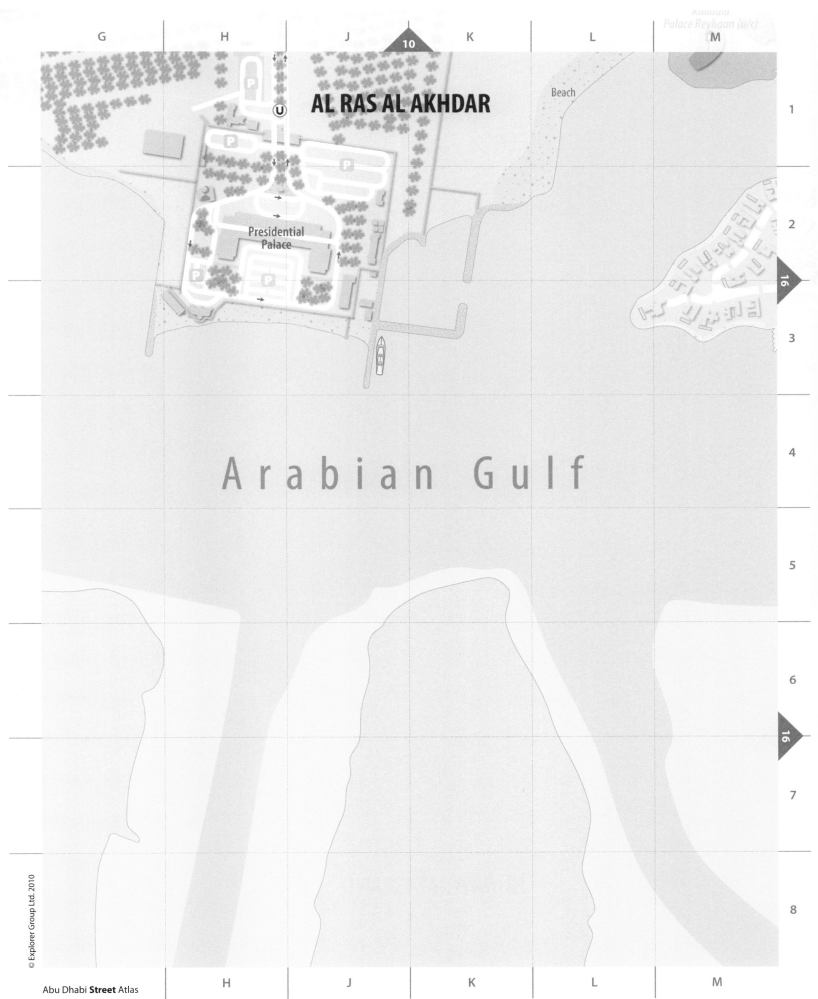

AL RAS AL AKHDAR

Beach

Presidential
Palace

Arabian Gulf

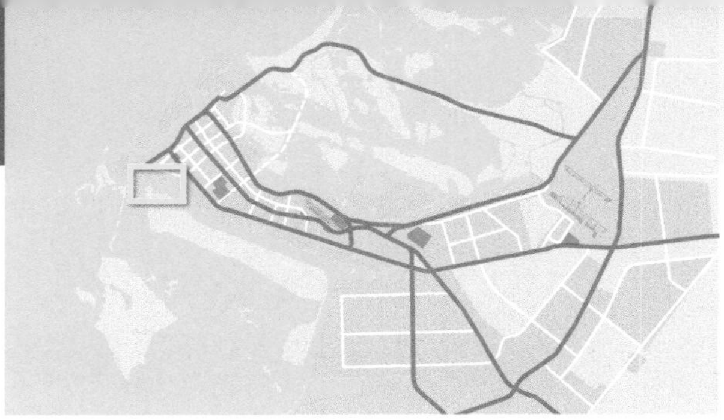

Scale 1: 6,500

0 — 250m
0 — 500ft

**N**

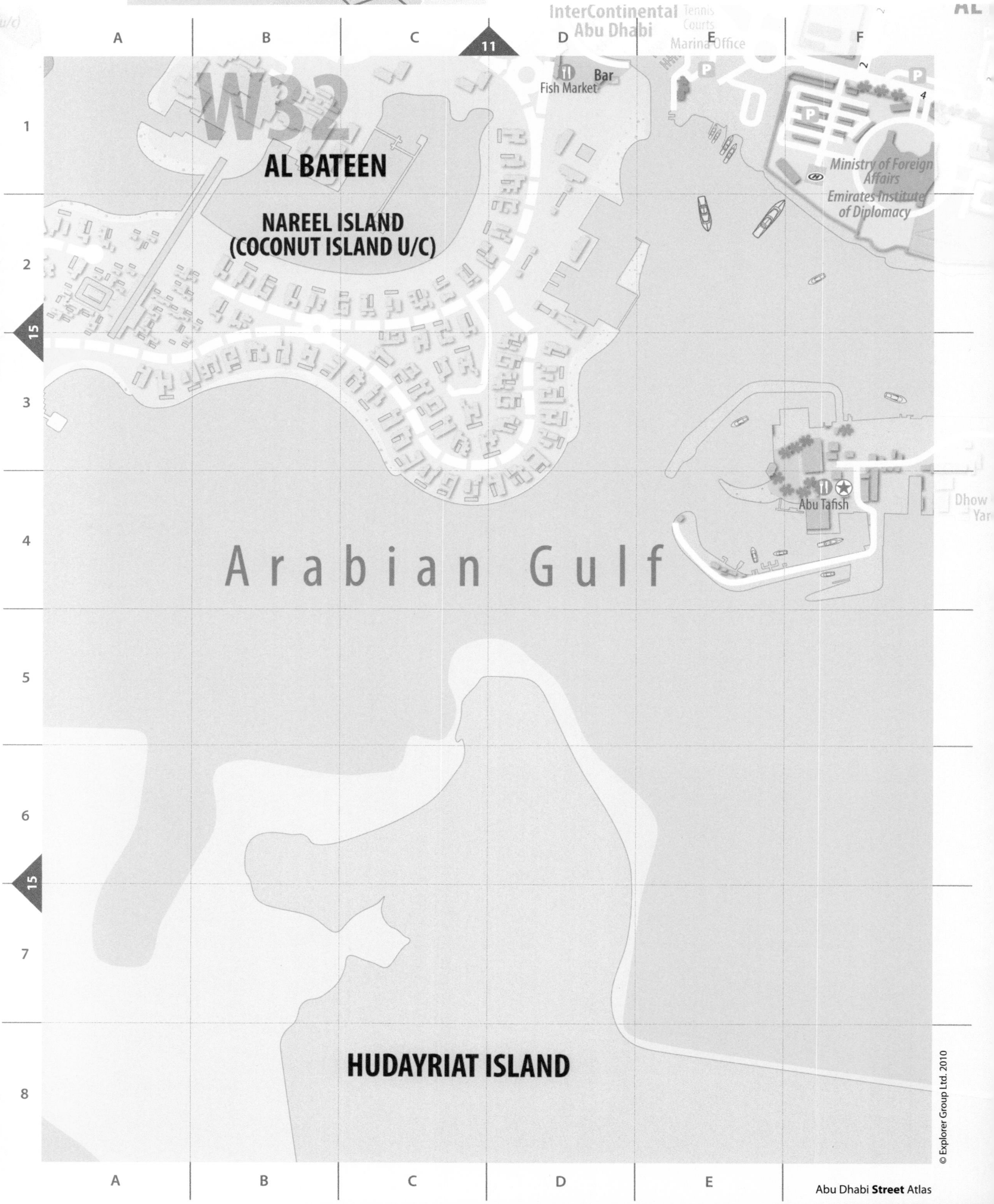

InterContinental Abu Dhabi

Tennis Courts
Marina Office

Fish Market

Bar

Ministry of Foreign Affairs

Emirates Institute of Diplomacy

**W32**

**AL BATEEN**

**NAREEL ISLAND
(COCONUT ISLAND U/C)**

Abu Tafish

Dhow Yard

# Arabian Gulf

**HUDAYRIAT ISLAND**

© Explorer Group Ltd. 2010

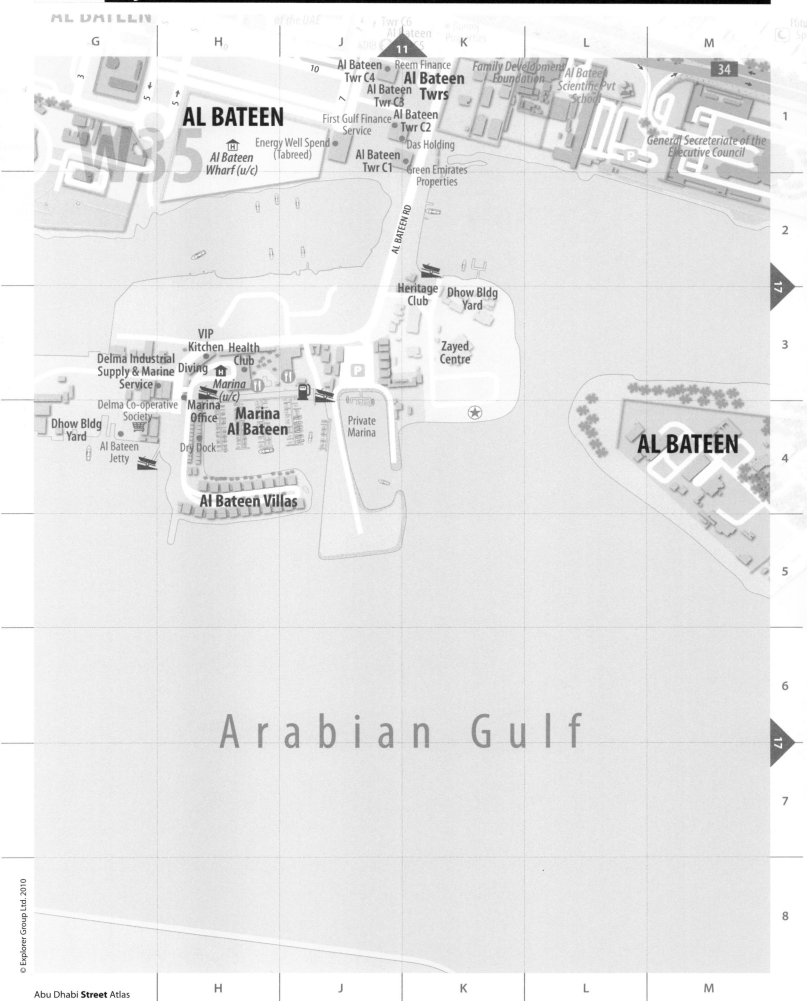

AL BATEEN

of the UAE

Twr C6
Al Bateen
Twr C5

**11**

34

G    H    J    K    L    M

Al Bateen
Twr C4

Reem Finance

Family Developments
Foundation

Al Bateen
Scientific Pvt
School

10

**Al Bateen
Twrs**

Al Bateen
Twr C3

**AL BATEEN**

First Gulf Finance
Service

Al Bateen
Twr C2

Das Holding

1

Energy Well Spend
(Tabreed)

General Secreteriate of the
Executive Council

Al Bateen
Wharf (u/c)

Al Bateen
Twr C1

Green Emirates
Properties

2

AL BATEEN RD

Heritage
Club

Dhow Bldg
Yard

17

VIP
Kitchen  Health
Club

Zayed
Centre

3

Delma Industrial
Supply & Marine
Service

Diving

Marina
(u/c)

Delma Co-operative
Society

Marina
Office

**Marina
Al Bateen**

Private
Marina

Dhow Bldg
Yard

**AL BATEEN**

Al Bateen
Jetty

Dry Dock

4

**Al Bateen Villas**

5

6

A r a b i a n   G u l f

17

7

© Explorer Group Ltd. 2010

8

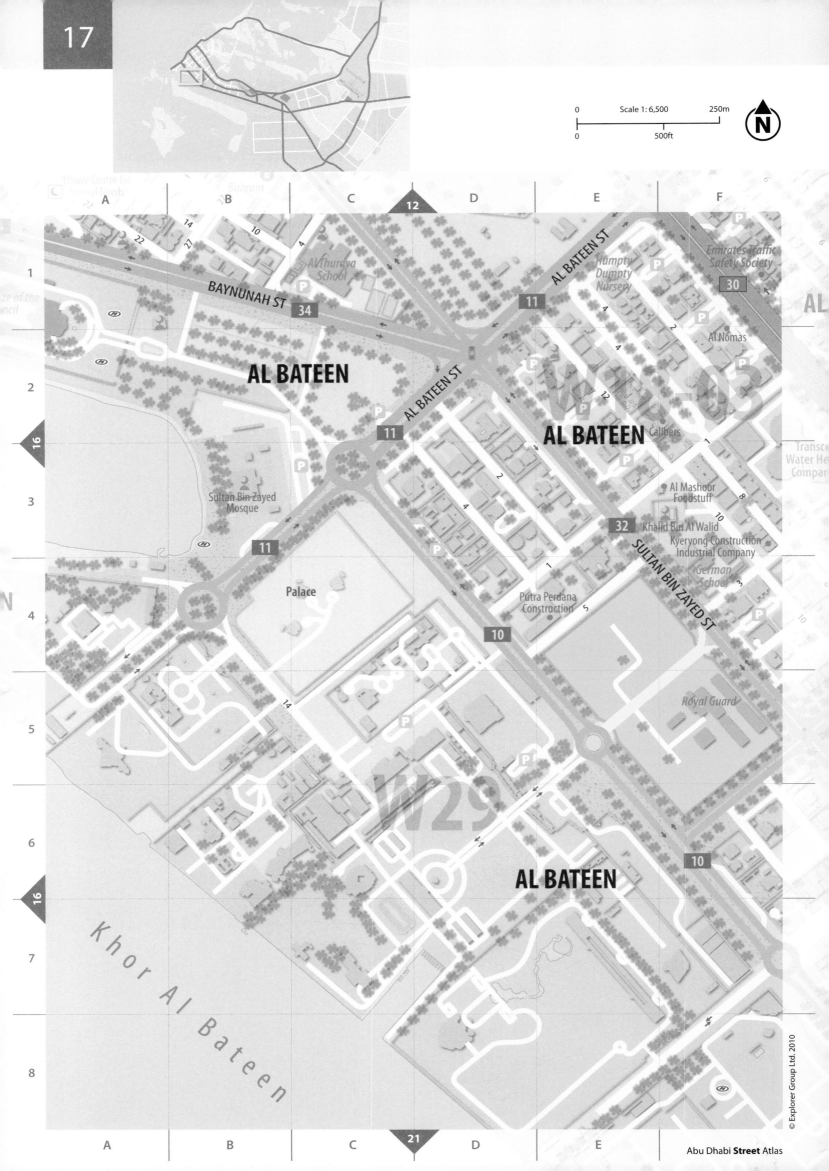

Scale 1: 6,500

0     250m

0     500ft

N

**AL BATEEN**

**AL BATEEN**

**AL BATEEN**

BAYNUNAH ST

AL BATEEN ST

AL BATEEN ST

SULTAN BIN ZAYED ST

Khor Al Bateen

Nature Centre for Special Needs

Al Thurqya School

Humpty Dumpty Nursery

Emirates Traffic Safety Society

Al Nomas

Calibers

Al Mashoor Foodstuff

Khalid Bin Al Walid Kyeryong Construction Industrial Company

German School

Putra Perdana Construction

Sultan Bin Zayed Mosque

Palace

Royal Guard

Transco Water Hea Compar

© Explorer Group Ltd. 2010

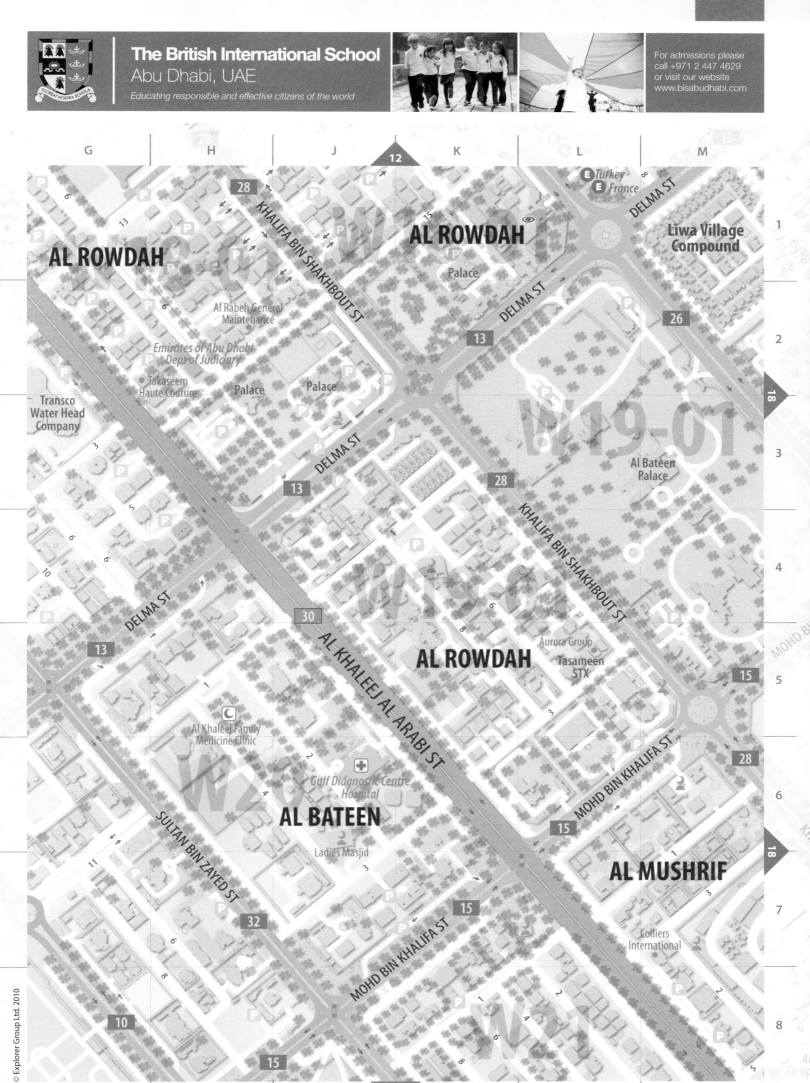

**The British International School**
Abu Dhabi, UAE
*Educating responsible and effective citizens of the world*

For admissions please
call +971 2 447 4629
or visit our website
www.bisabudhabi.com

**AL ROWDAH**

**AL ROWDAH**

KHALIFA BIN SHAKHBOUT ST

Al Rabeh General
Maintenance

Emirates of Abu Dhabi
Dept of Judiciary

Takaseem
Haute Couture

Palace

Palace

Palace

Transco
Water Head
Company

DELMA ST

DELMA ST

DELMA ST

DELMA ST

Turkey
France

Liwa Village
Compound

Al Bateen
Palace

KHALIFA BIN SHAKHBOUT ST

**AL ROWDAH**

Aurora Group
Tasameen
STX

AL KHALEEJ AL ARABI ST

Al Khaleej Family
Medicine Clinic

Gulf Diagnostic Centre
Hospital

**AL BATEEN**

Ladies Masjid

SULTAN BIN ZAYED ST

MOHD BIN KHALIFA ST

MOHD BIN KHALIFA ST

**AL MUSHRIF**

Colliers
International

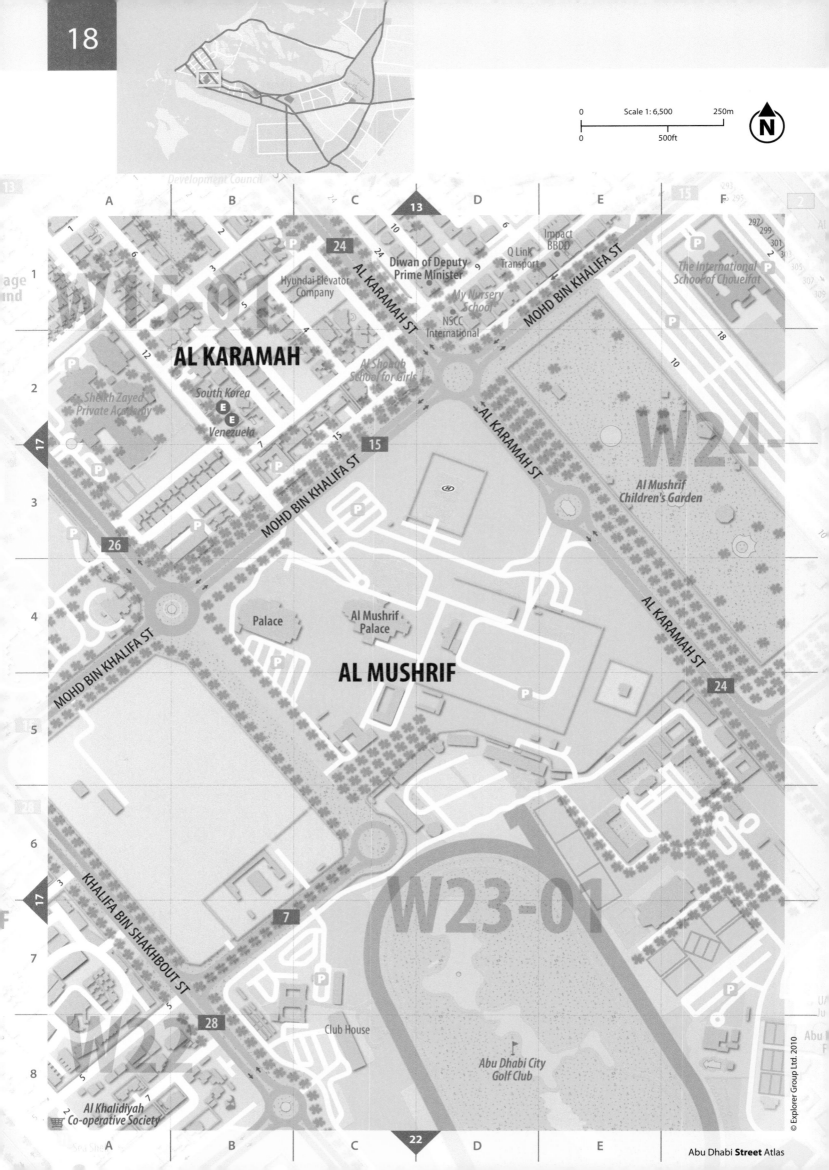

Scale 1: 6,500

0      250m

0      500ft

N

Development Council

A   B   C  **13**  D   E  **15**  F

**Diwan of Deputy Prime Minister**

Q Link Transport

Impact BBDD

The International School of Choueifat

Hyundai Elevator Company

AL KARAMAH ST

My Nursery School

MOHD BIN KHALIFA ST

**AL KARAMAH**

NSCC International

Al Shohub School for Girls

Sheikh Zayed Private Academy

South Korea

Venezuela

MOHD BIN KHALIFA ST

AL KARAMAH ST

W24-

Al Mushrif Children's Garden

**26**

Palace

Al Mushrif Palace

**AL MUSHRIF**

MOHD BIN KHALIFA ST

**24**

KHALIFA BIN SHAKHBOUT ST

W23-01

**7**

Club House

Abu Dhabi City Golf Club

Al Khalidiyah Co-operative Society

A   B   C  **22**  D   E

© Explorer Group Ltd. 2010

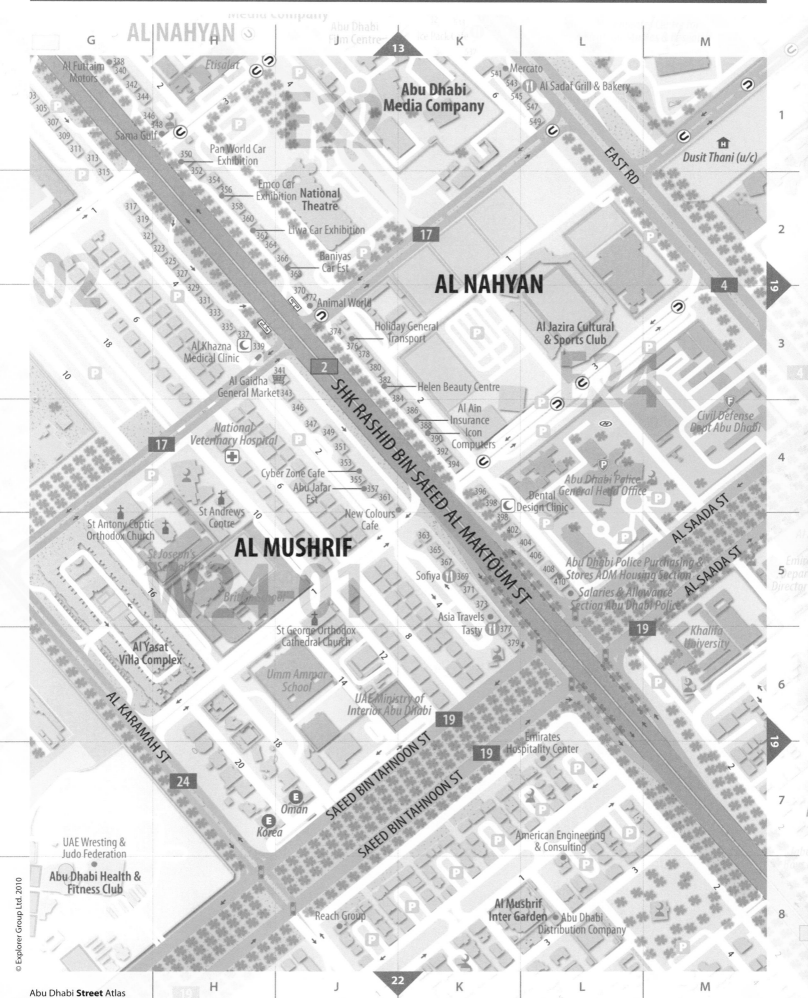

AL NAHYAN

Media Company

Abu Dhabi
Film Centre

Ice Packaging

Etisalat

Abu Dhabi
Media Company

13

Mercato
Al Sadaf Grill & Bakery

EAST RD

Dusit Thani (u/c)

Al Futtaim
Motors

Sama Gulf

Pan World Car
Exhibition

Emco Car
Exhibition

National
Theatre

Liwa Car Exhibition

Baniyas
Car Est

17

AL NAHYAN

Animal World

Holiday General
Transport

Al Jazira Cultural
& Sports Club

Al Khazna
Medical Clinic

Al Gaidha
General Market

Helen Beauty Centre

Al Ain
Insurance
Icon
Computers

Civil Defense
Dept Abu Dhabi

2

National
Veterinary Hospital

17

SHK RASHID BIN SAEED AL MAKTOUM ST

Cyber Zone Cafe
Abu Jafar
Est

Dental
Design Clinic

Abu Dhabi Police
General Head Office

Abu Dhabi Police Purchasing &
Stores ADM Housing Section

AL SAADA ST

AL SAADA ST

St Antony Coptic
Orthodox Church

St Andrews
Centre

New Colours
Cafe

AL MUSHRIF

Sofiya

Salaries & Allowance
Section Abu Dhabi Police

19

Khalifa
University

St Joseph's
School

British...

Asia Travels
Tasty

AL KARAMAH ST

Al Yasat
Villa Complex

St George Orthodox
Cathedral Church

Umm Ammar
School

UAE Ministry of
Interior Abu Dhabi

19

19

Emirates
Hospitality Center

24

Oman

Korea

SAEED BIN TAHNOON ST

SAEED BIN TAHNOON ST

American Engineering
& Consulting

UAE Wresting &
Judo Federation

Abu Dhabi Health &
Fitness Club

Reach Group

Al Mushrif
Inter Garden

Abu Dhabi
Distribution Company

22

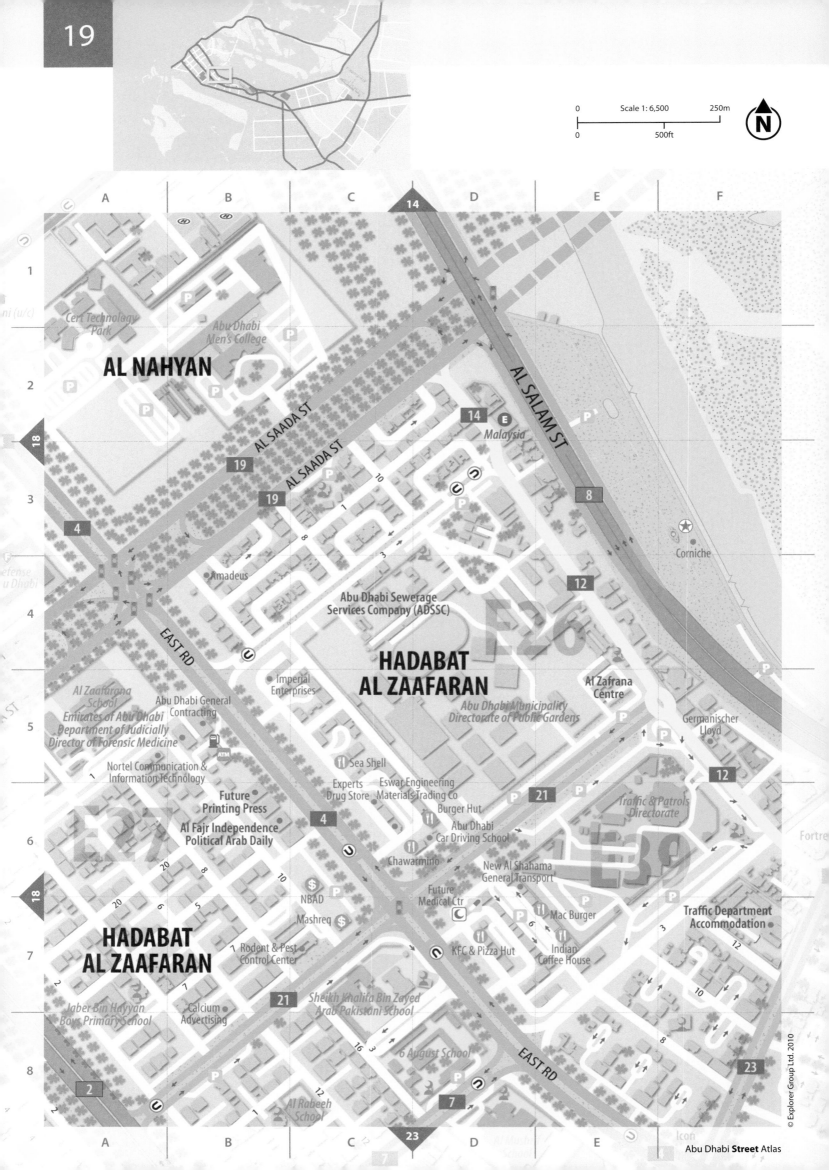

Scale 1: 6,500

0     250m

0     500ft

**N**

14

18

**AL NAHYAN**

Cert Technology Park

Abu Dhabi Men's College

AL SAADA ST

19

19

AL SAADA ST

4

Al Salam St

Malaysia

14

E

8

10

1

8

Amadeus

3

Abu Dhabi Sewerage Services Company (ADSSC)

Corniche

12

EAST RD

**HADABAT AL ZAAFARAN**

Imperial Enterprises

Al Zaafarana School

Emirates of Abu Dhabi Department of Judicially Director of Forensic Medicine

Abu Dhabi General Contracting

Al Zafrana Centre

Abu Dhabi Municipality Directorate of Public Gardens

Germanischer Lloyd

12

ATM

Sea Shell

Nortel Communication & Information Technology

Experts Drug Store

Eswar Engineering Materials Trading Co

Burger Hut

Traffic & Patrols Directorate

**Future Printing Press**

21

**Al Fajr Independence Political Arab Daily**

Abu Dhabi Car Driving School

4

Chawarmino

New Al Shahama General Transport

20

8

10

Future Medical Ctr

Mac Burger

**Traffic Department Accommodation**

18

$

NBAD

6

12

20

6

5

Mashreq

$

KFC & Pizza Hut

Indian Coffee House

3

**HADABAT AL ZAAFARAN**

Rodent & Pest Control Center

1

7

21

Sheikh Khalifa Bin Zayed Arab Pakistani School

10

Jaber Bin Hayyan Boys Primary School

Calcium Advertising

7

2

16

3

6 August School

8

EAST RD

23

12

7

Al Rabeeh School

1

23

Icon

G　　H　　J　　**14**　　K　　L　　M

1

2

**20**

3

**MANGROVES
(AL QURM)**

4

5

6

Fortress

Atlas Telecom

**8** AL SALAM ST

**23**

**20**

18

National Private School

**22**

Mashayil School (Arabic)

tment lation

Abu Dhabi Indian School

**HADABAT
AL ZAAFARAN**

The Model School Abu Dhabi

7

Little Bird School

14

20

16

Uzbekistan **E**

ABC Private School

26

8

8

Al Rawza Zahirah School

9

Aconex

**25**

**AL ZAHRA**

8

14

Jibreel Mosque

20

H　　J　　**23**　　K　　L　　M

Scale 1: 6,500

0      250m

0      500ft

N

1

2

19

3

# MANGROVES
# (AL QURM)

4

5

6

19

7

AL SALAM ST

8

**AL ZAHRA**

Al Manara Private School

Fajr Int'l School

26

Omnix International

40

29

24

110,000 Buildings, 3,000 Streets,
300 Pages, One Atlas

www.explorerpublishing.com

**Dubai**
street atlas

| G | H | J | K | L | M |

**MANGROVES
(AL QURM)**

Angsana Resort & Spa
Eastern Mangroves (u/c)

P

Bridge (u/c)

8

**AL ZAHRA**

Al Matar

J3

42

37

P

40

39

Sawaeed
Employment
Camp

31

**AL SALAM ST**

P

Scale 1: 6,500

N

A B C D E F

1

AL BATEEN

2

Khor Al Bateen

3

4

5

6

HUDAYRIAT ISLAND

7

8

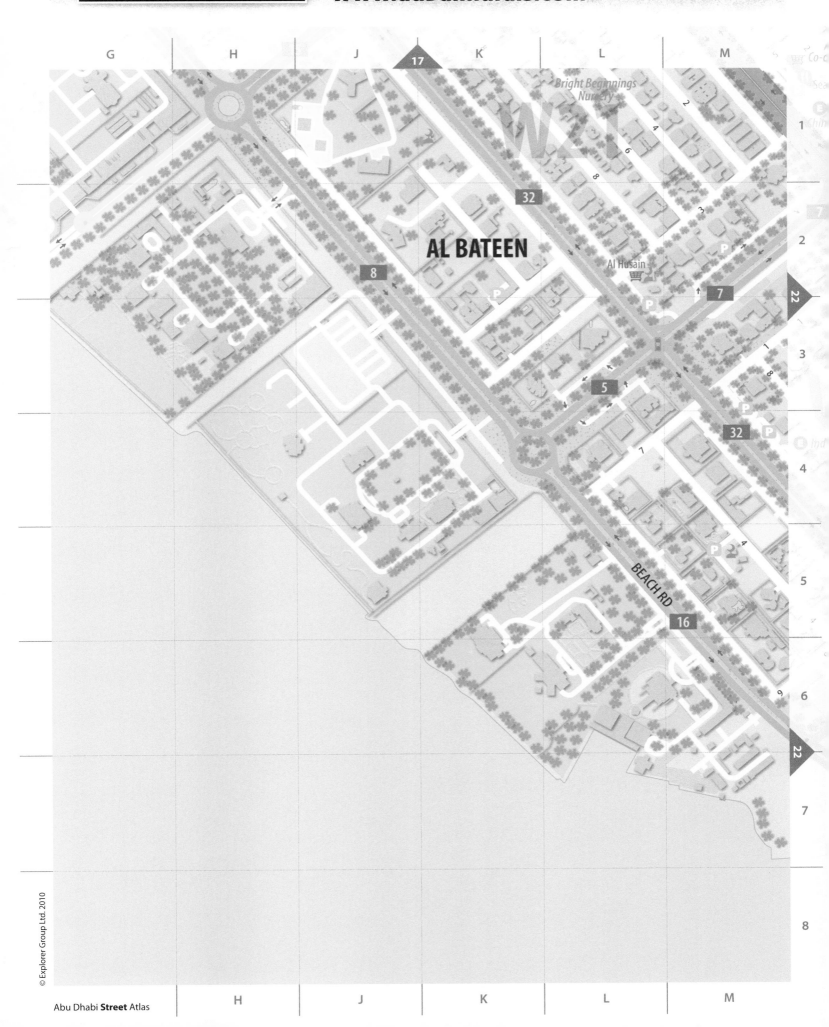

G H J 17 K L M

**AL BATEEN**

Bright Beginnings Nursery

Al Husain

BEACH RD

Scale 1: 6,500

0   250m

0   500ft

N

Al Khalidiyah
Co-operative Society

Sea Shell

China

Abu Dhabi City Golf Club

28

19

7

30

**AL MUSHRIF**

KHALIFA BIN SHAKHBOUT ST

SAEED BIN TAHNOON ST

SAEED BIN TAHNOON ST

W2.6

Indonesia

Libya

**AL BATEEN**

W2.5

19

28

16

KHALIFA BIN SHAKHBOUT ST

**AL MUSHRIF**

32

19

19

30

**Qasr Al Shati**

AL KHALEEJ AL ARABI ST (COAST RD)

14

**Qasr Al Shati**

**Qasr Al Shati**

BEACH RD

16

© Explorer Group Ltd. 2010

G    H    J    18    K    L    M

19

SAEED BIN TAHNOON ST

Al Arabia
Press & Media

Family Development
Foundation

W46

1

AL MUSHRIF

Nord Anglia
Education

2

23

3

24

10

AL KARAMAH ST

W52-01

Al Tawah
Private School

The Elite
Private School

4

5

Masjid & Quran
Study Center

Karlstorz
Endoscopy

Linde Gas
Middle East

6

Hamoodah
Bin Ali Model
School

19

23

30

AL KHALEEJ AL ARABI ST (COAST RD)

21

30

7

Picnic Area

ATM

8

Qasr Al Shati

Scale 1: 6,500

0   250m
0   500ft

N

A   B   C   **19**   D   E   F

1

Al Mushrif
School

Icon

**7**

**4**

Berlitz Language
Institute

Hayatt
Real Estate

**2**

Sheikh
Saif Mosque

13

Gulf
Coast

Al Mushrif
Marriage Hall

## HADABAT
## AL ZAAFARAN

Al Quadra
Industries

**22**

**23**

2

## AL MUSHRIF

China Petroleum
Pipeline Bureau

International
Community School

3

Al Nahda
National School

Haward Technology
Middle East

Municipality
Airport Road Markets

Municipality
Airport Road Markets

4

**19**

**21**

Al Mushrif
Medical Centre

**24**

Kazakhstan

Angola

5

Al Dhabiania
Model School

**24**

Abu Dhabi
Business

## AL KARAMAH ST

Adpesse Infra
Structure

Gov't
Office

6

Kuwait

**23**

## AL MUSHRIF

Vision Private
School

**22**

**80**

7

Khalifa Bin Zayed
Secondary School for Boys

## AL KARAMAH ST

Al Damam Foodstuff

8

Tasees
Consultancy

**30**

ZTE Corporation
Abu Dhabi

Public Prosecution of the
State Security

A   B   C   **26**   D   E   F

© Explorer Group Ltd. 2010

Abu Dhabi **Street** Atlas

# The British International School
## Abu Dhabi, UAE
*Educating responsible and effective citizens of the world*

For admissions please
call +971 2 447 4629
or visit our website
www.bisabudhabi.com

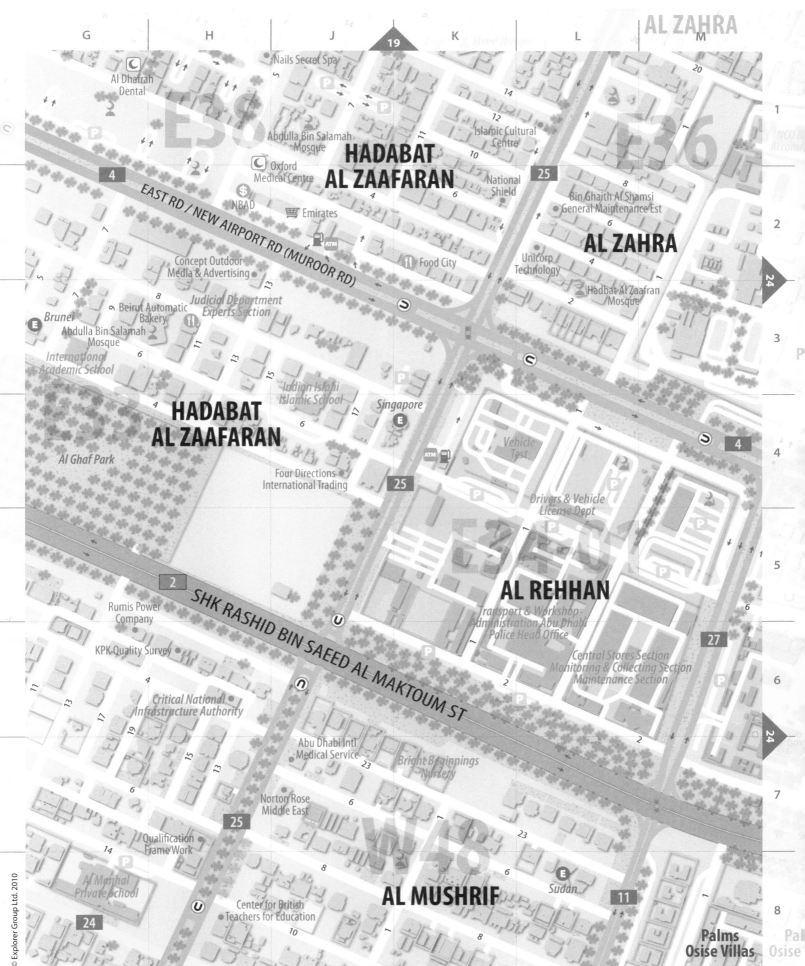

AL ZAHRA

Nails Secret Spa

Al Dhafrah
Dental

Abdulla Bin Salamah
Mosque

Oxford
Medical Centre

HADABAT
AL ZAAFARAN

Islamic Cultural
Centre

National
Shield

NBAD

Emirates

EAST RD / NEW AIRPORT RD (MUROOR RD)

Bin Ghaith Al Shamsi
General Maintenance Est

AL ZAHRA

Concept Outdoor
Media & Advertising

Food City

Unicorp
Technology

Hadbat Al Zaafran
Mosque

Brunei

Beirut Automatic
Bakery

Judicial Department
Experts Section

Abdulla Bin Salamah
Mosque

International
Academic School

HADABAT
AL ZAAFARAN

Indian Islahi
Islamic School

Singapore

Al Ghaf Park

Four Directions
International Trading

Vehicle
Test

Drivers & Vehicle
License Dept

AL REHHAN

SHK RASHID BIN SAEED AL MAKTOUM ST

Rumis Power
Company

Transport & Workshop
Administration Abu Dhabi
Police Head Office

KPK Quality Survey

Central Stores Section
Monitoring & Collecting Section
Maintenance Section

Critical National
Infrastructure Authority

Abu Dhabi Intl
Medical Service

Bright Beginnings
Nursery

Norton Rose
Middle East

Qualification
Frame Work

Al Manhal
Private School

Sudan

AL MUSHRIF

Center for British
Teachers for Education

Palms
Osise Villas

Scale 1: 6,500

0          250m

0          500ft

N

**A**     **B**     **C**     20     **D**     **E**     **F**

26

Al Dhafra
Private School

34

1

NCO & Soldier
Accommodation

General Directorate of
Financial Support Service
Purchasing & Store Dept

Al Noor Ce
Special

18

30

Diplomatic
Establishment Protection

16

9

13

28

23

2

Ministry of Interior General Directorate of
Eservices & Telecommuhication
General Directorate of Traffic
Coordination Police Judicial Council

14

22

24

20

3

5

3

Police College

12

**AL ZAHRA**

16

29

3

7

14

4

10

13

10

Zuama
Group Trading

8

Al Qadisiyah
School

ATM

4

**EAST RD**

Al Zafrana
Health Centre

Alam

Emirates NBD

5

5

UNB

Korfukan

ADIB

ADCB

2    4

6    8

8    10    12

16   18    20    22

6

Legal Affairs Dept
Police Court Section

10

Al Woroad
Academy School

**Al Aman**

Gate 6

5

29

French School
(Lycee Louis Massignan)

23

6

Government & Diplomatic
Protection Dept

3

Abu Dhabi Police

4

7

Burj Al Jewn
(u/c)

Gate 6

The American
International School

2

U

Al Bustan Complex,
Novotel (u/c)

**Danet
Abu Dhabi
(u/c)**

8

Al Ain University of
Science & Technology

**Palms
Osise Villas**

**SHK RASHID BIN SAEED AL MAKTOUM ST**

ATM

Palms
Osise Villas

**Municipality Old
Shopping Complex**
Al Haji Ahmed

Khamis Ali Saeed
Foodstuff

ms
Villas

**A**     **B**     **C**     27     **D**     **E**

Safran

Ministry of Foreign Trade

Pepsi
Company

© Explorer Group Ltd. 2010

Camp

20

G          H          J          K          L          M

1

Fatima Bint
Mubarak School

Al Noor Center for
Special Needs

Emirates
Private School

European
International College

25

Greece

AL ZAHRA

AL MATAR

31

2

3

Ministry of Interior
Private Security
Business Dept

International
Montessori
Nursery

Critical National
Infrastructure
Authority (CNIA)

AL BATEEN
AIRPORT

4

Sheikh Khalifa Bin Zayed
Bangladesh Islamia
School

Co-operative
Society

UAE
Exchange

5

Indian
Coffee House

DIB

Creation
Arts

ATM

6

EAST RD

25

40

Danet
Abu Dhabi (u/c)

Abu Dhabi
Municipality
Main Store

Public Garden

Abu Dhabi Judicial
Dept (ADJD)

7

AL REHHAN

Holiday Inn

Bin Hamoodah
Motors

Al Masood Motors
(Nissan Service Centre)

8

H          J          K          L          M

27

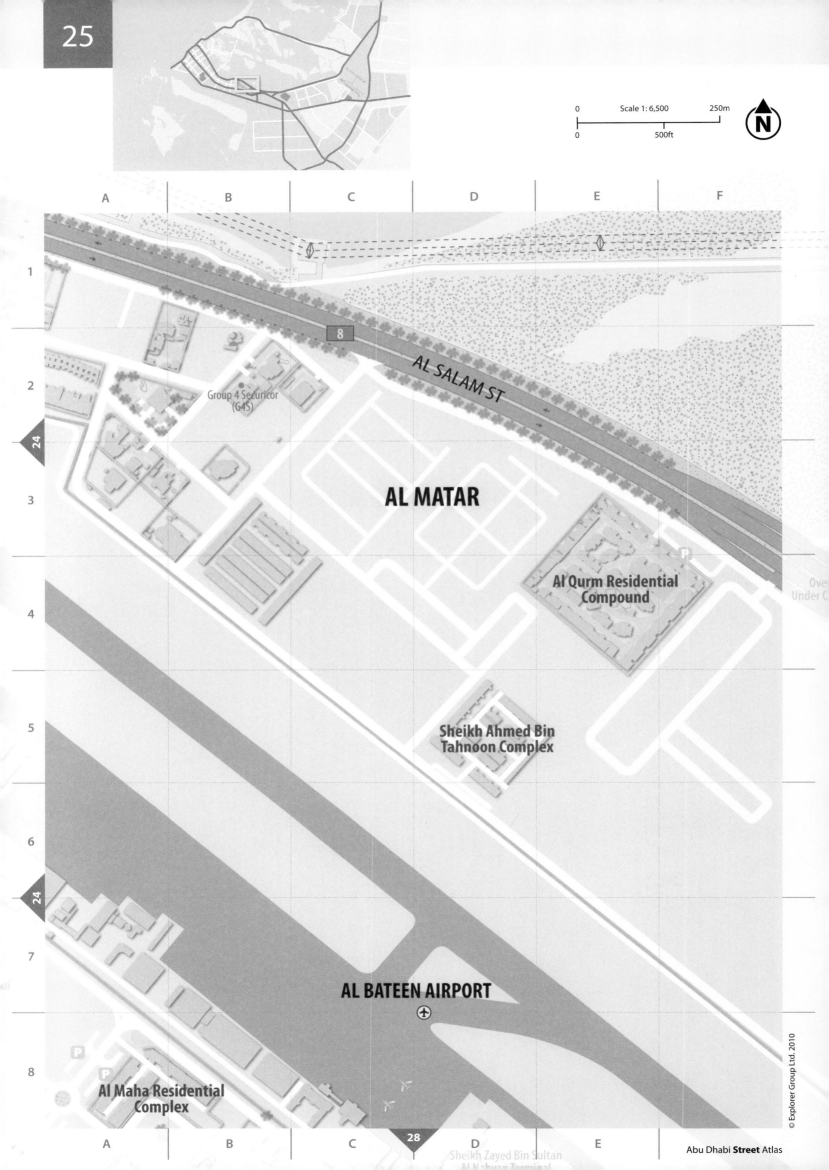

Scale 1: 6,500

0      250m

0      500ft

N

A    B    C    D    E    F

1

8

AL SALAM ST

2

Group 4 Securicor
(G4S)

24

3

**AL MATAR**

P

**Al Qurm Residential
Compound**

4

Ove
Under C

5

**Sheikh Ahmed Bin
Tahnoon Complex**

6

24

7

**AL BATEEN AIRPORT**

✈

8

P

P

**Al Maha Residential
Complex**

A    B    C    D    E

28

Sheikh Zayed Bin Sultan
Al Nahyan Terminal

G H J K L M

1

2

E49

Special Forces

49

3

Over Bridge
Under Construction

4

AL MATAR

5

8

AL SALAM ST

6

BLOOM
GARDENS (U/C)

49

Manazil

Qudra
HO (u/c)

W47

National
Transport
Authority

AL SALAM ST

7

$
AHB

Ministry of New
Head Office

Ministry of Labour — Yanah

Colombiano
Coffee House

Tasah EL
Al Qurm

Ministry of
Environment
& Water

Abu Dhabi Tourism
Authority (ADTA)

4

2

Twofour54

3

Abu Dhabi Transmission
& Dispatch Co (Transco)

1

Food United
National &
Agriculture

8

Twofour54

28

G H J K L M

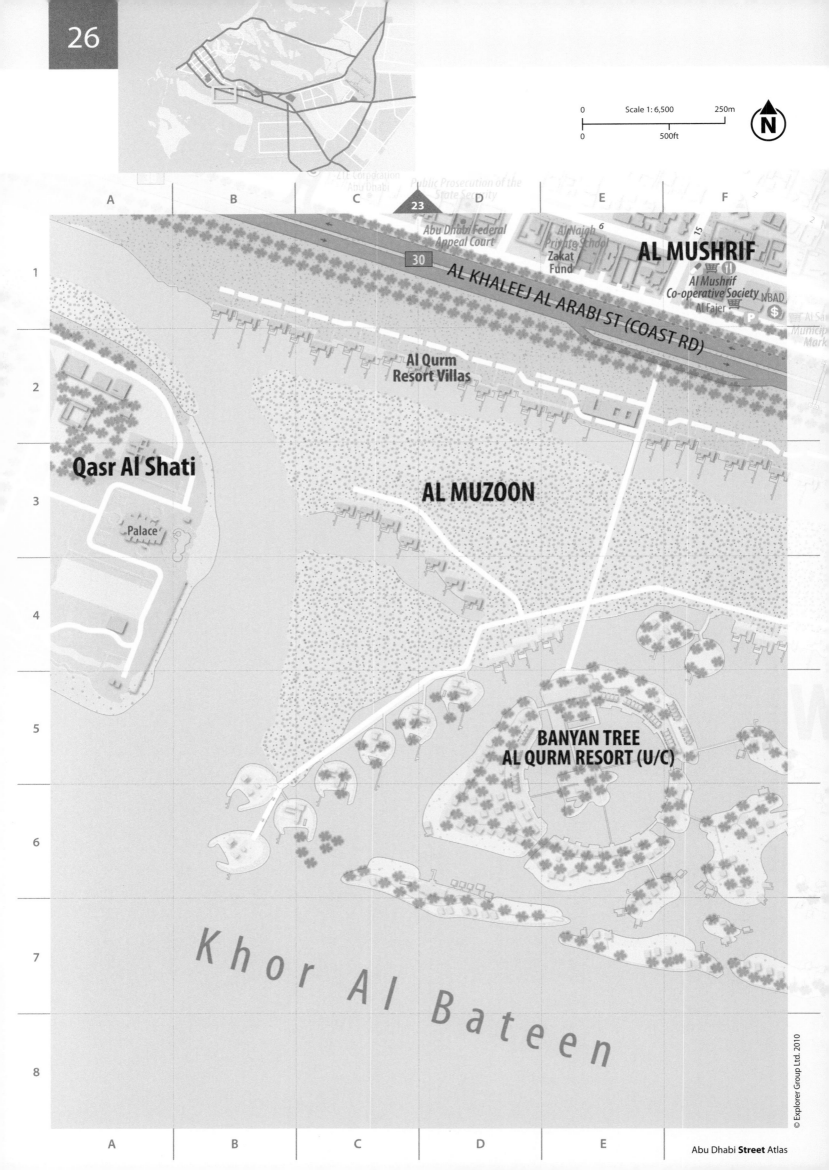

Scale 1: 6,500

0          250m

0          500ft

**N**

A    B    C    D    E    F

ZTE Corporation
Abu Dhabi

Public Proseution of the
State Security

**23**

Abu Dhabi Federal
Appeal Court

Al Najah
Private School

Zakat
Fund

**AL MUSHRIF**

Al Mushrif
Co-operative Society   NBAD

Al Fajer

1

**30**

**AL KHALEEJ AL ARABI ST (COAST RD)**

Al Qurm
Resort Villas

2

**Qasr Al Shati**

**AL MUZOON**

3

Palace

4

5

**BANYAN TREE
AL QURM RESORT (U/C)**

6

7

*Khor Al Bateen*

8

© Explorer Group Ltd. 2010

A    B    C    D    E

**The British International School**
Abu Dhabi, UAE
*Educating responsible and effective citizens of the world*

For admissions please
call +971 2 447 4629
or visit our website
www.bisabudhabi.com

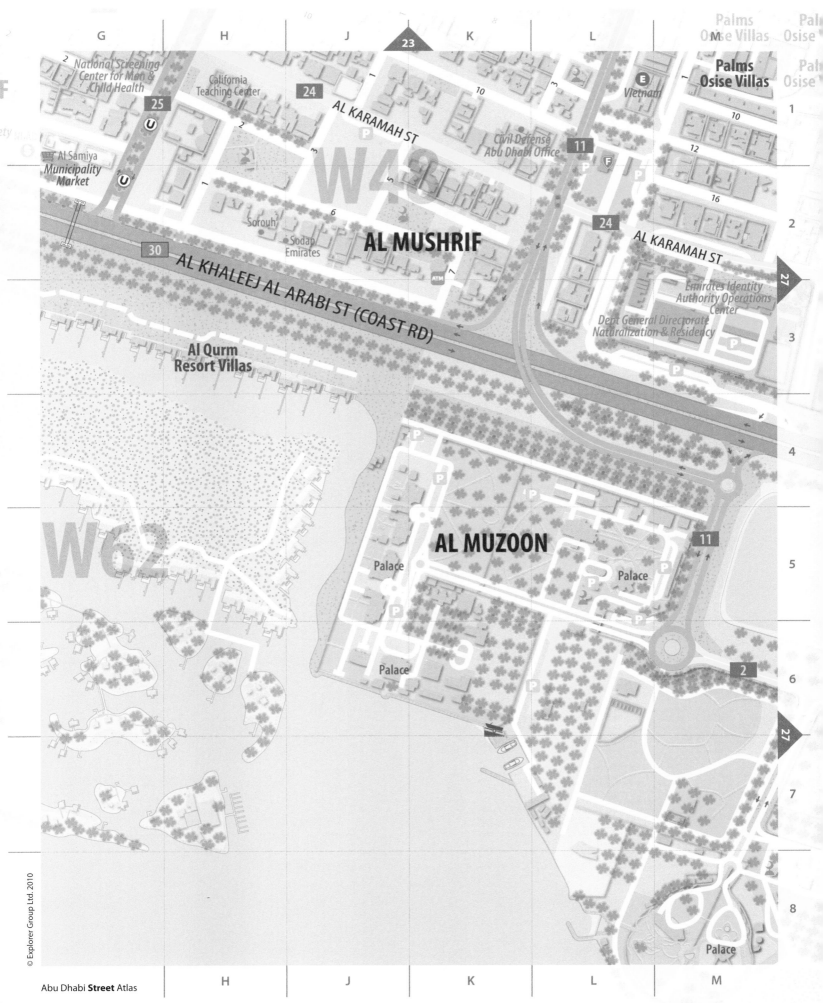

© Explorer Group Ltd. 2010

Scale 1: 6,500

0      250m

0      500ft

**N**

Ims
Palms
Osise Villas

Ims
Villas

Shopping Complex
Al Hajj Ahmed 雪

Khamis Ali Saeed
Foodstuff

**24**

Pepsi
Company

**P**

A   B   C   D   E   F

**Palms
Osise Villas**

6   Safran
Company

China Petroleum
Engineering & Construction
Group of Corporation

Ministry of Foreign Trade
Abu Dhabi Police GHQ
Human Resources General Directorate
Training Administration Education
& Scholarship Education

**E**
Afghanistan

1

5

8

8

7

**AL MUSHRIF**

**E**
Palestine

**E**
Jordan

**E**
Yemen

**E**
India

**E**
Saudi

14

14

W49

2

**26**

enthy
eration

**24**   AL KARAMAH ST

**29**

**P**

1

**P**

**E**
Lebanon

3

**E**
Pakistan

**E**
USA

W3

**National
security**

**E**
Qatar

**E**
Turkmenistan

**E**
Armenia

3

**24**   AL KARAMAH ST

Gate

**AL SAFARAT**

4

**Zayed Military
Hospital** ✚

**30**   AL KHALEEJ AL ARABI ST (COAST RD)

**U**

**C**
Imperial College
London Diabetes Centre

Picnic Site

**P**

Gate

5

**P**

**P**

**P**

Parki

**26**

**2**

Gate 3

Capita
Gate (u

6

**P**

**Marina**

7

**AL MUZOON**

**P**

**P**

**P**

13

**15**

**P**

8

**P**

**4**

**32**

A   B   C   D   E

© Explorer Group Ltd. 2010

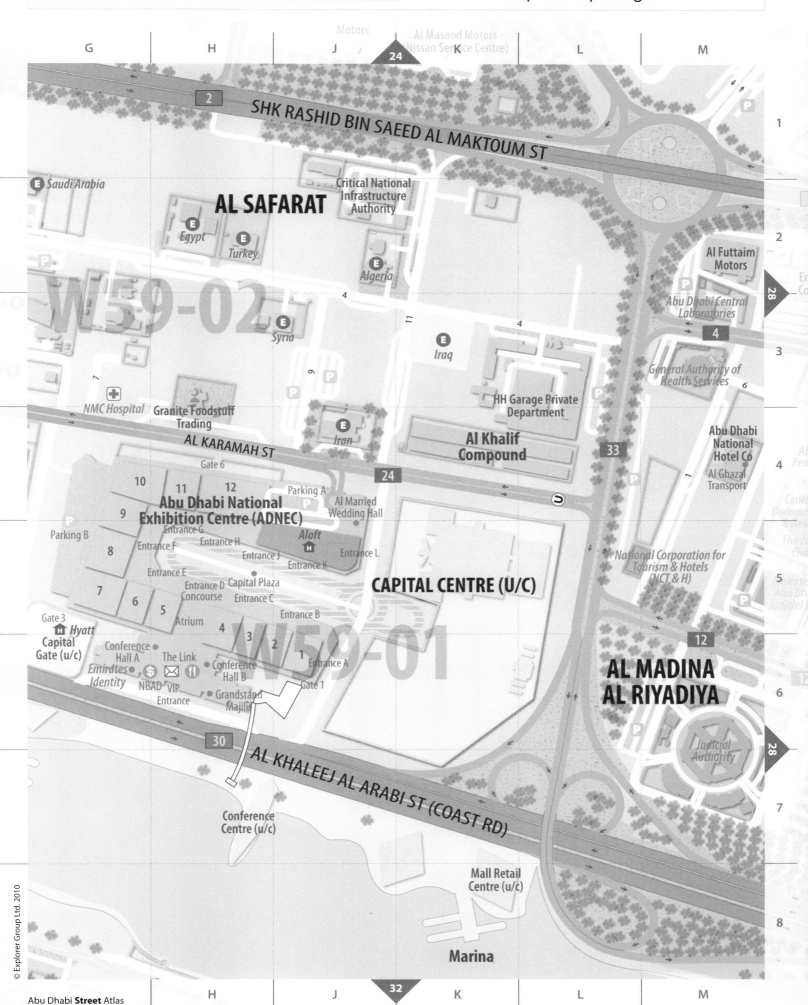

© Explorer Group Ltd. 2010

Scale 1: 6,500

0          250m

0          500ft

N

A B C **25** D E F

**1**

Sheikh Zayed Bin Sultan
Al Nahyan Terminal

AL BATEEN AIRPORT

**2**

**2**

**27**

Emirates Motor
Company (EMC)

**Island City
(u/c)**

World of
Furniture

**SHK RASHID BIN SAEED AL MAKTOUM ST**

**2**

2

**17**

Costa Cafe

**ATM**

*Carrefour*

**3**

**4**

Peugeot
Service Centre

UAE General
Secretariat of UAE General
Municipality Civil Aviation
Authority

6

19

Abu Dhabi Retirement
Pensions & Benefits Fund

**Arzanah
Heights (u/c)**

**Ministry of
Foreign Affairs**

21

**4**

**4**

8

Center for
Documentation
& Research

General Pensions
& Social Security
Authority

13

*Bridgeway
Abu Dhabi
(u/c)*

**11**

The Zayed Bin Sultan Al Nahyan
Charitable & Humanitarian
Foundation

**7**

KFC

*Old Airport
Garden*

**5**

Emirates of
Abu Dhabi
Judicial Dept

Department
of Thabreeth

Arzanah Medical
Complex

Sports
Centre

**AL MADINA
AL RIYADIYA**

**12**

**Arzanah
Heights (u/c)**

**4**

**6**

**27**

Entrance

Entrance

**W57**

**7**

Shk Zayed
Stadium

**ARZANAH (U/C)**

*Park*

**8**

**30**

**Arzanah
Lofts (u/c)**

Entrance

A B C **33** D E

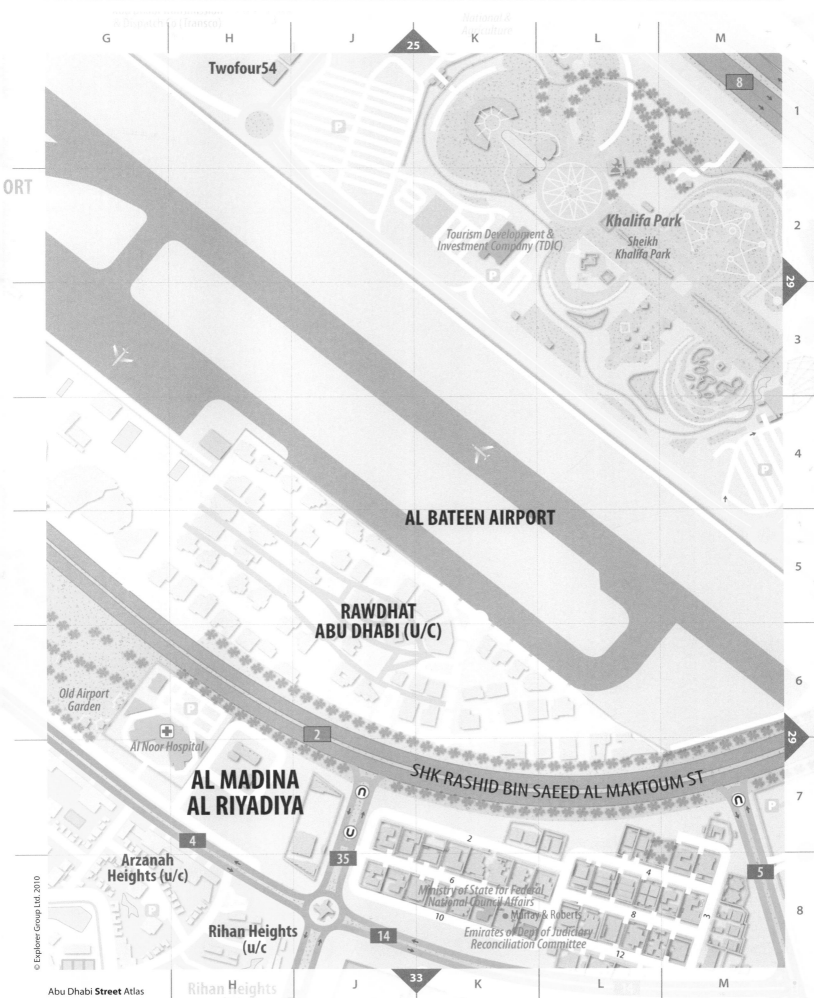

Twofour54

Tourism Development &
Investment Company (TDIC)

**Khalifa Park**

Sheikh
Khalifa Park

**AL BATEEN AIRPORT**

**RAWDHAT
ABU DHABI (U/C)**

Old Airport
Garden

Al Noor Hospital

SHK RASHID BIN SAEED AL MAKTOUM ST

**AL MADINA
AL RIYADIYA**

**Arzanah
Heights (u/c)**

Ministry of State for Federal
National Council Affairs

● Murray & Roberts

Emirates of Dept of Judiciary
Reconciliation Committee

**Rihan Heights
(u/c**

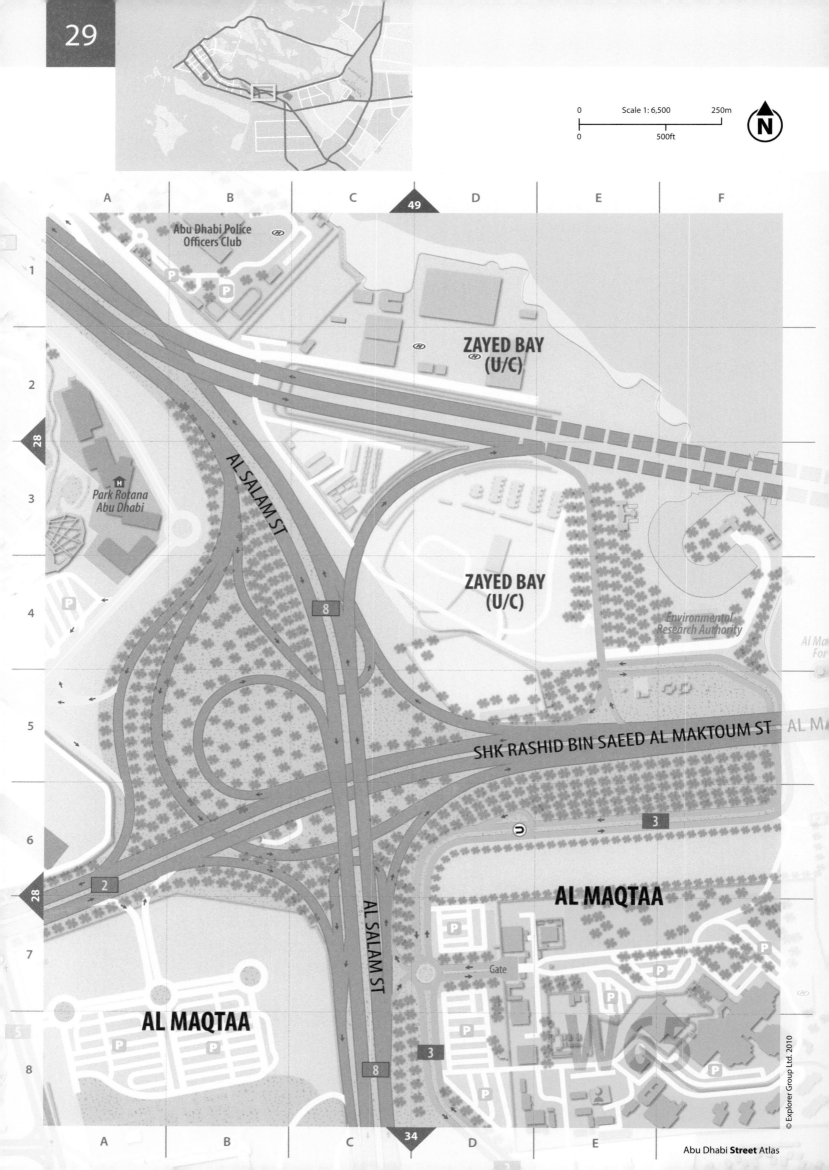

Scale 1: 6,500

0   250m

0   500ft

N

Abu Dhabi Police Officers Club

ZAYED BAY (U/C)

AL SALAM ST

Park Rotana Abu Dhabi

ZAYED BAY (U/C)

Environmental Research Authority

Al Ma For

SHK RASHID BIN SAEED AL MAKTOUM ST   AL M

AL MAQTAA

AL SALAM ST

Gate

AL MAQTAA

© Explorer Group Ltd. 2010

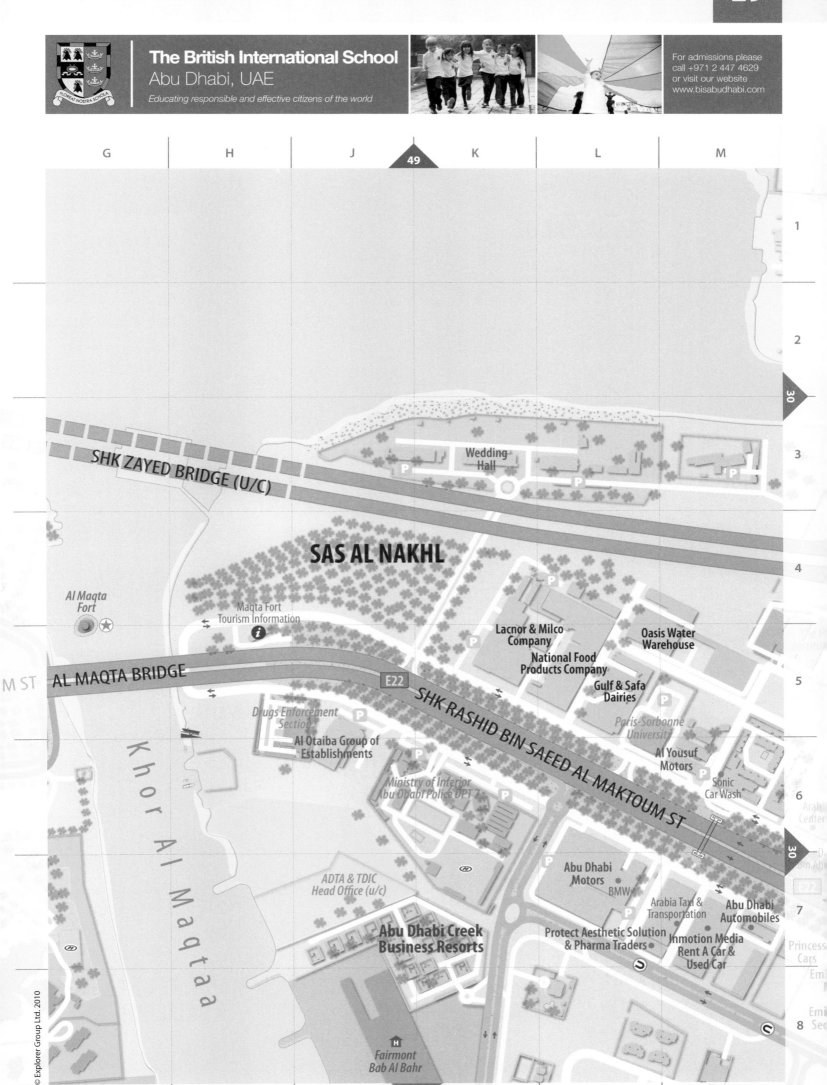

## The British International School
### Abu Dhabi, UAE
*Educating responsible and effective citizens of the world*

For admissions please
call +971 2 447 4629
or visit our website
www.bisabudhabi.com

49

SHK ZAYED BRIDGE (U/C)

Wedding
Hall

SAS AL NAKHL

Al Maqta
Fort

Maqta Fort
Tourism Information

Lacnor & Milco
Company

Oasis Water
Warehouse

National Food
Products Company

AL MAQTA BRIDGE

E22

Gulf & Safa
Dairies

SHK RASHID BIN SAEED AL MAKTOUM ST

M ST

Khor Al Maqtaa

Drugs Enforcement
Section

Paris-Sorbonne
University

Al Otaiba Group of
Establishments

Al Yousuf
Motors

Sonic
Car Wash

Ministry of Interior
Abu Dhabi Police DPT

Abu Dhabi
Motors
BMW

ADTA & TDIC
Head Office (u/c)

Arabia Taxi &
Transportation

Abu Dhabi
Automobiles

Abu Dhabi Creek
Business Resorts

Protect Aesthetic Solution
& Pharma Traders

Inmotion Media
Rent A Car &
Used Car

Princess
Cars

Fairmont
Bab Al Bahr

34

Scale 1 : 6,500

0 — 250m
0 — 500ft

N

A B C D E F

1

**SAS AL NAKHL**

49

29

2

3

ADNOC

*Onshore Affaire*
*Al Dafra Development*

P

4

Christian
Graveyard

*The Petroleum*
*Institute (Female)*

P

P

5

ADNOC

*The Petroleum*
*Institute*
*Administration*

**SAS AL NAKHL**

6

Arab
Center

**Tinkerer**
**Research**
**Centre**

E10

29

Darwish
Bin Ahmed & Sons

**Premier**
**Motors Ferrari**

*The Petroleum*
*Institute*

E22

Dhabi
mobiles

7

**SHK RASHID BIN SAEED AL MAKTOUM ST**

P

ABU DHABI-DUBAI RD

Princess
Cars

Emirates Intl
Motors

Emirates Gateway
Security Services

**MADINAT KHALIFA A**
**(KHALIFA CITY A)**

8

Bin Brook Motors
& Equipment

A B C D E

35

SHK R...

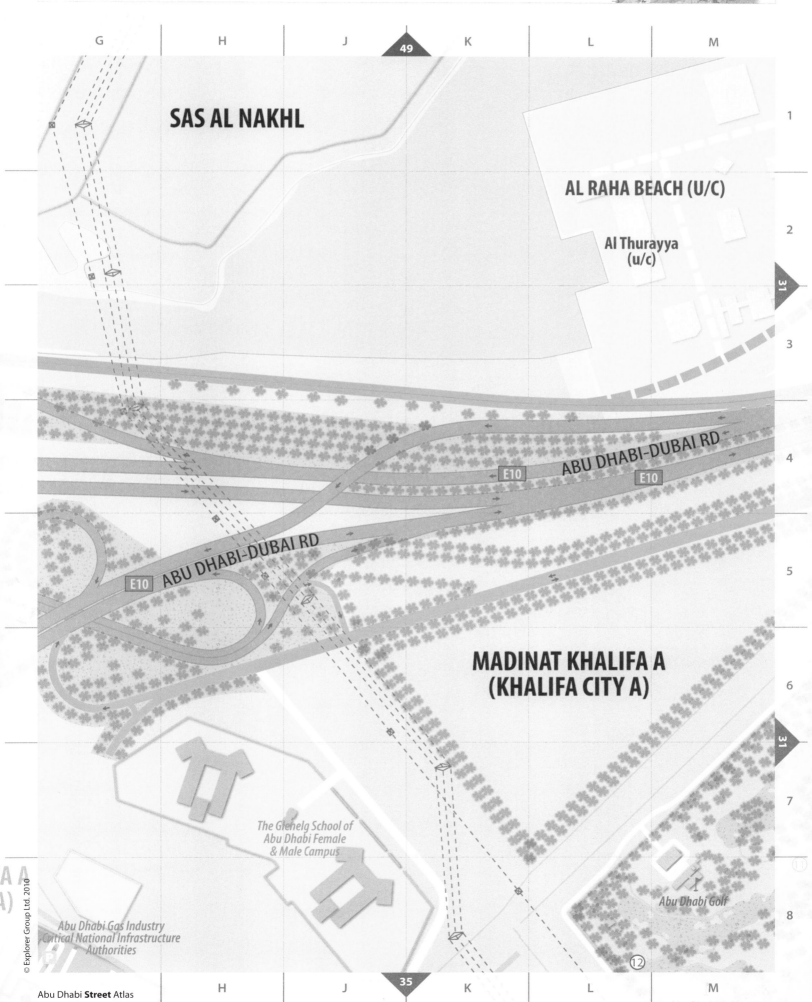

SAS AL NAKHL

AL RAHA BEACH (U/C)

Al Thurayya
(u/c)

ABU DHABI-DUBAI RD

E10

E10

ABU DHABI-DUBAI RD

E10

MADINAT KHALIFA A
(KHALIFA CITY A)

The Glenelg School of
Abu Dhabi Female
& Male Campus

Abu Dhabi Golf

Abu Dhabi Gas Industry
Critical National Infrastructure
Authorities

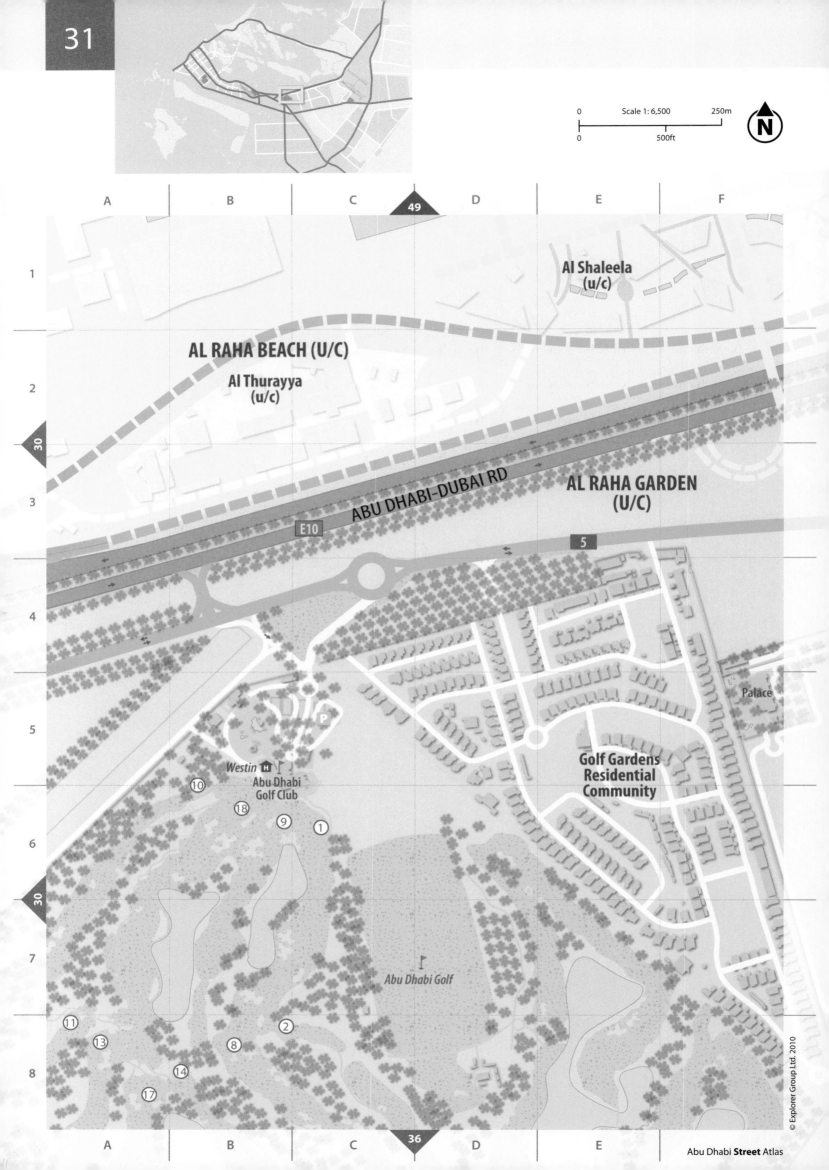

Scale 1:6,500

0      250m

0      500ft

N

49

30

30

A   B   C   D   E   F

1

2

3

4

5

6

7

8

**Al Shaleela (u/c)**

**AL RAHA BEACH (U/C)**

**Al Thurayya (u/c)**

ABU DHABI-DUBAI RD

E10

5

**AL RAHA GARDEN (U/C)**

Palace

**Golf Gardens Residential Community**

P

Westin H

Abu Dhabi Golf Club

10

18

9

1

Abu Dhabi Golf

11

13

8

2

14

17

36

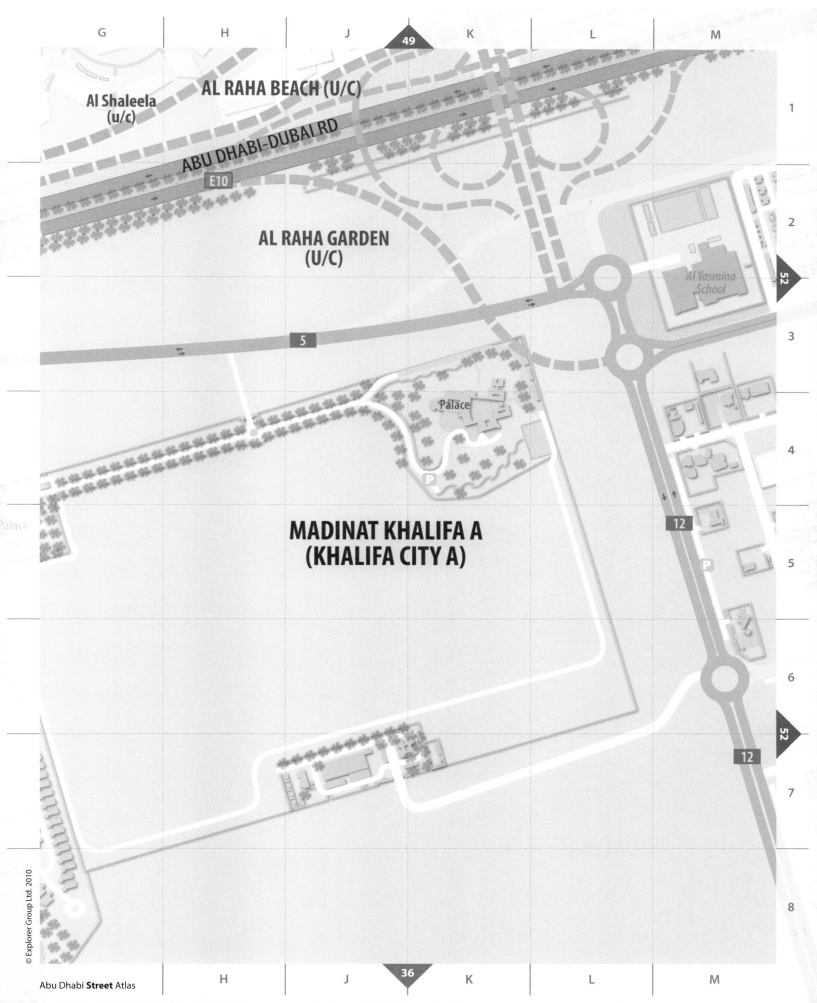

Al Shaleela (u/c)

**AL RAHA BEACH (U/C)**

ABU DHABI-DUBAI RD

E10

**AL RAHA GARDEN (U/C)**

Al Yasmina School

5

Palace

P

**MADINAT KHALIFA A (KHALIFA CITY A)**

12

P

Palace

49

52

12

52

12

36

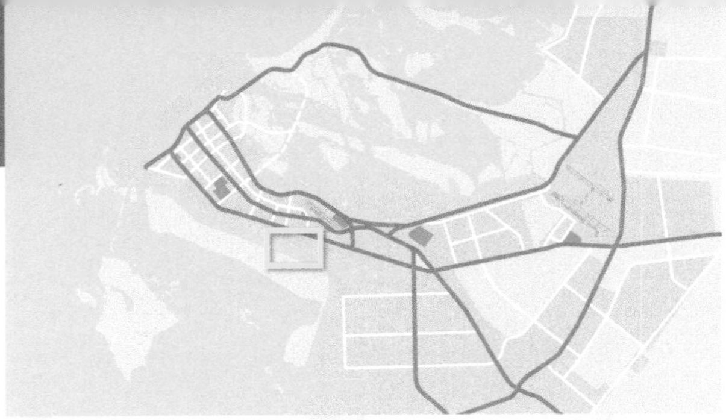

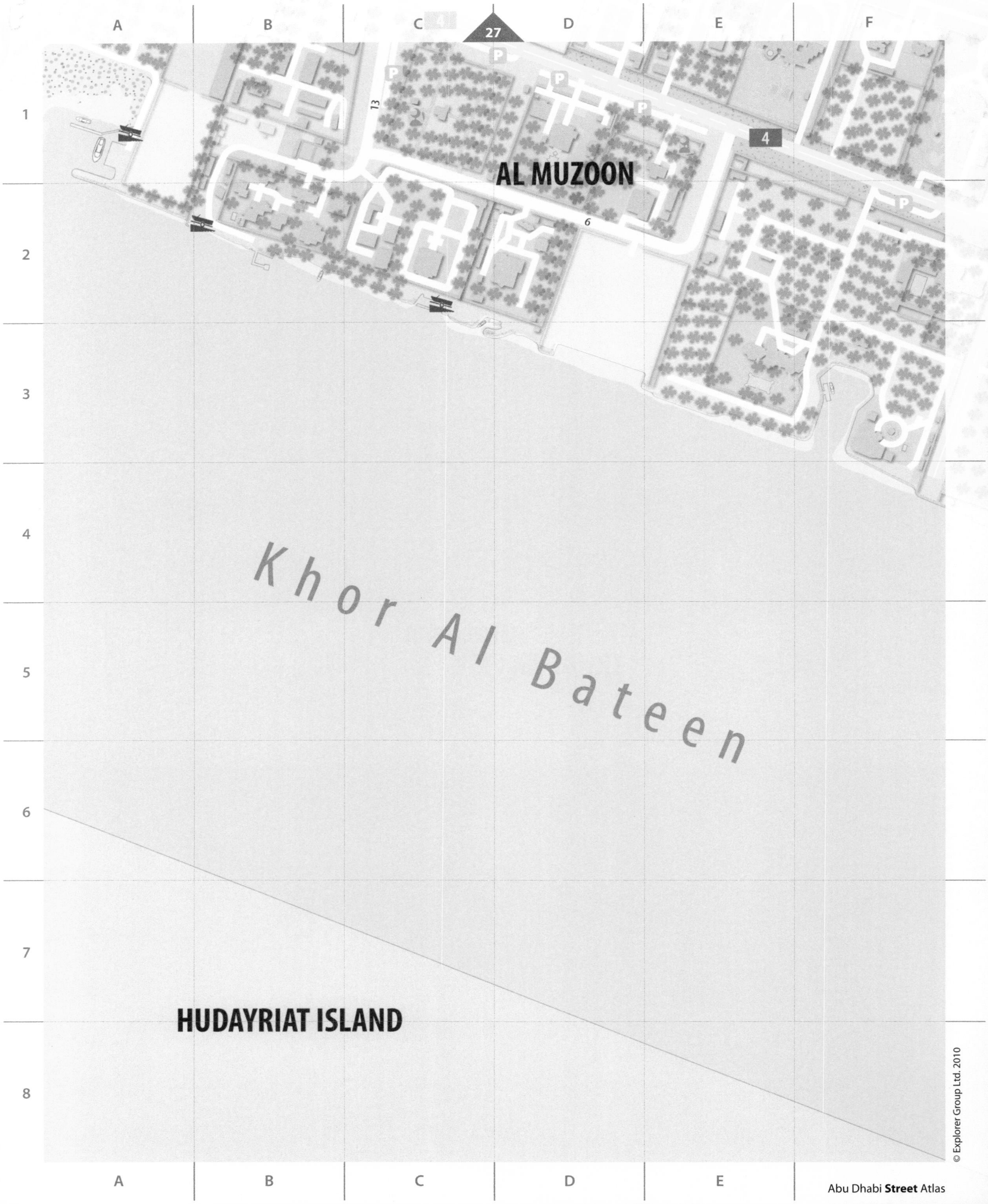

Scale 1:6,500

0       250m

0       500ft

N

A    B    C    D    E    F

1

2

3

4

5

6

7

8

**AL MUZOON**

*Khor Al Bateen*

**HUDAYRIAT ISLAND**

Marina

G H J K L M

27

Abu Dhabi Villa
& Majlis (u/c)

4

**AL MUZOON**

33

*Khor Al Bateen*

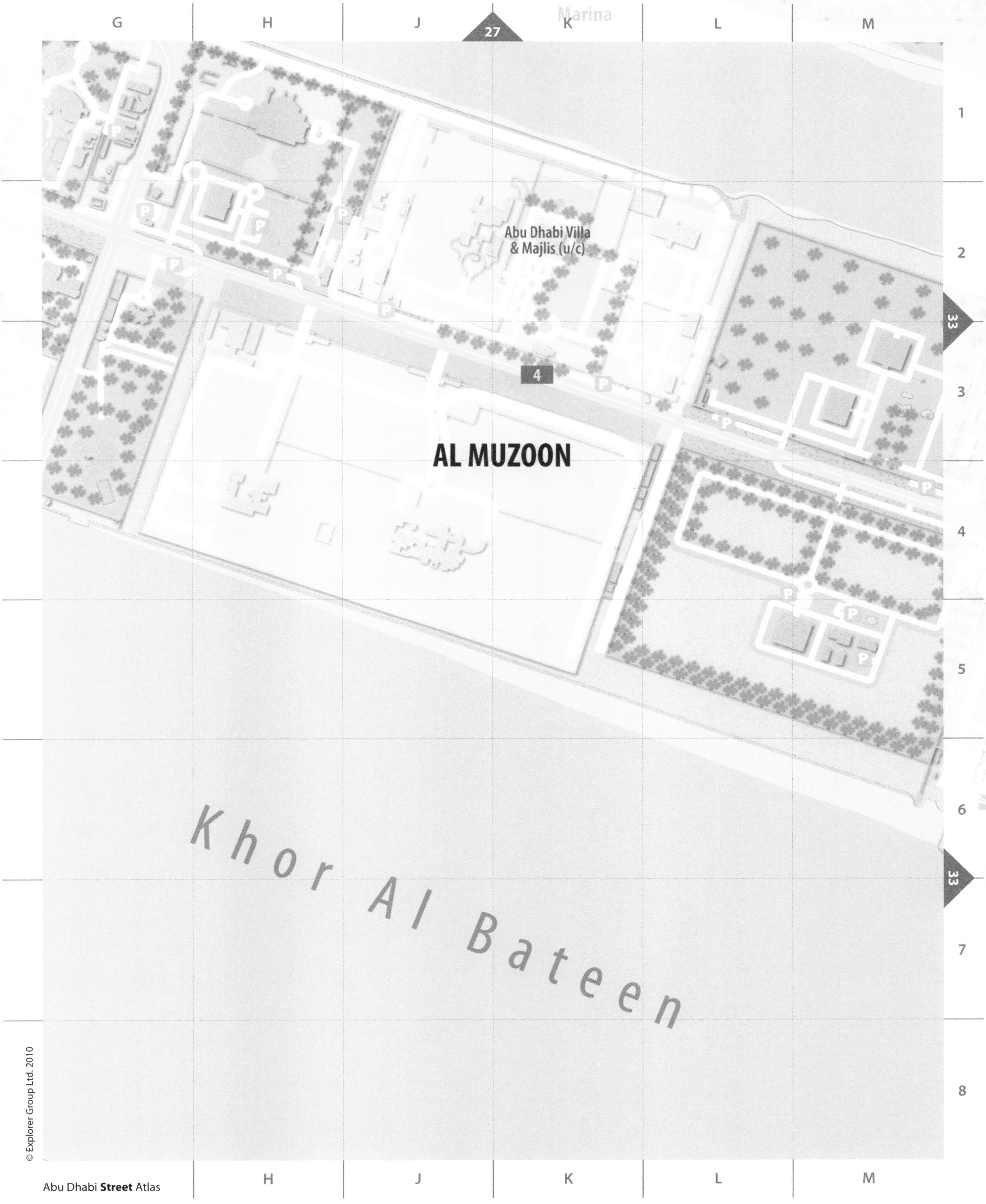

33

1
2
3
4
5
6
7
8

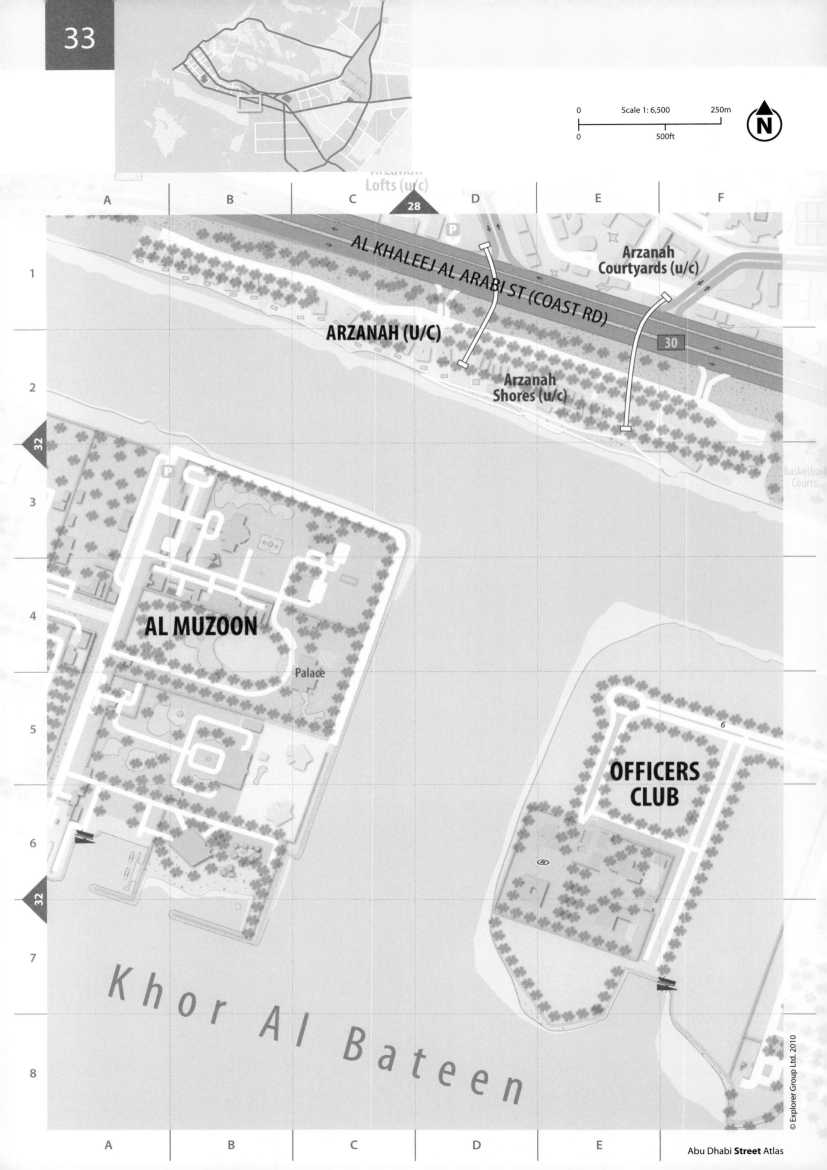

Scale 1 : 6,500

0      250m
0      500ft

N

Arzanah
Lofts (u/c)

Entrance

28

Arzanah
Courtyards (u/c)

AL KHALEEJ AL ARABI ST (COAST RD)

ARZANAH (U/C)

30

Arzanah
Shores (u/c)

32

Basketball
Courts

AL MUZOON

Palace

OFFICERS
CLUB

6

32

Khor Al Bateen

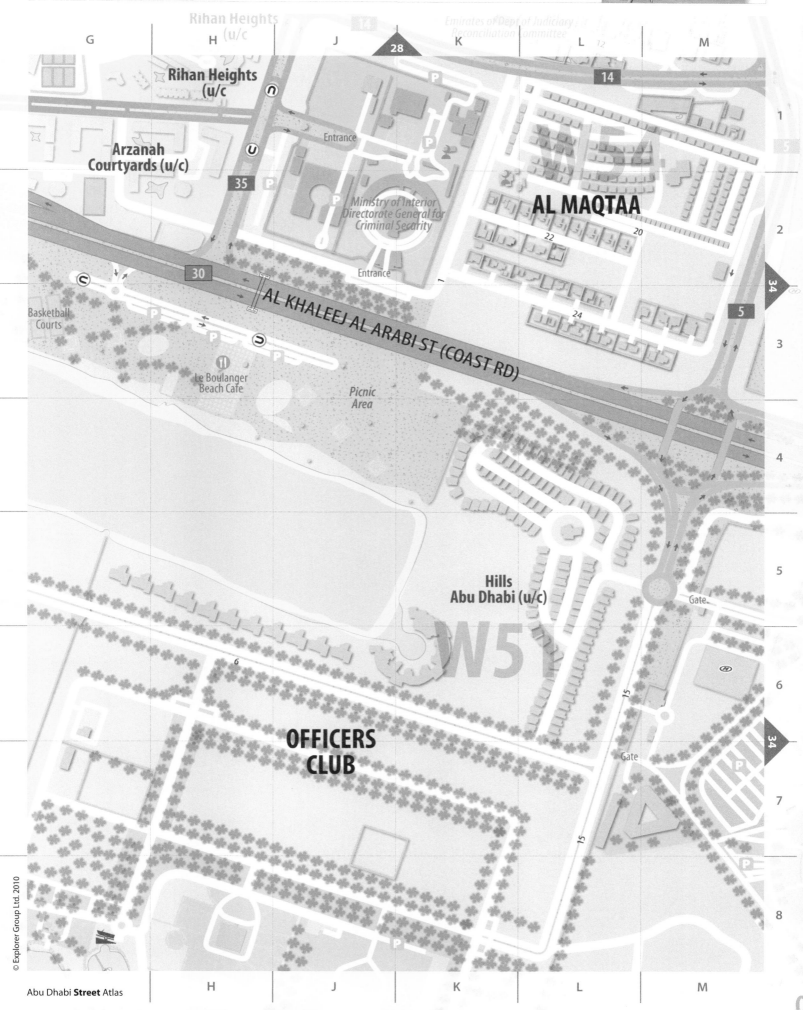

Rihan Heights (u/c)

Emirates of Dept of Judiciary
Reconciliation Committee

**Rihan Heights (u/c)**

**Arzanah Courtyards (u/c)**

Entrance

**AL MAQTAA**

Ministry of Interior
Directorate General for
Criminal Security

Entrance

**AL KHALEEJ AL ARABI ST (COAST RD)**

Basketball Courts

Le Boulanger Beach Cafe

Picnic Area

**W5**

Hills Abu Dhabi (u/c)

Gate

**OFFICERS CLUB**

Gate

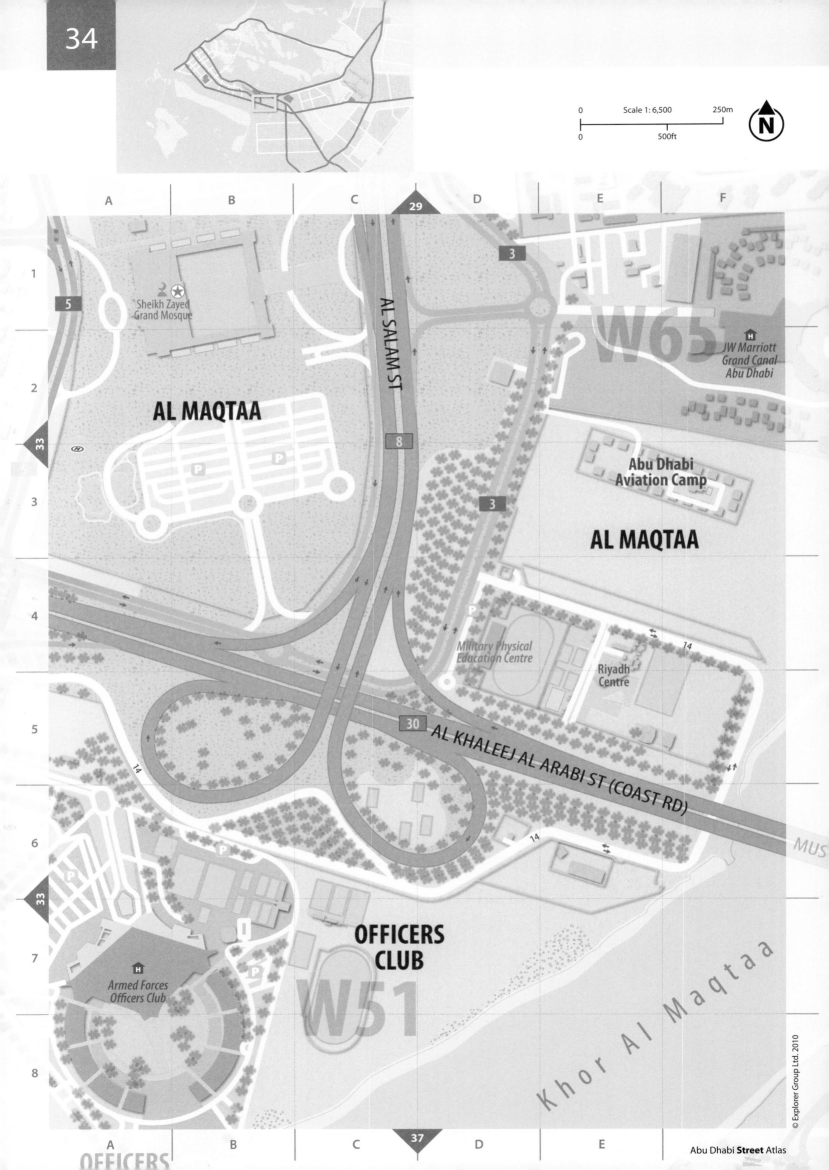

Scale 1:6,500

0      250m

0      500ft

**N**

29

3

**AL SALAM ST**

8

3

**W65**

**JW Marriott
Grand Canal
Abu Dhabi**

5

Sheikh Zayed
Grand Mosque

**AL MAQTAA**

33

P    P

**Abu Dhabi
Aviation Camp**

**AL MAQTAA**

P

Military Physical
Education Centre

14

Riyadh
Centre

30   *AL KHALEEJ AL ARABI ST (COAST RD)*

14

14

MUS

P

33

P

P

**OFFICERS
CLUB**

**W51**

H

*Armed Forces
Officers Club*

*Khor Al Maqtaa*

37

OFFICERS

A     B     C     D     E     F

The British International School
Abu Dhabi, UAE
Educating responsible and effective citizens of the world
FLOREAT NOSTRA SCHOLA
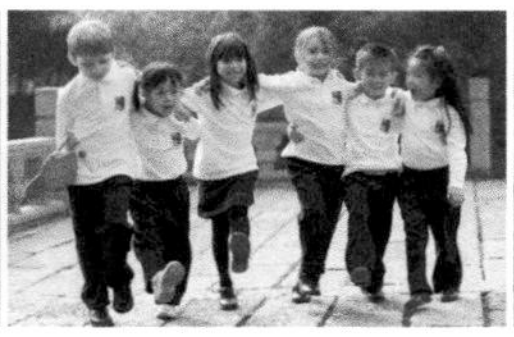
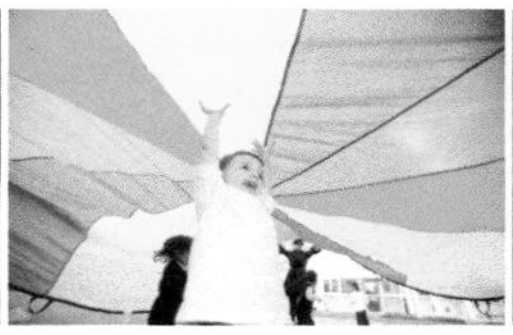
For admissions please call +971 2 447 4629 or visit our website www.bisabudhabi.com

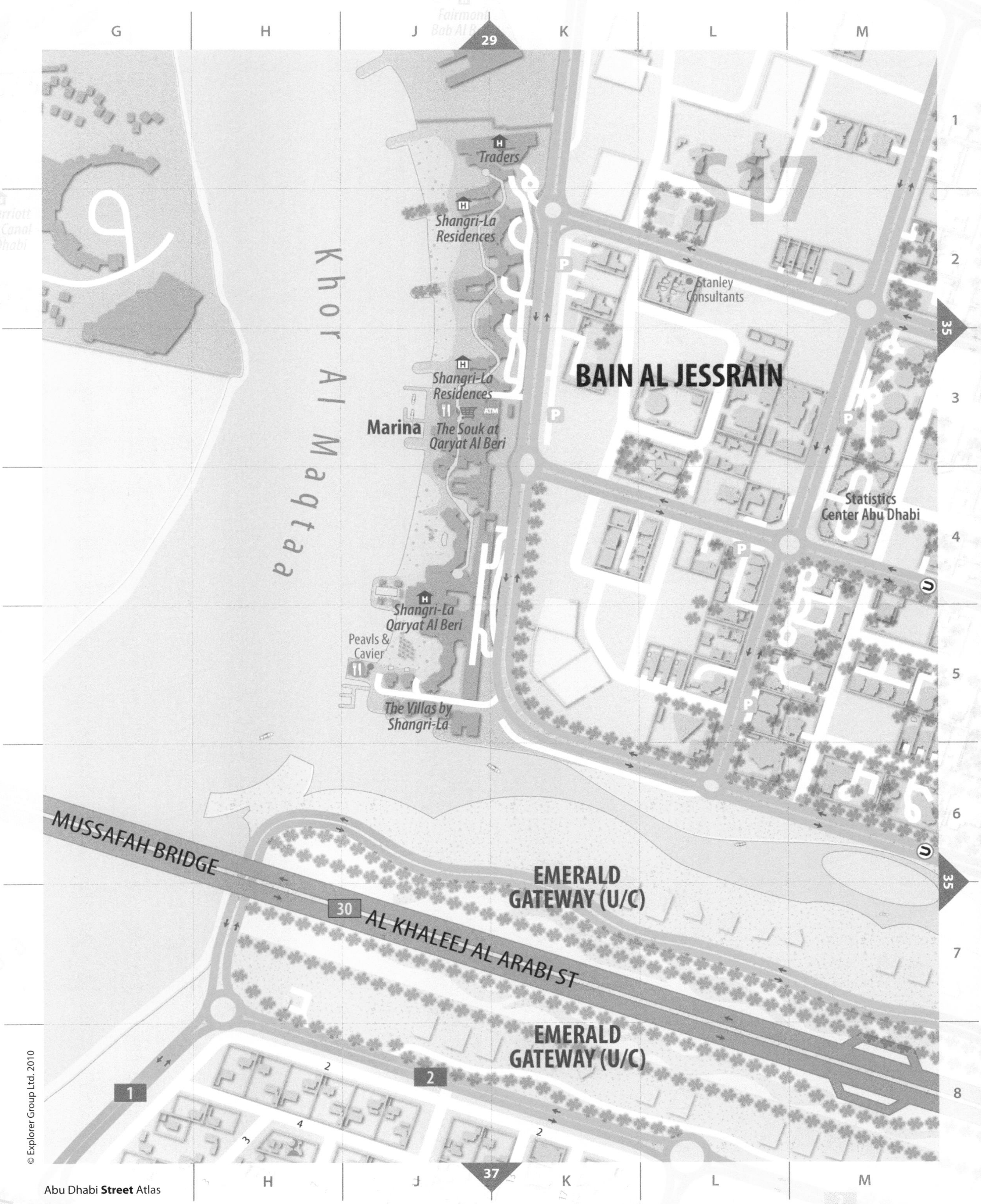
G
H
J
K
L
M
29
35
37
1
2
3
4
5
6
7
8
Fairmont Bab Al Bahr
Marriott Grand Canal Abu Dhabi
Traders
Shangri-La Residences
Shangri-La Residences
Khor Al Maqtaa
Marina
The Souk at Qaryat Al Beri
Shangri-La Qaryat Al Beri
Peavls & Cavier
The Villas by Shangri-La
Stanley Consultants
S17
BAIN AL JESSRAIN
Statistics Center Abu Dhabi
MUSSAFAH BRIDGE
30
AL KHALEEJ AL ARABI ST
EMERALD GATEWAY (U/C)
EMERALD GATEWAY (U/C)
1
2
P
ATM

© Explorer Group Ltd. 2010

Scale 1: 6,500

0     250m
0     500ft

N

A B C **30** D E F

Bin Brook Motors & Equipment

**E22** SHK RASHID BIN SAEED AL MAKTOUM ST

1

Oasis Car Wash

2

**34**

**BAIN AL JESSRAIN**

3

Bin Jessrain Park

Al Jessrain Medical Centre

**Al Maqta**

Abu Dhabi Educational Training Institute

4

National Bank of Abu Dhabi (NBAD) Academy

Pizza Way

NBAD

Bain Al Jesrain Co-operative Society

ATM

Nadreen Beauty & Fitness

Darwish Benkaram Secondary School

Fileh Inn

5

6

Stepping Stones Nursery Child Development

**34**

7

Ambulatory Health Care Centre

**EMERALD GATEWAY (U/C)**

8

**30**

A B **38** C D E

© Explorer Group Ltd. 2010

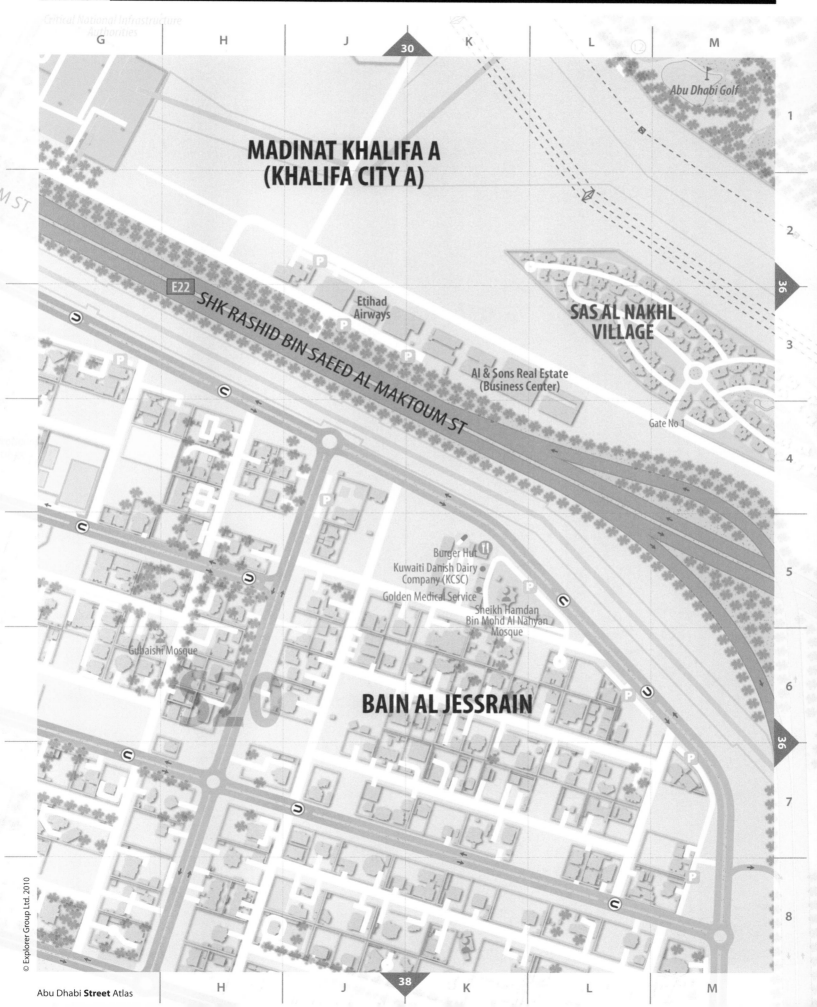

MADINAT KHALIFA A
(KHALIFA CITY A)

Abu Dhabi Golf

E22

SHK RASHID BIN SAEED AL MAKTOUM ST

Etihad
Airways

SAS AL NAKHL
VILLAGE

Al & Sons Real Estate
(Business Center)

Gate No 1

Burger Hut
Kuwaiti Danish Dairy
Company (KCSC)
Golden Medical Service

Sheikh Hamdan
Bin Mohd Al Nahyan
Mosque

Gubaishi Mosque

BAIN AL JESSRAIN

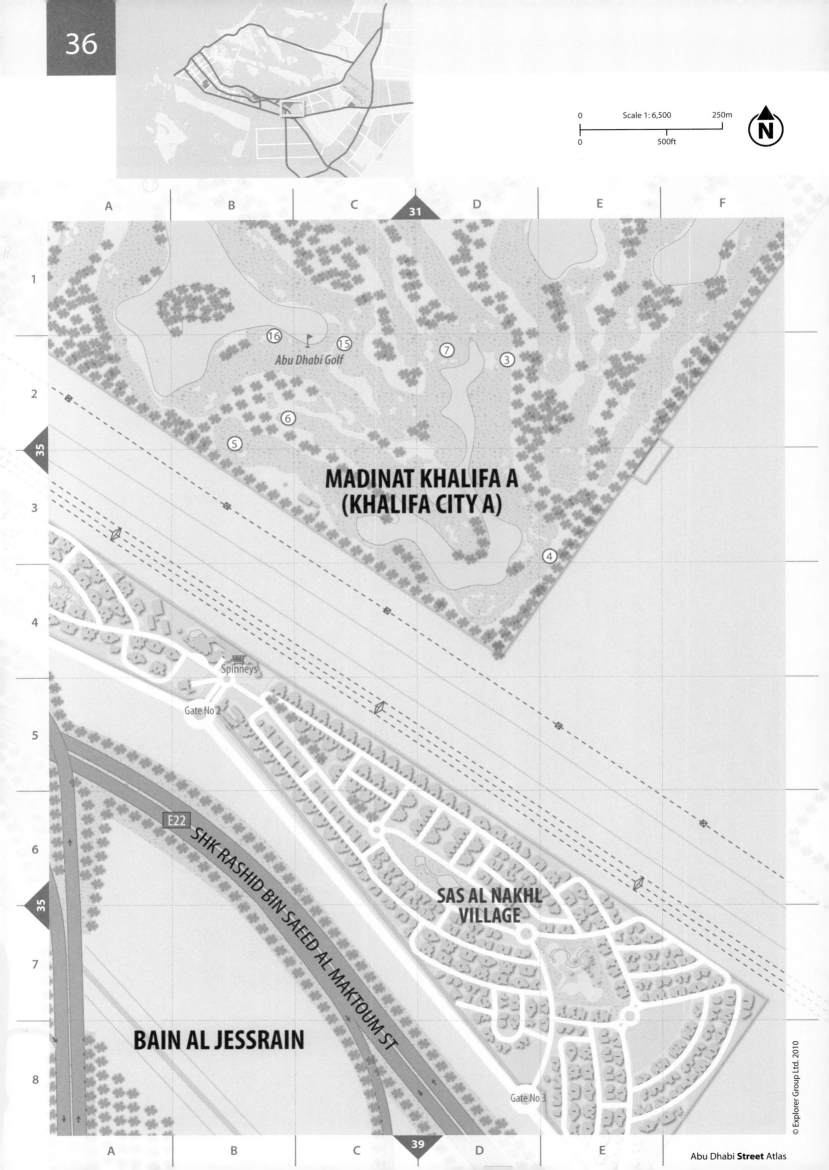

Scale 1: 6,500

0                        250m

0                   500ft

**N**

Abu Dhabi Golf

## MADINAT KHALIFA A
## (KHALIFA CITY A)

Spinneys

Gate No 2

E22

*SHK RASHID BIN SAEED AL MAKTOUM ST*

## SAS AL NAKHL
## VILLAGE

## BAIN AL JESSRAIN

Gate No 3

© Explorer Group Ltd. 2010

**Balloon Expeditions**
Into the **Heart of the Desert**

Abu Dhabi Bookings
call: 04 2854949
or visit www.ballooning.ae

Balloon
Adventures
Emirates

G  H  J  31  K  L  M

1

2

52

# MADINAT KHALIFA A
# (KHALIFA CITY A)

3

4

Crown Prince
Court (u/c)

5

## ABU DHABI INTERNATIONAL
## KART & MOTOCROSS COMPLEX (U/C)

6

## ADISC RESIDENTIAL
## PROJECT (U/C)

52  ADI
P

7

8

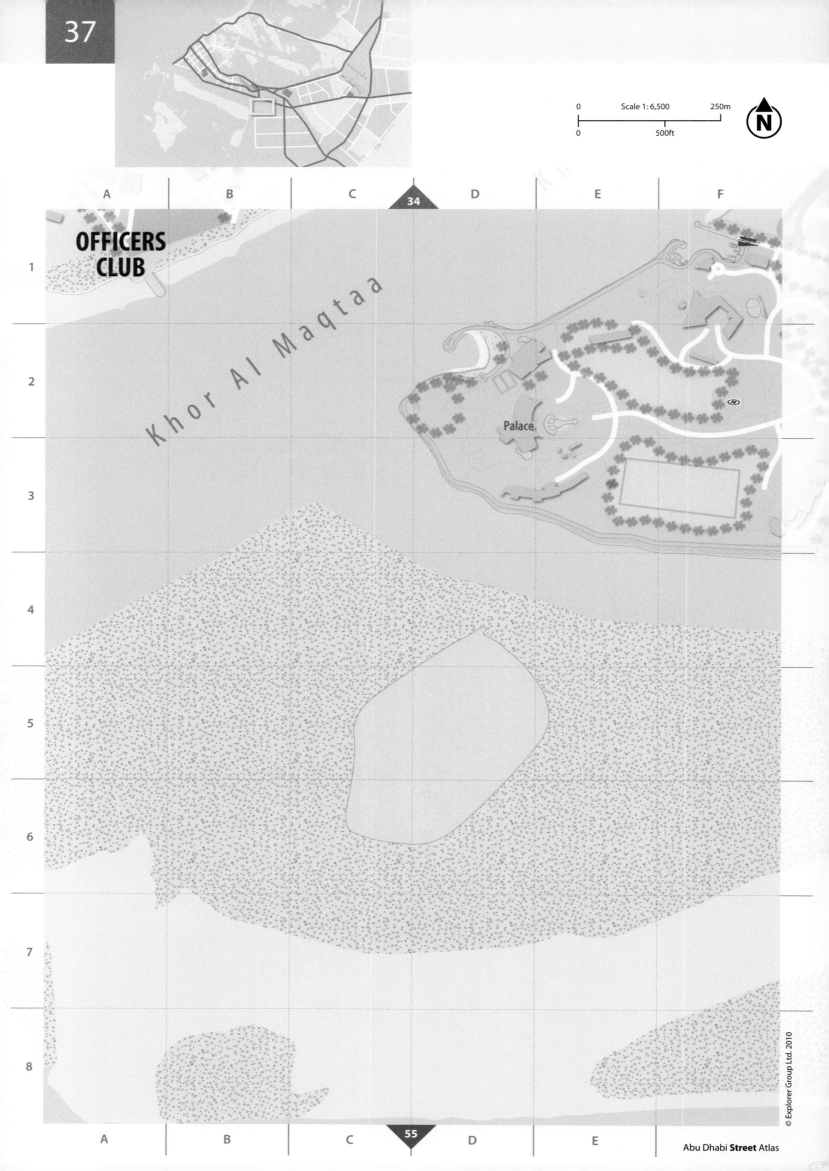

Scale 1:6,500

0     250m

0     500ft

N

A   B   C   D   E   F

OFFICERS CLUB

1

2

3

4

5

6

7

8

Khor Al Maqtaa

Palace

A   B   C   D   E

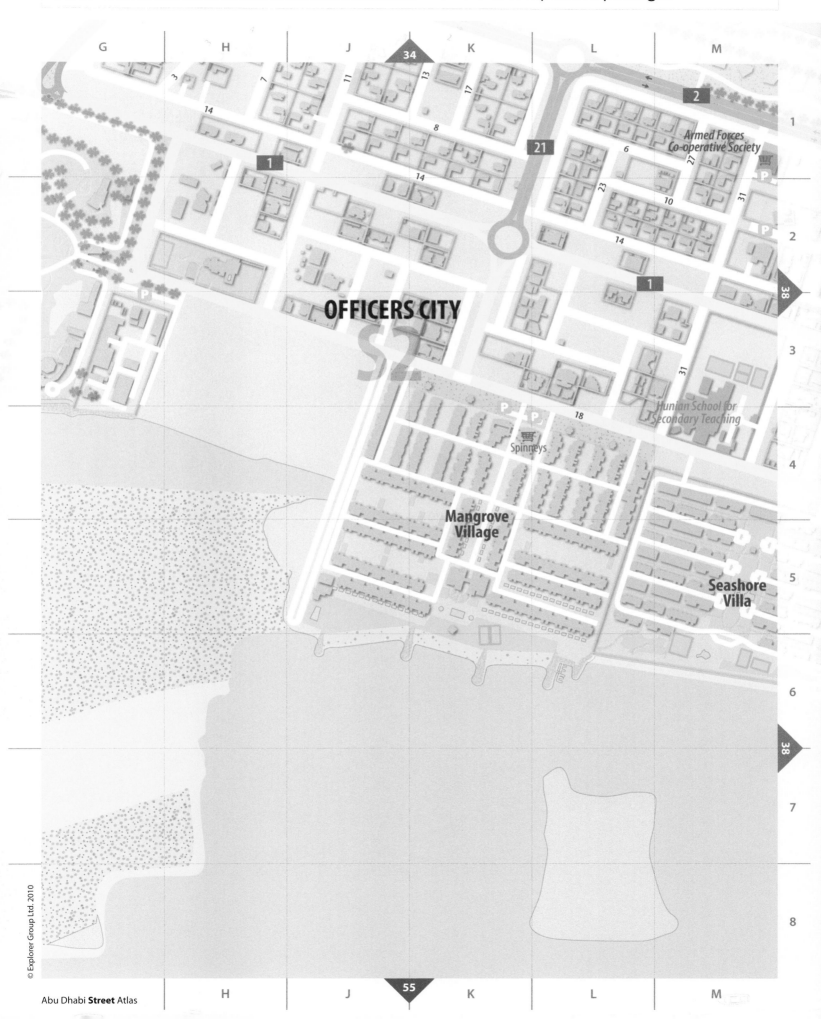

**OFFICERS CITY**

Armed Forces Co-operative Society

Hunian School for Secondary Teaching

Spinneys

Mangrove Village

Seashore Villa

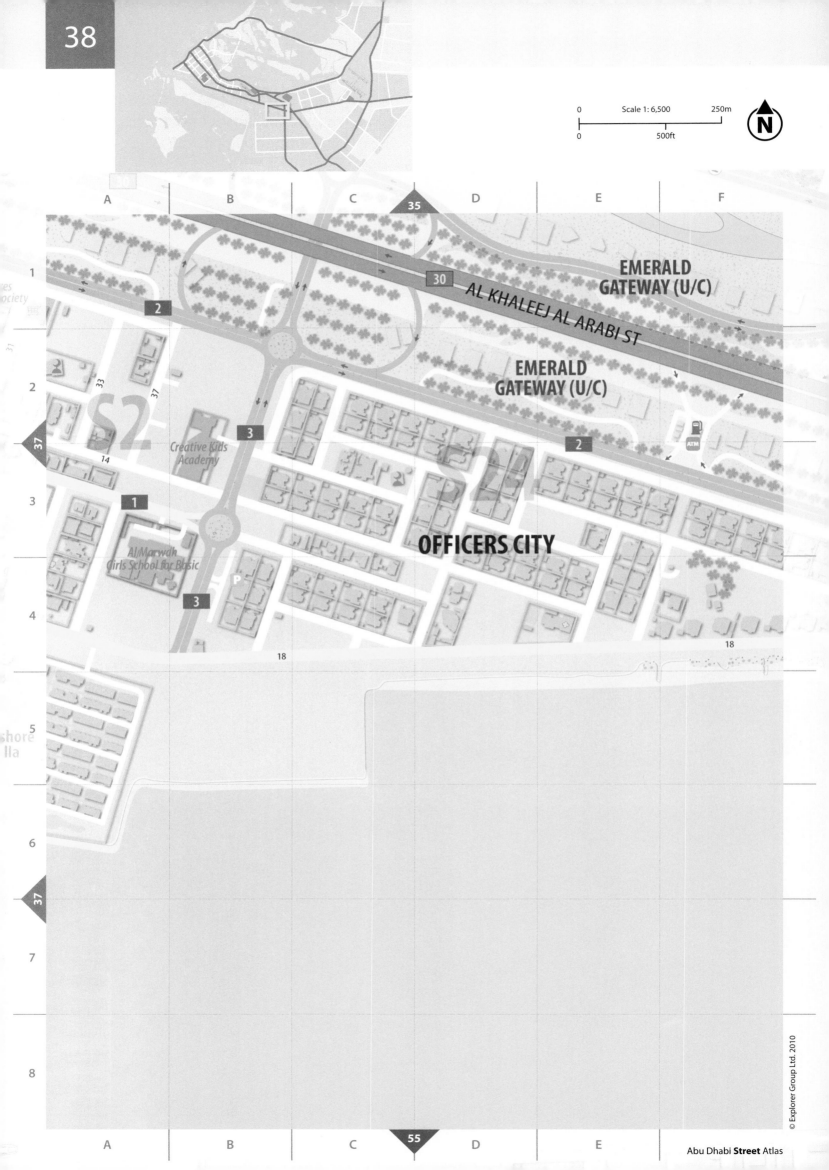

Scale 1: 6,500

0 — 250m
0 — 500ft

N

A  B  C  D  E  F

35

1

EMERALD
GATEWAY (U/C)

30

*AL KHALEEJ AL ARABI ST*

2

EMERALD
GATEWAY (U/C)

S2

33

37

2

37

*Creative Kids
Academy*

3

14

S2

ATM

2

3

1

*Al Marwah
Girls School for Basic*

OFFICERS CITY

P

3

4

18

18

5

shore
lla

6

37

7

8

A  B  C  D  E

55

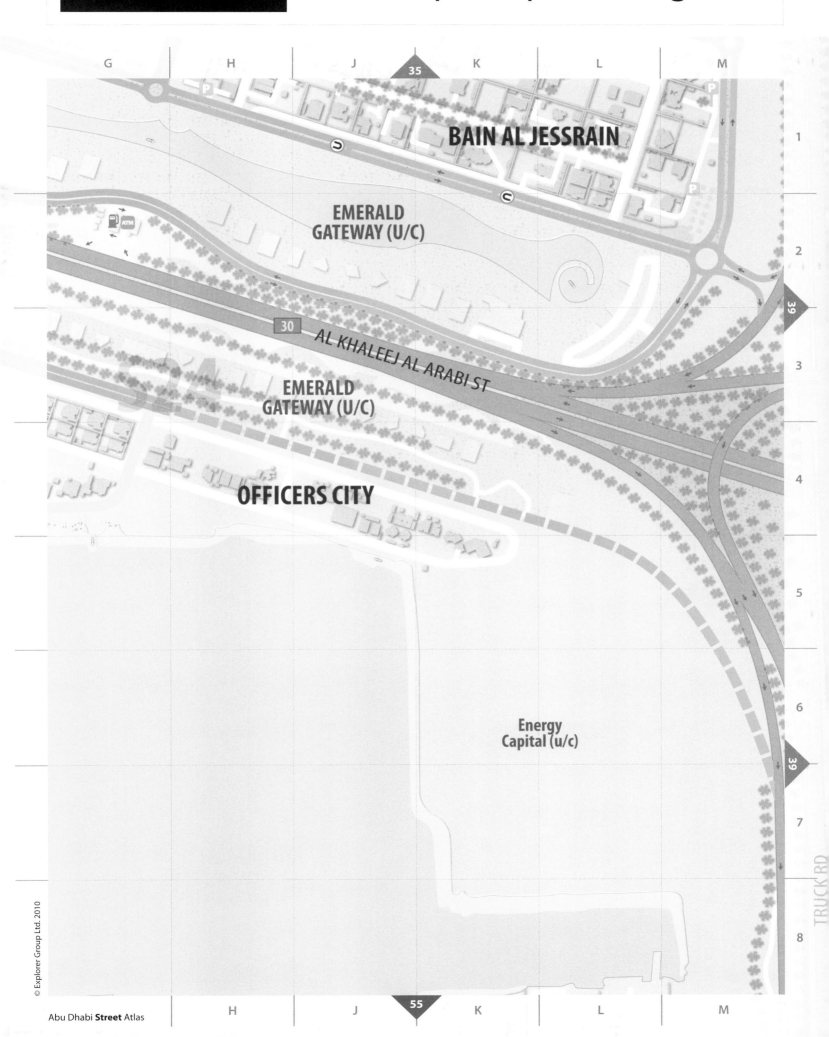

BAIN AL JESSRAIN

EMERALD
GATEWAY (U/C)

30 AL KHALEEJ AL ARABI ST

EMERALD
GATEWAY (U/C)

OFFICERS CITY

Energy
Capital (u/c)

TRUCK RD

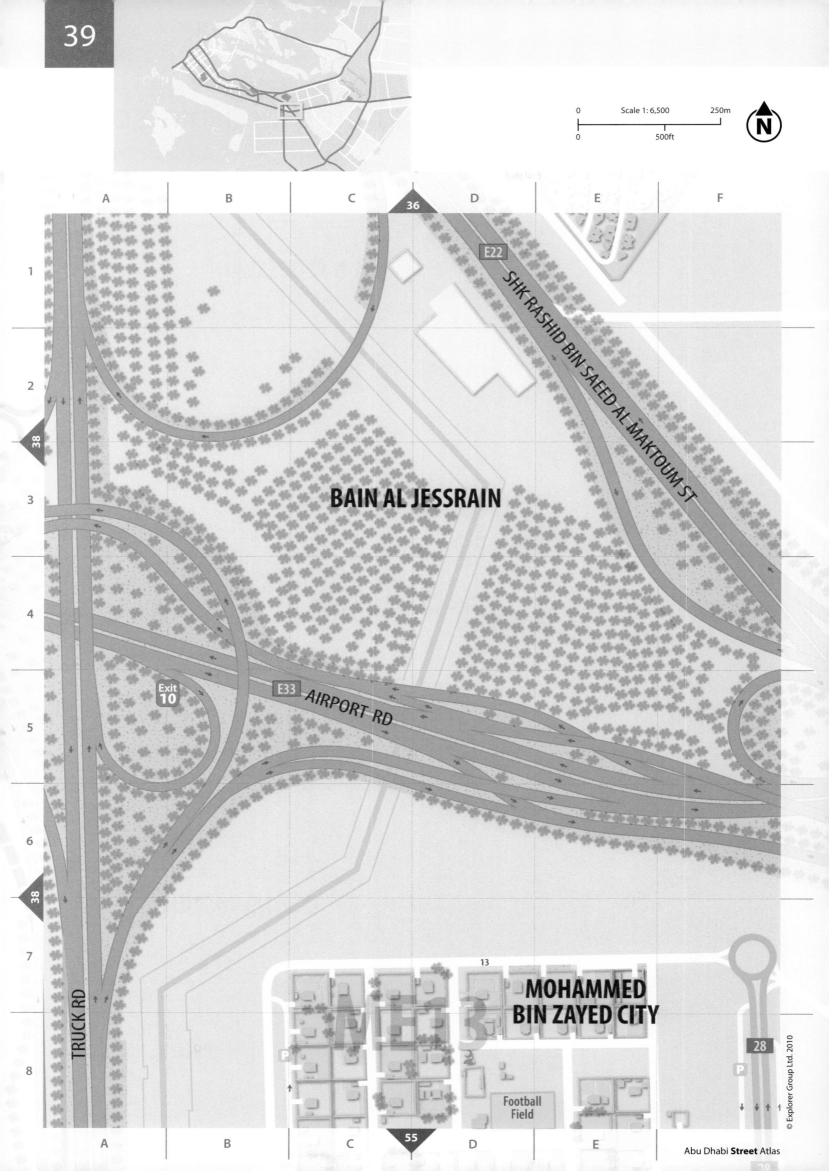

Scale 1: 6,500   250m
500ft

E22

SHK RASHID BIN SAEED AL MAKTOUM ST

**BAIN AL JESSRAIN**

Exit 10

E33 AIRPORT RD

TRUCK RD

**MOHAMMED BIN ZAYED CITY**

Football Field

© Explorer Group Ltd. 2010

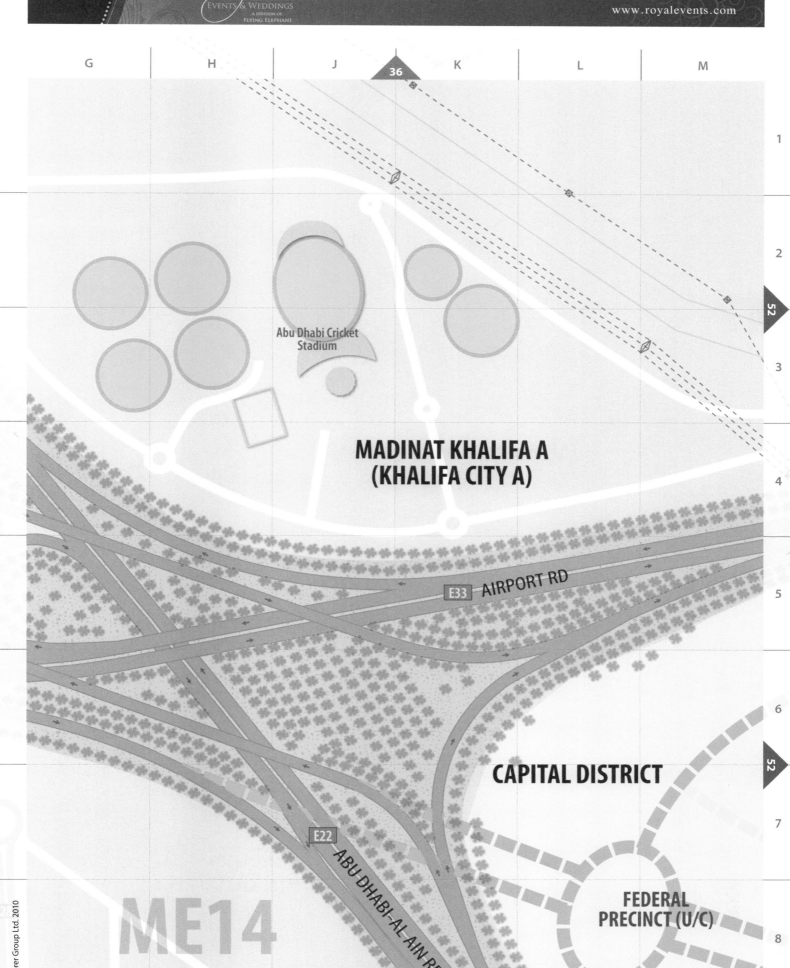

Abu Dhabi Cricket Stadium

**MADINAT KHALIFA A
(KHALIFA CITY A)**

E33 AIRPORT RD

**CAPITAL DISTRICT**

E22

ABU-DHABI-AL AIN RD

ME14

**FEDERAL
PRECINCT (U/C)**

Scale 1: 20,000

0        750m

0      1000ft

N

| | A | B | C | D | E | F |
|---|---|---|---|---|---|---|
| 1 | | | | | | |
| 2 | | | | | | |
| 3 | | | Arabian Gulf | | | |
| 4 | | | | | | |
| 5 | | | | | | |
| 6 | | | | | | |
| 7 | | | | | | |
| 8 | | | | | | |

**LULU ISLAND**

Abu Dhabi **Street** Atlas

| | G | H | J | K | L | M |
|---|---|---|---|---|---|---|

**1**

**2**

**41**

A r a b i a n   G u l f

**3**

**4**

Grand Mills

**Abu Dhabi Vegetable Oil Company**

**AL MEENA**

**5**

FREEZONE

**Cold Store Area**

Speed Line

AUH Commercial Co-operation

Al Razi

Jashanmal National Company

**Icon Cement Company**

**6**

Casttello Cafe

New Mina Market

AUH Tyre Co

Jabal Al Rahma Furniture

Al Ahlia Gulf Line

Crown Relocation

**PORT ZAYED**

Coast Guard Tower

**41**

Spinneys Warehouse

Juma Al Majid Customer Care Ctr

United Electronics Co

Force 10 Eng Warehouse

Bin Sagar Grp

Unifruitti Cold Store

FREEZONE

**AL MEENA**

**7**

ADCECO Group

Grand Store

Pan Emirates Foods Distribution

**Container Area**

AL M

GAC

Giffin Graphics

Barwil AUH Ruwais

ADMMI

Toys "R" Us

AUH Municipality Slaughter House

Dept of Transport Maritime Sector Municipal & Agricultural Dept

**DHOW HARBOUR**

Mina Centre

Al Futtaim Auto Mall

Gate 2

**Market Control Section**
Emirates of AUH Finance & Customs Administration Dept

**8**

Coast Guard Department

Marina Police

KM Trading Warehouse

EMKE Grp Warehouse

Jaber Khoory

Mina Plaza (u/c)

Al Mina Veg Mkt

Adnoc Tank

AUH National Hotel Warehouse

Shk Khalifa Medical City Warehouse

Free Zone Market (Iranian Market)

Food Distribution Center

LU AND

AUH Co-operative Society Warehouse

| | H | J | K | L | M |
|---|---|---|---|---|---|

Scale 1: 20,000

0      750m

0      1000ft

**N**

A    B    C    D    E    F

1

2

40

3

A r a b i a n   G u l f

4

*Rotana (u/c)*

**SAADIYAT BEACH (U/C)**

🏛 *Guggenheim Abu Dhabi Museum (u/c)*

*St Regis (u/c)*

🏛 *Zayed National Museum (u/c)*

5

**SAADIYAT CULTURAL DISTRICT (U/C)**

*Louvre Abu Dhabi (u/c)*

**SAADIYAT ISLAND**

6

40

*Coast Guard Tower*

*Performing Arts Centre (u/c)*

**SAADIYAT MARINA (U/C)**

7

E12

**AL MEENA**

SHEIKH KHALIFA BRIDGE

8

**Sadiyat Marina**

*Maritime Museum (u/c)* 🏛

**Adnoc Tank**

M

© Explorer Group Ltd. 2010

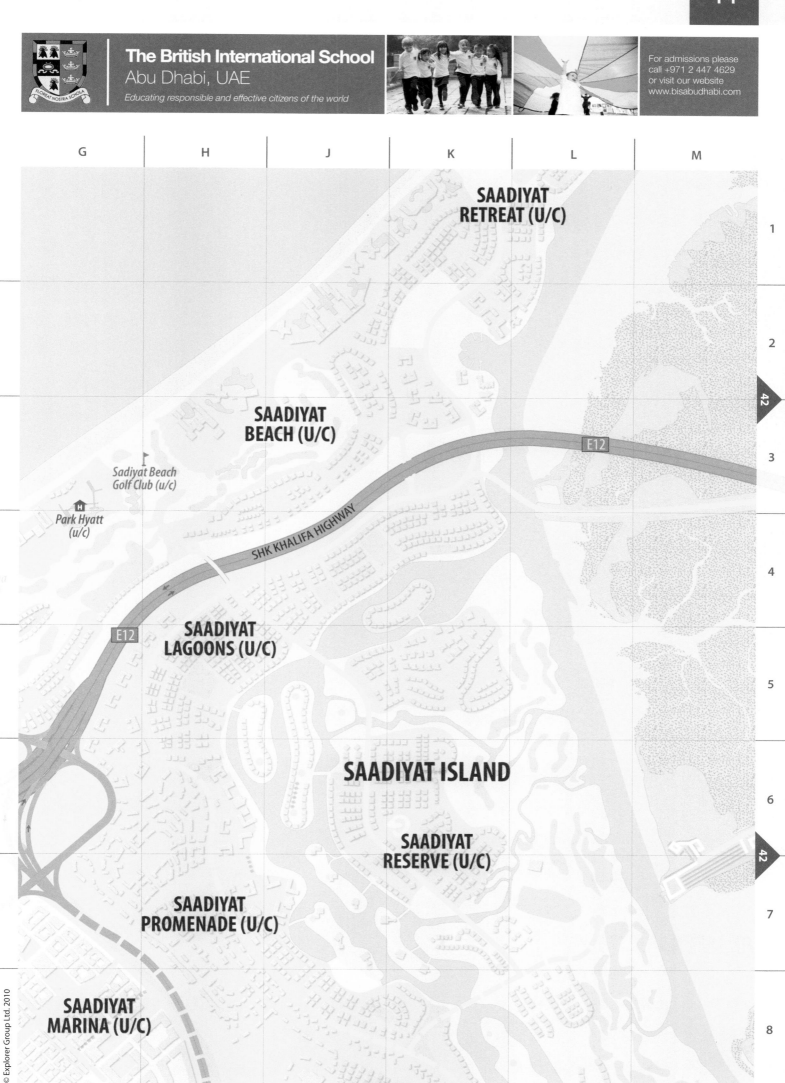

SAADIYAT RETREAT (U/C)

SAADIYAT BEACH (U/C)

Sadiyat Beach Golf Club (u/c)

E12

Park Hyatt (u/c)

Rotana (u/c)

SHK KHALIFA HIGHWAY

E12

SAADIYAT LAGOONS (U/C)

SAADIYAT ISLAND

SAADIYAT RESERVE (U/C)

SAADIYAT PROMENADE (U/C)

SAADIYAT MARINA (U/C)

Scale 1: 20,000

0 · · · · · 750m

0 · · · · · 1000ft

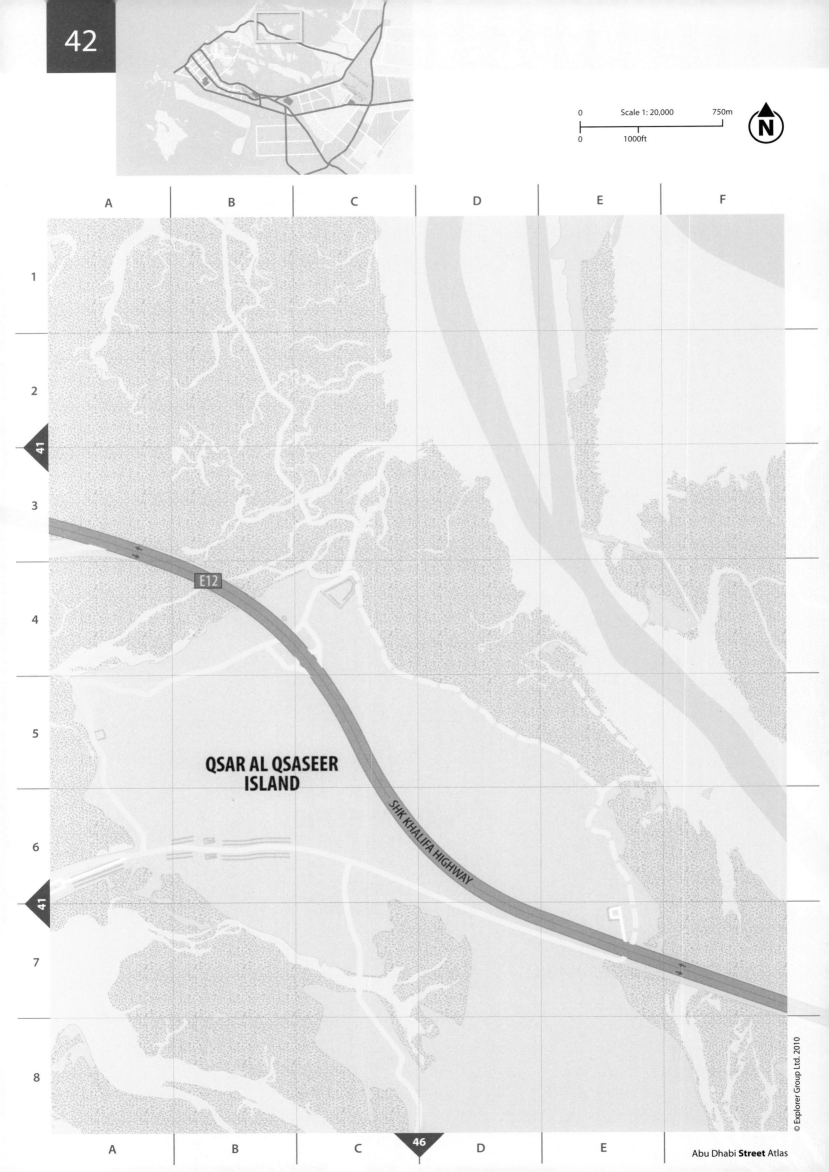

N

A B C D E F

1

2

41

3

E12

4

5

**QSAR AL QSASEER
ISLAND**

6

41

SHK KHALIFA HIGHWAY

7

8

A B C D E F

G    H    J    K    L    M

Arabian Gulf

**BAL GHELAM ISLAND**

1

2

43

3

4

**RAMHAN ISLAND**

5

6

43

7

E12

SHK KHALIFA HIGHWAY

8

H    J    46    K    L    M

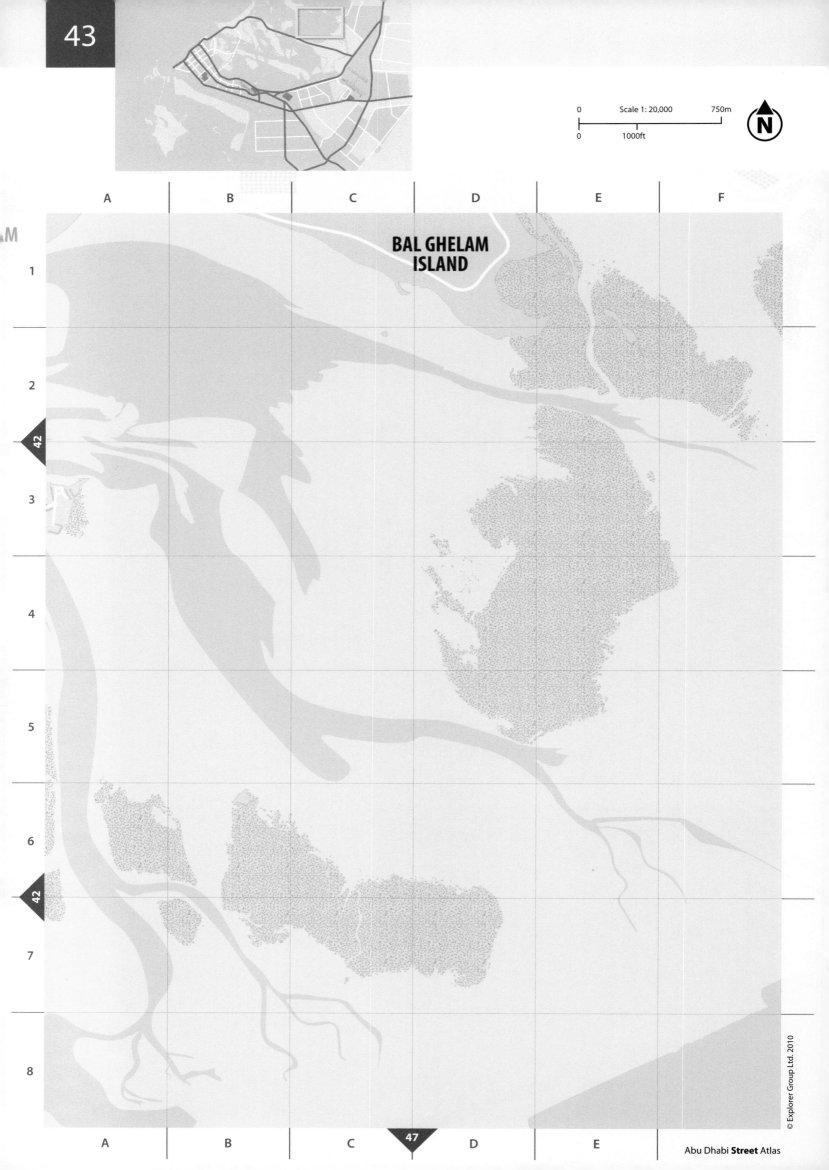

Scale 1: 20,000

0          750m

0       1000ft

N

**BAL GHELAM ISLAND**

A    B    C    D    E    F

1

2

42

3

4

5

6

42

7

8

A    B    C    D    E

G H J K L M

Arabian Gulf

Palace

AL BAHIA

1
2
44
3
4
5
6
44
7
8

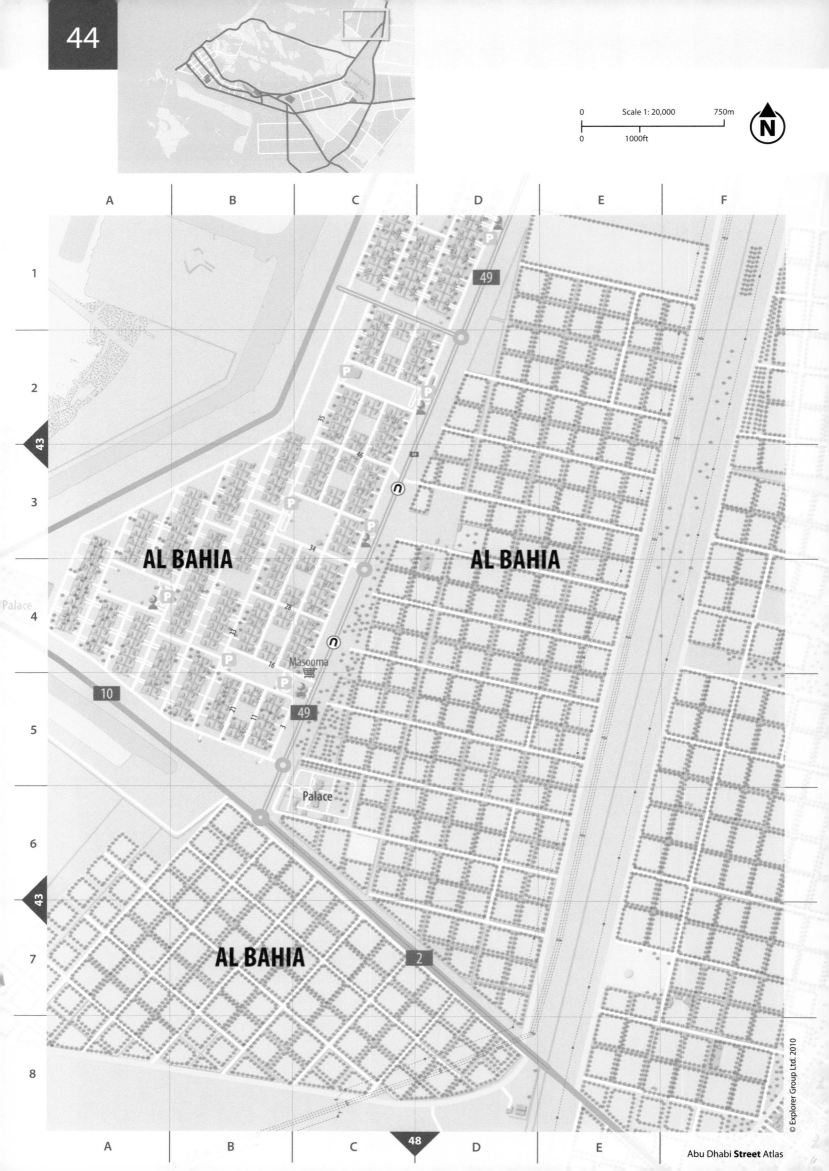

Scale 1: 20,000

0      750m

0      1000ft

N

A    B    C    D    E    F

1

2

43

3

AL BAHIA

49

AL BAHIA

Palace

4

34

28

33

16   Masooma

10

21   11   3

49

5

Palace

6

43

7

AL BAHIA

2

8

A    B    C    D    E

48

© Explorer Group Ltd. 2010

# CYCLONE TRAVEL & TOURS

Tel: +971 2 6276275 - Fax: +971 2 6273331
P.O.Box: 31740 - Abu Dhabi - U.A.E
www.cyclonetours.com

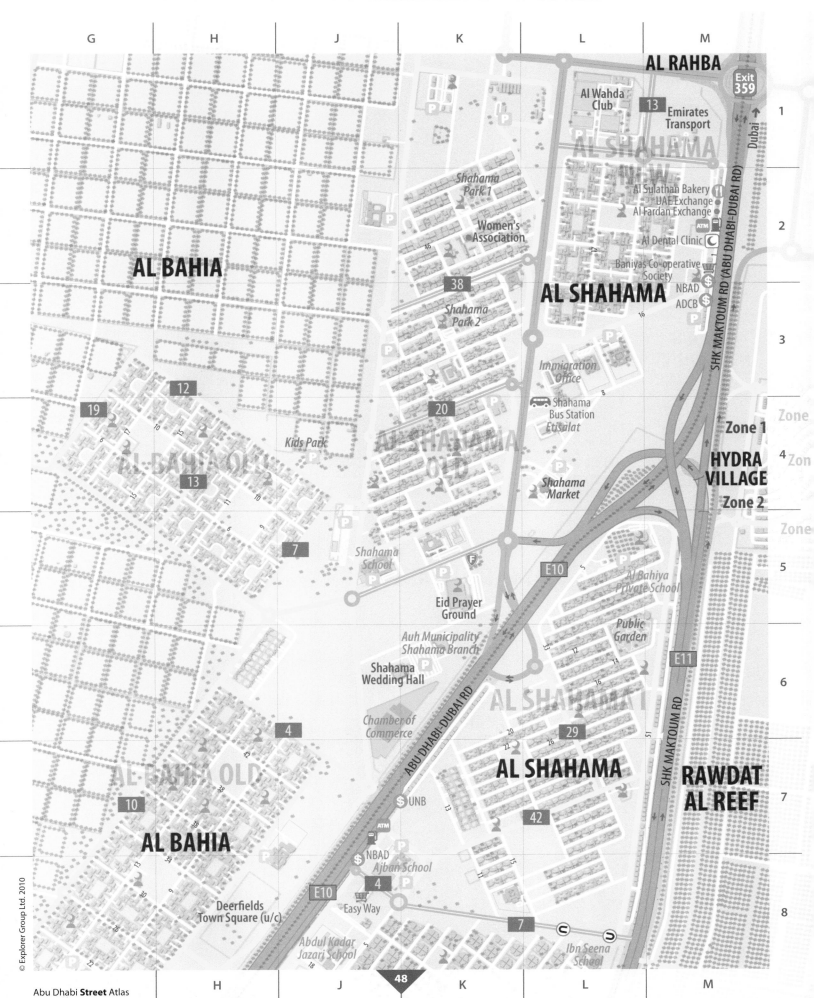

Scale 1: 20,000

0      750m

0      1000ft

N

Adnoc
Tank

*Maritime
Museum (u/c)*

41

A    B    C    D    E    F

K h o r   L a f f a n

**Eco Bay
Complex (u/c)**

Atlantis
Twr (u/c)

1

**Central Business
District (u/c)**

Hydra
Cubic (u/c)

Tameer
Twrs (u/c)

The Helix
(u/c)

2

**SHAMS
ABU DHABI (U/C)**

Al Odaid Beach
Residence (u/c)

**HALAT KHAMIS
ISLAND**

Onyx
Twr (u/c)

3

**TAMOUH
NORTH (U/C)**

Marina

Marina
Bay Twrs (u/c)

Triton
Twr (u/c)

*Hydra (u/c)*

Sigma 1

Hydra Avenue (u/c)

Addax Twr (u/c)

Omega Twr (u/c)

Ocean Pearl
Residence (u/c)

The Pearl
Twr (u/c)

Sigma 2
(u/c)

Pearl Bay
Residential

Reem Diamond (u/c)

Mangrove Place (u/c)

Royal
Palace

**ZUBROWKA
ISLAND**

Hydra Heights
Twrs (u/c)

**City of
Lights (u/c)**

Sky
Twr (u/c)

4

Synergy
Twr (u/c)

Hydra Corporate
Twrs

Sun Twr
(u/c)

**The Gate
District (u/c)**

5

Hydra Corporate
Twrs (u/c)

B   A

Hydra 55
(u/c)

Gate
Twrs (u/c)

REEM ISLAND

*Marina
Square (u/c)*

Julfar
Residence (u/c)

**AL REEM ISLAND**

5

Marina
Blue (u/c)

**UMM YIFENAH
ISLAND**

*Reem
Mall (u/c)*

RAK
Twrs (u/c)

Icon Twrs
(u/c)

REEM BRIDGE

Al Sharq
Twr 1 (u/c)

Solitaire
Twr (u/c)

**Carina
Views (u/c)**

The Wings
(u/c)

6

*Boutique
(u/c)*

**Central
Business
Bay Marina**

Marina
Bay (u/c)

**TAMOUH
SOUTH (U/C)**

11

**NAJMAT
ABU DHABI (U/C)**

*Boutique
(u/c)*

K h o r   A l   B a g h a l

Residential
Marina

7

9

**Qasr Al Bahar**

Resort
Marina

8

P   P

P

A    B    C    D    E

14

© Explorer Group Ltd. 2010

Qasr Al Bahar

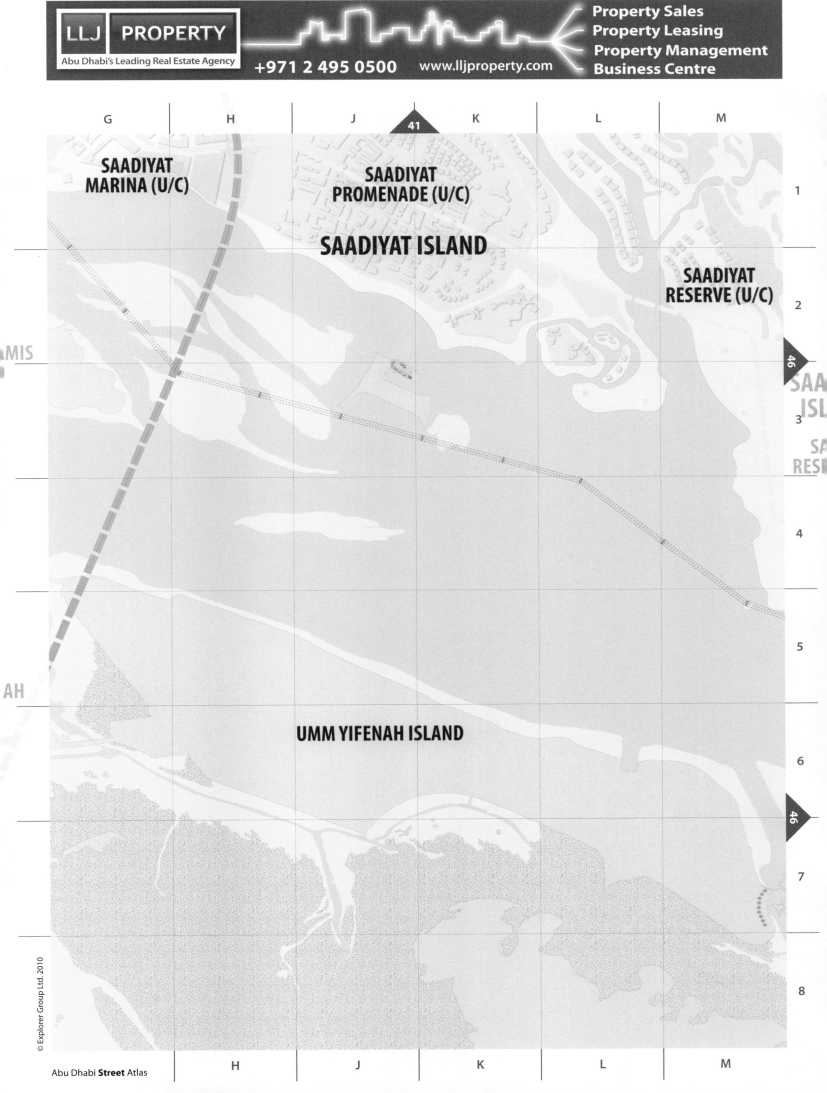

G   H   J   41   K   L   M

**SAADIYAT MARINA (U/C)**

**SAADIYAT PROMENADE (U/C)**

**SAADIYAT ISLAND**

**SAADIYAT RESERVE (U/C)**

1

2

46

SAA
ISL

SA
RES

3

4

5

**UMM YIFENAH ISLAND**

6

46

7

8

MIS

AH

Scale 1: 20,000

0        750m

0      1000ft

**N**

A   B   C   **42**   D   E   F

1

2

**QSAR AL QSASEER ISLAND**

**45**

**SAADIYAT ISLAND**

3

**SAADIYAT RESERVE (U/C)**

AT (U/C)

4

5

6

**Khor Laffan**

**45**

**Al Jaraf Fisheries**

7

**BALRMAD ISLAND**

**Horse Stables**

8

**AS SAMMALIYYAH ISLAND**

Marina **49**

A   B   C   D   E

# JASHANMAL BOOKSTORES

**Dubai:** Mall of the Emirates • Jashanmal-Wafi City • Caribou Coffee - Uptown Mirdiff, Dubai Marina Walk
The Village Mall • **Abu Dhabi:** Abu Dhabi Mall • **Sharjah:** Sahara Centre • **Bahrain:** Seef Mall • Al Aali Shopping Complex

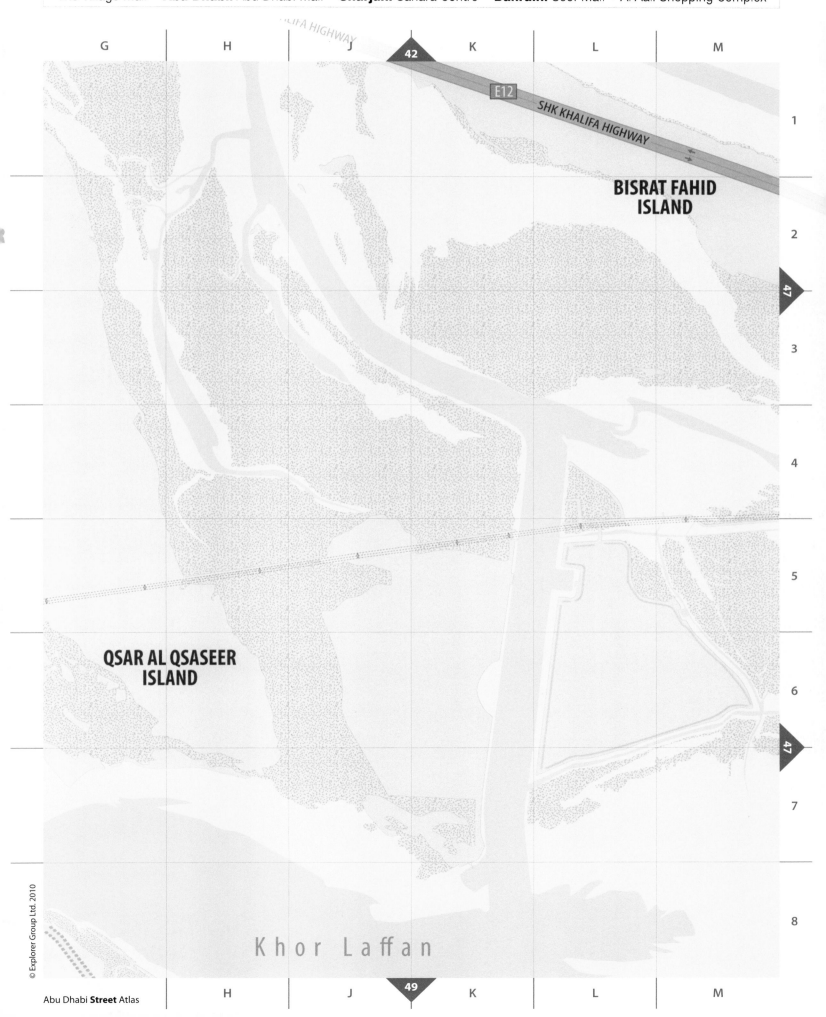

E12

SHK KHALIFA HIGHWAY

BISRAT FAHID
ISLAND

QSAR AL QSASEER
ISLAND

Khor Laffan

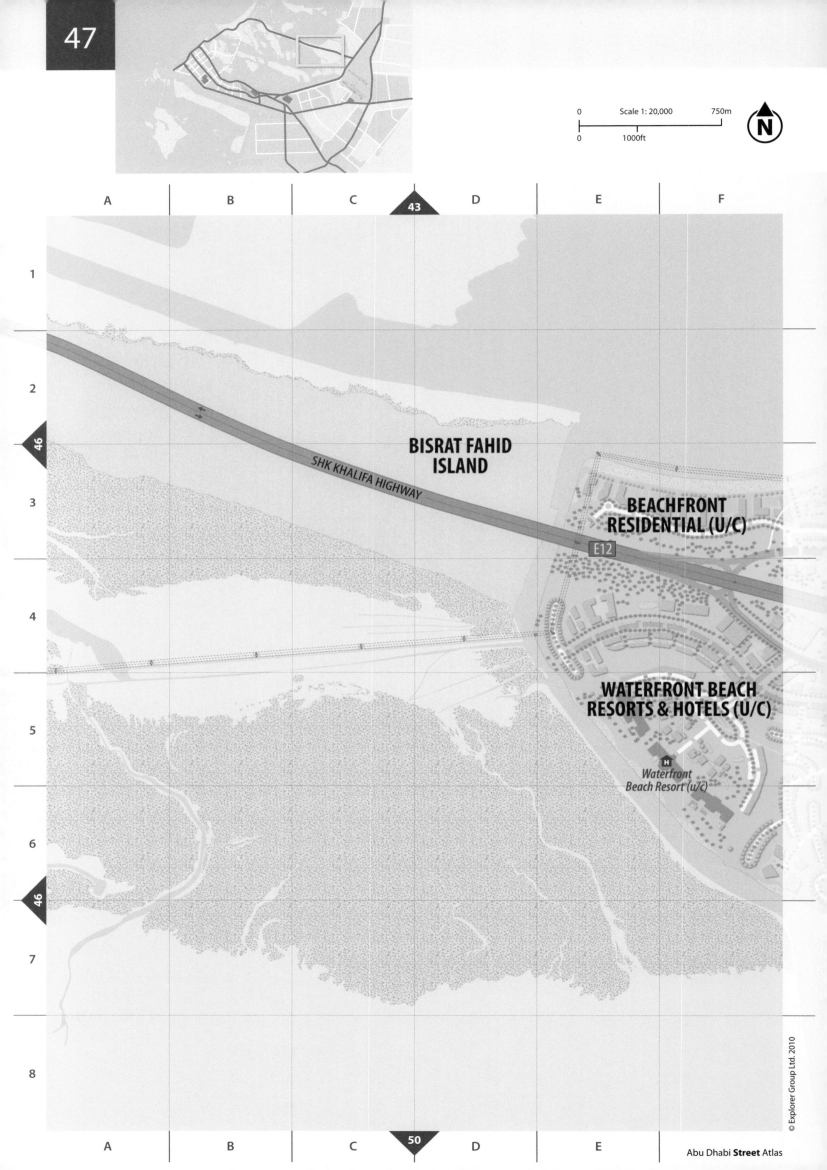

Scale 1: 20,000

0       750m

0      1000ft

N

A    B    C   43   D    E    F

1

2

46

**BISRAT FAHID ISLAND**

SHK KHALIFA HIGHWAY

**BEACHFRONT RESIDENTIAL (U/C)**

E12

3

4

**WATERFRONT BEACH RESORTS & HOTELS (U/C)**

5

*Waterfront Beach Resort (u/c)*

46

6

7

8

A    B    C   50   D    E

© Explorer Group Ltd. 2010

Abu Dhabi **Street** Atlas

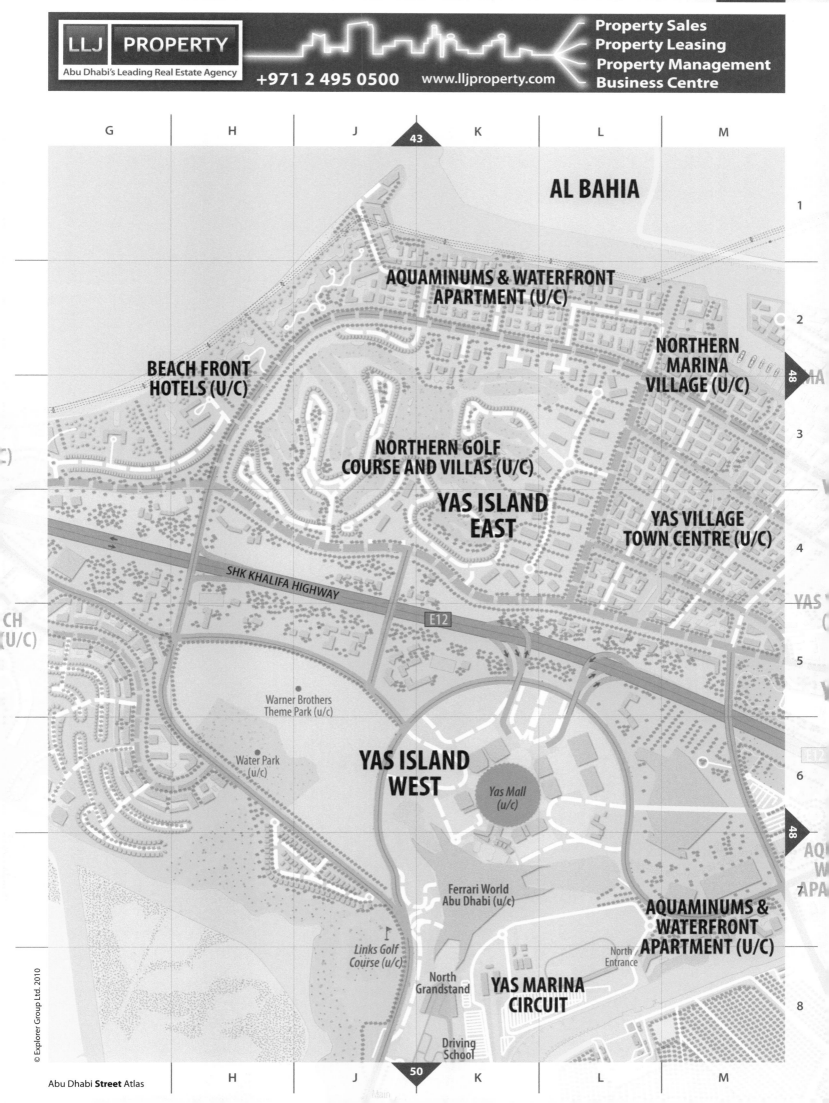

**AL BAHIA**

**AQUAMINUMS & WATERFRONT APARTMENT (U/C)**

**NORTHERN MARINA VILLAGE (U/C)**

**BEACH FRONT HOTELS (U/C)**

**NORTHERN GOLF COURSE AND VILLAS (U/C)**

**YAS ISLAND EAST**

**YAS VILLAGE TOWN CENTRE (U/C)**

SHK KHALIFA HIGHWAY

E12

Warner Brothers Theme Park (u/c)

Water Park (u/c)

**YAS ISLAND WEST**

Yas Mall (u/c)

Ferrari World Abu Dhabi (u/c)

**AQUAMINUMS & WATERFRONT APARTMENT (U/C)**

North Entrance

Links Golf Course (u/c)

North Grandstand

**YAS MARINA CIRCUIT**

Driving School

Scale 1: 20,000

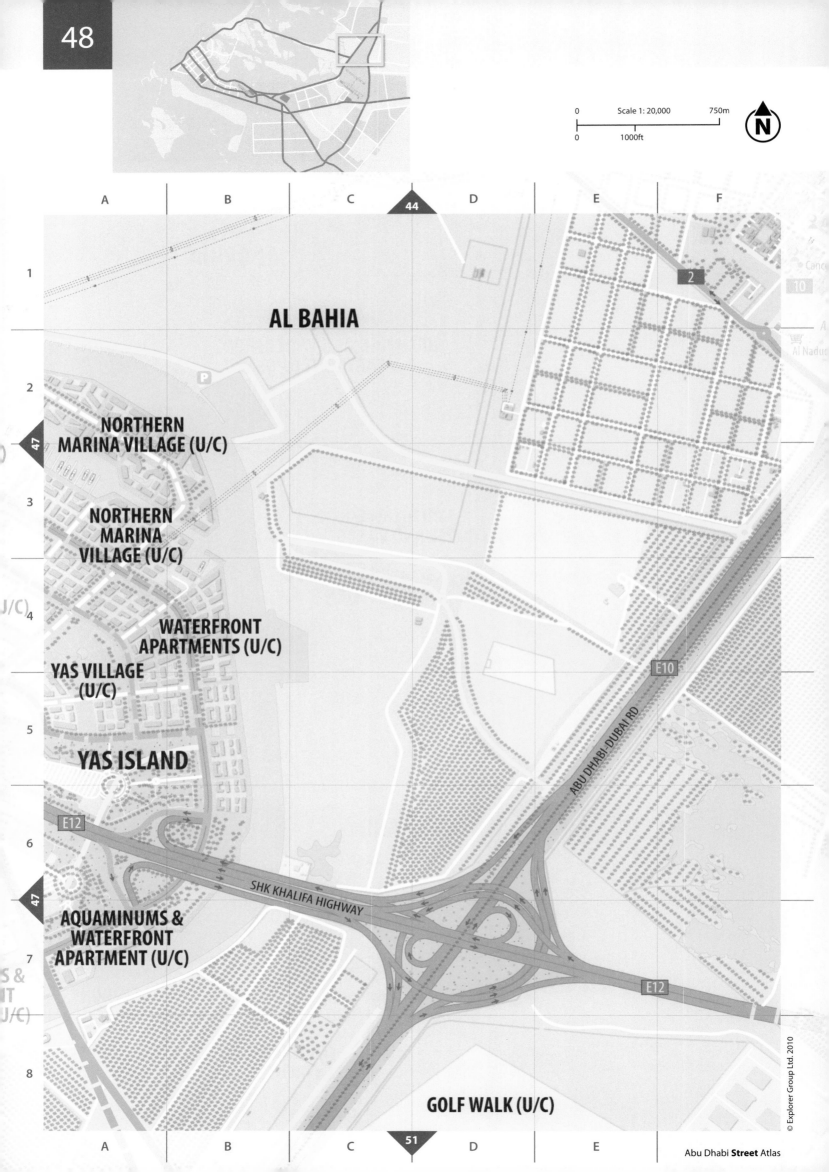

**AL BAHIA**

**NORTHERN
MARINA VILLAGE (U/C)**

**NORTHERN
MARINA
VILLAGE (U/C)**

**WATERFRONT
APARTMENTS (U/C)**

**YAS VILLAGE
(U/C)**

**YAS ISLAND**

E10

ABU DHABI-DUBAI RD

E12

SHK KHALIFA HIGHWAY

E12

**AQUAMINUMS &
WATERFRONT
APARTMENT (U/C)**

**GOLF WALK (U/C)**

© Explorer Group Ltd. 2010

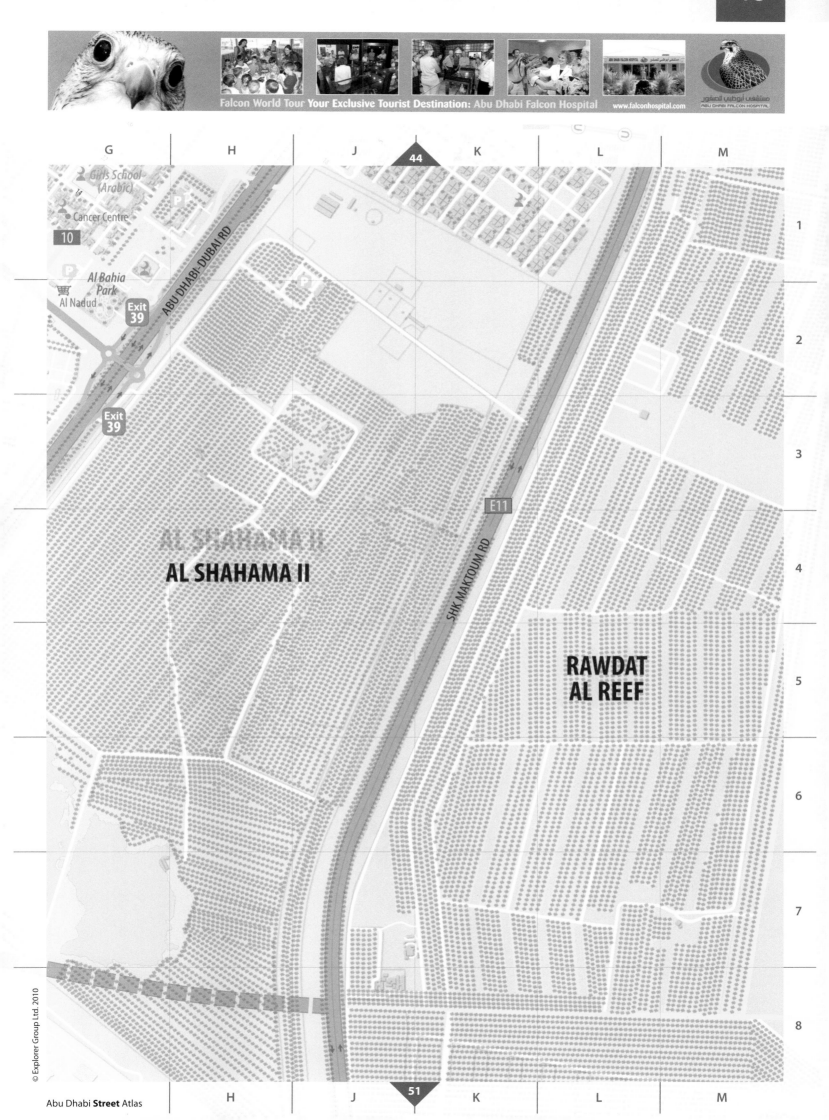

Falcon World Tour **Your** Exclusive Tourist Destination: Abu Dhabi Falcon Hospital    www.falconhospital.com

G    H    J    **44**    K    L    M

Girls School
(Arabic)

Cancer Centre

**10**

Al Bahia
Park

Al Nadud

**Exit
39**

ABU DHABI-DUBAI RD

**Exit
39**

1

2

3

AL SHAHAMA II

**AL SHAHAMA II**

E11

SHK MAKTOUM RD

4

**RAWDAT
AL REEF**

5

6

7

8

H    J    **51**    K    L    M

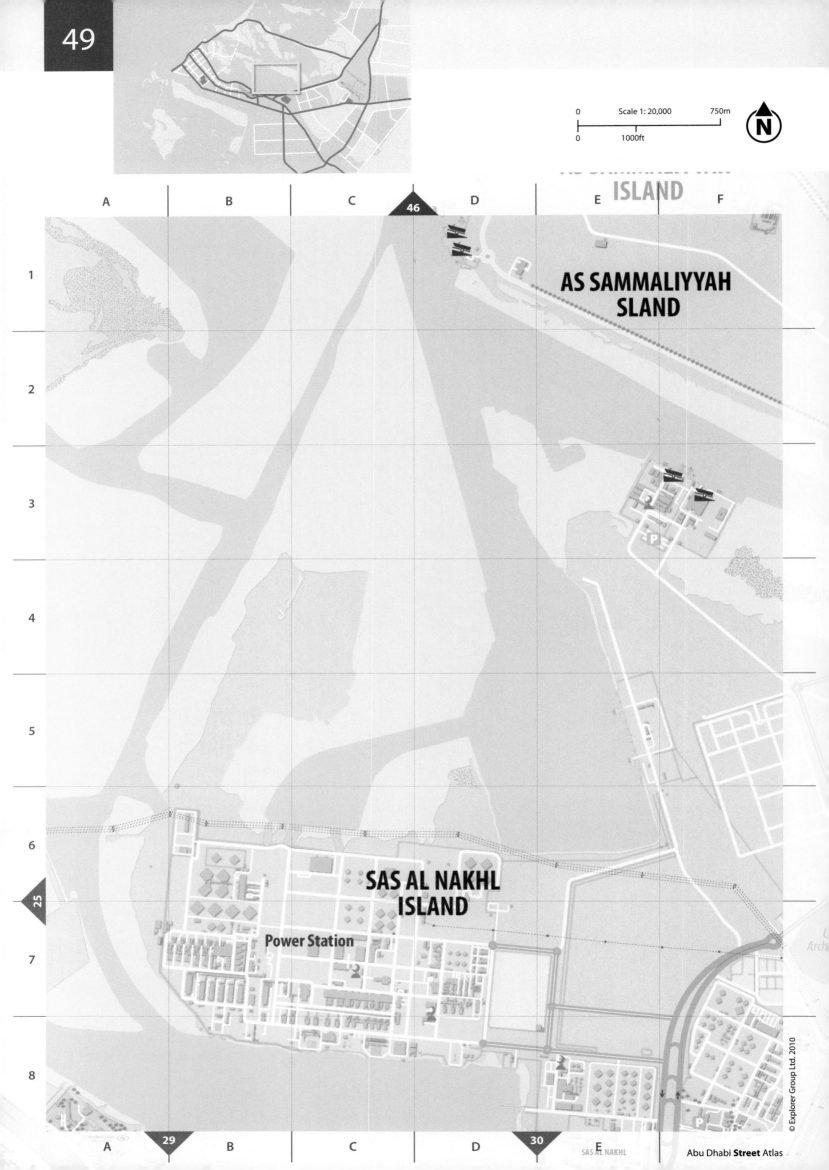

Scale 1: 20,000

0     750m

0     1000ft

**N**

ISLAND

# AS SAMMALIYYAH SLAND

# SAS AL NAKHL ISLAND

**Power Station**

SAS AL NAKHL

© Explorer Group Ltd. 2010

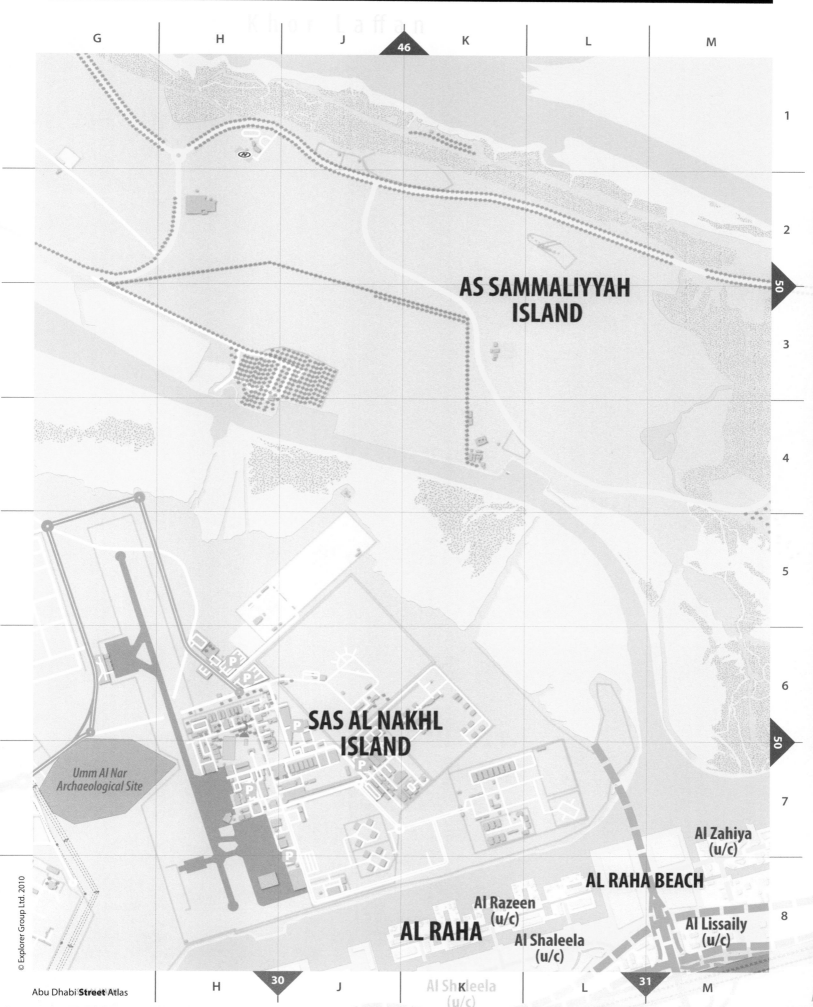

Khor Laffan

AS SAMMALIYYAH ISLAND

SAS AL NAKHL ISLAND

Umm Al Nar Archaeological Site

Al Zahiya (u/c)

AL RAHA BEACH

Al Razeen (u/c)

AL RAHA

Al Shaleela (u/c)

Al Lissaily (u/c)

Al Shaleela (u/c)

© Explorer Group Ltd. 2010

Abu Dhabi **Street** Atlas

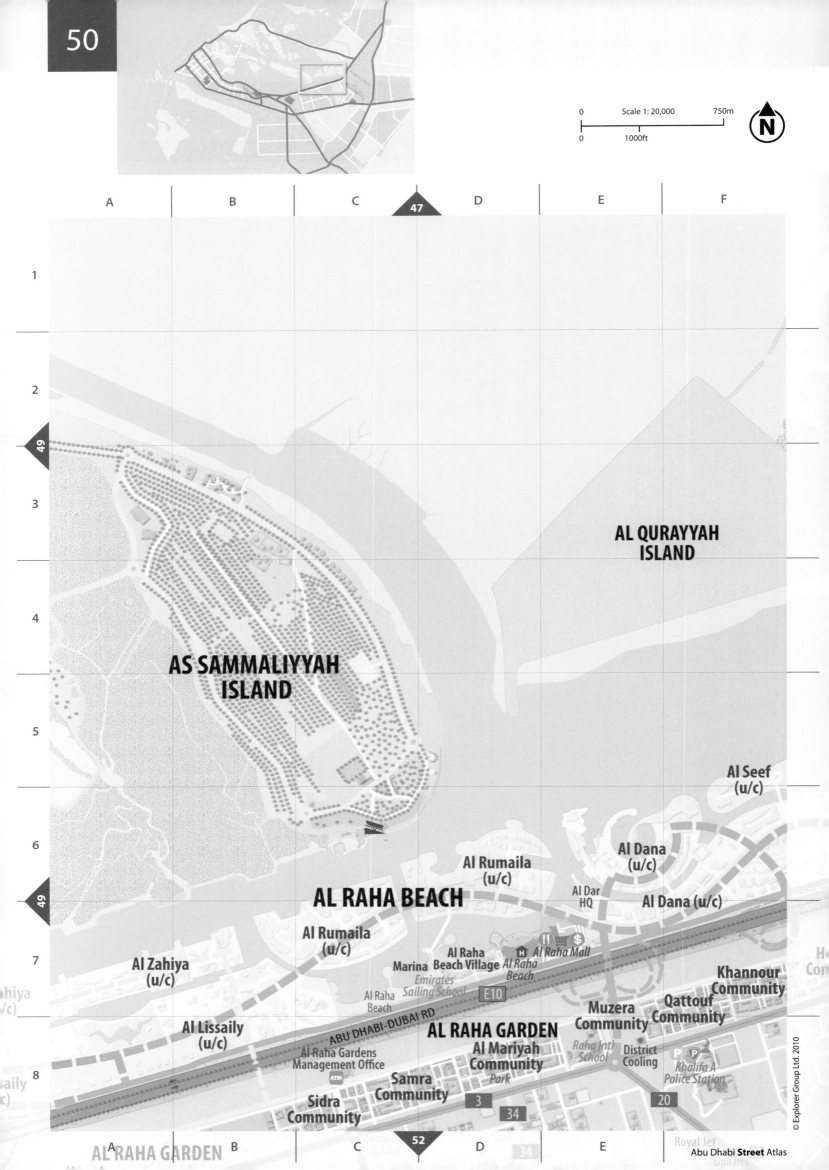

Scale 1: 20,000

0      750m

0      1000ft

**N**

A    B    C    D    E    F

1

2

49

3

**AL QURAYYAH ISLAND**

4

**AS SAMMALIYYAH ISLAND**

5

Al Seef (u/c)

6

Al Dana (u/c)

Al Rumaila (u/c)

49

**AL RAHA BEACH**

Al Dar HQ

Al Dana (u/c)

7

Al Rumaila (u/c)

Al Zahiya (u/c)

Al Raha Marina

Al Raha Beach Village

Al Raha Beach

Al Raha Mall

Khannour Community

ahiya (/c)

Emirates Sailing School

E10

Muzera Community

Qattouf Community

Al Raha Beach

Al Lissaily (u/c)

ABU DHABI-DUBAI RD

**AL RAHA GARDEN**

Raha Intl School

District Cooling

8

Al Raha Gardens Management Office

ATM

Al Mariyah Community

Park

Khalifa A Police Station

aily /c)

Sidra Community

Samra Community

3

20

**AL RAHA GARDEN**

A    B    C    D    E

52

34

Royal Jet

He Com

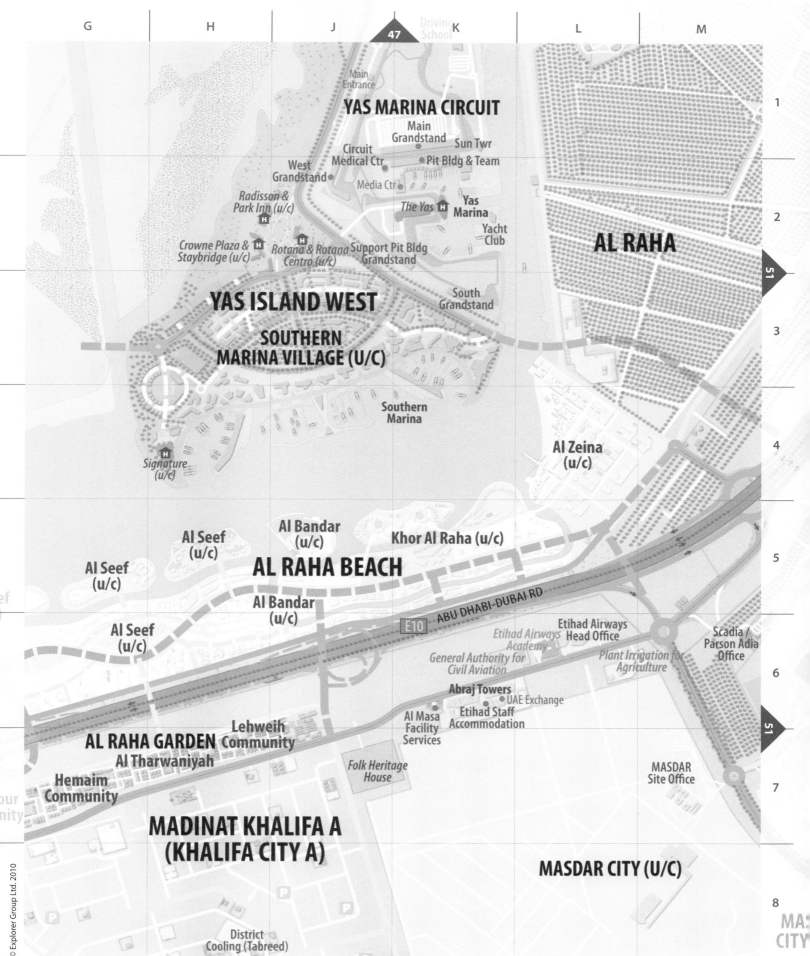

G    H    J    47    K    L    M

1

2

3

4

5

6

7

8

51

**YAS MARINA CIRCUIT**

Main Entrance

Main Grandstand
Sun Twr
Circuit Medical Ctr
Pit Bldg & Team
West Grandstand
Media Ctr
The Yas H    Yas Marina
Radisson & Park Inn (u/c)
Yacht Club
Crowne Plaza & Staybridge (u/c)
Rotana & Rotana Centro (u/c)
Support Pit Bldg Grandstand

**AL RAHA**

**YAS ISLAND WEST**

South Grandstand

**SOUTHERN MARINA VILLAGE (U/C)**

Southern Marina

Al Zeina (u/c)

Signature (u/c)

Al Bandar (u/c)
Al Seef (u/c)
Khor Al Raha (u/c)
Al Seef (u/c)

**AL RAHA BEACH**

Al Seef (u/c)
Al Bandar (u/c)

ABU DHABI-DUBAI RD
E10
Etihad Airways Academy
Etihad Airways Head Office
Scadia / Parson Adia Office
General Authority for Civil Aviation
Plant Irrigation for Agriculture
Al Seef (u/c)

Abraj Towers
UAE Exchange
Al Masa Facility Services
Etihad Staff Accommodation

Lehweih Community

**AL RAHA GARDEN**
Al Tharwaniyah
Folk Heritage House
MASDAR Site Office

Hemaim Community

**MADINAT KHALIFA A (KHALIFA CITY A)**

**MASDAR CITY (U/C)**

District Cooling (Tabreed)

H    J    52    K    L    M

Seef (u/c)
nnour unity

MAS CITY

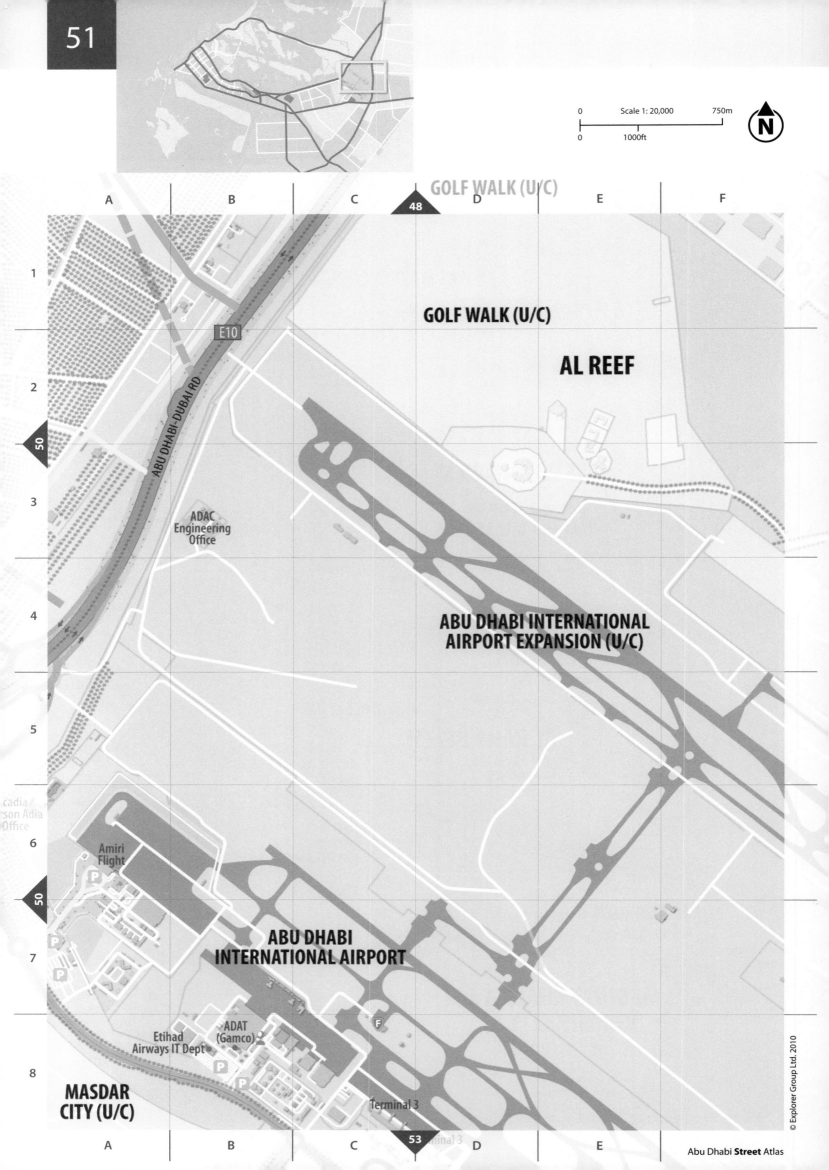

Scale 1: 20,000

0       750m

0       1000ft

N

GOLF WALK (U/C)

A    B    C    48    D    E    F

1

**GOLF WALK (U/C)**

**AL REEF**

E10

2

ABU DHABI-DUBAI RD

50

3

ADAC
Engineering
Office

4

**ABU DHABI INTERNATIONAL
AIRPORT EXPANSION (U/C)**

5

cadia /
son Adia
Office

6

Amiri
Flight

P

50

7

P

**ABU DHABI
INTERNATIONAL AIRPORT**

P

8

Etihad
Airways IT Dept

ADAT
(Gamco)

F

P

**MASDAR
CITY (U/C)**

P

Terminal 3

A    B    C    53    D    E

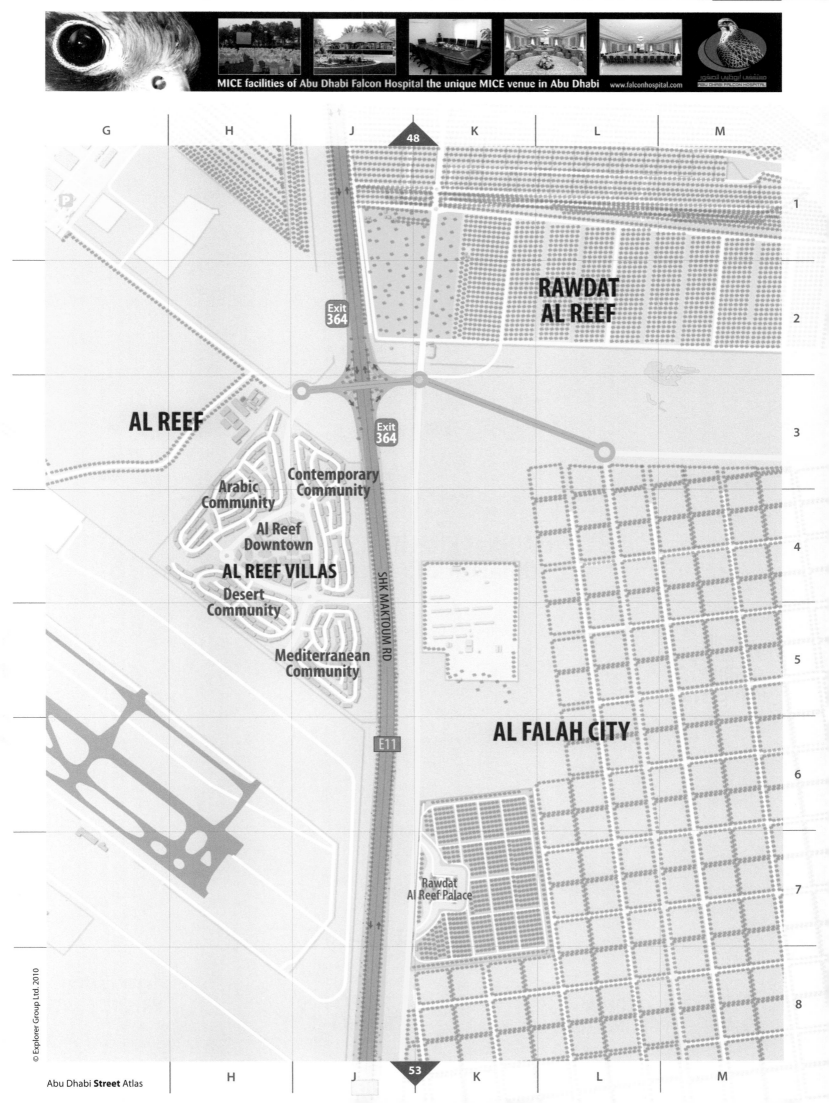

**RAWDAT AL REEF**

**AL REEF**

Contemporary Community

Arabic Community

Al Reef Downtown

**AL REEF VILLAS**

Desert Community

Mediterranean Community

Exit 364

Exit 364

48

SHK MAKTOUM RD

E11

**AL FALAH CITY**

Rawdat Al Reef Palace

**AL RAHA GARDEN**
**Yasmina Community**

Sidra Community

Community

Gems Intl School

Seha Ambulatory Health Care Centre

Knowledge Sun Training & Language Ctr
Dept of Private Security Business

ADCB

Khalifa City Market
Areej Dental Clinic

Khalifa City Co-operative Society
KFC

**SW12**

Landscapping
Gulf Nursery

Humpty Dumpty Nursery

Sas Al Nakhl School

The International School of Choueifat

Al Asayel Basic School

Royal Jet

Emirates Post

Gulf Dunes

**SE46**

Social Support Ctr

**MADINAT KHALIFA A
(KHALIFA CITY A)**

National Security Institute

**ADISC RESIDENTIAL PROJECT (U/C)**

**SW15**

Teddy Bear American Nursery

Sama Abu Dhabi Home Health Care Centre

**SE36**

Al Ittihad National Private School

E20 AIRPORT RD

New Zayed University Campus (u/c)

**CAPITAL DISTRICT**

Sheikh Khalifa Stadium (u/c)

**FEDERAL PRECINCT (U/C)**

**SPORTS HUB PRECINCT (U/C)**

**CITY CENTRE PRECINCT (U/C)**

FEDERAL PRECINCT (U/C)

© Explorer Group Ltd. 2010

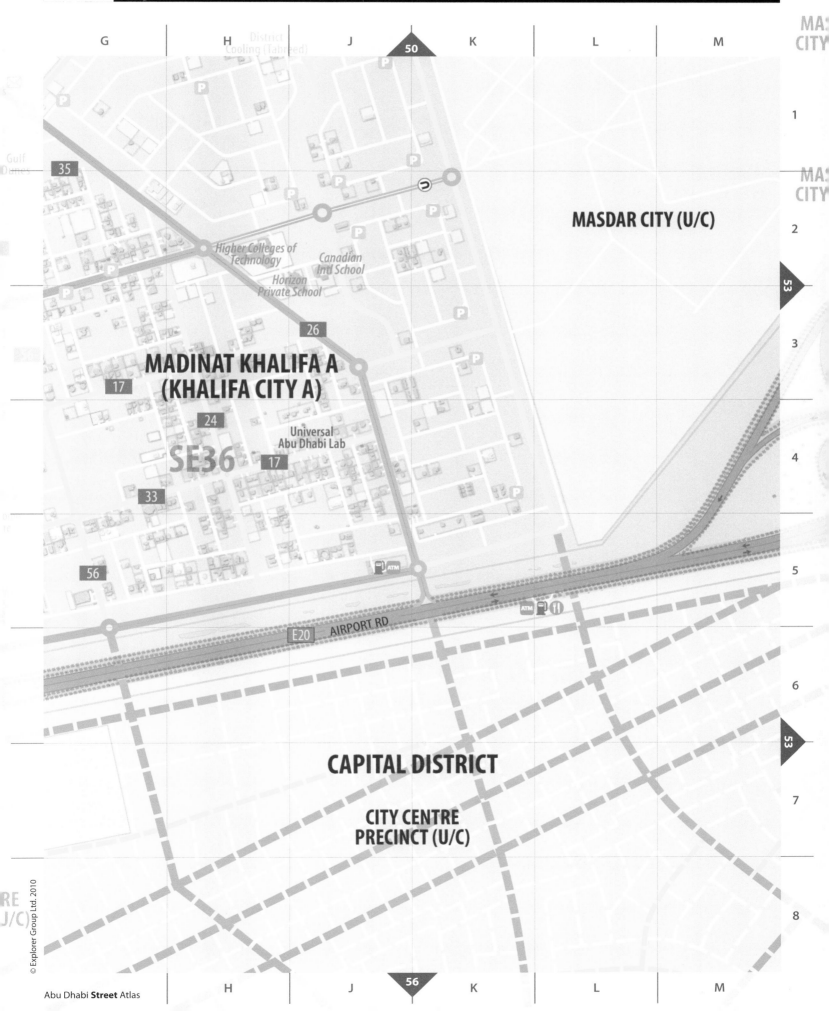

MASDAR CITY (U/C)

Higher Colleges of Technology

Canadian Intl School

Horizon Private School

**MADINAT KHALIFA A (KHALIFA CITY A)**

Universal Abu Dhabi Lab

SE36

District Cooling (Tabreed)

Gulf Dunes

E20 AIRPORT RD

**CAPITAL DISTRICT**

**CITY CENTRE PRECINCT (U/C)**

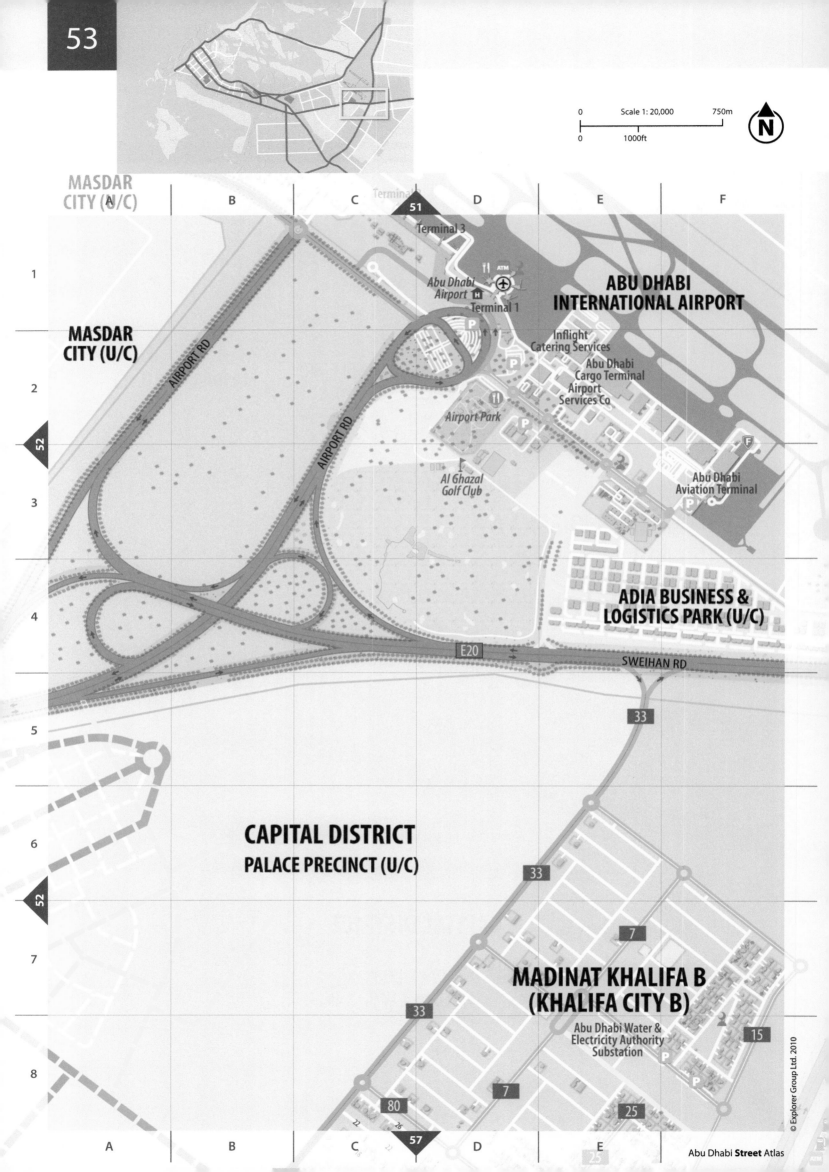

Scale 1: 20,000

0    750m

0    1000ft

**N**

**A**    **B**    **C**    Terminal    **D**    **E**    **F**

51

Terminal 3

**MASDAR
CITY (U/C)**

AIRPORT RD

Abu Dhabi
Airport

Terminal 1

**ABU DHABI
INTERNATIONAL AIRPORT**

ATM

Inflight
Catering Services

Abu Dhabi
Cargo Terminal
Airport
Services Co

Airport Park

Al Ghazal
Golf Club

Abu Dhabi
Aviation Terminal

**ADIA BUSINESS &
LOGISTICS PARK (U/C)**

E20

SWEIHAN RD

33

**CAPITAL DISTRICT
PALACE PRECINCT (U/C)**

33

33

7

**MADINAT KHALIFA B
(KHALIFA CITY B)**

Abu Dhabi Water &
Electricity Authority
Substation

15

33

80

7

25

52

52

1

2

3

4

5

6

7

8

**A**    **B**    **C**    **D**    **E**    **F**

57

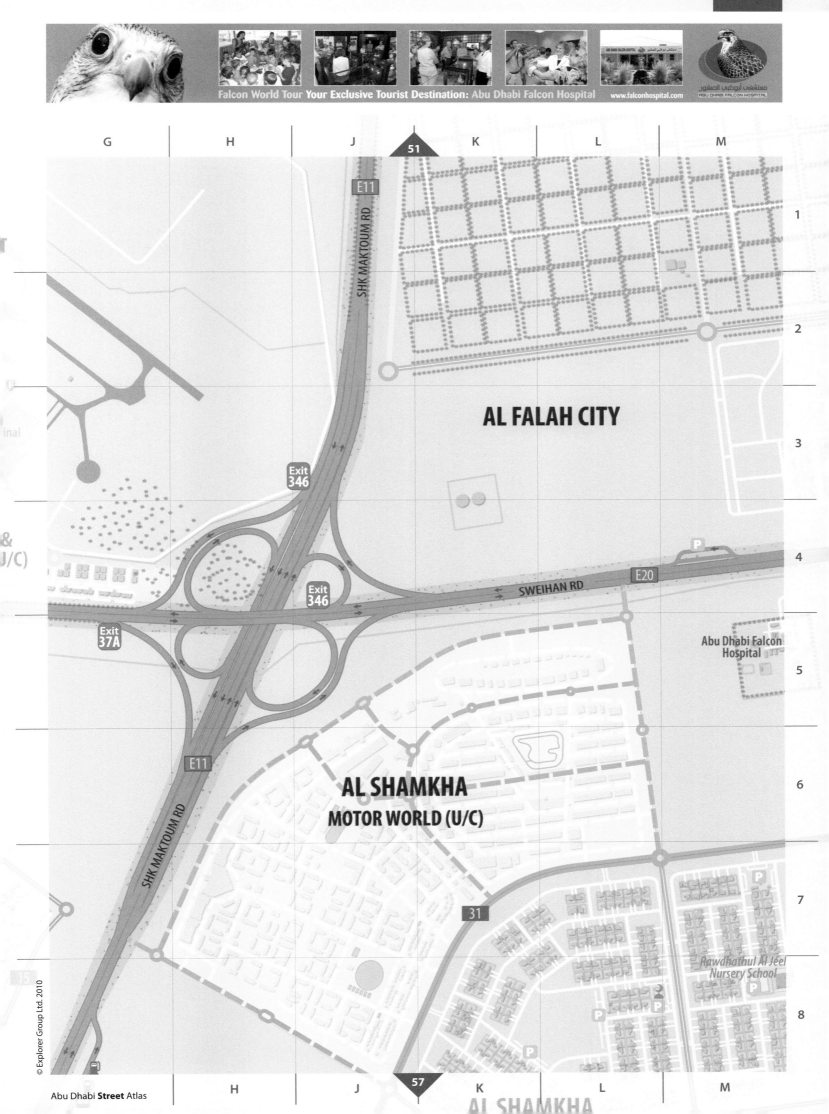

G    H    J    51    K    L    M

E11

SHK MAKTOUM RD

1

2

AL FALAH CITY

3

Exit 346

Exit 346

4

SWEIHAN RD    E20

Exit 37A

Abu Dhabi Falcon Hospital

5

E11

AL SHAMKHA
MOTOR WORLD (U/C)

6

SHK MAKTOUM RD

31

7

Rawdhathul Al Jeel Nursery School

8

H    J    57    K    L    M

AL SHAMKHA

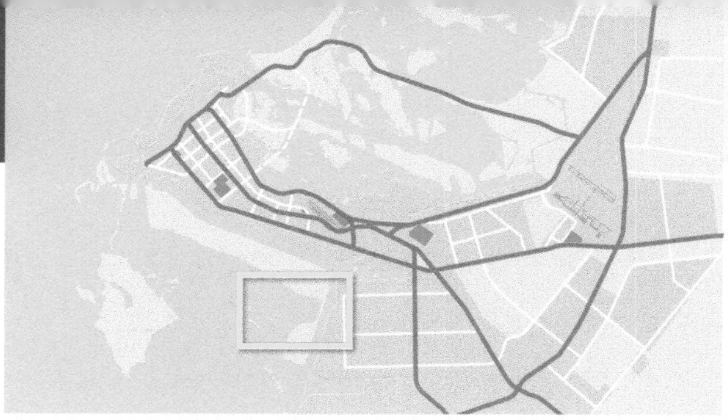

Scale 1: 20,000

0                                          750m

0            1000ft

N

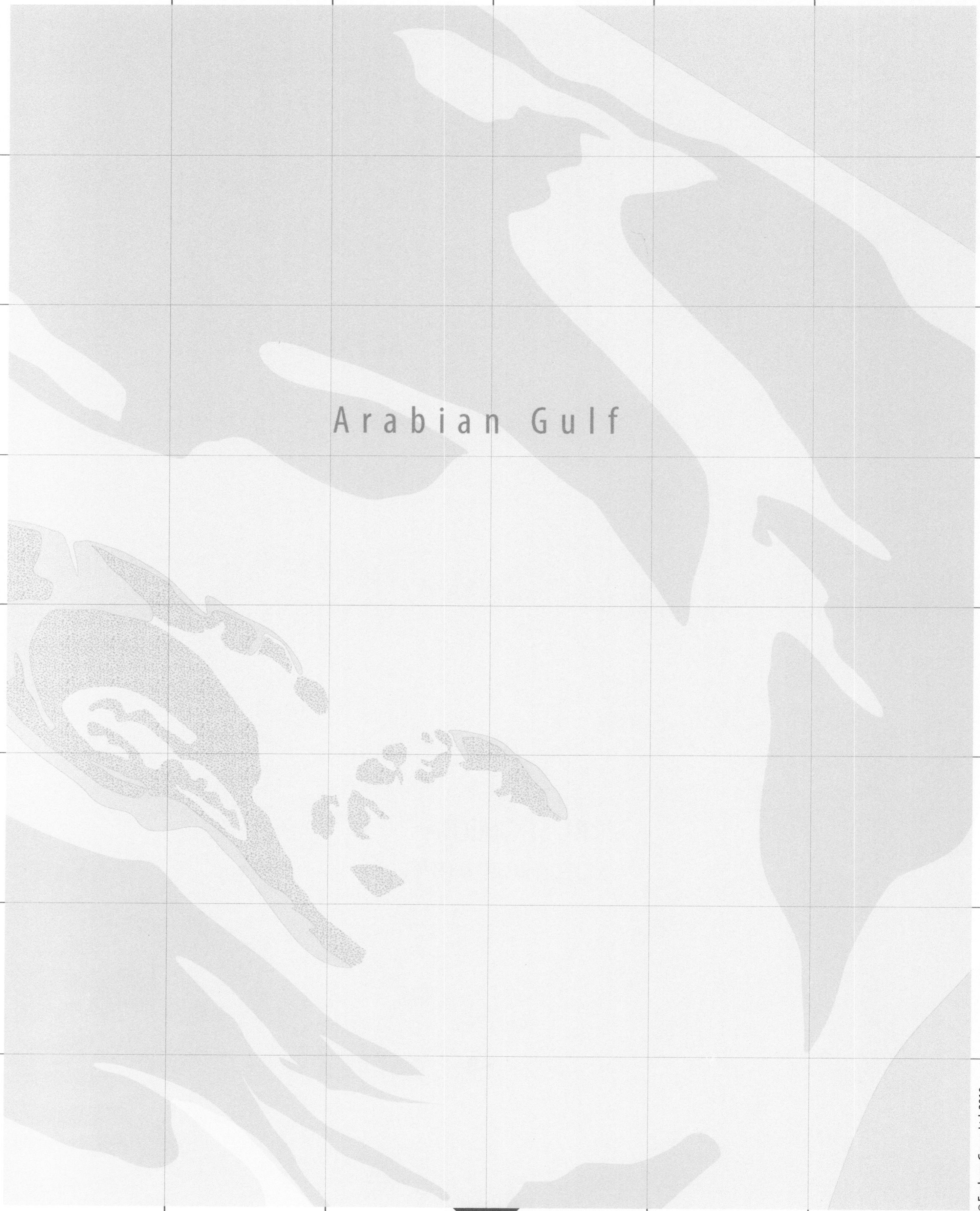

1

2

3

Arabian Gulf

4

5

6

7

8

G   H   J   K   L   M

**HUDAYRIAT ISLAND**

**Mussafah Port**
General Petroleum Services

1

7

Tremix Cement

**Al Jaber Group**

Gulf Star

Jazz

2

Global Marine Services

Al Jaber Energy

Gulf Filter

55

Ansoldo

Southern Gulf Marine Industries

Gulf Ind

3

Gulf Piping Company

Control Contracting & Trading Company

Al Ahlia General Trading

4

MW1

Gulf Piping Company

Bin Hamoodah Chevrolet & GMC Opel

**MUSSAFAH INDUSTRIAL AREA**

Defil Gulf Industries

5

12

Abu Dhabi Ship Building

7

Auh Garment Factory

Galfar Engineering

14

Jotun

6

Van Oord Middle East

Gulf Steel

ICE

Crystal Bin Moosa Grp

Gulf Ind Gases Co

55

Overseas AST Co

Royal Falcon

Galva Coat Industries

Sigma

Al Aurooba Plastic Factory

Emirates Steel

Al Panda

Kaddals

7

Baker Hughes Western Atlas Intl

MW4

Queenex

Fiber Flex Factory

Cosmoplast

Gulf Polymark

Seidco

Al Waleema

Al Khaleej Bitumen Co

Khalil Al Sayegh

16

SR Electrical

Giffin Traffiks Metal Fab Division

8

Abu Dhabi Precast

Fibrex

Baynounah Well Pipe Factory

7

**National Petroleum Construction Company**

Bin Mansour Plastic Factory

Metal Coating Ind

0  Scale 1: 20,000  750m
0  1000ft
N

**A** | 37 | **B** | **C** | 38 | **D** | **E** | **F**

1

International & Construction Co

Al Masaood Oil Industry Supplies & Services Co

Sheikh Sultan Bin Zayed Al Nahyan Personal Affairs

ADMA-OPCO Core Store

Protech

Ali & Sons

Redsea Aluminium

ADOS

6

Gulf Inspection Intl Co

Anabeeb Pipes

National Drilling Co

Madina

Sedana

Golden Spike

Galadari Trucks

EMC

Parker Store

Al Fatth

Universal Voltes

Bin Hamoodah Chevrolet & GMC Opel

Scania

Suhail Al Mazroui

Cape

Citroen

BOSCH Services Industries

Arabian Industries

ABG

Spinneys

German Gulf

Mission Marine

MINCO

Awafi Water Warehouse

Oasis Heavy Equipment

Al Masaood Trucks

Auh Laboratory

Honda & Suzuki Bike Service Ctr

Moraik

Emirates National Sack Co

ADMAK

Al Rakha

Food Time

Hitachi Power Tools

9

Galadari Automobiles Co

Chabros

Al Obaidali

Golden Tools

Apex Trading

Eldiar Furniture

Weatherford Bin Hamoodah Co

ADOS

Ready Mix Cement

Al Bustan Gulf

Etisalat

Juma Al Majid Est

UAE Exchange

Moopen's

The Kanoo Grp Machinery

Western Motors

Abu Dhabi Oxygen Co

Smith

Arab Market

ADIB

Intl Gas

Falcon Motors

8

Al Futtaim Motors

Ali & Sons Co

NBF, UBL

Royal Emirates

Ministry of Labour Mussafah Centre

Al Raha

Indoors Furniture

UNB, ENBD

Al Jaber Lighting

Mitsubishi

Emirates Identity Authority

Cemex

Mobile Marine

Golden Fork Bakery

Arabian Integrated Marine

Auh National Exhibition Co

Smart Design

Emirates Transport

3

Golden Stone

ATLAS

Inter Decor

Al Neda Ali Contracting

Hussain Yousuf General Transport

Jaber Industries

Al Hamra Group

Fence Intl

MBM Dallah

Popular Typing Office

10

SICHEM

City

RAK

Ideal Electro

Soul Stars

M18

UAE Enterprises Company

Al Jamea Trading Co

Al Hamood General Transport

City Car

NBB Group

Auh National Insurance Co

National Taxi

Arabian Construction Company

Etisalat Store

EMC

Easy Metal Trading

4

Mussafah City

Abu Dhabi Distribution Co

Crystal Steel

Prestige Steel Work

Oman Insurance Co

Hyundai Service

Bin Mansour Printing

Nova Intl

Markati

M12

Sara Trading Est

Al Hoty Stanger

Federal Switchgear

Al Amal Printing Ind

Al Masaood Automobiles

AVA

Mussaffa General Transport

Al Yamamah Heavy Equipment & Spare Parts

DUISCO Camp

Hamly Int

City Electrical Factory

Group 4 Securicor

5

MAI

HVAC

12

Advanced Pipes & Cast Co

Readyfix Middle East

National Bldg Materials

Liberty Auh Service Ctr

Al Kamal General Transport Co

Hyundai Service

Abu Dhabi Craft Factory

Chinese Palace

Golden City

Federal Transformers

Quick Mix Co

Regal Art Decor

Sinyar Logistics

Hafzco

Rapiscan Systems

Volvo Famco

Union Marble Engineering

Abu Dhabi Arch Contracting Co

Al Noor Hospital Stores

EMIDCO

Bitu Trade Industrial Co

Al-Futtain Auto & Machinery Co

Bldg Material Co

IBC

Al Ain Dairy

14

Al Naboodah Labour Camp

14

Modern ADOS Plastic

Automatic Engineering Co

DNA Motor

Abu Dhabi Distribution Co Central Store

Transco Musafah Stores

6

William Hare UAE

Abu Dhabi Distribution Co

Sorouh

Southern Aluminium & Glass

Sylhet

Al Jasim

M33

Dutest Trading Est

Private & Govt Co Vehicle License

Al Khazna Insurance Co Store

Emirates Oasis

Dr Moopen's

Sylhet

54

Rheem

Al Nahda LPG

New Al Majid Foodstuff

Castle Gate Timber Works

13

Air Condition Co

Al Hadaf Marble Cutting

IMECO

Well Gate

Zone

Al Maqam Corner

MUSSAFAH INDUSTRIAL AREA

Bin Ham Oil Group

9

Wintech Intl

Waste Paper

Cars Taxi

7

Technical Resources Est

City Gypsum

Penguin Cooling System

Marina Transport

M45

Dutch Foundation

Star Security Service

ARMEPCO

Global Logistic Solution

16

ADMAC

16

16

Advanced Pipes & Cast Company

16

SR Electrical Abu Dhabi

Al Madeena

New Alwafa

Aces Arab Center for Engineering Studies

SOWMCO

Saif Bin Darwish Carpentry

ASCORP

Crystal

Arabian Foundations

8

Liwa ICE Factory

M42

Special Catering

ICAD 1 Residential City

Gulf Center Group Cleaning Equipment

Al Falah Ready Mix

National Ready Mix

Seven Star

Chab Ind Co

Jumbo Filter Factory Plastics

Millennium

Topcare

Emirates Al Madina

M35

Al Ghafly

Golden Spike

Gulf Ready Mix

Al Khaleej Ready Mix

Adfert

**A** | **B** | 59 | **C** | **D** | **E** | **F**

© Explorer Group Ltd. 2010

© Explorer Group Ltd. 2010

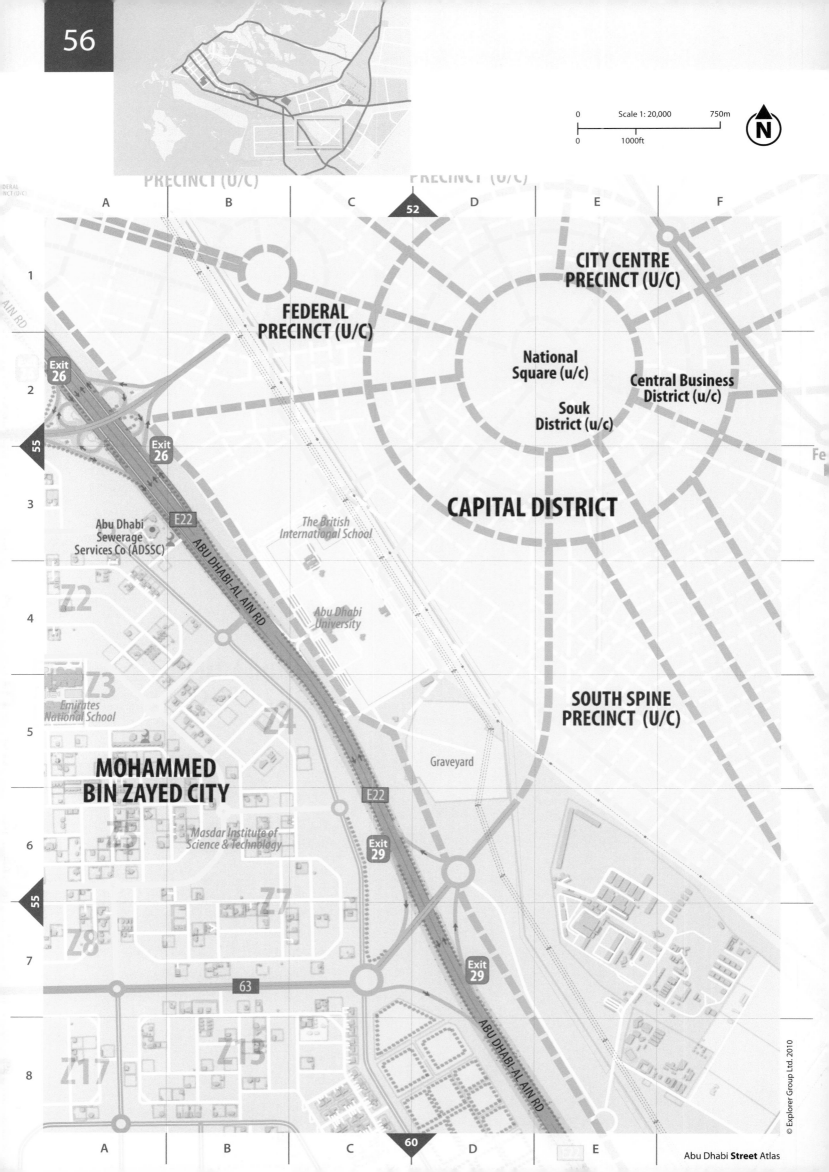

Scale 1: 20,000

0      750m

0      1000ft

**N**

PRECINCT (U/C)

PRECINCT (U/C)

**CITY CENTRE PRECINCT (U/C)**

**FEDERAL PRECINCT (U/C)**

**National Square (u/c)**

**Central Business District (u/c)**

**Souk District (u/c)**

**CAPITAL DISTRICT**

52

Exit 26

55

Exit 26

E22

**ABU DHABI-AL AIN RD**

Abu Dhabi Sewerage Services Co (ADSSC)

Z2

The British International School

Abu Dhabi University

Z3

Emirates National School

Z4

**SOUTH SPINE PRECINCT (U/C)**

**MOHAMMED BIN ZAYED CITY**

Graveyard

Masdar Institute of Science & Technology

55

Z7

Z8

E22

Exit 29

Exit 29

63

**ABU DHABI-AL AIN RD**

Z15

Z17

60

© Explorer Group Ltd. 2010

Abu Dhabi **Street** Atlas

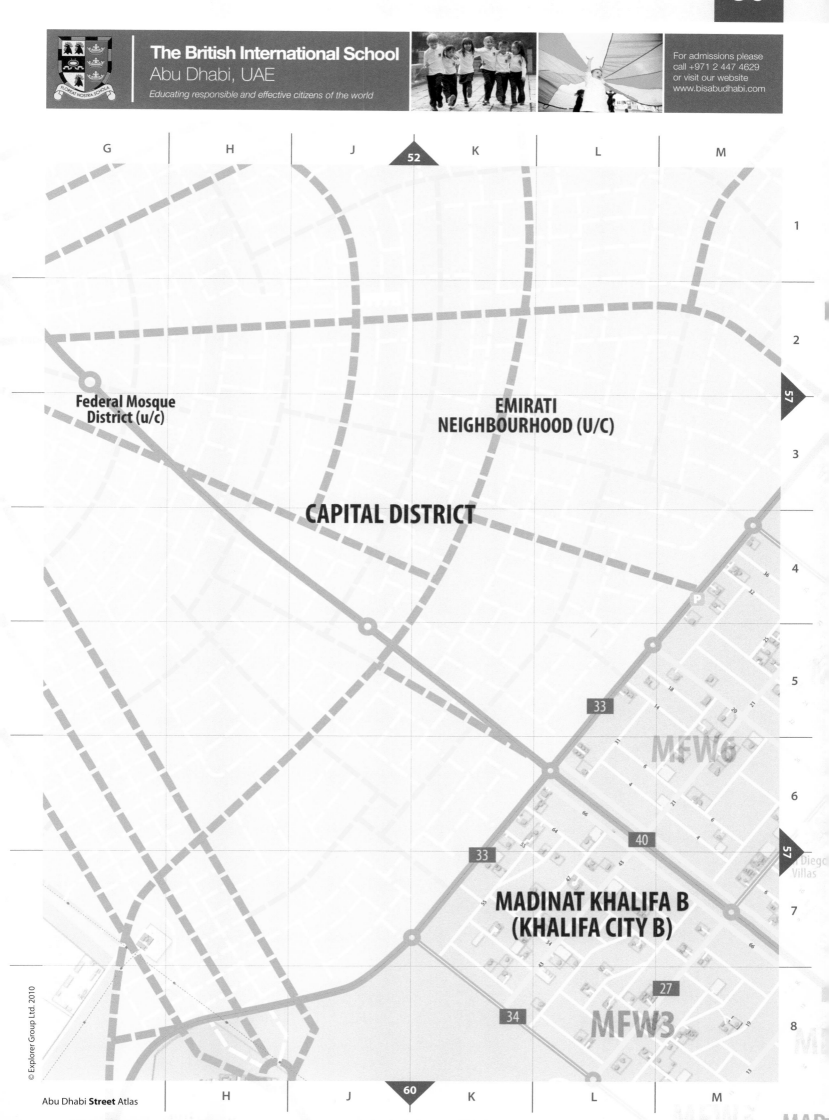

G | H | J | 52 | K | L | M

1

2

57

**Federal Mosque District (u/c)**

**EMIRATI NEIGHBOURHOOD (U/C)**

3

**CAPITAL DISTRICT**

4

5

MFW6

33

6

40

57

33

Diego Villas

**MADINAT KHALIFA B (KHALIFA CITY B)**

7

27

34

MFW3

8

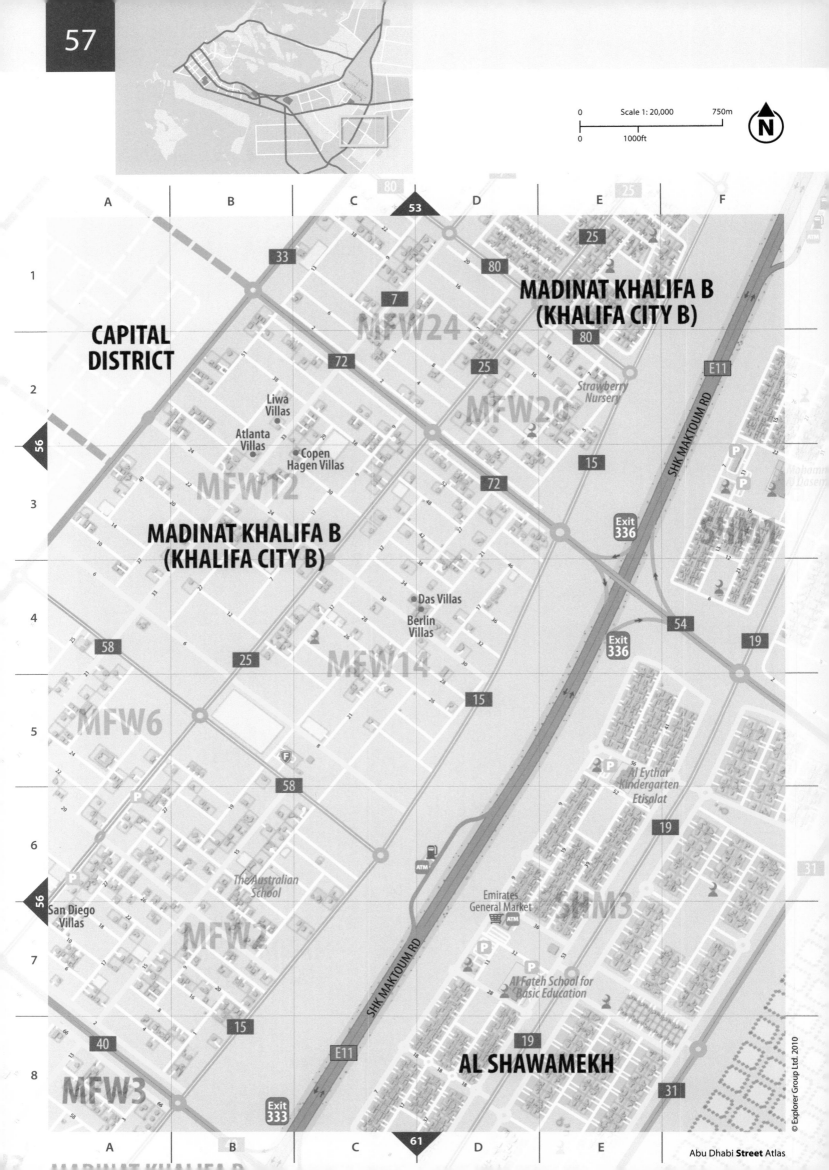

Scale 1: 20,000

0 ————————— 750m

0 ————————— 1000ft

**N**

| A | B | C | D | E | F |

33

7

25

**MADINAT KHALIFA B
(KHALIFA CITY B)**

1

MFW24

80

72

25

E11

**CAPITAL
DISTRICT**

80

2

Liwa
Villas

MFW20

Strawberry
Nursery

56

Atlanta
Villas

Copen
Hagen Villas

15

SHK MAKTOUM RD

MFW12

72

3

Exit
336

SHM

**MADINAT KHALIFA B
(KHALIFA CITY B)**

54

58

Das Villas

4

25

Berlin
Villas

Exit
336

19

MFW14

15

MFW6

5

Al Eythar
Kindergarten
Etisalat

F

58

19

6

31

P

The Australian
School

ATM

56

San Diego
Villas

Emirates
General Market

SHM3

MFW2

ATM

7

P

Al Fateh School for
Basic Education

15

40

19

8

MFW3

E11

**AL SHAWAMEKH**

31

Exit
333

| A | B | C | D | E |

Abu Dhabi **Street** Atlas

**The British International School**
Abu Dhabi, UAE
*Educating responsible and effective citizens of the world*

For admissions please
call +971 2 447 4629
or visit our website
www.bisabudhabi.com

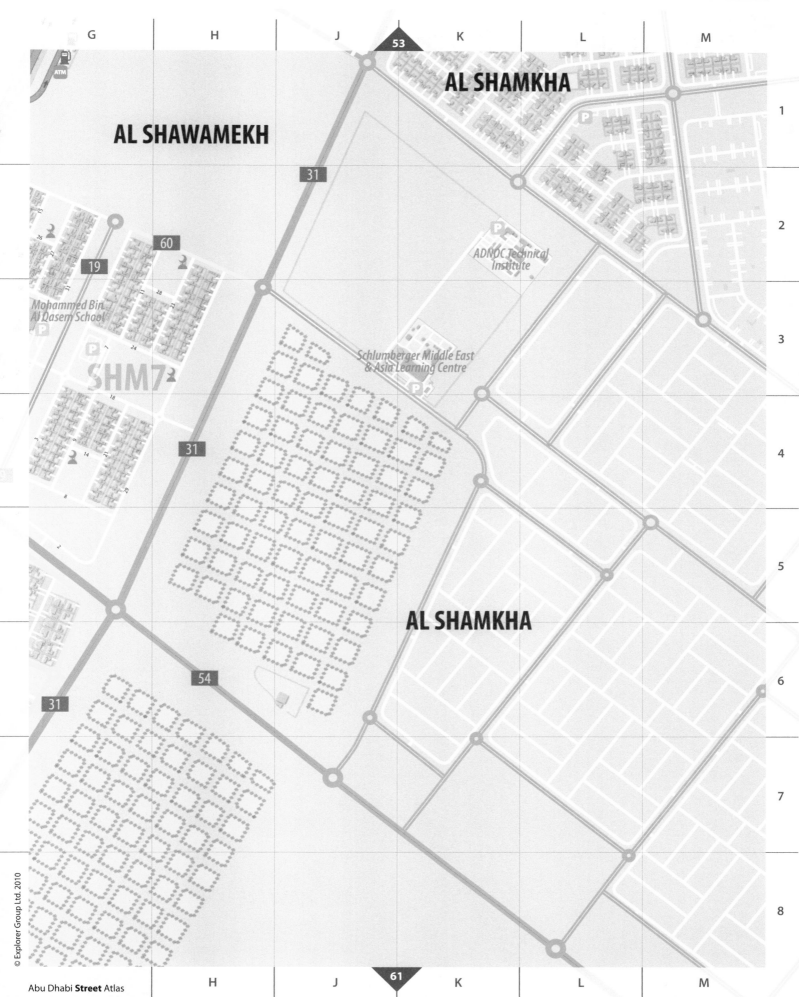

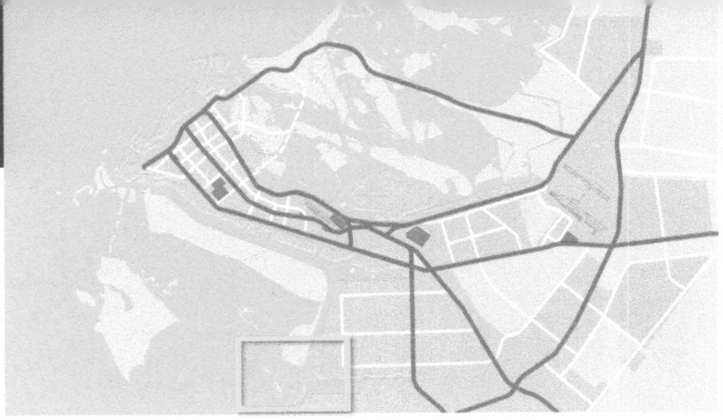

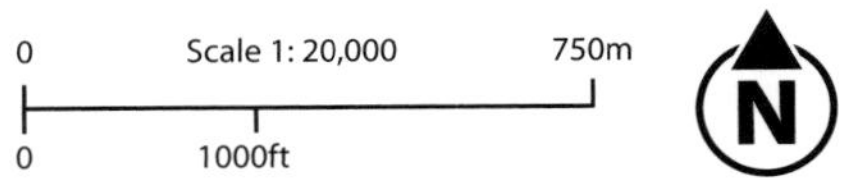

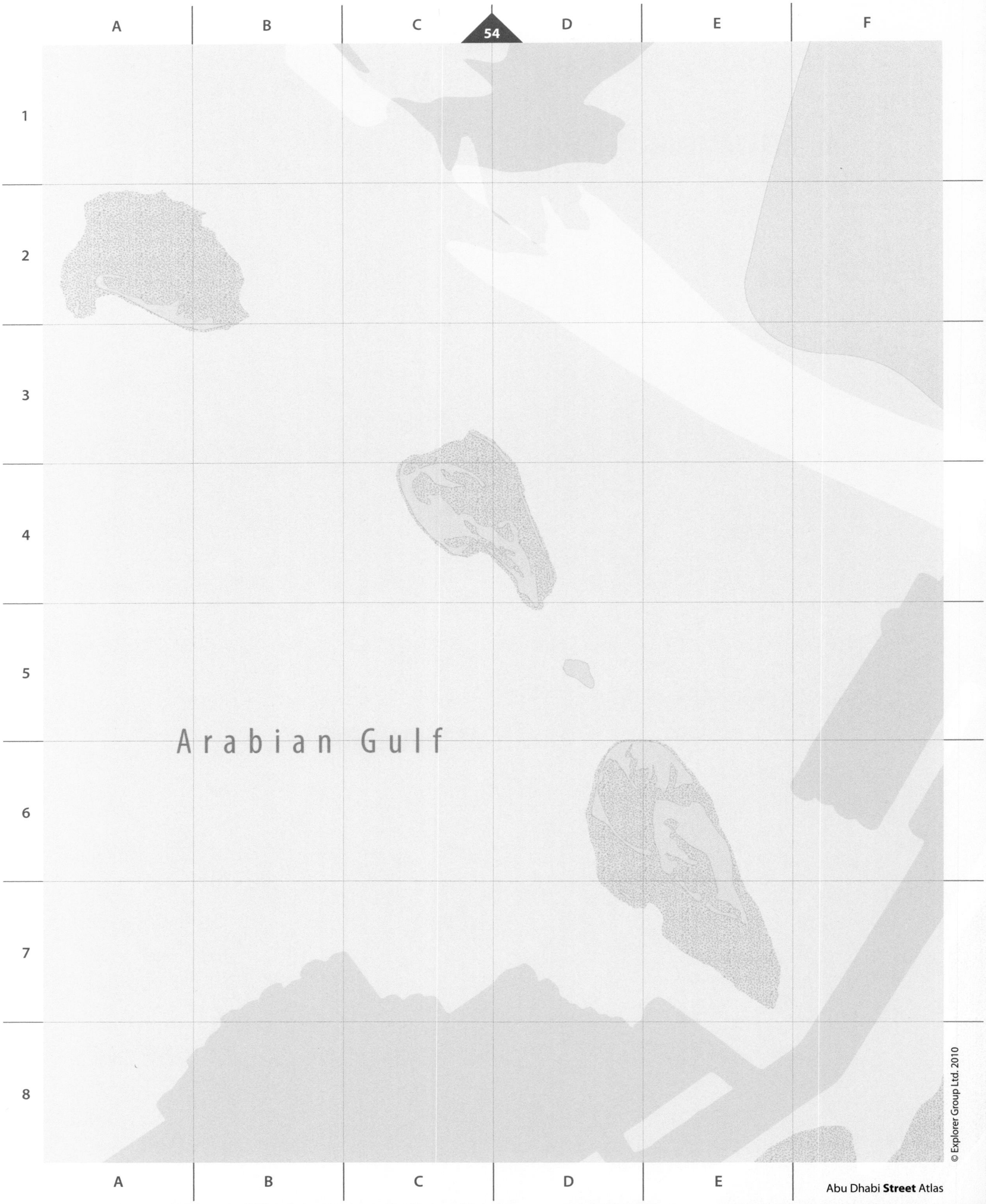

Scale 1: 20,000

0     750m

0     1000ft

N

| A | B | C | D | E | F |

1

2

3

4

5

Arabian Gulf

6

7

8

| A | B | C | D | E |

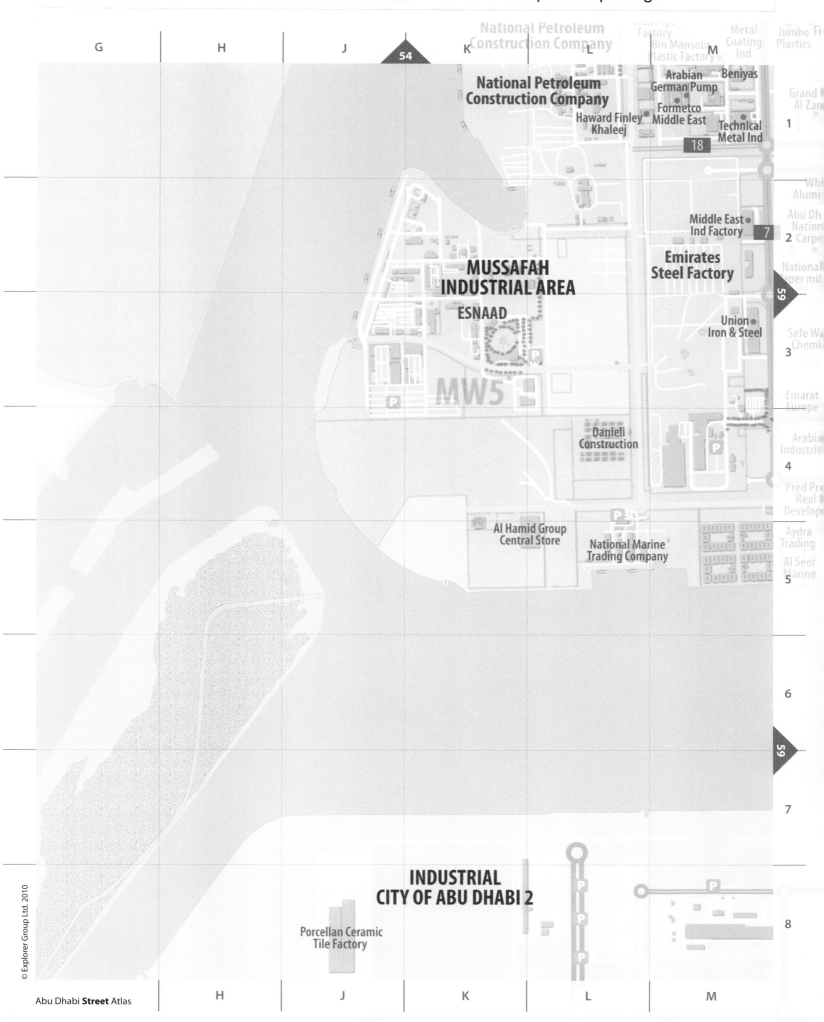

National Petroleum
Construction Company

**National Petroleum
Construction Company**

Haward Finley
Khaleej

Well Pipe
Factory

Bin Mansour
Plastic Factory

Metal
Coating
Ind

Jumbo Fi
Plastics

Arabian
German Pump

Beniyas

Formetco
Middle East

Technical
Metal Ind

18

Grand
Al Zam

1

Wh
Alumi

Abu Dh
Nation
Carpe

Middle East
Ind Factory

7

2

**Emirates
Steel Factory**

National
aper mill

59

**MUSSAFAH
INDUSTRIAL AREA**

**ESNAAD**

Union
Iron & Steel

Safe Wa
Chemi

3

MW5

Emarat
Europe

Arabia
Industrie

Danieli
Construction

4

Pred Pro
Real
Develop

Aydra
Trading

Al Hamid Group
Central Store

National Marine
Trading Company

Al Seer
Marine

5

59

6

7

**INDUSTRIAL
CITY OF ABU DHABI 2**

Porcelian Ceramic
Tile Factory

8

Scale 1: 20,000

0 ——— 750m

0 ——— 1000ft

**N**

55

18

M35

18

| | A | B | C | D | E | F |

Metal Coating Ind

eniyas

Jumbo Plastics

Filter Factory

Ind Co

Al Ghafly

Adrert

Millennium

Tracare

Golden Spike

Emirates Al Madina

Gulf Ready Mix

Al Khaleej Ready Mix

Grand Umm Al Zamoul

Al Manaa

Styrene

Bin Masood Plastic

Bildco

Dome

Giralda Emirates

Unibeton

United Precast Concrete

Trans Gulf

9

**1**

chnical etal Ind

East ory

White Aluminium

Abu Dhabi National Carpet

National Paper mill

**ADPICO**

W3 W2

W4

Abu Dhabi Precast Factory Phase 2

Auh Precast Factory Phase 1

Plaxit Dry Mix Company

CICON

GPCC

Middle East Garments Manufacturing

SCAFFCO

Bin Ajan

Al Ain Steel Factory

Gulf Ind

Al Sahar

Ro Clas

**INDUSTRIAL CITY OF ABU DHABI 1**

**2**

y

58

Safe Water Chemical

TMI

Al Masaood Bergum

Al Jaber Aluminium Composite Panels

SCHMDLIN

Ducab Dubai Cable Co

Union Rebar Factory

Exeed Aswar

Star Cements

Ghuzlan

Foresight Cement

Al Shoumukh Ind

Al Nibras

Noy

Auh Pallet Ind

Micoda Reem

Universal

Jazira Metal

Utmost

Qasem

Al Marzooqi

Space Age

Al Ain Acrylic

Northern Technical Power

Vision Steel

Poly Emirate Plastic Che

Exe Geote

nion & Steel

**3**

Emarat Europe

Auh Water & Electrical Authority

Auh National Cement Factory

Ogasco Oil & Gas Construction Co

Manazil Steel Framing

Hafilat

Tayco

Al Dhafra

Nova Plastic

EPPT

Arabian Industries Co

ABBA

Silent Vally

Agis Al Ghurair Iron & Steel

NPC

Reem Emirates Aluminium

Gulf Galvanizing Factory

Future Pipe Industries

Al Tamayoz Cement Product Factory

Dimensions Cement

Emirates Lime Factory

Firstchoice Fashion

Cosmo Plaster

Union Pipe

Excellent

Quickstep

GIC Substation

**4**

Pred Progressive Real Estate Development Co

GAC Marine Equipment Construction & Maintenance

Aydra Trading

Al Seer Marine

Phoenix Timber

Dry Mix Plant for M/s M&P Mortar & Plaster Dry Mix

Prompt Steel Bldg Contracting

National Cement Factory

**5**

Zamil Company

UAE Naval Force Naval School Security & Safety Wing

Takreer We Refine Right

AUH O & Oil P Dis

**Higher Corporation for Specialized Economic Zone**

**6**

58

**7**

**INDUSTRIAL CITY OF ABU DHABI 3**

**8**

| A | B | C | D | E |

CYCLONE TRAVEL & TOURS
Tel: +971 2 6276275 - Fax: +971 2 6273331
P.O.Box: 31740 - Abu Dhabi - U.A.E
www.cyclonetours.com

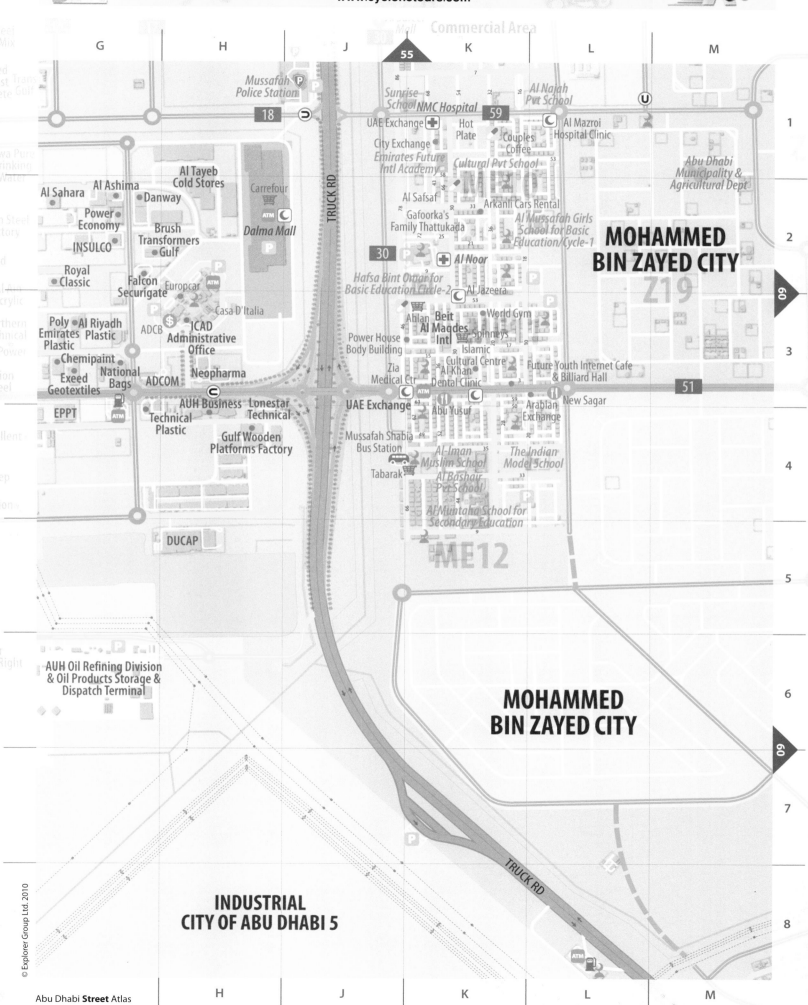

© Explorer Group Ltd. 2010

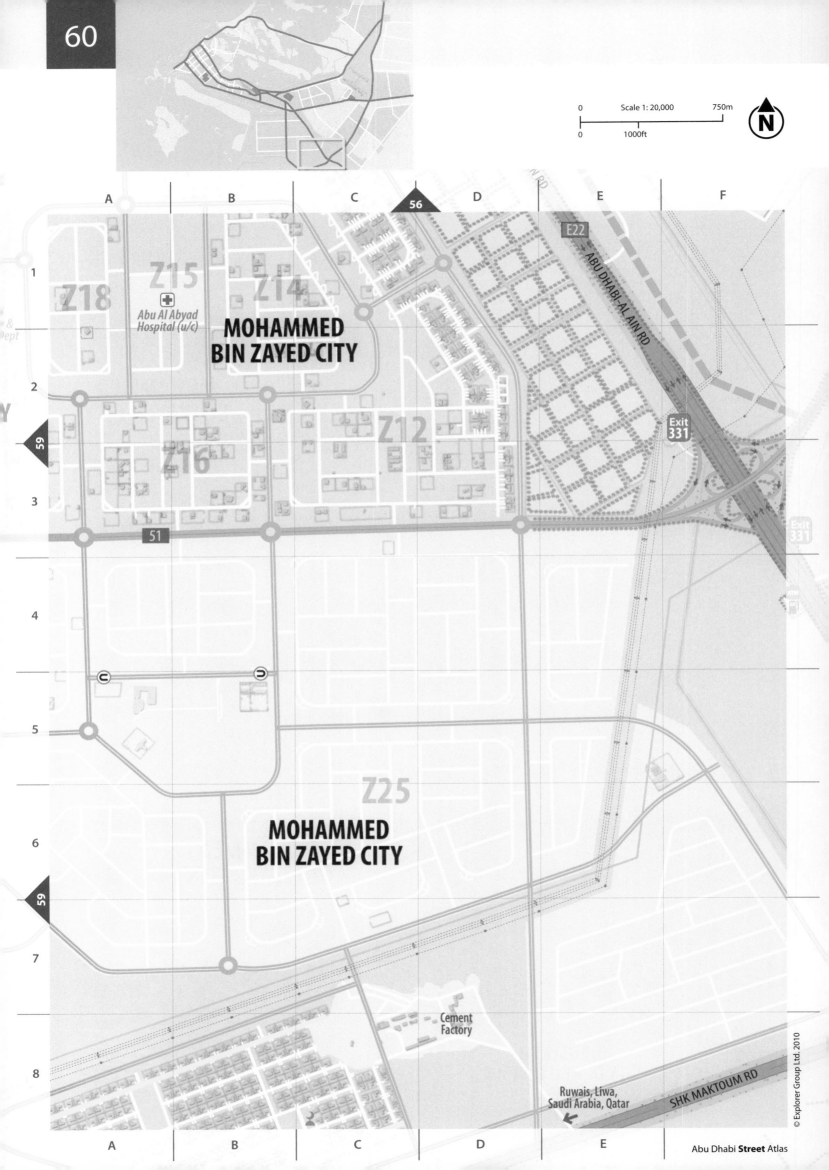

Scale 1: 20,000

0       750m

0     1000ft

**N**

**A** **B** **C** 56 **D** **E** **F**

E22

1

Z18

Z15

Z14

⊕

Abu Al Abyad
Hospital (u/c)

**MOHAMMED
BIN ZAYED CITY**

ABU DHABI-AL AIN RD

2

59

Z16

Z12

Exit
331

3

51

Exit
331

4

5

Z25

6

59

**MOHAMMED
BIN ZAYED CITY**

7

8

Cement
Factory

Ruwais, Liwa,
Saudi Arabia, Qatar

SHK MAKTOUM RD

© Explorer Group Ltd. 2010

**A** **B** **C** **D** **E**

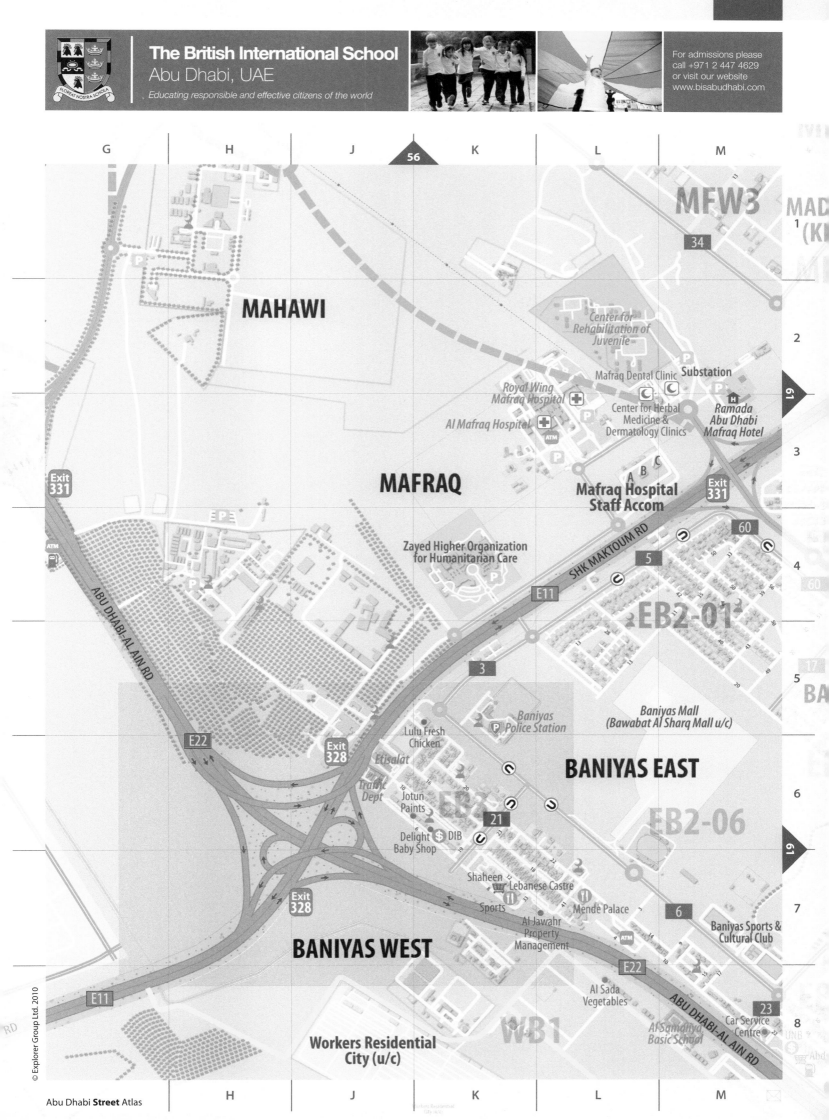

**The British International School**
Abu Dhabi, UAE
*Educating responsible and effective citizens of the world*

For admissions please
call +971 2 447 4629
or visit our website
www.bisabudhabi.com

MFW3

MAHAWI

Center for
Rehabilitation of
Juvenile

Mafraq Dental Clinic    Substation

Royal Wing
Mafraq Hospital

Al Mafraq Hospital

Center for Herbal
Medicine &
Dermatology Clinics

Ramada
Abu Dhabi
Mafraq Hotel

MAFRAQ

A  B  C

Mafraq Hospital
Staff Accom

Exit
331

Exit
331

Zayed Higher Organization
for Humanitarian Care

SHK MAKTOUM RD

E11

5

60

EB2-01

3

Baniyas Mall
(Bawabat Al Sharq Mall u/c)

Lulu Fresh
Chicken

Baniyas
Police Station

BANIYAS EAST

Etisalat

EB2-06

Traffic
Dept

Jotun
Paints

21

Delight
Baby Shop

DIB

Shaheen
Sports

Lebanese Castre

Mende Palace

6

Baniyas Sports &
Cultural Club

Al Jawahr
Property
Management

**BANIYAS WEST**

Exit
328

Exit
328

E22

Al Sada
Vegetables

E22

ABU DHABI-AL AIN RD

23

Car Service
Centre

E11

ABU DHABI-AL AIN RD

**Workers Residential
City (u/c)**

WB1

Al Sqndiyat
Basic School

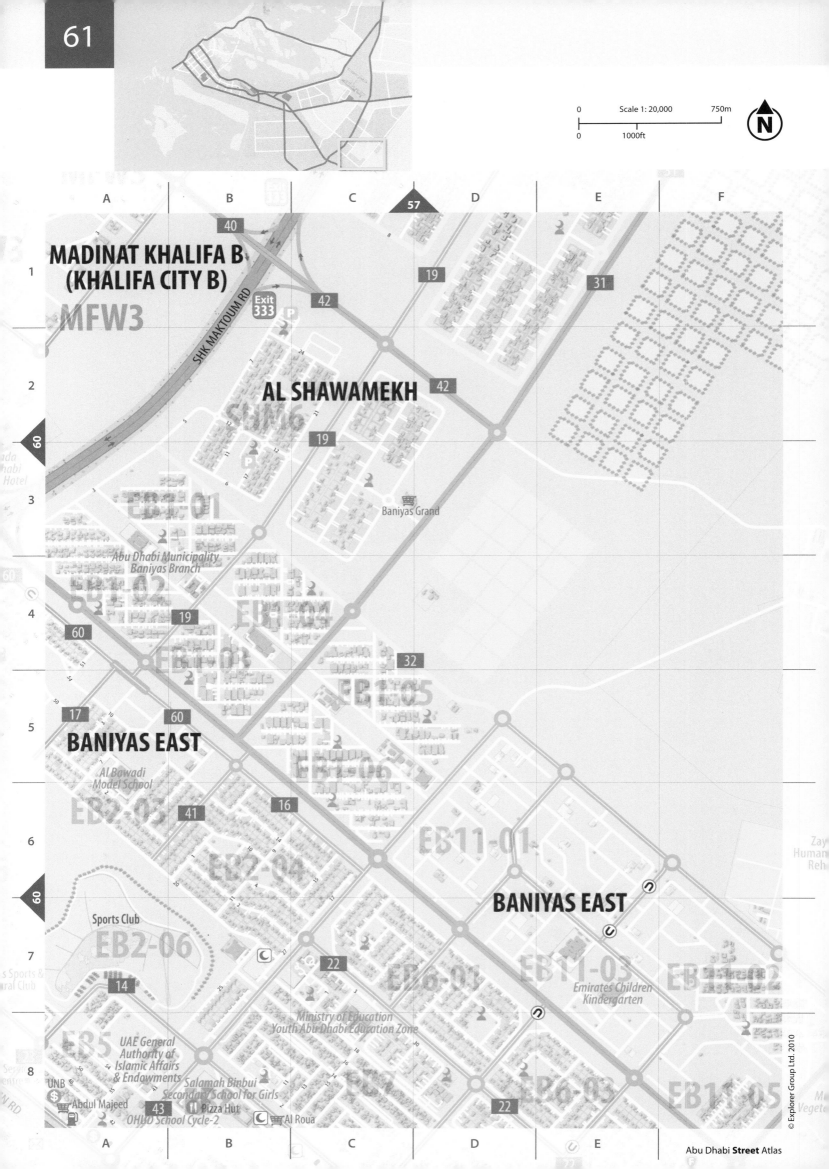

Scale 1: 20,000

0          750m

0          1000ft

N

A     B     C     D     E     F

57

40

# MADINAT KHALIFA B
# (KHALIFA CITY B)

MFW3

1

Exit
333

SHK MAKTOUM RD

P

42

42

19

19

31

## AL SHAWAMEKH

2

SHM6

19

P

EB1-01

Baniyas Grand

3

Abu Dhabi Municipality
Baniyas Branch

EB1-02

60

19

EB1-03

32

4

60

EB1-05

17

60

## BANIYAS EAST

EB1-06

5

Al Bawadi
Model School

EB2-05

41

16

EB11-01

EB2-04

6

60

Sports Club

EB2-06

## BANIYAS EAST

14

22

EB6-01

EB11-03

EB11-02

7

Sports &
ral Club

Emirates Children
Kindergarten

UAE General
Authority of
Islamic Affairs
& Endowments

Ministry of Education
Youth Abu Dhabi Education Zone

8

UNB

Abdul Majeed

Salamah Binbui
Secondary School for Girls

EB6-03

EB11-05

N RD

43

Pizza Hut

OHUD School Cycle-2

Al Roua

22

A     B     C     D     E

© Explorer Group Ltd. 2010

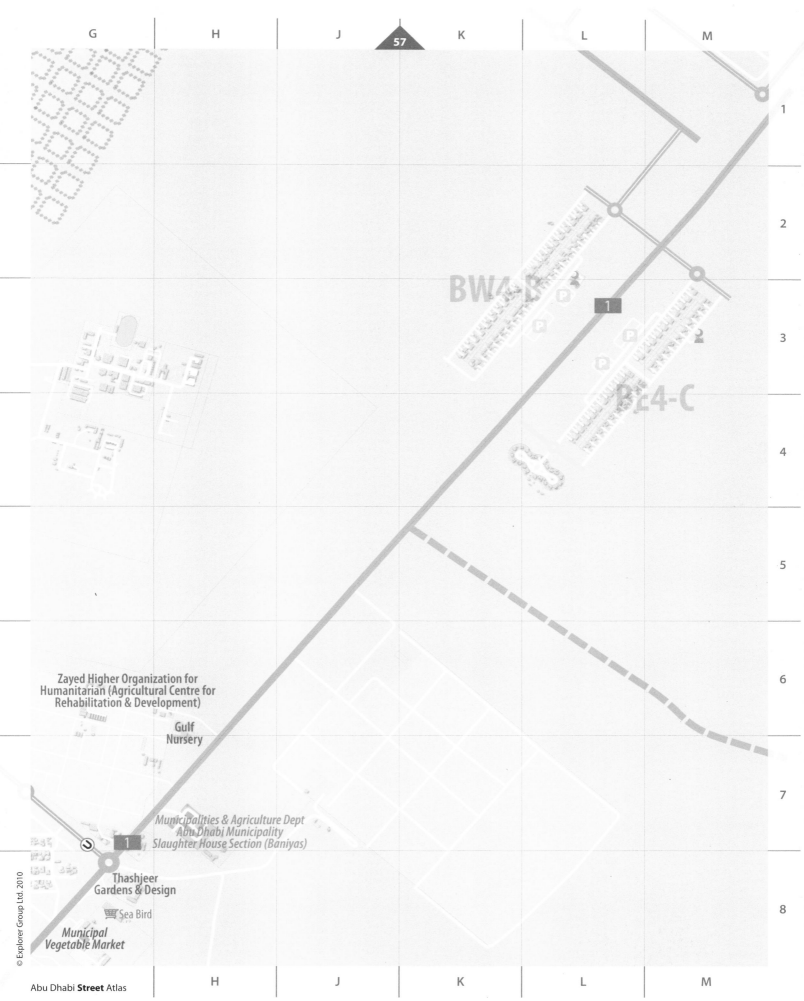

BW4-B

Bc4-C

Zayed Higher Organization for
Humanitarian (Agricultural Centre for
Rehabilitation & Development)

Gulf
Nursery

Municipalities & Agriculture Dept
Abu Dhabi Municipality
Slaughter House Section (Baniyas)

Thashjeer
Gardens & Design

Sea Bird

Municipal
Vegetable Market

...Madinat Zayed (E4_02) — 9-A3
...Markaziya East (E3) — 4-J8
...Markaziya East (E9) — 5-A3
...Markaziya East (E10) — 5-A5
...Markaziya West (W6) — 8-C5
...Mussafah Industrial Area (M20) — 54-M2
...Officers City (S2) — 37-K1
...Tourist Club Area (E13) — 2-B8
...Tourist Club Area (E15) — 5-D2
...Tourist Club Area (E16) — 5-E6

## 09
**9 Rd**
...Al Bahia (Al Bahya Old) — 44-G8
...Al Baladia (E11) — 5-B7
...Al Bateen — 21-M6
...Al Bateen (W17_01) — 12-F4
...Al Bateen (W37) — 11-K4
...Al Dhafrah (E18_01) — 8-M7
...Al Dhafrah (E18_02) — 9-C4
...Al Dhafrah (E18_03) — 9-F3
...Al Karamah (W14_01) — 12-M7
...Al Karamah (W14_02) — 12-M6
...Al Karamah (W15_02) — 13-E8
...Al Khubeirah (W38) — 11-H3
...Al Manhal (W4) — 8-D7
...Al Meena (Freezone) — 40-H8
...Al Mushrif (W46) — 22-M1
...Al Mushrif (W47) — 23-E8
...Al Mushrif (W52_01) — 22-G5
...Al Nahyan (E19) — 13-D2
...Al Nahyan (E20_02) — 13-F5
...Al Safarat (W59_02) — 27-J3
...Al Shawamekh (SHM3) — 57-D6
...Al Shawamekh (SHM7) — 57-G4
...Al Zahra (E36) — 24-E2
...Al Zahra (E41) — 24-G2
...Baniyas East (EB2_04) — 61-B6
...Baniyas East (EB5) — 60-M7
...Hadabat Al Zaafaran (E31) — 23-D1
...Hadabat Al Zaafaran (E33) — 23-G3
...Hadabat Al Zaafaran (E38) — 19-K8
...Madinat Khalifa B (MFW2) — 57-B7
...Madinat Khalifa B (MFW12) — 57-C2
...Madinat Khalifa B (MFW24) — 57-C1
...Madinat Zayed (E4_01) — 8-L3
...Madinat Zayed (E4_02) — 8-M2
...Markaziya East (E1) — 4-G6
...Markaziya East (E3) — 4-J8
...Markaziya East (E9) — 5-A3
...Markaziya West (W6) — 8-C5
...Mohammed Bin Zayed City (ME10) — 59-K2
...Mohammed Bin Zayed City (ME12) — 59-K5
...Mussafah Industrial Area (M3) — 55-G1

## 10
**10 Rd**
...Al Bahia (Al Bahya Old) — 44-G4
...Al Bateen (W17_01) — 12-D5
...Al Bateen (W18_03) — 17-F3
...Al Bateen (W35) — 11-H8
...Al Bateen (W37) — 12-A8
...Al Dhafrah (E18_02) — 9-C4
...Al Dhafrah (E18_03) — 9-F3
...Al Karamah (W14_02) — 12-M4
...Al Karamah (W15_02) — 18-C1
...Al Manhal (W13_02) — 12-J3
...Al Manhal (W4) — 8-F5
...Al Manhal (W9) — 12-C2
...Al Maqtaa (W54) — 28-K8
...Al Meena (E14) — 2-E4
...Al Meena (Freezone) — 40-H8
...Al Mushrif (W24_01) — 18-H4
...Al Mushrif (W24_02) — 18-F2
...Al Mushrif (W46) — 23-A2
...Al Mushrif (W47) — 23-D6
...Al Mushrif (W48) — 23-J8
...Al Mushrif (W49) — 26-M1
...Al Mushrif (W52_01) — 22-G3
...Al Nahyan (E19) — 13-C2
...Al Nahyan (E20_02) — 13-F4
...Al Rehhan (E40) — 24-E6
...Al Zahra (E36) — 24-D4
...Al Zahra (E41) — 24-F4
...Baniyas East (EB2_03) — 61-A5
...Baniyas East (EB2_04) — 61-B6
...Baniyas East (EB3) — 60-K6
...Baniyas East (EB5) — 60-M7
...Hadabat Al Zaafaran (E26) — 19-C3
...Hadabat Al Zaafaran (E27) — 19-B6
...Hadabat Al Zaafaran (E38) — 23-K1
...Hadabat Al Zaafaran (E39) — 19-F7
...Madinat Khalifa A (SW15) — 52-B5
...Madinat Khalifa B (MFW12) — 57-A3
...Madinat Khalifa B (MFW2) — 56-M7
...Madinat Zayed (E4_01) — 8-K4
...Madinat Zayed (E4_02) — 4-M7
...Markaziya East (E3) — 4-J8
...Markaziya East (E9) — 5-A1
...Markaziya East (E10) — 5-A5
...Markaziya West (W6) — 8-C5
...Mohammed Bin Zayed City (ME11) — 59-K3
...Mussafah Industrial Area (M20) — 54-M2
...Officers City (S2) — 37-M2
...Tourist Club Area (E12) — 1-M6
...Tourist Club Area (E13) — 5-C1
...Tourist Club Area (E15) — 5-D2
...Tourist Club Area (E16) — 5-F7
...Yas Island — 47-G4

## 11
**11 Rd**
...Al Bahia (Al Bahya Old) — 44-H4
...Al Bahia (Al Bahya) — 44-B5
...Al Baladia (E11) — 5-B6
...Al Bateen (W17_01) — 12-F5
...Al Bateen (W29) — 17-G7
...Al Dhafrah (E18_01) — 8-M7
...Al Dhafrah (E18_02) — 9-C5
...Al Karamah (W14_01) — 12-M8
...Al Khubeirah (W38) — 11-H2
...Al Manhal (W13_02) — 12-G3
...Al Manhal (W4) — 8-G4
...Al Meena (Freezone) — 40-H8
...Al Mushrif (W46) — 22-M2
...Al Mushrif (W47) — 23-E7
...Al Rowdah (W18_01) — 12-H8
...Al Safarat (W59_02) — 27-K3
...Al Shahama 2 (Al Shamama I) — 44-K8
...Al Shawamekh (SHM1) — 57-F3
...Al Shawamekh (SHM6) — 61-B3
...Al Shawamekh (SHM7) — 57-G3
...Al Zahra (E41) — 24-G3
...Baniyas East (EB2_04) — 61-B6
...Baniyas East (EB7) — 61-B8
...Hadabat Al Zaafaran (E31) — 23-D2
...Hadabat Al Zaafaran (E33) — 23-H3
...Hadabat Al Zaafaran (E38) — 23-K1
...Madinat Zayed (E4_02) — 9-A2
...Madinat Zayed (E11) — 5-B7
...Markaziya East (E9) — 5-A3
...Markaziya West (W6) — 8-C5
...Officers City (S2) — 37-J1

## 12
**12 Rd**
...Al Bateen (W17_01) — 12-F7
...Al Bateen (W18_03) — 17-E2
...Al Bateen (W37) — 11-L7
...Al Dhafrah (E18_02) — 9-C3
...Al Karamah (W15_01) — 18-A2
...Al Manhal (W13_02) — 12-J3
...Al Manhal (W4) — 8-E5
...Al Manhal (W9) — 12-B2
...Al Maqtaa (W54) — 28-L8
...Al Meena (Freezone) — 40-H7
...Al Mushrif (W24_01) — 18-J6
...Al Mushrif (W46) — 22-M1
...Al Mushrif (W47) — 23-F7
...Al Mushrif (W49) — 26-M1
...Al Mushrif (W52_01) — 22-G4
...Al Shahama 2 (Al Shamama I) — 44-L6
...Al Shawamekh (SHM1) — 57-F3
...Al Shawamekh (SHM6) — 61-B2
...Al Zahra (E36) — 24-D3
...Al Zahra (E41) — 24-H4
...Baniyas East (EB3) — 60-K7
...Hadabat Al Zaafaran (E31) — 19-C8
...Hadabat Al Zaafaran (E38) — 23-K1
...Hadabat Al Zaafaran (E39) — 19-F7
...Madinat Khalifa B (MFW12) — 57-B4
...Madinat Zayed (E4_01) — 8-K4
...Madinat Zayed (E4_02) — 5-A8
...Markaziya East (E1) — 4-G6
...Markaziya East (E3) — 4-J8
...Markaziya East (E9) — 5-A2
...Markaziya East (E10) — 5-A4
...Markaziya West (W6) — 8-C6
...Mussafah Industrial Area (M3) — 55-H1
...Mussafah Industrial Area (MW1) — 54-L5
...Tourist Club Area (E13) — 5-C1
...Tourist Club Area (E16) — 5-D4

## 13
**13 Rd**
...Al Bahia (Al Bahya Old) — 44-G8
...Al Bateen (W17_01) — 12-E6
...Al Dhafrah (E18_01) — 8-M7
...Al Dhafrah (E18_03) — 9-G4
...Al Madina Al Riyadiya (W57) — 28-A4
...Al Manhal (W9) — 12-A2
...Al Manhal (W13_02) — 12-H2
...Al Meena (Freezone) — 40-H8
...Al Mushrif (W46) — 22-M3
...Al Mushrif (W47) — 23-G6
...Al Muzoon (W62) — 27-C8
...Al Nahyan (E19) — 13-C3
...Al Rowdah (W18_01) — 17-G1
...Al Shahama 2 (Al Shamama I) — 44-K7
...Al Shawamekh (SHM1) — 57-F3
...Al Shawamekh (SHM3) — 57-D7
...Al Zahra (E36) — 24-E2
...Al Zahra (E41) — 20-G8
...Baniyas East (EB2_01) — 60-L5
...Baniyas East (EB7) — 61-C8
...Hadabat Al Zaafaran (E31) — 23-E3
...Hadabat Al Zaafaran (E33) — 23-H3
...Madinat Khalifa B (MFW3) — 56-M8
...Madinat Khalifa B (MFW24) — 57-C1
...Madinat Zayed (E4_01) — 8-K4
...Madinat Zayed (E4_02) — 8-M3
...Markaziya West (W6) — 8-E4
...Mohammed Bin Zayed City (ME13) — 39-D7
...Mussafah Industrial Area (M10) — 55-E2
...Mussafah Industrial Area (M20) — 55-B2
...Officers City (S2) — 37-K1
...Tourist Club Area (E16) — 5-E5

## 14
**14 Rd**
...Al Bahia (Al Bahya Old) — 44-F8
...Al Baladia (E11) — 5-C5
...Al Bateen (W17_01) — 12-D5
...Al Bateen (W29) — 17-B5
...Al Bateen (W37) — 12-A8
...Al Dhafrah (E18_02) — 9-C3
...Al Dhafrah (E18_03) — 9-F1
...Al Manhal (W4) — 8-E5
...Al Manhal (W13_02) — 12-J4
...Al Maqtaa (W65) — 34-F4
...Al Meena (Freezone) — 40-H7
...Al Mushrif (W24_01) — 18-J6
...Al Mushrif (W46) — 23-C5
...Al Mushrif (W47) — 23-G7
...Al Mushrif (W49) — 27-B2
...Al Mushrif (W52_01) — 22-G4
...Al Nahyan (E19) — 13-D3
...Al Nahyan (E20_02) — 13-F5
...Al Shahama 2 (Al Shamama I) — 44-L6
...Al Shawamekh (SHM7) — 57-G4
...Al Zahra (E36) — 24-D2
...Al Zahra (E41) — 24-F3
...Baniyas East (EB2_04) — 61-B6
...Baniyas East (EB5) — 60-L7
...Baniyas East (EB7) — 61-C8
...Hadabat Al Zaafaran (E31) — 23-D2
...Hadabat Al Zaafaran (E38) — 19-H8
...Madinat Khalifa B (MFW6) — 56-L5
...Madinat Khalifa B (MFW12) — 57-A3
...Madinat Zayed (E4_01) — 8-K2
...Madinat Zayed (E4_02) — 5-A7
...Markaziya East (E1) — 4-G5
...Markaziya East (E3) — 4-K8
...Markaziya East (E10) — 5-A4
...Officers City (S2) — 37-H1
...Officers Club (W51) — 34-A5
...Tourist Club Area (E16) — 5-F7

## 15
**15 Rd**
...Al Bahia (Al Bahya Old) — 44-G4
...Al Baladia (E11) — 5-D6
...Al Bateen (W17_01) — 12-E7
...Al Bateen (W37) — 11-K5
...Al Dhafrah (E18_01) — 9-A8
...Al Dhafrah (E18_02) — 9-C7
...Al Karamah (W15_01) — 18-C2
...Al Manhal (W9) — 12-B2
...Al Manhal (W13_02) — 12-G3
...Al Mushrif (W46) — 23-B2
...Al Mushrif (W47) — 23-H7
...Al Mushrif (W52_01) — 22-M4
...Al Nahyan (E19) — 13-D3
...Al Rowdah (W18_01) — 12-K8
...Al Shahama 2 (Al Shamama I) — 44-K8
...Al Shawamekh (SHM1) — 57-F2
...Al Zahra (E41) — 24-G4
...Baniyas East (EB2_04) — 61-C6
...Baniyas East (EB5) — 60-M8
...Baniyas East (EB7) — 61-C8
...Hadabat Al Zaafaran (E33) — 23-H3
...Madinat Khalifa B (MFW2) — 57-A7
...Madinat Zayed (E4_01) — 8-L4
...Madinat Zayed (E4_02) — 9-B3
...Markaziya West (W6) — 8-D5
...Mohammed Bin Zayed City (ME11) — 59-K3
...Officers Club (W51) — 33-L6
...Tourist Club Area (E16) — 5-F5

## 16
**16 Rd**
...Al Bahia (Al Bahya) — 44-B4
...Al Bateen (W17_01) — 12-E7
...Al Bateen (W37) — 11-K6
...Al Khubeirah — 11-D4
...Al Khubeirah (W38) — 11-E6
...Al Manhal (W4) — 8-D6
...Al Manhal (W9) — 12-B2
...Al Manhal (W13_02) — 12-J4
...Al Meena (Freezone) — 40-H7
...Al Mushrif (W24_01) — 18-G5
...Al Mushrif (W49) — 26-M2
...Al Mushrif (W52_01) — 22-F4
...Al Shahama 2 (Al Shamama I) — 44-L6
...Al Shahama 2 (Al Shahama New) — 44-L3
...Al Shawamekh (SHM1) — 57-F3
...Al Zahra (E36) — 24-D2
...Al Zahra (E41) — 24-F3
...Baniyas East (EB3) — 60-K6
...Baniyas East (EB7) — 61-C8
...Hadabat Al Zaafaran (E31) — 19-C8
...Hadabat Al Zaafaran (E38) — 19-K8
...Madinat Khalifa B (MFW2) — 57-B7
...Madinat Khalifa B (MFW20) — 57-D2
...Madinat Khalifa B (MFW24) — 57-D1
...Madinat Zayed (E4_01) — 8-L3
...Markaziya East (E10) — 5-A4
...Mohammed Bin Zayed City (ME9) — 59-K1
...Mohammed Bin Zayed City (ME10) — 59-K1
...Mussafah Industrial Area (M20) — 55-C2
...Tourist Club Area (E16) — 5-E4

## 17
**17 Rd**
...Al Bahia (Al Bahya Old) — 44-G3

## 18
**18 Rd**
...Al Bateen (W37) — 11-H5
...Al Dhafrah (E18_02) — 9-D3
...Al Manhal (W4) — 8-D6
...Al Manhal (W9) — 12-B3
...Al Manhal (W13_02) — 12-G3
...Al Mushrif (W24_01) — 18-J6
...Al Mushrif (W24_02) — 18-F2
...Al Mushrif (W46) — 22-M3
...Al Nahyan (E19) — 13-E3
...Al Nahyan (E20_02) — 13-F4
...Al Shahama 2 (Al Shamama II) — 44-J8
...Al Shawamekh (SHM3) — 57-C8
...Al Shawamekh (SHM7) — 57-G4
...Al Zahra (E36) — 24-D1
...Al Zahra (E41) — 24-H3
...Baniyas East (EB3) — 60-K7
...Baniyas East (EB7) — 61-C8
...Hadabat Al Zaafaran (E31) — 23-D1
...Hadabat Al Zaafaran (E38) — 19-H7
...Madinat Khalifa A (SW15) — 52-B6
...Madinat Khalifa B (MFW2) — 57-A7
...Madinat Khalifa B (MFW6) — 56-M5
...Madinat Khalifa B (MFW20) — 57-E2
...Madinat Khalifa B (MFW24) — 57-C1
...Madinat Zayed (E4_01) — 8-M4
...Markaziya East (E1) — 4-H5
...Markaziya East (E2) — 4-J6
...Markaziya East (E10) — 5-B4
...Mohammed Bin Zayed City (ME10) — 59-K2
...Officers City (S2) — 37-L4
...Officers City (S24) — 38-B4

## 14
**14 Rd**
...Al Baladia (E11) — 5-C8
...Al Bateen (W37) — 11-K5
...Al Dhafrah (E18_01) — 9-B7
...Al Manhal (W13_02) — 12-J2
...Al Manhal (W9) — 12-D2
...Al Meena (Freezone) — 40-J8
...Al Mushrif (W46) — 23-A4
...Al Mushrif (W47) — 23-G6
...Al Shahama 2 (Al Shahama New) — 44-L2
...Al Shawamekh (SHM3) — 57-C8
...Al Shawamekh (SHM6) — 61-B3
...Al Zahra (E41) — 24-G4
...Baniyas East (EB2_04) — 61-C6
...Baniyas East (EB5) — 60-M8
...Hadabat Al Zaafaran (E33) — 23-J4
...Madinat Khalifa A (SW15) — 57-A7
...Madinat Khalifa B (MFW12) — 57-C3
...Madinat Khalifa B (MFW14) — 57-D4
...Madinat Zayed (E4_01) — 8-K5
...Markaziya West (W6) — 8-E4
...Mohammed Bin Zayed City (ME11) — 59-K3
...Mussafah Industrial Area (M20) — 55-C2
...Officers City (S2) — 37-K1

## 19
**19 Rd**
...Al Bateen (W37) — 11-J5
...Al Madina Al Riyadiya (W57) — 28-D3
...Al Manhal (W13_02) — 12-G4
...Al Manhal (W9) — 12-C4
...Al Mushrif (W47) — 23-G6
...Al Shawamekh (SHM3) — 57-E6
...Al Zahra (E41) — 24-G2
...Baniyas East (EB3) — 60-K6
...Madinat Khalifa A (SW15) — 52-B5
...Madinat Khalifa B (MFW2) — 57-B6
...Madinat Khalifa B (MFW3) — 56-M8
...Madinat Zayed (E4_01) — 8-L5
...Markaziya West (W6) — 8-C6

## 20
**20 Rd**
...Al Bateen (W37) — 11-L7
...Al Manhal (W13_02) — 12-G3
...Al Manhal (W4) — 8-D7
...Al Meena (Freezone) — 40-J7
...Al Mushrif (W24_01) — 18-H7
...Al Mushrif (W46) — 22-L2
...Al Nahyan (E19) — 13-D2
...Al Nahyan (E20_02) — 13-F4
...Al Shahama 2 (Al Shamama I) — 44-K6
...Al Zahra (E36) — 19-L8
...Al Zahra (E41) — 24-F3
...Baniyas East (EB2_01) — 60-M5
...Baniyas East (EB2_03) — 61-A6
...Baniyas East (EB2_04) — 61-B7
...Baniyas East (EB3) — 60-K6
...Hadabat Al Zaafaran (E27) — 19-A6
...Hadabat Al Zaafaran (E38) — 19-K8
...Madinat Khalifa B (MFW6) — 56-M5
...Madinat Khalifa B (MFW12) — 57-B3
...Madinat Khalifa B (MFW24) — 57-D1
...Markaziya East (E2) — 4-J6
...Markaziya East (E10) — 5-B4
...Mohammed Bin Zayed City (ME9) — 55-K7
...Mohammed Bin Zayed City (ME11) — 59-K3
...Mohammed Bin Zayed City (ME12) — 59-K4
...Tourist Club Area (E16) — 5-E4

## 21
**21 Rd**
...Al Bahia (Al Bahya) — 44-B5
...Al Bateen (W37) — 11-L8

...Al Madina Al Riyadiya (W57) 28-E4
...Al Manhal (W4) 8-E7
...Al Manhal (W13_02) 12-J3
...Al Shawamekh (SHM1) 57-F3
...Al Shawamekh (SHM6) 61-C2
...Al Shawamekh (SHM7) 57-G4
...Al Zahra (E41) 24-H2
...Madinat Khalifa B (MFW6) 56-M5
...Madinat Khalifa B (MFW14) 57-C5
...Mohammed Bin Zayed City (ME9) 55-K8
...Mohammed Bin Zayed City (ME10) 59-K2
...Tourist Club Area (E16) 5-F7

## 22
**22 Rd**
...Al Bahia (Al Bahya Old) 44-G8
...Al Bateen (W37) 12-A8
...Al Manhal (W13_02) 12-H4
...Al Maqtaa (W54) 33-L2
...Al Mushrif (W46) 22-L2
...Al Mushrif (W52_01) 23-B6
...Al Nahyan (E20_02) 13-G5
...Al Shahama 2 (Al Shahama I) 44-K7
...Al Shawamekh (SHM1) 57-F3
...Al Zahra (E36) 24-C1
...Al Zahra (E41) 24-F2
...Baniyas East (EB3) 60-L7
...Baniyas East (EB5) 60-M8
...Madinat Khalifa B (MFW2) 57-A7
...Madinat Khalifa B (MFW6) 57-A5
...Madinat Khalifa B (MFW12) 57-B3
...Madinat Khalifa B (MFW24) 53-C8
...Markaziya East (E10) 5-B4
...Tourist Club Area (E16) 5-F5

## 23
**23 Rd**
...Al Bateen (W37) 11-M7
...Al Manhal (W13_02) 12-H4
...Al Mushrif (W46) 23-B4
...Al Mushrif (W48) 23-J7
...Al Shawamekh (SHM7) 57-H3
...Al Zahra (E41) 24-H3
...Baniyas East (EB3) 60-K6
...Madinat Khalifa A (SW15) 52-B6
...Mussafah Industrial Area (M10) 55-E2
...Officers City (S2) 37-L1
...Tourist Club Area (E16) 5-F7

## 24
**24 Rd**
...Al Bateen (W37) 11-H5
...Al Karamah (W15_02) 13-B8
...Al Maqtaa (W54) 33-L3
...Al Meena (Freezone) 40-J6
...Al Mushrif (W46) 23-C5
...Al Mushrif (W52_01) 23-B6
...Al Shawamekh (SHM6) 61-C2
...Al Shawamekh (SHM7) 57-G3
...Al Zahra (E36) 24-D1
...Al Zahra (E41) 24-F2
...Madinat Khalifa A (SW15) 52-B5
...Madinat Khalifa B (MFW6) 57-A5
...Madinat Khalifa B (MFW12) 57-B3
...Mussafah Industrial Area (M34) 55-G7
...Tourist Club Area (E16) 5-G6

## 25
**25 Rd**
...Al Bateen (W37) 11-M8
...Al Manhal (W13_02) 12-H4
...Al Meena (Freezone) 1-M1
...Al Mushrif (W46) 23-C5
...Al Zahra (E41) 24-H4
...Baniyas East (EB2_06) 61-B7
...Madinat Khalifa A (SW15) 52-D6
...Madinat Khalifa B (MFW6) 56-M5
...Mohammed Bin Zayed City (ME10) 59-K2

## 26
**26 Rd**
...Al Bahia (Al Bahya Old) 44-G8
...Al Bateen (W13_02) 12-G3
...Al Bateen (W37) 11-L7
...Al Manhal (W13_02) 12-F2
...Al Meena (Freezone) 40-J6
...Al Mushrif (W52_01) 22-M5
...Al Shahama 2 (Al Shahama I) 44-L7
...Al Shawamekh (SHM1) 57-G2
...Al Zahra (E36) 19-M8
...Al Zahra (E41) 24-H2
...Madinat Khalifa B (MFW2) 57-A6
...Madinat Khalifa B (MFW14) 57-C4
...Madinat Khalifa B (MFW24) 53-C8
...Tourist Club Area (E16) 5-E3

## 27
**27 Rd**
...Al Bateen (W37) 12-B8
...Al Manhal (W13_02) 12-J3
...Al Shawamekh (SHM1) 57-G2
...Al Zahra (E36) 24-A4
...Al Zahra (E41) 24-H5
...Baniyas East (EB2_04) 61-B7
...Madinat Khalifa B (MFW2) 57-A6
...Madinat Khalifa B (MFW12) 57-B4

...Madinat Khalifa B (MFW14) 57-D3
...Officers City (S2) 37-M1

## 28
**28 Rd**
...Al Bahia (Al Bahya) 44-B4
...Al Bateen (W37) 11-J7
...Al Shawamekh (SHM3) 57-D7
...Al Shawamekh (SHM7) 57-H3
...Al Zahra (E41) 24-F2
...Baniyas East (EB2_01) 60-L5
...Madinat Khalifa B (MFW14) 57-C4
...Mohammed Bin Zayed City (ME9) 55-K7
...Mohammed Bin Zayed City (ME12) 59-K4
...Mussafah Industrial Area (M24) 55-H4

## 29
**29 Rd**
...Al Manhal (W13_02) 12-H4
...Al Shawamekh (SHM7) 57-G4
...Al Zahra (E41) 24-J2
...Madinat Khalifa B (MFW12) 57-B3
...Mussafah Industrial Area (M3) 55-H1
...Tourist Club Area (E16) 5-G6

## 30
**30 Rd**
...Al Bahia (Al Bahya Old) 44-G8
...Al Bateen (W37) 11-J7
...Al Mushrif (W52_01) 22-M7
...Al Zahra (E41) 24-F1
...Baniyas East (EB7) 61-D8
...Madinat Khalifa B (MFW12) 57-C3
...Madinat Khalifa B (MFW14) 57-C4
...Mohammed Bin Zayed City (ME10) 59-K1
...Mohammed Bin Zayed City (ME11) 59-K3

## 31
**31 Rd**
...Al Manhal (W13_02) 12-H4
...Al Shawamekh (SHM1) 57-G2
...Al Zahra (E41) 24-J4
...Baniyas East (EB2_01) 60-M4
...Madinat Khalifa B (MFW6) 56-L5
...Mohammed Bin Zayed City (ME9) 55-K8
...Officers City (S2) 37-M2
...Tourist Club Area (E16) 5-G6

## 32
**32 Rd**
...Al Bateen (W37) 11-G7
...Al Shawamekh (SHM3) 57-D7
...Al Zahra (E41) 24-H2
...Madinat Khalifa B (MFW6) 56-M4
...Madinat Khalifa B (MFW14) 57-D4
...Mohammed Bin Zayed City (ME9) 59-K1
...Mohammed Bin Zayed City (ME10) 59-K1

## 33
**33 Rd**
...Al Bahia (Al Bahya) 44-B4
...Al Manhal (W13_02) 12-H4
...Al Shahama 2 (Al Shahama I) 44-L6
...Al Zahra (E41) 24-H4
...Baniyas East (EB2_01) 60-M4
...Baniyas East (EB3) 60-K7
...Madinat Khalifa B (MFW12) 57-A4
...Mohammed Bin Zayed City (ME10) 59-K2
...Mohammed Bin Zayed City (ME12) 59-K4
...Officers City (S2) 38-A2
...Tourist Club Area (E16) 5-G6

## 34
**34 Rd**
...Al Bahia (Al Bahya Old) 44-G7
...Al Bahia (Al Bahya) 44-C3
...Al Zahra (E41) 24-F1
...Madinat Khalifa B (MFW3) 56-K7
...Madinat Khalifa B (MFW14) 57-C4

## 35
**35 Rd**
...Al Bahia (Al Bahya) 44-C2
...Al Manhal (W13_02) 12-K3
...Al Meena (Freezone) 2-C6
...Al Zahra (E41) 24-J2
...Baniyas East (EB2_01) 60-M4
...Baniyas East (EB5) 61-A8
...Mohammed Bin Zayed City (ME12) 59-K4

## 36
**36 Rd**
...Al Shawamekh (SHM3) 57-D7
...Al Zahra (E41) 24-H1
...Madinat Khalifa B (MFW6) 56-M4
...Madinat Khalifa B (MFW14) 57-D4
...Mohammed Bin Zayed City (ME10) 59-K2
...Mohammed Bin Zayed City (ME11) 59-K3

## 37
**37 Rd**
...Al Manhal (W13_02) 12-J4

...Al Shawamekh (SHM3) 57-D8
...Al Zahra (E41) 20-H8
...Madinat Khalifa B (MFW12) 57-A3
...Madinat Khalifa B (MFW14) 57-C3
...Officers City (S2) 38-A2
...Tourist Club Area (E16) 5-G6

## 38
**38 Rd**
...Al Bahia (Al Bahya Old) 44-H7
...Madinat Khalifa B (MFW12) 57-B2
...Madinat Khalifa B (MFW14) 57-D4

## 39
**39 Rd**
...Al Shawamekh (SHM3) 57-E6
...Al Zahra (E41) 20-J8
...Baniyas East (EB2_01) 60-M4
...Madinat Khalifa A (SW15) 52-C6
...Mohammed Bin Zayed City (ME9) 55-K8
...Tourist Club Area (E16) 5-G6

## 40
**40 Rd**
...Al Zahra (E41) 20-F8
...Baniyas East (EB2_01) 60-M5

## 41
**41 Rd**
...Al Shawamekh (SHM3) 57-F5
...Baniyas East (EB3) 60-L7
...Mohammed Bin Zayed City (ME12) 59-K4

## 42
**42 Rd**
...Al Bahia (Al Bahya Old) 44-H6
...Al Zahra (E41) 20-H8
...Baniyas East (EB2_01) 60-M4
...Baniyas East (EB5) 61-A8
...Madinat Khalifa B (MFW14) 57-D3

## 43
**43 Rd**
...Baniyas East (EB2_01) 60-M5
...Baniyas East (EB5) 61-A8
...Madinat Khalifa B (MFW3) 56-K8
...Mohammed Bin Zayed City (ME10) 59-K1

## 44
**44 Rd**
...Mohammed Bin Zayed City (ME12) 59-K4

## 46
**46 Rd**
...Al Bahia (Al Bahya) 44-C3
...Al Shahama 2 (Al Shahama OLd) 44-K2
...Baniyas East (EB2_01) 60-M4
...Madinat Khalifa B (MFW14) 57-D4
...Mohammed Bin Zayed City (ME11) 59-J3

## 47
**47 Rd**
...Madinat Khalifa B (MFW3) 56-L7

## 48
**48 Rd**
...Baniyas East (EB5) 61-A8
...Madinat Khalifa B (MFW14) 57-D3

## 49
**49 Rd**
...Baniyas East (EB2_01) 60-M5
...Madinat Khalifa B (MFW12) 57-A3
...Mohammed Bin Zayed City (ME12) 59-K4

## 50
**50 Rd**
...Baniyas East (EB2_01) 60-M4
...Baniyas East (EB5) 61-A8
...Mohammed Bin Zayed City (ME12) 59-K4

## 51
**51 Rd**
...Al Shahama 2 (Al Shahama I) 44-L7
...Baniyas East (EB2_01) 61-A4
...Madinat Khalifa B (MFW12) 57-B1

## 52
**52 Rd**
...Al Shawamekh (SHM3) 57-E6
...Madinat Khalifa B (MFW14) 57-D3
...Mohammed Bin Zayed City (ME9) 55-K7
...Mohammed Bin Zayed City (ME12) 59-K4

## 53
**53 Rd**
...Al Shawamekh (SHM3) 57-E7

...Mohammed Bin Zayed City (ME10) 59-J3

## 54
**54 Rd**
...Baniyas East (EB2_01) 61-A5
...Baniyas East (EB5) 61-A8
...Mohammed Bin Zayed City (ME9) 59-K1

## 55
**55 Rd**
...Madinat Khalifa B (MFW3) 56-K6

## 56
**56 Rd**
...Al Shawamekh (SHM3) 57-E5
...Baniyas East (EB2_01) 60-M4

## 57
**57 Rd**
...Mohammed Bin Zayed City (ME12) 59-K4

## 58
**58 Rd**
...Madinat Khalifa B (MFW3) 57-A8
...Mohammed Bin Zayed City (ME10) 59-K1

## 59
**59 Rd**
...Mohammed Bin Zayed City (ME12) 59-K3

## 61
**61 Rd**
...Mohammed Bin Zayed City (ME12) 59-K3

## 62
**62 Rd**
...Mohammed Bin Zayed City (ME12) 59-K4

## 64
**64 Rd**
...Madinat Khalifa B (MFW3) 56-L6

## 65
**65 Rd**
...Mohammed Bin Zayed City (ME6) 55-K7

## 66
**66 Rd**
...Madinat Khalifa B (MFW3) 56-L6
...Mohammed Bin Zayed City (ME10) 59-K2
...Mohammed Bin Zayed City (ME12) 59-J4

## 68
**68 Rd**
...Mohammed Bin Zayed City (ME9) 59-K1

## 72
**72 Rd**
...Mohammed Bin Zayed City (ME10) 59-K2

## 78
**78 Rd**
...Mohammed Bin Zayed City (ME10) 59-J1

## 83
**83 Rd**
...Mohammed Bin Zayed City (ME1) 55-K2

## 86
**86 Rd**
...Mohammed Bin Zayed City (ME9) 55-J8

## A
**Abu Dhabi – Al Ain Rd**
...Baniyas East (EB5) 60-L7
...Baniyas West (EB3) 60-K7
...Baniyas West (EB5) 60-M8
...Capital District 39-J7
...Capital District (ME16) 56-A2
...Capital District (Z4) 56-C5
...Mahawi 60-G4
...Mohammed Bin Zayed City 39-H6
...Mohammed Bin Zayed City (Z1) 56-B4
...Mohammed Bin Zayed City (Z4) 56-C4
**Abu Dhabi – Dubai Rd**
...Abu Dhabi International Airport 48-C8
...Al Bahia (Al Bahya Old) 44-J8
...Al Raha 30-L2
...Al Shahama 2 48-E5
...Al Shahama 2 (Al Bahya Old) 44-H8
...Al Shahama 2 (Al Shahama New) 44-M4
...Al Shahama 2 (Al Shahama Old) 44-K6
...Madinat Khalifa A 30-D8

| | |
|---|---|
| ...Rawdat Al Reef | 44-M4 |
| ...Sas Al Nakhl | 30-D8 |
| ...Sas Al Nakhl Island | 30-D2 |

**Al Bateen Rd**, Al Bateen (W35) — 16-J2

**Al Falah St**
| | |
|---|---|
| ...Al Baladia (E11) | 9-D1 |
| ...Al Dhafrah (E11) | 9-D2 |
| ...Madinat Zayed (E4_01) | 8-L5 |
| ...Madinat Zayed (E4_02) | 9-C2 |

**Al Istiqalal St**
| | |
|---|---|
| ...Markaziya East (E1) | 4-F7 |
| ...Markaziya West (E1) | 4-F8 |
| ...Markaziya West (W1) | 4-D8 |

**Al Karamah St**
| | |
|---|---|
| ...Al Karamah (W14_02) | 12-L4 |
| ...Al Karamah (W15_02) | 13-B8 |
| ...Al Manhal (W13_01) | 12-J2 |
| ...Al Mushrif (W24_01) | 18-F5 |
| ...Al Mushrif (W24_02) | 18-D2 |
| ...Al Mushrif (W31) | 26-M2 |
| ...Al Mushrif (W47) | 23-C6 |
| ...Al Mushrif (W48) | 26-J1 |
| ...Al Mushrif (W49) | 26-L2 |
| ...Al Safarat (W59_02) | 27-E3 |

**Al Khaleej Al Arabi St**
| | |
|---|---|
| ... (W52_01) | 22-J7 |
| ...Al Bateen | 22-C5 |
| ...Al Bateen (W17_01) | 12-C6 |
| ...Al Bateen (W22) | 17-L7 |
| ...Al Bateen (W25) | 22-A2 |
| ...Al Madina Al Riyadiya (W57) | 27-L8 |
| ...Al Manhal (W4) | 12-F2 |
| ...Al Manhal (W9) | 12-A3 |
| ...Al Maqtaa | 34-G6 |
| ...Al Maqtaa (W54) | 33-H2 |
| ...Al Maqtaa (W65) | 34-D5 |
| ...Al Mushrif (W31) | 26-L3 |
| ...Al Mushrif (W47) | 26-D1 |
| ...Al Mushrif (W48) | 26-H2 |
| ...Al Mushrif (W52_01) | 23-A8 |
| ...Al Muzoon (W48) | 26-H2 |
| ...Al Rowdah (W18_01) | 12-F8 |
| ...Al Rowdah (W19_01) | 17-J5 |
| ...Al Safarat (W59_01) | 27-D5 |
| ...Bain Al Jessrain | 34-H6 |
| ...Bain Al Jessrain (S20) | 38-L3 |
| ...Bain Al Jessrain (S24) | 34-H6 |

**Al Khubeirah St**
| | |
|---|---|
| ...Al Khubeirah | 11-E4 |
| ...Al Khubeirah (W38) | 11-D5 |

**Al Manhal St**
| | |
|---|---|
| ...Al Bateen (W9) | 12-C5 |
| ...Al Bateen (W11) | 12-B6 |
| ...Al Manhal (W9) | 12-D3 |

**Al Meena St**
| | |
|---|---|
| ...Al Meena | 41-A8 |
| ...Al Meena (Freezone) | 2-C3 |
| ...Saadiyat Island | 41-B7 |
| ...Tourist Club Area (E12) | 2-B8 |

**Al Nahyan St**
| | |
|---|---|
| ...Al Rowdah (W14_01) | 12-J7 |
| ...Al Rowdah (W18_01) | 17-L1 |

**Al Nasr St**
| | |
|---|---|
| ...Al Khalidiya (W5) | 8-B6 |
| ...Markaziya West (W2) | 8-E1 |
| ...Markaziya West (W5) | 8-B5 |

**Al Saada St**
| | |
|---|---|
| ...Al Nahyan (E19_02) | 19-B2 |
| ...Al Nahyan (E24) | 18-M4 |
| ...Hadabat Al Zaafaran (E26) | 19-B3 |
| ...Hadabat Al Zaafaran (E27) | 18-M5 |

**Al Sharqi St**, Madinat Zayed (E4_02) — 8-L2

**Airport Rd**
| | |
|---|---|
| ...Abu Dhabi International Airport | 53-A2 |
| ...Bain Al Jessrain | 39-C5 |
| ...Capital District | 39-K5 |
| ...Capital District (SW15) | 52-C7 |
| ...Madinat Khalifa A (SE36) | 52-E6 |
| ...Mohammed Bin Zayed City | 39-H6 |

## B

**Bani Yas St**
| | |
|---|---|
| ...Al Baladia (E11) | 5-B8 |
| ...Madinat Zayed (E11) | 5-A6 |
| ...Markaziya East (E9) | 4-L4 |
| ...Markaziya East (E9_01) | 4-K2 |

**Bateen Rd**, Al Bateen (W35) — 16-J2

**Baynunah St**
| | |
|---|---|
| ...Al Bateen | 11-B6 |
| ...Al Bateen (W37) | 11-H7 |
| ...Al Khubeirah | 11-B6 |
| ...Al Khubeirah (W38) | 11-B5 |

**Beach Rd**, Al Bateen — 21-L5

## C

**Coast Rd**
| | |
|---|---|
| ... (W52_01) | 22-J7 |
| ...Al Bateen | 22-D5 |
| ...Al Madina Al Riyadiya (W57) | 27-L8 |
| ...Al Maqtaa | 34-G6 |
| ...Al Maqtaa (W54) | 33-H2 |
| ...Al Maqtaa (W65) | 34-D5 |
| ...Al Mushrif (W31) | 26-L3 |
| ...Al Mushrif (W47) | 26-D1 |
| ...Al Mushrif (W48) | 26-H2 |
| ...Al Mushrif (W52_01) | 23-A8 |
| ...Al Muzoon (W48) | 26-H2 |
| ...Al Safarat (W59_01) | 27-D5 |
| ...Bain Al Jessrain | 34-H6 |

**Corniche Rd**, Al Meena (Freezone) — 2-D3

**Corniche Rd East**
| | |
|---|---|
| ...Markaziya East (E1) | 4-D6 |
| ...Markaziya East (E7) | 4-G3 |
| ...Markaziya East (E9_01) | 4-J1 |
| ...Markaziya West (W1) | 4-C8 |
| ...Markaziya West (W5) | 8-A3 |

**Corniche Rd West**
| | |
|---|---|
| ...Al Khalidiya (W8) | 7-L7 |
| ...Al Khalidiya (W10) | 11-J1 |
| ...Al Khubeirah (W38) | 11-D3 |

**Corniche West St**, Al Ras Al Akhdar — 10-K7

## D

**Delma St**
| | |
|---|---|
| ...Al Bateen (W18_03) | 17-G5 |
| ...Al Karamah (W14_01) | 12-M8 |
| ...Al Karamah (W14_02) | 13-B6 |
| ...Al Nahyan (E19) | 13-E4 |
| ...Al Nahyan (E19_02) | 13-H1 |
| ...Al Rowdah (W18_01) | 17-J3 |

## E

**East Rd**
| | |
|---|---|
| ...Al Dhafrah (E18_02) | 9-B6 |
| ...Al Matar | 24-J6 |
| ...Al Nahyan (E19_02) | 13-D1 |
| ...Al Zahra (E36) | 23-L3 |
| ...Hadabat Al Zaafaran (E26) | 19-A4 |
| ...Hadabat Al Zaafaran (E38) | 23-G2 |
| ...Hadabat Al Zaafaran (E39) | 19-D8 |

**Eastern Ring Rd**
| | |
|---|---|
| ...Al Maqtaa (W54) | 34-C1 |
| ...Al Maqtaa (W65) | 29-C7 |
| ...Al Matar | 25-K7 |
| ...Al Matar (E49) | 29-B2 |
| ...Al Zahra (E36) | 20-C8 |
| ...Hadabat Al Zaafaran | 19-D2 |
| ...Hadabat Al Zaafaran (E26) | 19-E3 |
| ...Hadabat Al Zaafaran (E38) | 19-J6 |
| ...Mangroves (AL QURM) (E49) | 20-K8 |

**Electra St**
| | |
|---|---|
| ...Tourist Club Area (E14) | 5-F2 |
| ...Tourist Club Area (E15) | 5-C4 |

## F

**Falah St**
| | |
|---|---|
| ...Al Baladia (E11) | 9-D1 |
| ...Al Dhafrah (E11) | 9-D2 |
| ...Madinat Zayed (E4_01) | 8-L5 |
| ...Madinat Zayed (E4_02) | 9-C2 |

## H

**Hamdan Bin Mohammed St**
| | |
|---|---|
| ...Markaziya East (E8) | 4-L6 |
| ...Tourist Club Area (E13) | 5-C2 |
| ...Tourist Club Area (E14) | 5-E1 |

**Hazaa Bin Zayed The First St**
| | |
|---|---|
| ...Al Bateen (W17_01) | 12-F7 |
| ...Al Bateen (W17_03) | 12-E8 |
| ...Al Dhafrah (E18_02) | 9-D6 |
| ...Al Dhafrah (E18_03) | 9-F5 |
| ...Al Karamah (W13_02) | 12-K4 |
| ...Al Manhal (W13_01) | 12-L3 |
| ...Al Manhal (W13_02) | 12-J4 |
| ...Qasr Al Bahr | 9-L2 |
| ...Qasr Al Bahr (E17) | 9-K3 |

## I

**Istiqalal St**
| | |
|---|---|
| ...Markaziya East (E1) | 4-F7 |
| ...Markaziya West (E1) | 4-F8 |
| ...Markaziya West (W1) | 4-D8 |

## K

**Karamah St**
| | |
|---|---|
| ...Al Karamah (W14_02) | 12-L4 |
| ...Al Karamah (W15_02) | 13-B8 |
| ...Al Manhal (W13_01) | 12-J2 |
| ...Al Mushrif (W24_01) | 18-F5 |
| ...Al Mushrif (W24_02) | 18-D2 |
| ...Al Mushrif (W31) | 26-M2 |
| ...Al Mushrif (W46) | - |
| ...Al Mushrif (W47) | 23-C6 |
| ...Al Mushrif (W48) | 26-J1 |
| ...Al Mushrif (W49) | 26-L2 |
| ...Al Safarat (W59_02) | 27-E3 |

**Khaleej Al Arabi St**
| | |
|---|---|
| ... (W52_01) | 22-J7 |
| ...Al Bateen | 22-C5 |
| ...Al Bateen (W17_01) | 12-C6 |
| ...Al Bateen (W22) | 17-L7 |
| ...Al Bateen (W25) | 22-A2 |
| ...Al Madina Al Riyadiya (W57) | 27-L8 |
| ...Al Manhal (W4) | 12-F2 |
| ...Al Manhal (W9) | 12-A3 |
| ...Al Maqtaa | 34-G6 |
| ...Al Maqtaa (W54) | 33-H2 |
| ...Al Maqtaa (W65) | 34-D5 |
| ...Al Mushrif (W31) | 26-L3 |
| ...Al Mushrif (W47) | 26-D1 |
| ...Al Mushrif (W48) | 26-H2 |
| ...Al Mushrif (W52_01) | 23-A8 |
| ...Al Muzoon (W48) | 26-H2 |
| ...Al Rowdah (W18_01) | 12-F8 |
| ...Al Rowdah (W19_01) | 17-J5 |

| | |
|---|---|
| ...Al Safarat (W59_01) | 27-D5 |
| ...Bain Al Jessrain | 34-H6 |
| ...Bain Al Jessrain (S20) | 38-L3 |
| ...Bain Al Jessrain (S24) | 34-H6 |

**Khalid Bin Waleed St**
| | |
|---|---|
| ...Al Manhal (W4) | 8-F5 |
| ...Markaziya West (W2) | 8-D1 |
| ...Markaziya West (W3) | 8-E2 |

**Khalifa Bin Shakhbout St**
| | |
|---|---|
| ...Al Bateen | 22-G6 |
| ...Al Bateen (W17_01) | 12-E5 |
| ...Al Mushrif (W23_01) | 17-M6 |
| ...Al Mushrif (W52_01) | 22-E3 |
| ...Al Rowdah (W18_01) | 12-G7 |
| ...Al Rowdah (W19_01) | 17-K2 |

**Khalifa Bin Zayed St**
| | |
|---|---|
| ...Markaziya East (E7) | 4-J5 |
| ...Markaziya East (E9) | 4-L3 |
| ...Markaziya East (E9_01) | 4-L2 |
| ...Tourist Club Area (E12) | 1-L8 |

**Khubeirah St**
| | |
|---|---|
| ...Al Khubeirah | 11-E4 |
| ...Al Khubeirah (W38) | 11-D5 |

**King Khalid Bin Abdel Aziz St**
| | |
|---|---|
| ...Al Khalidiya (W6) | 8-C6 |
| ...Al Manhal (W4) | 12-D1 |
| ...Markaziya West (W5) | 8-A5 |

## L

**Liwa St**
| | |
|---|---|
| ...Markaziya East (E1) | 4-F5 |
| ...Markaziya East (E2) | 4-G7 |

**Lulu St**
| | |
|---|---|
| ...Markaziya East (E7) | 4-H4 |
| ...Markaziya East (E8) | 4-J6 |

## M

**Manhal St**
| | |
|---|---|
| ...Al Bateen (W9) | 12-C5 |
| ...Al Bateen (W11) | 12-B6 |
| ...Al Manhal (W9) | 12-D3 |

**Meena St**
| | |
|---|---|
| ...Al Meena | 41-A8 |
| ...Al Meena (Freezone) | 2-C3 |
| ...Saadiyat Island | 41-B7 |
| ...Tourist Club Area (E12) | 2-B8 |

**Mohd Bin Khalifa St**
| | |
|---|---|
| ... (W20) | 17-J8 |
| ...Al Karamah (W15_01) | 18-B3 |
| ...Al Karamah (W15_02) | 13-E8 |
| ...Al Mushrif (W15_01) | 18-B3 |
| ...Al Mushrif (W19_01) | 17-L6 |
| ...Al Nahyan (E19_02) | 13-J6 |
| ...Al Nahyan (E20_02) | 13-G7 |
| ...Al Rowdah (W19_01) | 17-L6 |

## N

**Nahyan St**
| | |
|---|---|
| ...Al Rowdah (W14_01) | 12-J7 |
| ...Al Rowdah (W18_01) | 17-L1 |

**Nasr St, Al**
| | |
|---|---|
| ...Al Khalidiya (W5) | 8-B6 |
| ...Markaziya West (W2) | 8-E1 |
| ...Markaziya West (W5) | 8-B5 |

## R

**Rashid Bin Al Maktoum Rd**
| | |
|---|---|
| ...Al Matar | 27-M1 |
| ...Al Rehhan (E42) | 27-L1 |
| ...Madinat Zayed (E4_01) | 8-H3 |

**Reem Bridge**, Qsar Al Qsaseer Island — 42-E7

## S

**Saada St**
| | |
|---|---|
| ...Al Nahyan (E19_02) | 19-B2 |
| ...Al Nahyan (E24) | 18-M4 |
| ...Hadabat Al Zaafaran (E26) | 19-B3 |
| ...Hadabat Al Zaafaran (E27) | 18-M5 |

**Saeed Bin Tahnoon St**
| | |
|---|---|
| ...Al Mushrif (W23_01) | 22-E2 |
| ...Al Mushrif (W24_01) | 18-J7 |
| ...Al Mushrif (W46) | 18-J7 |
| ...Al Mushrif (W52_01) | 18-H8 |
| ...Al Mushrif (W46) | 18-L6 |
| ...Hadabat Al Zaafaran (E27) | 18-L6 |

**Salam St**
| | |
|---|---|
| ...Al Baladia (E16) | 5-D6 |
| ...Al Dhafrah (E18_03) | 9-G2 |
| ...Al Nahyan (E19_02) | 13-L1 |
| ...Tourist Club Area (E13) | 5-B2 |
| ...Tourist Club Area (E15) | 5-C3 |
| ...Tourist Club Area (E16) | 5-C4 |

**Sharqi St**, Madinat Zayed (E4_02) — 8-L2

**Shk Maktoum Rd**
| | |
|---|---|
| ...Al Falah City | 51-J7 |
| ...Al Shahama 2 | 51-J1 |
| ...Al Shamkha | 53-G6 |
| ...Al Shawamekh (MFW2) | 57-C7 |
| ...Al Shawamekh (MFW3) | 61-B1 |
| ...Al Shawamekh (MFW14) | 57-E5 |
| ...Al Shawamekh (SHM3) | 57-E4 |
| ...Baniyas East | 61-A2 |
| ...Baniyas East (MFW3) | 61-A2 |
| ...Madinat Khalifa B | 57-F1 |
| ...Madinat Khalifa B (MFW2) | 61-B1 |
| ...Mahawi | 60-L4 |
| ...Rawdat Al Reef | 48-K4 |

| | |
|---|---|
| ...Al Safarat (W59_01) | 27-D5 |
| ...Bain Al Jessrain | 34-H6 |
| ...Bain Al Jessrain (S20) | 38-L3 |
| ...Bain Al Jessrain (S24) | 34-H6 |

| | |
|---|---|
| ...Rawdat Al Reef (Al Shahama I) | 44-M6 |

**Shk Rashid Bin Saeed Al Maktoum St**
| | |
|---|---|
| ...Al Manhal (E4_01) | 8-K6 |
| ...Al Manhal (W4) | 8-K6 |
| ...Al Maqtaa (E49) | 29-E5 |
| ...Al Matar | 28-C2 |
| ...Al Mushrif (E24) | 18-J3 |
| ...Al Mushrif (E27) | 18-M6 |
| ...Al Mushrif (E31) | 23-B2 |
| ...Al Mushrif (E35) | 24-A8 |
| ...Al Mushrif (W49) | 23-M7 |
| ...Al Nahyan (E19) | 13-B2 |
| ...Al Nahyan (E20_02) | 13-D5 |
| ...Al Nahyan (E22) | 13-G8 |
| ...Al Rehhan (E34_01) | 23-K6 |
| ...Al Rehhan (E35) | 24-C8 |
| ...Al Safarat (E40) | 24-E8 |
| ...Al Safarat (E42) | 27-H1 |
| ...Bain Al Jessrain | 35-K3 |
| ...Hadabat Al Zaafaran (E27) | 18-M8 |
| ...Hadabat Al Zaafaran (E31) | 23-C2 |
| ...Hadabat Al Zaafaran (E33) | 23-F2 |
| ...Hadabat Al Zaafaran (E38) | 23-H2 |
| ...Madinat Khalifa A | 30-D8 |
| ...Madinat Zayed (E4_01) | 8-J5 |
| ...Mangroves (Al Qurm) (E49) | 29-D5 |
| ...Markaziya East | 4-D5 |
| ...Markaziya East (E1) | 4-E6 |
| ...Markaziya East (E2) | 4-F8 |
| ...Markaziya East (E3) | 8-G1 |
| ...Sas Al Nakhl Island | 30-A2 |

**Shk Zayed First St**
| | |
|---|---|
| ...Al Bateen (W10) | 11-K2 |
| ...Al Bateen (W37) | 11-G6 |
| ...Al Bateen (W38) | 11-J3 |
| ...Al Khalidiya (W10) | 11-K2 |
| ...Al Khalidiya (W8) | 11-M1 |
| ...Al Khubeirah (W38) | 11-G6 |
| ...Al Manhal (W6) | 8-D6 |
| ...Markaziya East (E3) | 4-J8 |
| ...Markaziya West (W3) | 8-G2 |
| ...Markaziya West (W6) | 8-D6 |

**Shk Zayed Second St**
| | |
|---|---|
| ...Markaziya East (E3) | 4-K8 |
| ...Markaziya East (E10) | 5-B5 |

**Sultan Bin Zayed St**
| | |
|---|---|
| ... (W20) | 17-G5 |
| ...Al Bateen (W11) | 11-K3 |
| ...Al Bateen (W17_03) | 12-A6 |
| ...Al Bateen (W18_03) | 17-E3 |
| ...Al Bateen (W21) | 17-J8 |
| ...Al Khalidiya (W10) | 11-J1 |

**Sweihan Rd**
| | |
|---|---|
| ...Abu Dhabi International Airport | 53-F4 |
| ...Al Shamkha | 53-K4 |

## T

**Tourist Club St**
| | |
|---|---|
| ...Tourist Club Area (E14) | 2-D7 |
| ...Tourist Club Area (E16_01) | 5-F2 |

**Truck Rd**
| | |
|---|---|
| ...Industrial City of Abu Dhabi | 59-J4 |
| ...Mohammed Bin Zayed City | 59-L8 |
| ...Mohammed Bin Zayed City (ME5) | 55-J4 |
| ...Mohammed Bin Zayed City (ME10) | 59-J2 |
| ...Mohammed Bin Zayed City (ME11) | 59-J3 |
| ...Mussafah Industrial Area (M3) | 55-J1 |
| ...Mussafah Industrial Area (M28) | 55-J7 |
| ...Officers City (M3) | 39-A8 |
| ...Officers City (S24) | 39-A7 |

## Z

**Zayed Bridge**
| | |
|---|---|
| ...Mangroves (Al Qurm) | 29-F2 |
| ...Mangroves (Al Qurm) (E49) | 29-D2 |
| ...Sas Al Nakhl Island | 29-G2 |

# #

**007 Mechanical Electrical Accessories Bldg,**
Mussafah Industrial Area ........................................... 55-G2
**4 All Rent A Car,** Al Nahyan ...................................... 9-H5
**4 Bldg,** Al Matar ................................................... 25-H7
**6 August School,** Hadabat Al Zaafaran ........................ 19-D8
**18Oz,** (One To One Hotel – The Village), Al Nahyan .......... 9-J6
**49er's The Gold Rush,** (Al Diar Dana Hotel), Tourist Club Area ... 5-E3

# A

**A to Z Rent A Car,** Al Nahyan .................................... 13-G8
**ABB Transmission & Distribution,** Mussafah Industrial Area ... 55-B1
**ABBA Herbal Preparation Bldg,** Industrial City of Abu Dhabi ... 59-A4
**ABC Private School,** Al Zahra .................................... 19-M8
**Abdul Kadar Jazari School,** Al Shahama 2 ...................... 44-J8
**Abdul Majeed Supermarket,** Baniyas East ...................... 61-A8
**Abdul Monem Al Rashed Steel Industries Bldg,** Industrial
City of Abu Dhabi ................................................... 59-A3
**Abdul Wahab Auto Electrical Shope Bldg,** Mussafah
Industrial Area ..................................................... 55-G2
**Abdulla Bin Salamah Mosque,** Hadabat Al Zaafaran .......... 23-H3
**Abdullah Bin Moseyed School**
...Mohammed Bin Zayed City ....................................... 55-L1
...Mussafah Industrial Area ....................................... 55-G2
**Abdullah Bin Toiba School,** Madinat Zayed .................... 8-L4
**Abela Super Store,** Al Khalidiya ................................ 8-A6
**ABG Al Badie Group Bldg,** Mussafah Industrial Area ......... 55-E1
**Abi Alfida Restaurant,** Tourist Club Area ..................... 5-F5
**Abraj Medical Service Bldg, Al,** Mussafah Industrial Area ... 55-H2
**Abraj Towers,** Madinat Khalifa A
...Etihad Staff Accommodation Bldg ............................... 50-K6
...UAE Exchange ...................................................... 50-K6
**Abu Al Abyad Automatic Laundry Bldg,** Mussafah
Industrial Area ..................................................... 55-D3
**Abu Al Abyad Hospital,** Mohammed Bin Zayed City ............ 60-A1
**Abu Ameer Furniture Bldg,** Al Meena .......................... 40-J8
**Abu Amir Furniture,** Al Nahyan ................................. 13-G5
**Abu Azooz Trading,** Tourist Club Area ......................... 5-D5
**Abu Dhabi Airport City Terminal Bldg,** Tourist Club Area ... 5-G4
**Abu Dhabi Airport Hotel,** Abu Dhabi International Airport ... 53-D1
**Abu Dhabi Al Jaleel Al Faheem Primary School,** Al Dhafrah ... 9-D5
**Abu Dhabi Arch Contracting Company Bldg,** Mussafah
Industrial Area ..................................................... 55-D6
**Abu Dhabi Arts Bldg,** Mussafah Industrial Area .............. 55-F3
**Abu Dhabi Automobiles Bldg,** Bain Al Jessrain ............... 29-M7
**Abu Dhabi Aviation Camp,** Al Maqtaa .......................... 34-E3
**Abu Dhabi Aviation Terminal Bldg,** Abu Dhabi
International Airport ............................................... 53-F3
**Abu Dhabi Business,** Al Mushrif ................................ 23-B6
**Abu Dhabi Car Driving School,** Hadabat Al Zaafaran ......... 19-D6
**Abu Dhabi Car Service Station Bldg,** Mussafah Industrial Area ... 55-G1
**Abu Dhabi Cargo Terminal Bldg,** Abu Dhabi
International Airport ............................................... 53-E2
**Abu Dhabi Carnation Metal Industries Bldg,** Mussafah
Industrial Area ..................................................... 54-M6
**Abu Dhabi Central Laboratories Bldg,** Al Madina Al Riyadiya ... 27-M3
**Abu Dhabi Centre For Housing & Services Facilities**
**Department,** Al Karamah .......................................... 13-C6
**Abu Dhabi Centre for Languages & Speech Disorders,**
Al Manhal ........................................................... 12-B1
**Abu Dhabi Chamber of Commerce & Industry Bldg,**
Markaziya West ...................................................... 4-D7
**Abu Dhabi Chess Club,** Madinat Zayed ......................... 5-A8
**Abu Dhabi Children's Kindergarten,** Al Karamah ............. 12-L4
**Abu Dhabi City Golf Club,** Al Mushrif ......................... 18-D8
**Abu Dhabi Co-operative Hypermarket,** Tourist Club Area ... 5-G3
**Abu Dhabi Co-operative Society**
...Al Baladia ........................................................ 5-C5
...Al Bateen ......................................................... 12-H5
...Al Khalidiya ...................................................... 8-A7
...Al Manhal ......................................................... 12-A2
**Abu Dhabi Commercial Bank**
...Al Baladia ........................................................ 5-C5
...Al Karamah ........................................................ 13-A1
...Al Rehhan ......................................................... 24-F6
...Al Shahama 2 ...................................................... 44-M3
...Industrial City of Abu Dhabi .................................... 59-H3
...Madinat Khalifa A ................................................ 52-C2
...Madinat Zayed ..................................................... 8-L1
...Markaziya East .................................................... 4-G5
...Mussafah Industrial Area ........................................ 55-H2
...Tourist Club Area ................................................ 5-E5
**Abu Dhabi Commercial Corporation,** Markaziya East ......... 4-L6
**Abu Dhabi Construction & Showroom Bldg,** Mussafah
Industrial Area ..................................................... 55-D2
**Abu Dhabi Craft Factory Bldg,** Mussafah Industrial Area .... 55-E5
**Abu Dhabi Creek Business Resorts,** Bain Al Jessrain ........ 29-K7
**Abu Dhabi Cricket Stadium Bldg,** Madinat Khalifa A ......... 39-J3
**Abu Dhabi Customs & Immigration Department Bldg,**
Al Meena ............................................................. 2-F1
**Abu Dhabi Dental Centre,** Madinat Zayed ...................... 8-J2
**Abu Dhabi Distribution Company (ADDC) Bldg,**
...Al Dhafrah ........................................................ 9-D2
...Al Mushrif ........................................................ 18-L8
...Al Nahyan ......................................................... 13-F5
...Madinat Zayed ..................................................... 8-J2
...Mussafah Industrial Area ........................................ 55-C6
...Tourist Club Area ................................................ 5-E6
**Abu Dhabi Distribution Company Central Store,**
Mussafah Industrial Area ........................................... 55-F6
**Abu Dhabi Education Council,** Al Karamah ...................... 13-E7
**Abu Dhabi Education Zone (ADEZ)**
...Al Karamah ........................................................ 12-L7

...Al Khalidiya ....................................................... 8-B6
**Abu Dhabi Educational Training Institute,** Bain Al Jessrain ... 35-F4
**Abu Dhabi Falcon Hospital,** Al Shamkha ....................... 53-M5
**Abu Dhabi Federal Appeal Court,** Al Mushrif .................. 26-D1
**Abu Dhabi Fiber Glass Factory Bldg,** Mussafah Industrial Area ... 58-M1
**Abu Dhabi Financial Services & Ministry of Public Works,**
Markaziya East ...................................................... 4-G5
**Abu Dhabi Folklore & Theatre Society Bldg,** Al Nahyan ...... 13-D4
**Abu Dhabi Food Control Authority (ADFCA) Bldg**
...Al Baladia ........................................................ 5-D6
...Al Karamah ........................................................ 13-B5
**Abu Dhabi Fund for Development (ADFD) Bldg,** Al Bateen ..... 11-H8
**Abu Dhabi Garment Factory Bldg,** Mussafah Industrial Area ... 54-M6
**Abu Dhabi Gas Industry Critical National Infrastructure**
**Authorities Bldg,** Madinat Khalifa A ........................... 30-F8
**Abu Dhabi General Contracting,** Hadabat Al Zaafaran ........ 19-B5
**Abu Dhabi Golf Club,** Madinat Khalifa A ....................... 31-B5
**Abu Dhabi Health & Fitness Club Bldg,** Al Mushrif ........... 18-G8
**Abu Dhabi Indian School,** Hadabat Al Zaafaran ................ 19-G7
**Abu Dhabi Industrial Supplies Company Bldg,** Al Meena ...... 2-D1
**Abu Dhabi International Airport** ................................ 53-D1
**Abu Dhabi International Airport Catering Bldg,** Mussafah
Industrial Area ..................................................... 55-G6
**Abu Dhabi International Center for Organizational**
**Excellence (ADICOE),** Al Bateen ................................. 11-M7
**Abu Dhabi International Kart & Motocross Complex**
...Crown Prince Court Bldg .......................................... 36-K5
...Madinat Khalifa A ................................................ 36-G4
**Abu Dhabi International Marine Sports Club,** Breakwater ..... 7-D5
**Abu Dhabi International Medical Service,** Al Mushrif ......... 23-J7
**Abu Dhabi International Metal Casting Factory Bldg,**
Mussafah Industrial Area ........................................... 55-G7
**Abu Dhabi Investment Authority (ADIA) Bldg,** Markaziya West ... 4-D8
**Abu Dhabi Investment Council,** Markaziya East ................ 4-G5
**Abu Dhabi Islamic Bank**
...Al Manhal ......................................................... 8-B7
...Al Meena .......................................................... 2-E4
...Al Nahyan ......................................................... 13-B1
...Al Rehhan ......................................................... 24-E6
...Breakwater ........................................................ 7-A5
...Markaziya East .................................................... 4-G6
...Mussafah Industrial Area ........................................ 55-F2
**Abu Dhabi Judicial Department (ADJD) Bldg,** Al Matar ....... 24-M7
**Abu Dhabi Junior Academy,** Al Nahyan ......................... 13-D2
**Abu Dhabi Laboratory Bldg,** Mussafah Industrial Area ....... 55-D2
**Abu Dhabi Ladies Club Bldg,** Al Ras Al Akhdar ................ 10-F7
**Abu Dhabi Main Terminal Bus Station,** Al Nahyan ............. 13-D1
**Abu Dhabi Maintenance & Construction Company**
**(ADMAC) Bldg,** Mussafah Industrial Area ....................... 55-B7
**Abu Dhabi Malayalee Samajam,** Al Manhal ...................... 12-B2
**Abu Dhabi Mall**
...Il Forno .......................................................... 5-G3
...Tourist Club Area ................................................ 5-F3
**Abu Dhabi Marble Bldg,** Mussafah Industrial Area ............ 55-B7
**Abu Dhabi Marina,** Tourist Club Area .......................... 5-G2
**Abu Dhabi Media Company**
...Al Nahyan ......................................................... 13-J8
...Abu Dhabi Film Centre Bldg ...................................... 13-J8
...E22 ............................................................... 18-K1
**Abu Dhabi Media Company Bldg,** Al Nahyan ..................... 13-H7
**Abu Dhabi Motor Sport Management (ADMM) Bldg,**
Al Karamah .......................................................... 13-A7
**Abu Dhabi Motors**
...Al Bateen ......................................................... 11-K3
...Bain Al Jessrain .................................................. 29-K7
...Markaziya East .................................................... 4-M1
...Mussafah Industrial Area ........................................ 55-H4
**Abu Dhabi Municipality Bldg**
...Agriculture Centre Bldg, Mussafah Industrial Area ............ 55-G1
...Al Baladia ........................................................ 5-D7
...Al Meena .......................................................... 40-K8
...Al Rehhan ......................................................... 24-J7
...Al Shahama 2 ...................................................... 44-K6
...Baniyas East ...................................................... 61-A4
...Hadabat Al Zaafaran .............................................. 19-D5
...Mussafah Industrial Area ........................................ 55-H1
**Abu Dhabi National Cement Factory Bldg,** Industrial
City of Abu Dhabi ................................................... 59-B3
**Abu Dhabi National Exhibition Centre,** Al Safarat
...Al Married Wedding Hall .......................................... 27-J5
...Aloft Hotel ....................................................... 27-J5
...Capital Centre .................................................... 27-F5
...Capital Gate Bldg ................................................. 27-G5
...Capital Plaza ..................................................... 27-H5
...Conference Hall A ................................................. 27-H6
...Conference Hall B ................................................. 27-H6
...Emirates Identity Authority ...................................... 27-G6
...Grandstand Majilis ............................................... 27-H6
...Hyatt Hotel ....................................................... 27-G5
...National Bank of Abu Dhabi ....................................... 27-H6
**Abu Dhabi National Exhibition Company Bldg,** Mussafah
Industrial Area ..................................................... 55-E3
**Abu Dhabi National Hotel Company Bldg,** Al Madina
Al Riyadiya .......................................................... 27-M4
**Abu Dhabi National Insurance Company Bldg,** Mussafah
Industrial Area ..................................................... 55-B4
**Abu Dhabi National Islamic Finance (ADNF),** Markaziya East ... 4-F6
**Abu Dhabi National Scaffolding Factory Bldg,** Mussafah
Industrial Area ..................................................... 54-L7
**Abu Dhabi Oil Refining Division & Oil Products Storage**
**& Dispatch Terminal Bldg,** Industrial City of Abu Dhabi ...... 59-G6
**Abu Dhabi Oxygen Company Bldg,** Mussafah Industrial Area ... 55-C2
**Abu Dhabi Pallet Industries Bldg,** Industrial City of Abu Dhabi ... 59-E3
**Abu Dhabi Plaza Hotel Apartment,** Markaziya East ........... 4-M6

**Abu Dhabi Police**
...Al Nahyan (Abu Dhabi Police General Head Office) ............. 18-L4
...Al Rehhan ......................................................... 24-D7
...GHQ Human Resources General Directorate Training Administration
Education & Scholarship Education, Al Mushrif ................... 27-D1
...Officers Club Bldg, Mangroves (Al Qurm) ....................... 29-B1
...Purchasing & Stores ADM Housing Section, Al Nahyan .......... 18-L5
**Abu Dhabi Police DPT 7,** Bain Al Jessrain ..................... 29-J6
**Abu Dhabi Ports Company Bldg,** Al Meena ...................... 2-G1
**Abu Dhabi Precast Factory Phase 1 Bldg,** Industrial
City of Abu Dhabi ................................................... 59-C2
**Abu Dhabi Precast Factory Phase 2 Bldg,** Industrial
City of Abu Dhabi ................................................... 59-C2
**Abu Dhabi Rehabilitation Center,** Al Manhal ................. 8-K8
**Abu Dhabi Retirement Pensions & Benefits Fund Bldg,**
Al Madina Al Riyadiya ............................................... 28-A4
**Abu Dhabi Scaffolding Factory Bldg,** Industrial
City of Abu Dhabi ................................................... 59-E3
**Abu Dhabi School for Secondary Education,** Al Karamah ....... 12-L7
**Abu Dhabi Sewerage Services Company (ADSSC)**
...Al Rowdah ......................................................... 12-J8
...Hadabat Al Zaafaran .............................................. 19-C4
...Mohammed Bin Zayed City ......................................... 56-A3
**Abu Dhabi Ship Building Bldg,** Mussafah Industrial Area .... 54-L5
**Abu Dhabi Stock Exchange,** Markaziya East ..................... 4-K6
**Abu Dhabi Switchgear Factory Bldg,** Industrial
City of Abu Dhabi ................................................... 59-G3
**Abu Dhabi Taxi Stand,** Al Nahyan ............................... 9-C8
**Abu Dhabi Technical Garage Bldg,** Mussafah Industrial Area ... 55-G2
**Abu Dhabi Theatre Bldg,** Breakwater ........................... 7-G4
**Abu Dhabi Tourism Authority (ADTA),** Al Matar ............... 25-K8
**Abu Dhabi Traffic Control Centre Bldg,** Al Baladia .......... 5-D7
**Abu Dhabi Transmission & Dispatch Company (Transco) Bldg**
...Al Matar .......................................................... 25-G8
...Al Nahyan ......................................................... 9-H5
**Abu Dhabi University,** Capital District ........................ 56-C4
**Abu Dhabi Vegetable Oil Company Bldg,** Al Meena ............. 40-L5
**Abu Dhabi Villa & Majlis Bldg,** Al Muzoon ..................... 32-K2
**Abu Dhabi Waste Management Center,** Al Nahyan ............... 9-J7
**Abu Dhabi Water & Electrical Authority Bldg,**
...Al Dhafrah ........................................................ 9-D2
...Industrial City of Abu Dhabi .................................... 59-A3
...Substation Bldg, Madinat Khalifa B ............................. 53-E8
**Abu Dhabi Womens College,** Al Dhafrah ......................... 9-C5
**Abu Jafar Establishment,** Al Mushrif ........................... 18-J4
**Abu Mansor Plastic Factory Bldg,** Industrial City of Abu Dhabi ... 59-G3
**Abu Saeed Ali Khoory Supermarket,** Al Karamah ............... 13-C4
**Abu Saeed Trading Company (Honeywell),** Mussafah
Industrial Area ..................................................... 55-G7
**Abu Shakra Restaurant,** Markaziya West ....................... 4-E8
**Abu Tafish Restaurant,** Al Bateen ............................. 16-F4
**Abu Tariq Supermarket,** Al Karamah ............................ 13-A2
**Abudhabi National Carpet Bldg,** Industrial City of Abu Dhabi ... 59-A2
**Abunasr General Transport Company Bldg,** Mussafah
Industrial Area ..................................................... 55-C6
**Aces Arab Center for Engineering Studies Bldg,** Mussafah
Industrial Area ..................................................... 55-D8
**Aconex,** Hadabat Al Zaafaran ................................... 19-K8
**ADAC Engineering Office Bldg,** Abu Dhabi
International Airport ............................................... 51-B3
**Adams Medical Center,** Markaziya East ......................... 5-B5
**ADAT Gamco Bldg,** Abu Dhabi International Airport ........... 51-B8
**ADCB Bldg,** Tourist Club Area .................................. 5-D5
**ADCO Compound**
...Abu Dhabi For Onshore Oil Operations (ADCO) Bldg ............ 7-M7
...Al Khalidiya ...................................................... 7-M7
...Environment Conservation Centre Bldg ........................... 7-M8
...W8 ................................................................ 7-L8
**ADCOM Bldg,** Industrial City of Abu Dhabi ..................... 59-H3
**ADCP,** Markaziya East ........................................... 4-M5
**Adfert Bldg,** Mussafah Industrial Area ......................... 55-A8
**ADGAS Marine Operating Company,** Markaziya East ............. 4-K4
**ADIA Bldg,** Markaziya West ...................................... 4-D8
**ADIA Business & Logistics Park**
...Abu Dhabi International Airport .................................. 53-C1
...Al Ghazal Golf Club .............................................. 53-D3
**ADICOE,** Al Bateen .............................................. 11-M7
**ADMA & ADGAS Bldg,** Markaziya East ............................ 4-K3
**ADMA-OPCO Core Store Bldg,** Mussafah Industrial Area ....... 55-F1
**ADMAK General Contracting Company Bldg,** Mussafah
Industrial Area ..................................................... 55-B2
**Admiral Foodstuff,** Al Rowdah .................................. 12-H7
**ADMM Bldg,** Al Karamah .......................................... 13-A7
**ADNIC Bldg,** Markaziya East ..................................... 4-J4
**ADNOC**
...Al Baladia ........................................................ 5-C5
...Al Khubeirah ...................................................... 11-C5
...Al Meena .......................................................... 2-A3
...Khalidia Compound, Al Bateen .................................... 11-L2
...Lubes Western Bianoona Group Bldg, Mussafah Industrial Area ... 55-B6
...Markaziya East .................................................... 4-L2
...Sas Al Nakhl ...................................................... 30-C3
...Tank Bldg, Al Meena .............................................. 41-A8
...Technical Institute, Al Shamkha .................................. 57-K2
**ADOS Abu Dhabi Oil Field Service Bldg,** Mussafah
Industrial Area ..................................................... 55-B2
**ADOS Engineering Industries Bldg,** Mussafah Industrial Area ... 55-B6
**ADOS Klinger Gasket Factory Bldg,** Mussafah Industrial Area ... 55-E1
**ADSA Cargo Centre,** Tourist Club Area .......................... 5-F6
**ADSSC Bldg,** Hadabat Al Zaafaran ............................... 19-C4
**ADTA,** Al Matar ................................................... 25-K8
**Adu Dhabi International Private School,** Al Karamah ......... 12-K5
**Advanced American Dental Centre,** Al Bateen ................. 11-K4
**Advanced Pipes & Cast Company Bldg,** Mussafah
Industrial Area ..................................................... 55-B5

Advanced Travel Tourism, Markaziya West 8-E3
ADX Exchange, Markaziya East 4-K6
Afghanistan Embassy, Al Safarat 27-F1
Afghanistan Restaurant, Al Nahyan 13-J7
African & Eastern, Tourist Club Area 5-E2
Agis Al Ghurair Iron & Steel Bldg, Industrial City of Abu Dhabi 59-B4
Agriculture Research Laboratory Bldg, Al Manhal 8-E8
AGS School, Tourist Club Area 5-F5
Ahalia Exchange, Al, Markaziya East 4-H7
Ahalia Hospital, Al, Markaziya East 4-H7
Ahalya Medical Centre, Al, Al Dhafrah 9-C6
Ahamed Bin Hamza Spare Parts Bldg, Mussafah Industrial Area 55-G3
Ahamed Mubarak Salem General Transport Bldg, Mussafah
   Industrial Area 55-C6
Ahamed Taye Marble Establishment Bldg, Mussafah
   Industrial Area 55-D7
Ahasan Heavy Equipment Bldg, Mussafah Industrial Area 55-G3
Ahlan Supermarket, Mohammed Bin Zayed City 59-K3
Ahli Bank Bldg, Al, Al Nahyan 13-L8
Ahli Bank, Al, Al Nahyan 13-L8
Ahlia General Trading Bldg, Al, Mussafah Industrial Area 54-M4
Ahmadiah Labour Camp Bldg, Al, Mussafah Industrial Area 55-H7
Ain Acrylic Tubs Factory Bldg, Al, Industrial City of Abu Dhabi 59-F2
Ain Commercial Printing Press, Al, Al Nahyan 13-J8
Ain Dairy Bldg, Al, Mussafah Industrial Area 55-E6
Ain Insurance, Al, Al Nahyan 18-K4
Ain International Group, Al, Al Khubeirah 11-H3
Ain Palace Hotel, Al
   ...Ally Pally Corner 4-K2
   ...Markaziya East 4-K2
   ...Taste of Thailand 4-K2
   ...Zen 4-K2
Ain Steel Factory Bldg, Al, Industrial City of Abu Dhabi 59-F2
Ain Supermarket, Al, Markaziya West 4-E8
Ain University of Science & Technology, Al, Al Mushrif 24-A8
Ain Villas, Al, Al Nahyan 13-G8
Air India, Markaziya East 4-E7
Air Line Restaurant, Madinat Zayed 8-L4
Airlines Tower Bldg, Markaziya East 4-G7
Airport Park, Abu Dhabi International Airport 53-D3
Airport Services Company Bldg, Abu Dhabi
   International Airport 53-E2
Ajban School, Al Shahama 2 44-J7
Ajman Bank, Tourist Club Area 5-F4
Ajman Mineral Water Supply, Al Manhal 8-G4
Akai Bldg, Al Karamah 13-B3
Akai Showroom, Al Karamah 13-B3
Ala Kalifa Restaurant, Al Nahyan 13-A1
Alafaq Junior Model School, Al Karamah 12-L7
Alain Factory for Metal Casting & Electroplating Bldg,
   Mussafah Industrial Area 55-C3
Alam Steel Industrial Company Bldg, Mussafah Industrial Area 55-E6
Alam Supermarket
   ...Al Zahra 24-E5
   ...Markaziya East 4-J8
Ale Middle East Bldg, Mussafah Industrial Area 55-B2
Algeria Embassy, Al Safarat 27-J2
Ali & Sons (Porsche Car Showroom & Service Centre),
   Mussafah Industrial Area 55-H3
Ali & Sons Company, Al Khalidiya 8-A6
Ali & Sons Company Bldg
   ...Mussafah Industrial Area 55-E6
   ...Tourist Club Area 5-C3
Ali & Sons Motors, Al Khalidiya 7-L8
Ali & Sons Oilfield Suppliers & Service Bldg, Mussafah
   Industrial Area 55-B1
All Prints Book Shop Bldg, Markaziya West 8-D3
Allied Factory Outlet, Tourist Club Area 5-G7
Ally Pally Corner, (Al Ain Palace Hotel), Markaziya East 4-K2
ALP Emirates Panel Manufacturing Bldg, Mussafah
   Industrial Area 55-A6
Alpha General Transport Bldg, Mussafah Industrial Area 55-G3
Alqurm School, Mohammed Bin Zayed City 55-L2
Alumco Architecture Facade Specialist Bldg, Mussafah
   Industrial Area 55-H3
Amaali School, Al, Al Bateen 12-C6
Amadeus, Hadabat Al Zaafaran 19-B4
Amal Printing Industries Bldg, Al, Mussafah Industrial Area 55-D4
Amalfi, (Le Royal Méridien Abu Dhabi), Markaziya West 4-L3
Aman Supermarket, Al, Markaziya East 4-F8
Amana Contracting & Steel Bldg, Mussafah Industrial Area 55-B4
Amanath Financial Service, Al Khubeirah 11-H3
Amani, Tourist Club Area 5-G6
Ambulatory Health Care Centre, Bain Al Jessrain 35-D7
Ameen Boys School for Basic Education Cycle, Al, Al Karamah 12-K6
Ameen Medical Centre, Al, Madinat Zayed 4-L8
Ameen Rent A Car, Al, Al Manhal 12-B1
Ameerah Printing Press, Al, Mussafah Industrial Area 55-H2
Ameeri Tower Bldg, Al, Markaziya East 4-F7
American Centre for Psychiatry & Neurology, Al Manhal 12-D2
American Community School, Al Karamah 11-K4
American Crescent Health Care, Al Manhal 8-F4
American Engineering & Consulting, Al Mushrif 18-L8
American European Medical Centre, Al Nahyan 13-E6
American Gulf Medical Centre, Al Bateen 12-C5
American International School, The, Al Rehhan 24-E7
American Veterinary Clinic, Al Manhal 12-C4
Amin Transport Bldg, Al, Mussafah Industrial Area 55-E3
Amir Modern Workshop Bldg, Al, Mussafah Industrial Area 55-G2
Amiri Flight Bldg, Abu Dhabi International Airport 51-A6
AMIT International Link, Al Nahyan 9-E6
Amplex Emirates
   ...Al Khalidiya 12-L3
   ...Al Manhal 12-B2
Amritha Medical Centre, Markaziya West 8-B5
Amry General Transport Bldg, Al, Mussafah Industrial Area 55-D1
Amwaj Tower Bldg, Al Khalidiya 8-A8

Amwah Holding Bldg, Markaziya East 4-H6
Anabeeb Pipes Manufacturing Bldg, Mussafah Industrial Area 55-B1
Anarkali Plaza, Markaziya East 4-J8
Andaus Bookshop, Al, Al Manhal 8-L8
Angola Embassy, Al Mushrif 23-D5
Angsana Resort & Spa Eastern Mangroves Htl,
   Mangroves (Al Qurm) 20-H6
Animal Market Bldg, Al Meena 2-F4
Animal World, Al Nahyan 18-J3
Ansari Travels, Al, Tourist Club Area 5-B2
Ansoldo Thamassen Gulf Bldg, Mussafah Industrial Area 54-M3
Antonio, Markaziya West 8-D4
Apex Trading Bldg, Mussafah Industrial Area 55-F2
Appolo Medical Centre, Markaziya East 4-K7
Arab African International Bank, Markaziya West 8-C3
Arab Bank, Markaziya West 8-E2
Arab Bank Bldg, Markaziya West 8-E2
Arab Center, Sas Al Nakhl 30-A6
Arab Establishment for Manufacturing of Body Car Bldg,
   Mussafah Industrial Area 55-A8
Arab Market Bldg, Mussafah Industrial Area 55-E2
Arab Tower Rent A Car, Al Nahyan 13-H5
Arab Udupi Restaurant
   ...Markaziya East 5-A3
   ...Mohammed Bin Zayed City 59-K1
Arabia Press & Media Bldg, Al, Al Mushrif 22-G2
Arabia Taxi & Transportation, Bain Al Jessrain 29-M7
Arabian  House Restaurant, Al Karamah 13-D6
Arabian Construction Company Bldg, Mussafah Industrial Area 55-C4
Arabian Exchange, Markaziya East 4-G7
Arabian Foundations Bldg, Mussafah Industrial Area 55-E8
Arabian German Pump Bldg, Mussafah Industrial Area 58-M1
Arabian Home Health Care, Al Manhal 8-M8
Arabian House Refreshment, Al Khubeirah 11-J3
Arabian Industries Bldg, Mussafah Industrial Area 55-E2
Arabian Industries Company Bldg, Industrial City of Abu Dhabi 59-A4
Arabian Integrated Marine Services Bldg, Mussafah
   Industrial Area 55-C3
Arabian Oud Perfumes, Al Manhal 8-G4
Arabian Palace Restaurant, Markaziya West 8-C2
Arabian Printing Press, Markaziya East 4-G6
Arabic School, Al Dhafrah 9-E2
Aramex
   ...Al Nahyan 9-D8
   ...Mussafah Industrial Area 55-G2
Aramoun General Contracting, Al Nahyan 9-H7
Arcantia Furniture Bldg, Mussafah Industrial Area 55-B4
Area Boutique, Madinat Zayed 8-H2
Areej Dental Clinic, Madinat Khalifa A 52-C2
Areej Tower Bldg, Al Khalidiya 7-M8
Areen Tower Bldg, Al, Al Khalidiya 8-B7
Argentina Embassy, Al Karamah 12-M8
Arjwan Furniture, Markaziya East 4-J8
Arkanli Cars Rental, Mohammed Bin Zayed City 59-K2
Armani Cafe, Al Manhal 8-G5
Armed Force Passport Office Bldg, Al Nahyan 13-M4
Armed Forces Co-operative Society, Officers City 37-M1
Armed Forces Officers Club & Hotel, Officers Club 34-A7
Armenia Embassy, Al Safarat 27-F3
Artco Building Design Materials, Al Nahyan 9-G5
Arzanah
   ...Al Madina Al Riyadiya 28-A6
   ...Arzanah Medical Complex Bldg 28-C5
   ...Shk Zayed Stadium Bldg 28-C7
Arzanah Heights W57, Al Madina Al Riyadiya (Arzanah) 28-E7
Arzanah Medical Complex Bldg, Al Madina Al Riyadiya 28-C5
Arzanah Tower Bldg, Tourist Club Area 5-D4
Asaf General Transport Company Bldg, Al, Mussafah
   Industrial Area 55-C7
Asaian Heavy Equipment Bldg, Mussafah Industrial Area 55-G5
Asala Caffe, Al, Breakwater 7-F5
Asala Phones, Al, Al Nahyan 9-D7
ASAYEL (Shares & Bonds) Bldg, Al Bateen 12-A5
Asayel Basic School, Al, Madinat Khalifa A 52-D3
Asfar Engineering Equipments Trading Bldg, Mussafah
   Industrial Area 54-M6
Ashima Aluminium Factory Bldg, Al, Industrial
   City of Abu Dhabi 59-G2
Asia Travels, Al Mushrif 18-K5
Asian International School, Al Dhafrah 9-F4
Asmat Dental Medical Centre, Markaziya West 4-D8
Atif Engineering Bldg, Mussafah Industrial Area 55-F4
Atlanta Villas Bldg, Madinat Khalifa B 57-B3
ATLAS Aluminium Company Bldg, Mussafah Industrial Area 55-C3
Atlas Telecom, Hadabat Al Zaafaran 19-H6
Atmosphere Furnishing, Markaziya West 8-C5
Aurooba Plastic Factory Bldg, Al, Mussafah Industrial Area 54-L7
Aurora Group, Al Rowdah 17-L5
Australia Embassy, Al Manhal 8-G4
Australian School of Abu Dhabi, The, Madinat Khalifa B 57-B6
Auto Link Rent A Car, Al Nahyan 13-G6
Auto Star Trading, Al Nahyan 13-F7
Automatic Engineering Company Bldg, Mussafah
   Industrial Area 55-C6
Automatic System Corporation (ASCORP) Bldg, Mussafah
   Industrial Area 55-A8
Automech Machine & Tools Trading Bldg, Mussafah
   Industrial Area 55-C2
Automobile & Touring Club, Markaziya West 8-D3
AVA National Scaffolding Factory Bldg, Mussafah
   Industrial Area 55-E5
Awafi Trading, Al Karamah 13-C4
Awafi Water Warehouse, Mussafah Industrial Area 55-B2
Awtar, Tourist Club Area 5-F7
Axis Insurance Brokers, Al Manhal 12-B4
Aydra Trading (Vision Furniture 7 Decoration Factory) Bldg,
   Mussafah Industrial Area 59-A5

Ayisha Ummul Muhmineen School, Al Manhal 12-C4
Azher Used Auto Bldg, Al, Mussafah Industrial Area 55-G4
Azna Supermarket, Al, Al Nahyan 13-J8
Azzam Travels, Markaziya West 8-E3

## B

Bab Al Qasr Hotel, Al Bateen 10-M7
Baba Sweets Restaurant, Al, Tourist Club Area 5-E3
Baby City, Madinat Zayed 4-M6
Baby Shop, Madinat Zayed 8-J4
Badar Exchange, Al, Mohammed Bin Zayed City 59-K3
Baddad International, Al, Al Dhafrah 9-E5
Bader Exchange, Al
   ...Madinat Zayed 8-K2
   ...Mussafah Industrial Area 55-G3
Badie Travel Agency, Al, Markaziya West 8-D3
Badr Al Kobra Private School, Madinat Zayed 8-M1
Badsha Used Cars Bldg, Mussafah Industrial Area 55-G4
Baheya Hotel Apartment, Al, Al Baladia 5-C6
Bahia Park, Al, Al Bahia 48-G1
Bahia Private School, Al, Al Shahama 2 44-M5
Bahrain Air, Markaziya East 4-L6
Bahrain Embassy, Al Bateen 12-B8
Bahya Old, Al, Al Bahia 44-G4
Bahya, Al, Al Bahia 44-A4
Bain Al Jesrain Co-operative Society, Bain Al Jessrain 35-E4
Bainoona Power Company E14, Al Meena 2-D6
Bainunah Fountain, Al Bateen 11-F7
Bainunah Roundabout, Al, Al Khubeirah 11-F7
Baker Hughes Western Atlas International Bldg, Mussafah
   Industrial Area 54-L7
Bandar, Al
   ...Al Raha 50-J5
Bangladesh Embassy, Al Karamah 12-M8
Baniya Grand Supermarket & Hypermarket, Al Shawamekh 61-C3
Baniyas Car Establishment, Al Nahyan 18-J2
Baniyas Co-operative Society, Al Shahama 2 44-M2
Baniyas Mall (Bawabat Al Sharq Mall u/c) Bldg, Baniyas East 60-L5
Baniyas Police Station, Baniyas East 60-K5
Baniyas Sports & Cultural Club Bldg, Baniyas East 60-M7
Baniyas Tower Bldg, Al Baladia 5-C8
Bank Melli Iran, Markaziya East 4-K6
Bank of Baroda, Mussafah Industrial Area 55-G2
Bank of Oman, Markaziya East 4-M5
Bank of Sharjah, Tourist Club Area 5-B1
Bank Saderat Iran, Markaziya East 4-G8
Bar Bldg, Al Bateen 16-D1
Barbanel Middle East, Al Karamah 13-A6
Barclays Bank, Markaziya East 4-K5
Basma Studio, Al, Tourist Club Area 5-D5
Bateen Airport, Al
   ...Al Bateen Airport 25-D8
   ...Al Matar 25-D8
   ...Sheikh Zayed Bin Sultan Al Nahyan Terminal Bldg 28-D1
Bateen Family Medical Clinic, Al, Al Bateen 11-L6
Bateen Jetty, Al, Al Bateen 16-G4
Bateen Mall, Al, Al Bateen 12-B6
Bateen Municipality Centre Bldg, Al, Al Bateen 12-A6
Bateen Palace Bldg, Al, Al Rowdah 17-L3
Bateen Scientific Private School, Al, Al Bateen 16-L1
Bateen Towers, Al, Al Bateen
   ...Abu Dhabi Islamic Bank 11-J8
   ...Al Bateen Tower Bldg 11-J8
   ...Al Bateen Towers (6Towers) 16-K1
   ...Das Holding 16-J1
   ...First Gulf Finance Service 16-J1
   ...Green Emirates Properties 16-K1
   ...Reem Finance 16-J1
Bateen Villas, Al, Al Bateen 16-H4
Bateen Wharf Apartment, Al, Al Bateen 16-H1
Bawadi Model School, Al, Baniyas East 61-A5
Bay View, (Beach Rotana Hotel & Towers), Tourist Club Area 5-G4
Bayan Arabic News Paper Bldg, Al, Al Rowdah 12-H6
Baynounah Well Pipe Factory Bldg, Mussafah Industrial Area 54-M8
Beach Real Estate, Al Manhal 8-H4
Beach Rotana Hotel & Towers, Tourist Club Area
   ...Bay View 5-G4
   ...Benihana 5-G4
   ...Brauhaus 5-G4
   ...FINZ 5-G4
   ...Indigo 5-G4
   ...L.A.B. – Lounge At The Beach Bar 5-G4
   ...Prego's 5-G4
   ...Rodeo Grill 5-G4
   ...Rosebuds 5-G4
   ...Trader Vic's 5-G4
Beauty Palace Furniture, Al Nahyan 13-D4
Bees Kingdom Establishment, Markaziya West 8-D5
Beirut Automatic Bakery, Hadabat Al Zaafaran 23-H3
Beit Al Maqdes International Bldg, Mohammed Bin Zayed City 59-K3
Bel Ghailam Tower Bldg, Al Khalidiya 7-L8
Bel Mondo Cafe, Markaziya East 5-B3
Belgium Embassy, Markaziya East 4-K6
Benihana, (Beach Rotana Hotel & Towers), Tourist Club Area 5-G4
Beniyas Concrete Bldg, Mussafah Industrial Area 58-M1
Benkaram Tower Bldg, Markaziya East 5-A4
Berlin Auto Repair Workshop Bldg, Mussafah Industrial Area 55-G4
Berlin Villas Bldg, Madinat Khalifa B 57-D4
Berlitz Language Institute, Hadabat Al Zaafaran 23-D1
Besco Dental Clinic, Markaziya West 8-C3
Best Auto Repair Bldg, Mussafah Industrial Area 55-G2
Best Trailer Bldg, Mussafah Industrial Area 55-E2
BiCE, (Hilton Abu Dhabi), Al Khubeirah 11-D5
Bildco Cement Products Bldg, Mussafah Industrial Area 59-E1
Bildo Cement Product Bldg, Mussafah Industrial Area 55-E8
Bin Ajan Metal Industries Bldg, Industrial City of Abu Dhabi 59-F2

Bin Al Shaiba Workshop Bldg, Mussafah Industrial Area ... 55-G4
Bin Brook Motors & Equipment Bldg, Bain Al Jessrain ... 30-B8
Bin Ghaith Al Shamsi General Maintenance Establishment,
Al Zahra ... 23-L2
Bin Hafeez Establishment Bldg, Mussafah Industrial Area ... 55-H5
Bin Ham Oil Group Bldg, Mussafah Industrial Area ... 55-A7
Bin Hamoodah Chevrolet & GMC Opel Bldg, Mussafah
Industrial Area ... 54-M5
Bin Hamoodah Motors Bldg
...Al Khubeirah ... 11-J1
...Al Rehhan ... 24-J8
Bin Hasim Plastic Industries Bldg, Mussafah Industrial Area ... 54-M8
Bin Jessrain Park, Bain Al Jessrain ... 35-C3
Bin Mansour Plastic Factory Bldg, Mussafah Industrial Area ... 54-M8
Bin Mansour Printing Bldg, Mussafah Industrial Area ... 55-E4
Bin Masood Plastic Bldg, Mussafah Industrial Area ... 59-B1
Bin Mehran Ready Mix Concrete Bldg, Mussafah
Industrial Area ... 55-F8
Bin Moosa Group Furniture Factory Bldg, Mussafah
Industrial Area ... 54-M6
Bin Murshid Holding Bldg 2 Bldg, Markaziya West ... 8-C4
Bin Salama Tower Bldg, Markaziya West ... 4-E8
Bin Suroor Tower Bldg, Markaziya East ... 4-J5
Bin Talib General Contracting Bldg, Mussafah Industrial Area ... 55-G6
Binjuma Al Suwaidi Group, Al Khalidiya ... 7-L8
Birds Market Bldg, Al Meena ... 2-E4
Birkeh, Al, (Le Meridien Abu Dhabi), Tourist Club Area ... 5-F2
Bite Rite Cafe, Al Nahyan ... 13-E1
Bitu Trade Industrial Company Bldg, Mussafah Industrial Area ... 55-A6
BJ Sanitaryware Factory Bldg, Mussafah Industrial Area ... 54-M6
Black Cavaliero Readymade, Markaziya West ... 8-D6
Black Phantom, Al Bateen ... 12-C5
BLC Bank, Markaziya East ... 4-E6
Bliss House, Markaziya East ... 4-L3
Bloom Gardens, Al Matar ... 25-F5
Blue Line Stationery, Madinat Zayed ... 4-L8
Blue Marine, Markaziya East ... 4-M4
Blue Star Advertising Bldg, Mussafah Industrial Area ... 55-C1
Blue Tower Bldg, Al Dhafrah ... 9-A5
Blue White Car Glasses Bldg, Mussafah Industrial Area ... 55-G4
BMW, Bain Al Jessrain ... 29-L7
BNP Paribas Bldg, Al Bateen ... 11-M5
Boccaccio, (InterContinental Abu Dhabi), Al Bateen ... 11-D8
Bohra Islamic Cultural Complex Bldg, Mohammed Bin
Zayed City ... 55-L5
Boom Tracks, Mussafah Industrial Area ... 55-G3
Boracally Island Restaurant, Tourist Club Area ... 2-D8
Bord Eau, (Shangri-La Hotel, Qaryat Al Beri), Bain Al Jessrain ... 34-J4
BOSCH Services Bldg, Mussafah Industrial Area ... 55-D2
Boundary Wall of National Kharafi Bldg, Mussafah
Industrial Area ... 54-L8
Brass Light, Al Nahyan ... 13-F8
Brauhaus, (Beach Rotana Hotel & Towers), Tourist Club Area ... 5-G4
Bravo Tapas Bar (Sheraton Abu Dhabi Hotel & Resort),
Tourist Club Area ... 4-M1
Brazil Embassy, Madinat Zayed ... 8-M1
Bricco Cafe, Al Nahyan ... 13-B1
Bridge Stone Tyres, Al Dhafrah ... 9-E1
Bridgeway Abu Dhabi Apartment, Al Madina Al Riyadiya ... 28-E4
Bridgeway Garage & Equipment Bldg, Mussafah
Industrial Area ... 55-E3
Bright Beginnings Nursery
...Al Bateen ... 21-L1
...Al Mushrif ... 23-K7
Brightway Steel & Welding Bldg, Mussafah Industrial Area ... 55-F2
British Club Bldg, The, Al Meena ... 2-K2
British Council, Markaziya West ... 8-C4
British Dental Clinic, Markaziya East ... 5-A4
British International School, The, Capital District ... 56-C3
British School, Al Mushrif ... 18-H5
British Veterinary Centre, Al Manhal ... 12-B4
Brokerage House Securities, Al Bateen ... 12-B4
Brunei Embassy, Hadabat Al Zaafaran ... 23-G3
Brush Transformers Gulf Bldg, Industrial City of Abu Dhabi ... 59-G2
Building Materials City, Mohammed Bin Zayed City
...ME2 ... 55-K2
...Prestige Tower Bldg ... 55-K2
Building Metals International Bldg, Mussafah Industrial Area ... 54-M7
Buqubai Tower Bldg, Al, Markaziya West ... 8-E4
Burak Supermarket, Al, Al Karamah ... 13-E7
Burger Hut
...Bain Al Jessrain ... 35-K5
...Hadabat Al Zaafaran ... 19-D6
Burger King, Al Khalidiya ... 8-A8
Burhani Engineering Bldg, Mussafah Industrial Area ... 55-E2
Burooj Properties, Al Bateen ... 11-K8
Business & Technology Education Centre, Tourist Club Area ... 5-C3
Business Centre Bldg, Tourist Club Area ... 5-B2
Bustan Complex, Novotel, Al, Al Rehhan ... 24-D7
Bustan Gulf Bldg, Al, Mussafah Industrial Area ... 55-D2
Busy Bees Nursery, Madinat Zayed ... 9-A1
Butain Model School, Al, Al Bateen ... 11-M6
Butterfly Montessori Nursery, Al Bateen ... 12-E5
Bynuna Flower, Tourist Club Area ... 5-H6

**C**

C&J Engineering Bldg, Mussafah Industrial Area ... 55-H1
Cafe Bldg, Tourist Club Area ... 5-F2
Cafe du Roi Restaurant, Al Khalidiya ... 7-K8
Cafe Marina Al Yakhoot, Breakwater ... 7-C5
Calcium Advertising, Hadabat Al Zaafaran ... 19-B7
Calibers, Al Bateen ... 17-F2
California Teaching Center, Al Mushrif ... 26-H1
Cambridge High School, Mohammed Bin Zayed City ... 55-J7
Canada Embassy, Tourist Club Area ... 5-G4
Canadian French Consulate Bldg, Mussafah Industrial Area ... 55-G5

Canadian International School, Madinat Khalifa A ... 52-J2
Canadian Medical Centre, Al Karamah ... 13-D6
Cancer Centre, Al Bahia ... 48-G1
Canon, Markaziya East ... 4-L4
Cape Bldg, Mussafah Industrial Area ... 55-D1
Capital Centre, Al Safarat ... 27-F7
...Conference Centre Bldg ... 27-H8
...Mall Retail Centre Bldg ... 27-J7
Capital Garden, Markaziya East ... 4-J5
Capital Hills Building, Tourist Club Area ... 2-C7
Captain Cafe, Markaziya West ... 4-E7
Captain's Arms, (Le Meridien Abu Dhabi), Tourist Club Area ... 5-F2
Car Service Centre, Baniyas East ... 60-M8
Carewell Modern Medical Centre, Madinat Zayed ... 8-K3
Carpet Market Bldg, Al Meena ... 2-E2
Carpet Souk Bldg, Al Meena ... 2-E3
Carrefour
...Al Madina Al Riyadiya ... 28-C3
...Breakwater ... 7-A5
...Industrial City of Abu Dhabi ... 59-H2
Cars Rent A Car, Al Karamah ... 13-C5
Cars Taxi Bldg, Mussafah Industrial Area ... 55-D7
Casa D'Italia, Industrial City of Abu Dhabi ... 59-H3
Casa Goa, (Zakher Hotel), Markaziya East ... 4-L4
Casa Mobile Furniture, Al Nahyan ... 13-C4
Castle Gate Timber Works Bldg, Mussafah Industrial Area ... 55-D7
Castle Private School, Al Dhafrah ... 9-A6
Casttello Cafe & Restaurant, Al Meena ... 40-H6
Cement Factory Bldg, Mohammed Bin Zayed City ... 60-D7
Cemex Bldg, Mussafah Industrial Area ... 55-C3
Center for British Teachers for Education, Al Mushrif ... 23-H8
Center for Documentation & Research Bldg, Al Madina
Al Riyadiya ... 28-A4
Center for Herbal Medicine & Dermatology Clinics, Mahawi ... 60-L3
Center for Rehabilitation of Juvenile Bldg, Mahawi ... 60-L2
Central Bank of UAE, Al Bateen ... 11-H8
Central Business District, Capital District
...City Centre Precinct ... 52-D8
Central Hospital, Al Manhal ... 8-K8
Central Market
...Cassells Hotel Apartment ... 4-G8
...Markaziya East ... 4-F6
...Residential (The Domain) ... 4-G7
...Retail Emporium ... 4-G8
...Souk ... 4-F7
...Trust Tower Bldg ... 4-G8
Central Motors & Equipment Bldg, Mussafah Industrial Area ... 55-C2
Central Stores Section Monitoring & Collecting Section
Maintenance Section Bldg, Al Rehhan ... 23-L6
Central Tent, Tourist Club Area ... 5-E5
Centre Point Bldg, Breakwater ... 7-A4
Century Cinema, Tourist Club Area ... 5-G3
Century Hotel, Tourist Club Area ... 5-E6
Cert Technology Park, Al Nahyan ... 18-M1
Chab Industrial Company Bldg, Mussafah Industrial Area ... 55-B8
Chabros Bldg, Mussafah Industrial Area ... 55-D2
Chamas Brazilian Churrascaria Restaurant & Bar,
(InterContinental Abu Dhabi), Al Bateen ... 11-E7
Chamber of Commerce Bldg, Al Shahama 2 ... 44-J6
Chawarmino Restaurant, Hadabat Al Zaafaran ... 19-C6
Chemipaint Bldg, Industrial City of Abu Dhabi ... 59-G3
China Embassy, Al Mushrif ... 22-A1
China Petroleum Engineering & Construction Group of
Corporation, Al Mushrif ... 27-A1
China Petroleum Pipeline Bureau, Hadabat Al Zaafaran ... 23-E3
Chinese Palace Furniture Factory Bldg, Mussafah
Industrial Area ... 55-F5
Choise Restaurant, Al Dhafrah ... 8-L6
Choithram Supermarket
...Al Khalidiya ... 11-K1
...Al Manhal ... 8-C7
Chowking Restaurant, Markaziya East ... 4-L6
Christian Graveyard, Sas Al Nakhl ... 30-F4
CICON Bldg, Industrial City of Abu Dhabi ... 59-D2
Cicon Epoxy & Steel Cutting Plant Bldg, Mussafah
Industrial Area ... 58-M1
Cine Royal, Al Manhal ... 12-D1
Cinestar Cinema, Breakwater ... 7-B5
Cinnabar, (Hilton Abu Dhabi), Al Khubeirah ... 11-D5
Circuit Medical Centre Bldg, Yas Island ... 50-J2
Ciro's Pomodoro, (Al Diar Capital Hotel), Tourist Club Area ... 2-C7
Citroen Bldg, Mussafah Industrial Area ... 55-D1
Citroen French Automobile, Al Karamah ... 13-A2
City Burger, Al Manhal ... 8-B8
City Car Transport Bldg, Mussafah Industrial Area ... 55-F4
City Centre Shopping Mall, Markaziya East ... 4-K5
City Clinic, Al Dhafrah ... 8-M5
City Electrical Factory Bldg, Mussafah Industrial Area ... 55-E5
City Exchange, Mohammed Bin Zayed City ... 59-K1
City Gypsum Bldg, Mussafah Industrial Area ... 55-B7
City Police Station, Al Meena ... 2-E1
City Ready Mix Bldg, Mussafah Industrial Area ... 55-E8
City Restaurant
...Al Meena ... 40-K8
...Mussafah Industrial Area ... 55-D3
City Seasons Al Hamra Hotel Apartment, Al Baladia ... 5-A6
Civil Defense
...Abu Dhabi Office, Al Mushrif ... 26-K1
...Department Abu Dhabi Bldg, Al Nahyan ... 18-K4
Classic Printing, Al Manhal ... 8-H4
Clock Tower Bldg, Al Baladia ... 5-C8
Cloud Nine – Cigar & Bottle Club, (Sheraton Abu Dhabi
Hotel & Resort), Tourist Club Area ... 4-M1
Cloud Nine – Cigar & Bottle Club, Tourist Club Area ... 4-M1
Club Bldg, The, Al Meena ... 2-K1
CNIA Bldg, Al Matar ... 24-K4
Co-operative Society, Al Matar ... 24-J5

Coast Guard Department Bldg, Al Meena ... 40-G8
Coast Guard Tower Bldg, Al Meena ... 40-M6
Coconut Bay, (Hilton Abu Dhabi), Al Khubeirah ... 11-D5
Colliers International, Al Mushrif ... 17-M7
Colombiano Coffee House
...Al Matar ... 25-K8
...Markaziya West ... 4-D7
Color lines Wedding Cards, Markaziya West ... 8-D4
Colours Fashion, Tourist Club Area ... 5-D3
Comassat Bldg, Al Dhafrah ... 9-F4
Comma, Al Bateen ... 12-B4
Commercial Bank International, Al Khalidiya ... 7-K8
Commercial Bank of Dubai
...Al Manhal ... 8-B7
...Markaziya East ... 4-H4
...Mussafah Industrial Area ... 55-G3
Compressor Controls Corporation, Al Karamah ... 13-A5
Concept Outdoor Media & Advertising, Hadabat Al Zaafaran ... 23-H2
Concrete Walls Contracting Bldg, Mussafah Industrial Area ... 55-C7
Conference Centre Bldg, Al Safarat ... 27-H8
Continental Tyres, Tourist Club Area ... 5-C4
Control Contracting & Trading Company Bldg, Mussafah
Industrial Area ... 54-M4
Copen Hagen Villas Bldg, Madinat Khalifa B ... 57-C3
Corner Al Hawamir Seafood Restaurant, Al Nahyan ... 9-D7
Corner Stone Real Estate, Al Manhal ... 12-D3
Corniche Public Beach, Al Khalidiya ... 7-K6
Corniche Towers Residence, Al Dhafrah ... 9-B6
Corniche, The
...Markaziya East ... 4-G3
...Markaziya West ... 4-C8
...Tourist Club Area ... 1-M7
Corpo Fine SPA & Slimming Centre, Al Nahyan ... 13-C3
CosmeSurge & Emirates Hospital, Al Karamah ... 13-B7
Cosmo Plaster Inter Plaster Bldg, Industrial City of Abu Dhabi ... 59-E4
Cosmoplast Pipeline System Bldg, Mussafah Industrial Area ... 54-L7
Cosmopolitan Medical Centre, Markaziya East ... 4-L7
Cosmos ITL Group, Tourist Club Area ... 2-D7
Costa Cafe, Al Madina Al Riyadiya ... 28-C3
Costa Coffee, Al Dhafrah ... 9-B6
Couples Coffee, Mohammed Bin Zayed City ... 59-K1
Creation Arts, Al Rehhan ... 24-H6
Creative Kids Academy, Officers City ... 38-B2
Crescent Tower Bldg, Al Khalidiya ... 11-L1
Cristal City Lights, Al Dhafrah ... 9-B5
Cristal Hotel, Madinat Zayed ... 8-K1
Critical National Infrastructure Authority
...Al Mushrif ... 23-H6
...Al Matar ... 24-K4
...Al Safarat ... 27-J2
Crown Prince Court Bldg, Madinat Khalifa A ... 36-K5
Crowne Plaza & Staybridge Hotels, Yas Island ... 50-H2
Crowne Plaza Htl, Markaziya East ... 4-L6
Crystal Steel Company Bldg, Mussafah Industrial Area ... 55-E4
Cultural Foundation, Markaziya West
...Al Hosn Fort Bldg ... 8-E2
...Al Hosn Palace ... 8-E2
...Museum ... 8-E2
...W3 ... 8-F2
Cultural Private School, Mohammed Bin Zayed City ... 59-K1
Cure Advanced Diagnostic Centre, Al Bateen ... 12-C7
Current Electric Jupiter Aluminium Bldg, Mussafah
Industrial Area ... 55-B3
Cyber Zone Cafe, Al Mushrif ... 18-J4
Cyclone Electronics, Al Nahyan ... 9-E6
Czech Embassy, Markaziya East ... 4-M1

**D**

Dafra Restaurant, Al, Al Meena ... 2-A3
Dalma Mall, Industrial City of Abu Dhabi ... 59-H1
Dalma Motors TATA, Mussafah Industrial Area ... 55-H3
Damac Properties
...Al Manhal ... 8-B7
...Al Khalidiya ... 8-A6
Damam Foodstuff, Al, Al Mushrif ... 23-E7
Daman National Insurance, Madinat Zayed ... 8-H3
Damas Jewellery, Markaziya East ... 4-H8
Dana Plaza Bldg, Al Khalidiya ... 8-A7
Dana Private Kindergarten, Al, Madinat Zayed ... 9-A1
Dana Style Office Furniture, Al Nahyan ... 13-B3
Dana Tower Bldg, Al, Al Khalidiya ... 11-J1
Dana, Al
...Al Raha ... 50-E6
...ALDAR HQ Bldg ... 50-E6
Danet Abu Dhabi
...Al Rehhan ... 24-F7
...Burj Al Jewn Bldg ... 24-F7
...E40 ... 24-G7
...Holiday Inn Hotel & Resorts ... 24-H8
Danieli Construction Bldg, Mussafah Industrial Area ... 58-L4
Danik Restaurant & Bar, Tourist Club Area ... 5-G1
Danway Fusion Glass Bldg, Industrial City of Abu Dhabi ... 59-G2
Dar Al Ain Furniture Bldg, Al Meena ... 40-J8
Dar Al Shifa Hospital, Al Dhafrah ... 9-F5
Dar Al Shifa Medical Centre, Tourist Club Area ... 5-E3
Dar Doors Factory Bldg, Mussafah Industrial Area ... 55-F6
Dar Properties Bldg, Al, Al Meena ... 2-C4
Darbar Restaurant, Tourist Club Area ... 5-E4
Darwesh Welding Shop Bldg, Mussafah Industrial Area ... 55-G4
Darwish Benkaram Secondary School, Bain Al Jessrain ... 35-C5
Darwish Bin Ahamed & Sons Bldg, Mussafah Industrial Area ... 55-B1
Darwish Bin Ahamed & Sons Warehouse, Mussafah
Industrial Area ... 55-A2
Darwish Bin Ahmed & Sons, Sas Al Nakhl ... 30-A7
Das Aluminium Kitchens & False Ceiling Bldg, Mussafah
Industrial Area ... 55-E5

Das Textorium Bldg, Markaziya East 4-H8
Das Villas Bldg, Madinat Khalifa B 57-C4
Dawn Medical Centre, Markaziya East 4-J8
Deerfields Town Square, Al Bahia 44-H8
Defil Gulf Industries Bldg, Mussafah Industrial Area 54-M5
Delight Baby Shop, Baniyas East 60-K6
Delma Brokerage, Markaziya East 4-K6
Delma Co-operative Society
...Al Bateen 16-G4
...Al Meena 1-M2
Delma Industrial Supply & Marine Service Bldg, Al Bateen 16-G3
Delmon Furniture, Al Nahyan 13-F4
Delta for Heavy Equipment Bldg, Mussafah Industrial Area 55-F1
Deluxe Arabian Gents Tailor, Al Nahyan 9-C7
Deluxe Mobile Phones, Al Nahyan 9-D7
Dental Art Clinic, Al Khubeirah 11-H3
Dental Clinic & Child Clinic Centre, Al Dhafrah 8-L7
Dental Clinic, Al, Al Shahama 2 44-M2
Dental Design Clinic, Al Nahyan 18-K4
Department General Directorate Naturalization
 & Residency Bldg, Al Mushrif 26-L3
Department of
...Economic Development, Al Baladia 5-D8
...Municipal Affairs, Al Baladia 5-C7
...Presidents Affairs Abu Dhabi, Al Bateen 11-F8
...Private Affairs, Al Bateen 12-A4
...Private Security Business, Madinat Khalifa A 52-C2
...Social Service & Commercial Bldg, Markaziya West 8-C2
...Social Services & Commercial Bldg, Al Karamah 13-A1
...The Zayed Bin Sultan Al Nahyan Charitable & Humanitarian Foundation,
 Thabreeth, Al Madina Al Riyadiya 28-B5
...Transport Maritime Sector, Al Meena 40-K8
Deral Dhasi Cafe, Al Manhal 8-E6
Derma Beauty Laser Medical Clinic, Markaziya West 4-E8
Dhabi Tower Bldg, Markaziya East 4-K4
Dhabia Trading Establishment Bldg, Mussafah Industrial Area 55-C7
Dhabiania Model School, Al, Al Mushrif 23-A5
Dhabyania Private School, Al, Al Bateen 12-F6
Dhafir Technology Bldg, Mussafah Industrial Area 55-G6
Dhafra Compound, Al, Al Karamah 13-A5
Dhafra Insurance, Al, Al Baladia 5-B5
Dhafra Irrigation Systems, Al, Al Nahyan 9-G6
Dhafra Pipes Factory Bldg, Al, Industrial City of Abu Dhabi 59-E4
Dhafra Private School, Al, Al Zahra 24-C1
Dhafrah Dental, Al, Hadabat Al Zaafaran 23-G1
Dhaham Watches Gallery, Al, Markaziya West 8-E3
Dhaheri Rent A Car, Al, Al Nahyan 13-G8
Dhiyafa, Al Manhal 8-C7
DHL
...Al Karamah 13-B3
...Madinat Zayed 8-K5
Dhow Harbour
...Al Meena 1-G1
...Abu Ameer Furniture Bldg 40-J8
...Abu Dhabi Industrial Supplies Company Bldg 2-D1
...ADNOC Bldg 2-A3
...Al Dafra Restaurant 2-A3
...City Police Station 2-E1
...Coast Guard Department Bldg 40-G8
...Dar Al Ain Furniture Bldg 40-J8
...Delma Co-operative Society 1-M2
...Food Distribution Center Bldg 40-K8
...Free Zone Market (Iranian Market) Bldg 40-J8
...Jaber Khoory Bldg 40-J8
...Marina Police 40-G8
...Mina Fish Market Bldg 2-C1
...Mina Plaza Bldg 40-J8
...Morka Restaurant 2-B2
...Police Station 2-E1
...Saudi Kitchen 2-C2
Diamond Palace, Tourist Club Area 5-F5
Diar Capital Hotel, Al
...Ciro's Pomodoro 2-C7
...Rock Bottom Café 2-C7
...The Palm 2-C7
...Tourist Club Area 2-C7
Diar Dana Hotel, Al
...Tourist Club Area 5-E3
...49er's The Gold Rush 5-E3
Diar Mina Hotel, Al
...Tourist Club Area 5-A1
...Wasabi 5-A1
Diar Palm Hotel Apartment, Al, Al Dhafrah 9-A5
Diar Regency Hotel, Al, Tourist Club Area 5-A1
Diar Sands Hotel, Al, Madinat Zayed 4-M7
Dimension Data Middle East, Al Nahyan 9-G7
Dimensions Cement Factory Bldg, Industrial City of Abu Dhabi 59-E4
Dina Tower Bldg, Markaziya East 4-J4
Diplomatic Establishment Protection Bldg, Al Zahra 24-B2
Directorate General for Criminal Security, Al Maqtaa 33-J2
Dirham Plaza, Markaziya East 4-M5
Discount Emirates Market Bldg, Al Dhafrah 9-B7
Discovery Building Materials Bldg, Mussafah Industrial Area 55-E2
Diving Bldg, Al Bateen 16-H3
Diwan of Deputy Prime Minister Bldg, Al Karamah 18-C1
DNA Motor Engineering Works Bldg, Mussafah Industrial Area 55-D6
Dnata Travel, Markaziya East 5-B3
Dock Side Pool Bar, (Marina Al Bateen Resort), Al Bateen 16-H4
Doctors Centre Bldg, Mohammed Bin Zayed City 59-K2
Dollar Tower Bldg, Tourist Club Area 2-D7
Dolphin Oilfield Equipment Services Bldg, Mussafah
 Industrial Area 55-C3
Dome General Contracting Company Bldg, Mussafah
 Industrial Area 59-E1
Dominican Embassy, Al Bateen 11-H7
Dr Adna Merih Dental Clinic, Tourist Club Area 5-A1
Dr Ahmed Abu Sharia Medical Centre, Al Manhal 12-D2

Dr Moopen's Medical Centre, Mussafah Industrial Area 55-D6
Dr Moosa Abu Saeed Dental Clinic, Markaziya East 5-B2
Dr Nisar Younus Clinic, Markaziya West 4-E8
Dream Tech Computer, Al Nahyan 13-F4
Drivers & Vehicle License Department Bldg, Al Rehhan 23-L4
Driving School Bldg, Yas Island 47-K8
Drugs Enforcement Section Bldg, Bain Al Jessrain 29-H5
Dry Dock
...Al Bateen 16-H4
...Tourist Club Area 5-G2
Dry Mix Plant for M/s M&P Mortar & Plaster Dry Mix Bldg,
 Mussafah Industrial Area 59-A4
DT DCL Business Communication, Mussafah Industrial Area 55-H2
Du Office, Markaziya East 4-H8
Du Office Bldg, Markaziya East 4-G7
Du Tower Bldg, The, Madinat Zayed 8-H2
Dubai Bank
...Al Karamah 13-C5
...Markaziya East 4-F5
...Mussafah Industrial Area 55-H3
...Tourist Club Area 5-G3
Dubai Islamic Bank
...Al Khalidiya 7-L8
...Al Rehhan 24-H6
...Baniyas East 60-K6
...Mussafah Industrial Area 55-H3
...Tourist Club Area 5-D5
Ducab, Markaziya East 4-L7
Ducab Dubai Cable Company Bldg, Industrial
 City of Abu Dhabi 59-B3
DUCAP Bldg, Industrial City of Abu Dhabi 59-H5
DUISCO Camp Bldg, Mussafah Industrial Area 55-B5
Dunkin Donuts, Al Manhal 12-D1
Dusit Thani Htl, Al Nahyan 18-M1
Dutch Foundation Bldg, Mussafah Industrial Area 55-D7
Dutest Trading Establishment Bldg, Mussafah Industrial Area 55-A6
Dyna Trade Auto Services Bldg, Mussafah Industrial Area 55-E5

E

E4U Electronics, Al Nahyan 13-C3
Eagle Printing Press Bldg, Mussafah Industrial Area 55-D2
East Light Restaurant, Al Manhal 8-B8
Eastern Blue, Al Baladia 9-D1
Easy Metal Trading Bldg, Mussafah Industrial Area 55-F4
Easy Way Supermarket, Al Shahama 2 44-J8
Eclipse Boutique Suites, The, Markaziya East 4-G6
Educare Centre Villa Bldg, Markaziya West 8-B6
Eduscan Edutainment Home Birds of Hope Nursery,
 Madinat Zayed 9-A3
Eduscan Nursery, Markaziya West 8-C4
Egypt Embassy, Al Safarat 27-H2
Eid Prayer Ground
...Al Shahama 2 44-K5
...Mohammed Bin Zayed City 55-K4
Eidgah Ground Bldg, Al Karamah 13-E8
Eifel Tower Bldg, Al Nahyan 13-B2
Eiffel Supermarket, Markaziya East 4-M6
Eissa Engineering Bldg, Mussafah Industrial Area 55-F2
Ekhails Private School, Al, Al Dhafrah 9-A8
El Darawi Advertising, Al Manhal 8-D6
El Sombrero, (Sheraton Abu Dhabi Hotel & Resort),
Tourist Club Area 4-M1
Elastogran Kanoo Polyurethane System, Mussafah
 Industrial Area 55-H3
Eldiar Furniture Bldg, Mussafah Industrial Area 55-A2
Eldorado Cinema, Markaziya East 5-A5
Electra Abu Dhabi, Tourist Club Area 2-D8
Electra Park, Tourist Club Area 5-C2
Electro Mechanical Company Bldg, Mussafah Industrial Area 55-B2
Electronic & Engineering Industries Company Bldg,
 Industrial City of Abu Dhabi 59-G2
Electronic Stock Brokerage Company, Al Manhal 12-B4
Elenco Emirates Group Bldg, Tourist Club Area 5-C2
Elite Factory for Precast & Cement Product Holding Group,
 Al Bateen 12-B4
Elite Furnishing, Markaziya West 8-B5
Elite Modern Restaurant, Markaziya East 5-A2
Elite Motors, Al Dhafrah 9-A5
Elite Music Institute, Al Karamah 13-C8
Elite Optical, Al Manhal 8-C6
Elite Private School, The, Al Mushrif 22-M4
Elite Rent A Car, Al Nahyan 9-E6
Emarald Tower Bldg, Markaziya East 4-K3
Emarat Europe Bldg, Industrial City of Abu Dhabi 59-A3
EMC (Benz Showroom), Mussafah Industrial Area 55-G3
EMC Emirates Motors Company, Mussafah Industrial Area 55-D1
EMCC Bldg, Tourist Club Area 5-C3
Emco Car Exhibition, Al Nahyan 18-H2
Emco Rent A Car, Markaziya West 8-D3
EMIDCO Engineering Services Bldg, Mussafah Industrial Area 55-F6
Emirates Abu Dhabi Municipality & Agricultural
 Department Bldg, Mohammed Bin Zayed City 59-M1
Emirates Autism Center, Al Dhafrah 9-D3
Emirates Canadian Auto Works & Repair Bldg, Mussafah
 Industrial Area 55-G5
Emirates Centre for Strategic Studies & Research, The,
 Al Nahyan 13-L8
Emirates Children Kindergarten, Baniyas East 61-E7
Emirates College for Advance Education, Al Nahyan 13-K4
Emirates College of Technology, Markaziya East 4-J6
Emirates Colour Advertising Company Bldg, Mussafah
 Industrial Area 55-E6
Emirates Computers, Al Dhafrah 9-E1
Emirates Driving Company, Mussafah Industrial Area 55-H8
Emirates Electrical & Plastic Industries Bldg, Industrial
 City of Abu Dhabi 59-G3

Emirates Express Printing, Markaziya West 4-E7
Emirates Filament Bldg, Industrial City of Abu Dhabi 59-G3
Emirates Flights, Al Khalidiya 8-A5
Emirates for American & European Cars Bldg, Mussafah
 Industrial Area 55-H3
Emirates Furniture & Factory Decoration Bldg, Mussafah
 Industrial Area 58-M1
Emirates Future International Academy, Mohammed
 Bin Zayed City 59-K1
Emirates Gateway Security Services Bldg, Bain Al Jessrain 30-A8
Emirates General Market
...Al Shawamekh 57-D7
...Hadabat Al Zaafaran 23-J2
...Madinat Zayed 4-M7
...Markaziya East 4-K6
Emirates Heritage Club Bldg, Al Nahyan 13-D2
Emirates Hospital Supply, Tourist Club Area 5-C1
Emirates Hospitality Center, Al Mushrif 18-L7
Emirates Identity Authority
...Mussafah Industrial Area 55-B3
...Operations Center, Al Mushrif 26-M3
Emirates Industrial Laboratory Bldg, Mussafah Industrial Area 55-D2
Emirates Institute for Banking & Financial Studies Bldg,
 Al Nahyan 13-K7
Emirates Institute of Diplomacy, Al Bateen 16-F1
Emirates Insurance Company Bldg, Mussafah Industrial Area 55-H6
Emirates International Exchange, Mussafah Industrial Area 55-G3
Emirates International Motors Bldg, Bain Al Jessrain 30-A7
Emirates International Real Estate, Al Karamah 12-J7
Emirates Islamic Bank
...Al Karamah 13-F8
...Tourist Club Area 5-G5
Emirates Lighting Factory Bldg, Mussafah Industrial Area 55-D2
Emirates Lime Factory Bldg, Industrial City of Abu Dhabi 59-E4
Emirates Motor Company Bldg
...Al Madina Al Riyadiya 28-A2
...Breakwater 7-A6
...Mussafah Industrial Area 55-D4
Emirates National Sack Company Bldg, Mussafah
 Industrial Area 55-A2
Emirates National School, Mohammed Bin Zayed City 55-M5
Emirates National School for Girls, Al Nahyan 9-F6
Emirates National School K.G. & Primary, Al Nahyan 13-G1
Emirates NBD Bank
...Al Baladia 5-B7
...Al Khalidiya 7-M8
...Al Zahra 24-F5
...Markaziya East 4-G6
...Mussafah Industrial Area 55-E3
...Tourist Club Area 5-E3
Emirates Oasis Supermarket, Mussafah Industrial Area 55-D6
Emirate of Abu Dhabi Department of Judicially Director
 of Forensic Medicine, Hadabat Al Zaafaran 19-B5
Emirate of Abu Dhabi Finance & Customs Administration
 Department, Al Meena 40-K8
Emirates of Bldg
...Al Karamah 13-B8
...Al Madina Al Riyadiya 27-M5
...Al Maqtaa 28-K8
...Al Rowdah 17-H2
Emirates Palace Hotel, Al Ras Al Akhdar 10-L5
...Havana Club 10-L5
...Le Vendôme Brasserie 10-L5
...Mezzaluna 10-L5
...Sayad 10-L5
Emirates Plaza Hotel, Tourist Club Area 2-C8
Emirates Post
...Al Bateen 12-B6
...Al Khalidiya 11-L1
...Madinat Khalifa A 52-F1
...Madinat Zayed 8-L3
...Markaziya East 4-L3
Emirates Private School, Al Zahra 24-G1
Emirates Spanish Furnishing, Al Nahyan 13-F7
Emirates Steel Bldg, Mussafah Industrial Area 54-M7
Emirates Steel Factory, Industrial City of Abu Dhabi
...Emirates Steel Factory 58-M3
Emirates Steel Wool Manufacturing Establishment Bldg,
 Mussafah Industrial Area 55-B3
Emirates Technical & Safety Development Centre Bldg,
 Mussafah Industrial Area 55-G1
Emirates Technical & Thermal Systems Bldg, Mussafah
 Industrial Area 55-G6
Emirates Technical Service Bldg, Mussafah Industrial Area 55-G3
Emirates Tools Bldg, Mussafah Industrial Area 55-F2
Emirates Tower Bldg, Markaziya East 5-A3
Emirates Trading Agency Bldg, Mussafah Industrial Area 55-C4
Emirates Traffic Safety Society, Al Rowdah 17-F1
Emirates Transport Bldg
...Al Shahama 2 44-M1
...Mussafah Industrial Area 55-F3
Emirates Transport Mussafah Station 2 Bldg, Mussafah
 Industrial Area 55-B6
EMKE Bldg, Al Nahyan 13-H3
EMKE Group, Al Nahyan 9-D8
EMKE Stores Supermarket & Department Store,
 Madinat Zayed 8-L4
Emmar Properties Bldg, Al Dhafrah 9-A4
Emperor Arts, Tourist Club Area 2-C7
Emsons Bldg, Markaziya East 4-M6
Energy Capital, Officers City 38-K6
Energy Well Spend (Tabreed), Al Bateen 16-J1
Engineering Building Material Company Bldg, Mussafah
 Industrial Area 55-C6
Environmental Research Authority Bldg,
 Mangroves (Al Qurm) 29-F4
Envitech Middle East, Al Bateen 12-C5

**EPPT Bldg**, Industrial City of Abu Dhabi — 59-G4
**Eritrea Embassy**, Madinat Zayed — 4-M7
**Eros Digital Home**, Madinat Zayed — 8-M3
**Erricson Bldg**, Al Nahyan — 9-D7
**Escape Lounge**, (Hilton Abu Dhabi), Al Khubeirah — 11-D5
**ESNAAD MW5**, Mussafah Industrial Area — 58-K3
**Eswar Engineering Materials Trading Company**, Hadabat Al Zaafaran — 19-C6
**Etihad Airways**
...*Academy*, Madinat Khalifa A — 50-L6
...*Bldg*, Madinat Khalifa A — 35-J3
...*IT Dept Bldg*, Abu Dhabi International Airport — 51-B8
**Etihad Bldg**, Madinat Zayed — 8-M2
**Etihad Towers**, Al Bateen — 11-A7
**Etisalat Bldg**
...Al Baladia — 5-C6
...Al Bateen — 12-E6
...Al Dhafrah — 9-A6
...Al Manhal — 12-C3
...Al Nahyan — 13-H8
...Al Shahama 2 — 44-L4
...Al Shawamekh — 57-E6
...Baniyas East — 60-J6
...Markaziya East — 8-G1
...Mussafah Industrial Area — 55-D2
**Etisalat Store Bldg**, Mussafah Industrial Area — 55-D4
**Ettihad Square, Al**, Markaziya East — 4-E7
**Euro Hotel Apartment**, Al Dhafrah — 9-B6
**Euro Mechanical Contracting Company Factory Bldg**, Industrial City of Abu Dhabi — 59-G2
**Europcar**
...Industrial City of Abu Dhabi — 59-H3
...Markaziya East — 4-H5
**European International College**, Al Matar — 24-K1
**Eva Beauty SPA**, Al Nahyan — 13-H5
**Excellent Pipe Company Bldg**, Industrial City of Abu Dhabi — 59-F4
**Exeed Aswar Bldg**, Industrial City of Abu Dhabi — 59-D3
**Exeed Geotextiles Bldg**, Industrial City of Abu Dhabi — 59-G3
**Exotica Emirates**, Tourist Club Area — 5-F5
**Experts Drug Store**, Hadabat Al Zaafaran — 19-C6
**Eythar Kindergarten, Al**, Al Shawamekh — 57-E6
**Ezzat Heavy Duty Equipment Bldg**, Mussafah Industrial Area — 55-G4

**F**

**Fahra Bakery Bldg, Al**, Mussafah Industrial Area — 55-F2
**Fairmont Bab Al Bahr Htl**, Bain Al Jessrain — 29-J8
**Faiza Fjhani International Car Workshop Bldg**, Mussafah Industrial Area — 55-G2
**Fajer Securities, Al**, Al Bateen — 12-A6
**Fajer Supermarket, Al**, Al Mushrif — 26-F1
**Fajr Independence Political Arab Daily Bldg, Al**, Hadabat Al Zaafaran — 19-B6
**Fajr International School, Al**, Al Zahra — 20-B8
**Falah Exchange, Al**
...Markaziya East — 4-L5
...Mussafah Industrial Area — 55-H3
**Falah Ready Mix Bldg, Al**, Mussafah Industrial Area — 55-F8
**Falcon Motors Bldg**, Mussafah Industrial Area — 55-A2
**Falcon Securigate Bldg**, Industrial City of Abu Dhabi — 59-G2
**Family Development Foundation Bldg**
...Al Bateen — 11-L8
...Al Mushrif — 22-K1
**Family Park**, Markaziya West — 8-B3
**Fanar, Al**, (Le Royal Méridien Abu Dhabi), Markaziya East — 4-L3
**Faras Engineering Consultant**, Al Nahyan — 9-H6
**Fardan Bldg, Al**, Al Karamah — 13-B3
**Fardan Exchange, Al**
...Al Shahama 2 — 44-M2
...Markaziya East — 4-G7
**Faris Furniture**, Al Karamah — 13-E6
**Farmazan Furniture Design Bldg**, Mussafah Industrial Area — 54-M7
**Farooq International Stationery**, Markaziya East — 4-K7
**Farsan Blacksmith Welding Workshop Bldg, Al**, Mussafah Industrial Area — 55-G4
**Fast Rent A Car**
...Al Karamah — 13-C5
...Markaziya West — 4-D8
...Tourist Club Area — 5-E6
**Fast Service Centre**, Mussafah Industrial Area — 55-H2
**Fateh School for Basic Education, Al**, Al Shawamekh — 57-D7
**Fathima Supermarket**
...Al Dhafrah — 9-B4
...Al Karamah — 13-A2
...Al Nahyan — 13-E6
...Tourist Club Area — 5-E4
**Fathima Trading & Departmental Stores**, Al Manhal — 8-F5
**Fatima Bint Mubarak School**, Al Zahra — 24-G1
**Fatth Engineering Works Bldg, Al**, Mussafah Industrial Area — 55-F1
**Fawar Restaurant, Al**, Al Manhal — 8-B8
**Federal Environment Agency**, Madinat Zayed — 9-A3
**Federal Mosque District**, Capital District
...*City Centre Precinct* — 56-F4
**Federal National Council Bldg**, Al Khubeirah — 11-F4
**Federal Precinct**
...*Capital District* — 39-L7
...*National Square* — 56-E2
**Federal Switchgear Bldg**, Mussafah Industrial Area — 55-C5
**Federal Transformers Bldg**, Mussafah Industrial Area — 55-A5
**Fence International Bldg**, Mussafah Industrial Area — 55-B3
**Ferrari World Abu Dhabi Bldg**, Yas Island — 47-J7
**Fiber Flex Factory Bldg**, Mussafah Industrial Area — 54-L7
**Fibrex Industries Bldg**, Mussafah Industrial Area — 54-M8
**Figaro's Pizza**, (Marina Mall), Breakwater — 7-A6
**Fileh Inn**, Bain Al Jessrain — 35-D5
**Finance Department Bldg**, Markaziya West — 8-C5
**Finance House**, Markaziya West — 8-E4

**Finland Embassy**, Markaziya East — 4-K6
**FINZ**, (Beach Rotana Hotel & Towers), Tourist Club Area — 5-G4
**Fire Fighting & Safety Company Bldg**, Al Nahyan — 13-J7
**Fire Service**, Al Maqtaa — 28-K8
**First Choice Plastic Production**, Mussafah Industrial Area — 55-G3
**First Gate Blacksmith Bldg**, Mussafah Industrial Area — 55-G3
**First Gulf Bank**
...Al Khubeirah — 11-H4
...Markaziya East — 4-E6
...Markaziya West — 4-D8
...Mussafah Industrial Area — 55-H2
...Tourist Club Area — 5-D6
**First Rent A Car**, Tourist Club Area — 5-F6
**First Steps School**, Al Karamah — 12-M6
**First Touch Uniform**, Al Nahyan — 13-G5
**Firstchoice Fashion Bldg**, Industrial City of Abu Dhabi — 59-E4
**Fischer Emirates Bldg**, Mussafah Industrial Area — 55-E6
**Fish Market Restaurant**, Al Bateen — 16-D1
**Fishmarket**, (InterContinental Abu Dhabi), Al Bateen — 11-E7
**Flamingo Hotel Apartment**, Madinat Zayed — 8-L4
**Flavours**, (Sheraton Abu Dhabi Hotel & Resort), Tourist Club Area — 4-M1
**Folcra Beach Industries Company Bldg**, Mussafah Industrial Area — 54-M7
**Folk Heritage House**, Madinat Khalifa A — 50-J7
**Food City Restaurant**, Hadabat Al Zaafaran — 23-K2
**Food Distribution Center Bldg**, Al Meena — 40-K8
**Food Time Restaurant**, Mussafah Industrial Area — 55-E2
**Food United National & Agriculture**, Al Matar — 25-K8
**Foodlands Restaurant**, Madinat Zayed — 8-J4
**Football Cafe Shop**, Al Karamah — 13-A2
**Foresight Cement Industries Bldg**, Industrial City of Abu Dhabi — 59-D3
**Formal Park**, Markaziya East — 4-G3
**Formetco Middle East Bldg**, Mussafah Industrial Area — 58-M1
**Formula 1 (F1)**, Markaziya West — 8-E5
**Fortress Bldg**, Hadabat Al Zaafaran — 19-F6
**Fortune Hotel Apartment**, Tourist Club Area — 5-E4
**Fotouh Al Khair Bldg**, Markaziya East — 8-G1
**Four Directions International Trading**, Hadabat Al Zaafaran — 23-J4
**France Embassy**, Al Karamah — 17-L1
**Free Zone Market (Iranian Market) Bldg**, Al Meena — 40-J8
**Free Zone Store**, Al Meena — 40-J8
**Free Zone Store**, Al Meena (Dhow Harbour)
...*Abu Dhabi Co-operative Society* — 40-J8
...*Abu Dhabi Co-operative Society Warehouse* — 1-K1
...*Abu Dhabi Maritime & Mercantile International (ADMMI) Bldg* — 40-H7
...*Abu Dhabi National Foodstuff Company Bldg* — 40-J8
...*Abu Dhabi National Hotel Warehouse* — 40-H8
...*Abu Dhabi Tyre Company Bldg* — 40-H6
...*ADCECO Group Bldg* — 40-H7
...*Al Ahlia Gulf line General Trading Bldg* — 40-J6
...*Al Dhafra Tourist Village (Hareb)* — 40-J7
...*Al Fada Trading Bldg* — 40-J6
...*Al Futtaim Auto Mall* — 40-J8
...*Al Meena (Port Zayed)* — 40-K7
...*Al RDEM Building Materials Bldg* — 1-K1
...*Alpha Data Bldg* — 40-J6
...*Baniyas Co-operative Society Warehouse* — 1-L1
...*Barwil Abu Dhabi Ruwais Bldg* — 40-J7
...*Bin Sagar Group Bldg* — 40-J7
...*Bin Sror Trading Bldg* — 1-L1
...*Control & Applications Emirates & John Brown Offshore Bldg* — 1-K1
...*Crown Relocation Bldg* — 40-J6
...*Dhow Harbour* — 40-J7
...*Electrical Lighting Company Warehouse* — 40-H8
...*Emirates Specialties Company Bldg* — 1-L1
...*Emirates Trade Centre Bldg* — 40-J8
...*EMKE Group Warehouse* — 40-J8
...*Euro Mechanical Warehouse* — 40-H8
...*Force 10 Engineering Warehouse* — 40-H6
...*Freezone* — 40-K7
...*GAC Bldg* — 40-H7
...*Games Action Zone* — 40-J8
...*Giffin Graphics Bldg* — 40-H7
...*Grand Store Bldg* — 40-J7
...*Gulf Paints Warehouse* — 40-H8
...*Jashanmal National Company Bldg* — 40-J6
...*Khalidia Co-operative Society Warehouse* — 40-J6
...*KM Trading Warehouse* — 40-H8
...*Lebanese Fruit Warehouse* — 40-H8
...*Masafi Bldg* — 1-M1
...*Mina Centre Bldg* — 40-J8
...*Modern Bakery Bldg* — 40-H8
...*Pan Emirates Foods Distribution Bldg* — 40-J7
...*Popeyes Chicken & Seafood Warehouse* — 40-J6
...*Port Zayed* — 40-H7
...*Pro-Tect Middle East Bldg* — 1-K1
...*Sheikh Khalifa Medical City Warehouse* — 40-H8
...*Spinneys Warehouse* — 40-J7
...*Speed Line Bldg* — 40-J6
...*Toys R Us Bldg* — 40-J8
...*United Book Store* — 40-J8
**French School (Lycee Louis Massignon)**, Al Rehhan — 24-E7
**Fuala Home Needs**, Al Bateen — 11-K7
**Fuala Restaurant**, Al Nahyan — 13-E1
**Futtaim Electronics, Al**, Markaziya West — 4-D8
**Futtaim Engineering Bldg, Al**, Tourist Club Area — 5-D4
**Futtaim Motors, Al**
...Al Madina Al Riyadiya — 27-M2
...Al Nahyan — 18-G1
...Mussafah Industrial Area — 55-B2
**Future Cafe**, Tourist Club Area — 5-G6
**Future Centre for Special Needs**, Al Bateen — 12-A8
**Future Medical Centre**, Hadabat Al Zaafaran — 19-D7
**Future Model School**, Al Nahyan — 13-F6
**Future Nursery School**, Al Karamah — 13-A2
**Future Pipe Industries Bldg**, Industrial City of Abu Dhabi — 59-C4

**Future Printing Press Bldg**, Hadabat Al Zaafaran — 19-B5
**Future Tower 1 Bldg**, Al Dhafrah — 9-A5
**Future Youth Internet Cafe & Billiard Hall**, Mohammed Bin Zayed City — 59-L3

**G**

**G Club**, (Le Meridien Abu Dhabi), Tourist Club Area — 5-F2
**GAC Marine Equipment Construction & Maintenance Bldg**, Industrial City of Abu Dhabi — 59-B4
**Gafoorka's Family Thattukada Restaurant**, Mohammed Bin Zayed City — 59-K2
**Gaidha General Market, Al**, Al Mushrif — 18-J3
**Galadari Automobiles Company Bldg**, Mussafah Industrial Area — 55-B2
**Galadari Trucks Equipment Bldg**, Mussafah Industrial Area — 55-D1
**Galadhari Automobiles**, Al Baladia — 5-A6
**Galaxy Carpets**, Al Karamah — 13-B4
**Galaxy Electrical Factory Bldg**, Mussafah Industrial Area — 55-B3
**Galaxy Electronic Trading Company**, Markaziya West — 8-D3
**Galaxy Tower Bldg**, Markaziya East — 4-J4
**Galfar Engineering Construction Company Bldg**, Mussafah Industrial Area — 54-L6
**Gallery Art Trading**, Al Manhal — 8-E5
**Gallery Bldg, The**, Tourist Club Area — 2-A8
**Galva Coat Industries Bldg**, Mussafah Industrial Area — 54-M7
**Ganadah Tower Bldg, Al**, Al Khalidiya — 8-B7
**Gantoot Group Bldg**, Markaziya East — 4-H8
**Garden City Tower Bldg**, Al Khalidiya — 8-A7
**Garden Tower Bldg**, Markaziya East — 4-K4
**Garden View Hotel Apartment**, Markaziya East — 4-J5
**Gardenia Internet**, Al Manhal — 8-E5
**Gardens Landscape**, Al Dhafrah — 9-H3
**GASCO**, Markaziya East — 4-L2
**Gate Real Estate, The**, Al Manhal — 8-F5
**Gava Forwarding**, Al Karamah — 12-M3
**Gava Hotel**, Al Dhafrah — 9-F5
**Gemini Trading**, Al Dhafrah — 9-H3
**Gems American Academy**, Al Dhafrah — 9-E3
**Gems International School**, Madinat Khalifa A — 52-C1
**General Authority for Civil Aviation Bldg**, Madinat Khalifa A — 50-K6
**General Authority for Health Service for The Emirate of Abu Dhabi Bldg**, Al Karamah — 12-K5
**General Directorate of Traffic Coordination Police Judicial Council**, Al Zahra — 24-D2
**General Information Authority**, Markaziya East — 4-G5
**General Petroleum Services Bldg**, Mussafah Industrial Area — 54-M1
**Genovac & Isuzu Bldg**, Mussafah Industrial Area — 55-A2
**German Gulf Enterprises Bldg**, Mussafah Industrial Area — 55-F1
**German Home**, Al Baladia — 5-C6
**German Rent A Car**, Al Karamah — 13-A7
**German School**, Al Bateen — 17-F4
**Germanischer Lloyd**, Hadabat Al Zaafaran — 19-F3
**Germany Embassy**, Tourist Club Area — 5-G3
**Germen International School**, Al Manhal — 12-H2
**GFC**, Madinat Zayed — 8-L5
**Ghadheer Specialized Medical Centre, Al**, Al Nahyan — 13-F4
**Ghaf Park, Al**, Hadabat Al Zaafaran — 23-F3
**Ghafly Group of Companies Bldg, Al**, Mussafah Industrial Area — 55-B8
**Ghafly Ready Mix Bldg, Al**, Mussafah Industrial Area — 55-F8
**Ghaith Oilfield Supplies & Services Company Bldg, Al**, Mussafah Industrial Area — 55-C2
**Ghaith Tower Bldg, Al**, Markaziya East — 4-K6
**Ghanthoot Mussafah Camp Bldg**, Mussafah Industrial Area — 55-H4
**Ghantoot Flowers**, Al Manhal — 8-D6
**Ghawas, Al**, Madinat Zayed — 8-L5
**Ghazal Golf Club, Al**, Abu Dhabi International Airport — 53-D3
**Ghazal Model School, Al**, Al Bateen — 11-K7
**Ghazal Rent A Car, Al**, Markaziya West — 8-D2
**Ghazal Service Station Bldg, Al**, Mussafah Industrial Area — 55-G2
**Ghazal Specialized Medical Centre, Al**, Markaziya East — 8-J1
**Ghazal Transport, Al**, Al Madina Al Riyadiya — 27-M4
**Ghazal Travels, Al**, Tourist Club Area — 5-E4
**Ghubairah Palace Attorney General Office Bldg, Al**, Al Khubeirah — 11-G5
**Ghuzlan Emirates Furniture & Decor Bldg**, Industrial City of Abu Dhabi — 59-E2
**Giant Billiards Nursery**, Tourist Club Area — 5-D1
**Giffin Traffiks Metal Fab Division Bldg**, Mussafah Industrial Area — 54-M8
**Giggles English Nursery**
...Al Dhafrah — 8-M7
...Al Meena — 2-C6
**Giralda Emirates Bldg**, Mussafah Industrial Area — 59-F1
**Girls School (Arabic)**, Al Bahia — 44-G8
**Global Logistic Solution Bldg**, Mussafah Industrial Area — 55-C7
**Global Marine Services Bldg**, Mussafah Industrial Area — 54-L2
**Global Office Tower Bldg**, Al Baladia — 5-A6
**Gold Centre Bldg**, Madinat Zayed — 8-L2
**Gold Garden Flowers**, Markaziya East — 4-M3
**Golden Calligraphy & Printing Bldg**, Mussafah Industrial Area — 55-F3
**Golden City Supermarket**, Mussafah Industrial Area — 55-F5
**Golden Falcon Tower Bldg**, Markaziya East — 4-G8
**Golden Fork**, Markaziya East — 4-H5
**Golden Fork Bakery Bldg**, Mussafah Industrial Area — 55-C3
**Golden Fork New Bldg**, Markaziya West — 8-C6
**Golden Goal Undertaking & Services**, Al Nahyan — 9-J6
**Golden Holidays Travels**, Markaziya West — 8-E2
**Golden Medical Service**, Bain Al Jessrain — 35-K5
**Golden Motors**, Al Nahyan — 9-D7
**Golden Spike & Wheat Establishment**, Mussafah Industrial Area — 55-G1
**Golden Spike Supermarket**, Mussafah Industrial Area — 55-D1
**Golden Stone Aluminium & Glass Bldg**, Mussafah Industrial Area — 54-M3
**Golden Ticket Travels**, Al Dhafrah — 9-D3
**Golden Tools Bldg**, Mussafah Industrial Area — 55-F2

Golden Tower Rent A Car, Al Nahyan — 13-F2
Golden Tulip Dalma Suites, Markaziya East — 4-H8
Golf Gardens Residential Community, Madinat Khalifa A — 31-E5
Government & Diplomatic Production Department Bldg,
 Al Rehhan — 23-M6
Government Departments Sports Association Bldg,
 Al Karamah — 13-C7
Government of Abu Dhabi Municipality Sewerage Projects
Committee Bldg, Mussafah Industrial Area — 55-H5
Government Office Bldg, Al Mushrif — 23-E6
GPCC Bldg, Industrial City of Abu Dhabi — 59-E2
Grace Medical Centre, Al Karamah — 12-J6
Granada Fibre Glass Factory Bldg, Mussafah Industrial Area — 54-L7
Grand Al Mariah Cinema, Markaziya East — 4-L4
Grand Cinema, Mohammed Bin Zayed City — 55-J8
Grand Continental Flamingo Hotel, Markaziya East — 4-L5
Grand Millenium Htl, The, Al Nahyan — 9-C8
Grand Millennium Corniche Hotel, Markaziya West — 8-B6
Grand Mills Bldg, Al Meena — 40-L5
Grand Store, Markaziya West — 8-F4
Grand Supermarket, Al Khalidiya — 11-L1
Grand Umm Al Zamoul Construction & Factory for
 Polystyrene Bldg, Mussafah Industrial Area — 59-A1
Granite Foodstuff Trading Bldg, Al Safarat — 27-H4
Granite Supermarket, Al Nahyan — 9-E7
Gray Mackenzie & Partners (GMP), Al Baladia — 9-C1
Greece Embassy, Al Matar — 24-L2
Green House Supermarket, Al Dhafrah — 8-M7
Green Land Trading Company Bldg, Mussafah Industrial Area — 58-M1
Green Oasis Company, Tourist Club Area — 5-F5
Green Rent A Car, Markaziya West — 8-C5
Group 4 Securicor (G4S), Al Matar — 25-B2
Group 4 Securicor Bldg, Mussafah Industrial Area — 55-E5
Guggenheim Abu Dhabi Museum, Saadiyat Island — 41-A4
Gulf & Safa Dairies Bldg, Sas Al Nakhl — 29-L5
Gulf Air Building, Madinat Zayed — 8-J4
Gulf Autism Centre, Al Manhal — 12-C3
Gulf Center Group Cleaning Equipment Bldg, Mussafah
 Industrial Area — 55-D8
Gulf Chinese Medical Centre & Ansari Medical Centre,
 Markaziya West — 8-F1
Gulf City Real Estate, Markaziya West — 8-C6
Gulf Coast Bldg, Al Mushrif — 23-A2
Gulf Commercial Group Bldg, Tourist Club Area — 5-F7
Gulf Drug Establishment, Al Manhal — 8-G5
Gulf Dunes Bldg, Madinat Khalifa A — 52-F1
Gulf Filter Factory Bldg, Mussafah Industrial Area — 54-M2
Gulf Galvanizing Factory Bldg, Industrial City of Abu Dhabi — 59-C4
Gulf Horizon My Little Angel, Al Bateen — 12-A3
Gulf Industrial Gases Company Bldg, Mussafah Industrial Area — 54-M6
Gulf Industries & Metal Profile Bldg, Industrial
 City of Abu Dhabi — 59-F2
Gulf Industries Bldg, Mussafah Industrial Area — 54-M3
Gulf Inspection International Company Bldg, Mussafah
 Industrial Area — 55-A1
Gulf KN Aluminium & Glass Bldg, Mussafah Industrial Area — 55-G6
Gulf Manufacturing Company Bldg, Mussafah Industrial Area — 54-M8
Gulf Marine Services Bldg, Mussafah Industrial Area — 55-H1
Gulf Navigation Holding, Markaziya East — 4-L7
Gulf Palace Property Bldg, Al Nahyan — 13-H5
Gulf Palace Restaurant, Markaziya East — 4-K7
Gulf Palace Trading Establishment, Al Nahyan — 13-F5
Gulf Pearl Dental Clinic, Markaziya West — 8-D3
Gulf Piping Company, Mussafah Industrial Area — 54-M3
Gulf Piping Company Bldg, Mussafah Industrial Area — 54-L5
Gulf Polymark Bldg, Mussafah Industrial Area — 54-M7
Gulf Radiology & Laboratories, Markaziya East — 4-K8
Gulf Readymade Garment Manufacturing Bldg, Mussafah
 Industrial Area — 54-M8
Gulf Ready Mix Bldg, Mussafah Industrial Area — 55-E8
Gulf Sea Electrical & Automobile Bldg, Mussafah
 Industrial Area — 55-G1
Gulf Sky Rent A Car, Al Nahyan — 13-H5
Gulf Star Coffee Shop, Al Manhal — 8-G4
Gulf Star Cooling Work Bldg, Mussafah Industrial Area — 54-M2
Gulf Steel Factory Bldg, Mussafah Industrial Area — 54-L6
Gulf Travel Training Center, Al Bateen — 12-A8
Gulf Way Rent A Car, Tourist Club Area — 5-D2
Gulfab Decor Bldg, Mussafah Industrial Area — 55-F2
Gulistan Steel Works Bldg, Mussafah Industrial Area — 55-G4

H

Habara House Hotel Apartment, Al Nahyan — 13-C3
Habib Bank, Markaziya East — 4-E6
Habib Bank AG Zurich, Al Dhafrah — 8-M5
Habib Exchange, Markaziya East — 4-H7
Hadaf Marble Cutting Bldg, Al, Mussafah Industrial Area — 55-B6
Hadbat Al Zaafran Mosque, Al Zahra — 23-L3
Hafilat Industries Bldg, Industrial City of Abu Dhabi — 59-D3
Hafsa Bint Omar for Basic Education Circle-2, Mohammed
 Bin Zayed City — 59-K2
Hafzco Trading Bldg, Mussafah Industrial Area — 55-F5
Haji Ahmed Supermarket, Al Mushrif — 24-B8
Hamdan Centre Bldg, Markaziya East — 4-J7
Hamed Centre Bldg, Madinat Zayed — 8-J1
Hamid Group Bldg, Al, Mussafah Industrial Area — 55-H4
Hamliworks Bldg, Al, Mussafah Industrial Area — 55-C1
Hamly International Bldg, Mussafah Industrial Area — 55-B5
Hamood General Transport Bldg, Al, Mussafah Industrial Area — 55-E4
Hamoodah Bin Ali Model School, Al Mushrif — 22-M6
Hamra Group Bldg, Al, Mussafah Industrial Area — 55-B3
Hamra Plaza Residence Bldg, Al, Al Baladia — 5-A6
Hana Shopping Centre Bldg, Al, Al Khalidiya — 7-K8
Hana Supermarket, Al, Al Karamah — 13-C7
Hanayen Company Middle East, Al Karamah — 13-A6
Hanin Restaurant, Al Bateen — 12-D4

Hanover International Trading, Mussafah Industrial Area — 55-H2
Hanyouna Tower Bldg, Al, Al Khalidiya — 7-M8
Hapco Geaco Company Bldg, Mussafah Industrial Area — 55-F6
Happy Chocolates, Al Manhal — 8-D7
Happy Days Garments, Al Karamah — 13-E6
Hard Rock Internet, Tourist Club Area — 5-D2
Harib Sultan Bldg, Madinat Zayed — 8-H2
Harley Davidson Motorcycle, Al Dhafrah — 5-F8
Haroline Car Service Bldg, Mussafah Industrial Area — 55-G1
Hashem Arts, Mussafah Industrial Area — 55-F2
Hashim Contracting General Maintenance Bldg, Mussafah
 Industrial Area — 55-B7
Hathboor Electrical Bldg, Al, Mussafah Industrial Area — 55-F1
Havana Caffe, Breakwater — 7-C6
Havana Club, (Emirates Palace), Al Ras Al Akhdar — 10-L5
Haven Fire & Safety Bldg, Mussafah Industrial Area — 55-D3
Hawai Office Furniture & Equipment, Al, Al Karamah — 13-F8
Haward Finley Khaleej Bldg, Mussafah Industrial Area — 58-L1
Haward Technology Middle East, Hadabat Al Zaafaran — 23-F4
Hayatt Real Estate, Hadabat Al Zaafaran — 23-F2
Hazza Bin Zayed Mosque, Tourist Club Area — 5-C2
Health Care International Centre Clinic, Markaziya East — 5-B3
Health Club Bldg, Al Bateen — 16-H3
Health Quest Medical Centre, Al Karamah — 13-D6
Heel Tower Bldg, Al, Al Manhal — 8-D7
Heidel Berg Abu Dhabi Branch, Al Nahyan — 13-H6
Helen Beauty Centre, Al Nahyan — 18-J3
Hemingway's, (Hilton Abu Dhabi), Al Khubeirah — 11-D5
Heris Bader Mohamed Saeed Al Muraiki Bldg, Al Nahyan — 13-C3
Heritage Club Bldg, Al Bateen — 16-K2
Heritage Park, Al Meena — 2-A5
Heritage Village
...Al Asala Restaurant — 7-F6
...Breakwater — 7-F5
Hertz Car Rental Bldg, Mussafah Industrial Area — 55-F5
Hertz Rent A Car, Al Baladia — 9-D2
HH Garage Private Department Bldg, Al Safarat — 27-K3
Hidaya Kindergarten Nursery, Al, Al Nahyan — 13-D3
High Class International Training, Al Manhal — 12-B1
Higher College of Technology
...Al Khalidiya — 11-K1
...Madinat Khalifa A — 52-H2
Higher Corporation for Specialized Economic Zone,
 Industrial City of Abu Dhabi — 59-D6
Hilal Auto, Al, Al Khubeirah — 11-H2
Hilal Bank, Al
...Al Khubeirah — 11-H2
...Al Matar — 25-J7
...Markaziya East — 4-H5
Hills Abu Dhabi (u/c)
...Officers Club — 33-K5
...W51 — 33-K6
Hilton Abu Dhabi Htl
...Al Khubeirah — 11-D5
...BiCE — 11-D5
...Cinnabar — 11-D5
...Coconut Bay — 11-D5
...Escape Lounge — 11-D5
...Hemingway's — 11-D5
...La Terrazza — 11-D5
...Mawal — 11-D5
...Royal Orchid — 11-D5
...The Jazz Bar & Dining — 11-D5
...Vasco's — 11-D5
Hilton Baynunah Htl, Markaziya West — 8-C2
Hilton Corniche Hotel Apartment, Markaziya East — 4-J4
Hiltonia Beach Club Bldg, Al Khubeirah — 11-C4
Himd Engineering Bldg, Mussafah Industrial Area — 55-G4
Hitachi Power Tools Bldg, Mussafah Industrial Area — 55-E3
HMC Dental Clinic, Markaziya East — 4-M4
Hoi An, (Shangri-La Hotel, Qaryat Al Beri), Bain Al Jessrain — 34-J4
Holiday General Transport, Al Nahyan — 18-J3
Holidays Tourism, Markaziya East — 4-J6
Homeopathic Medical Centre, Markaziya East — 4-K7
Honda & Suzuki Bike Service Centre Bldg, Mussafah
 Industrial Area — 55-E1
Horizon Private School, Madinat Khalifa A — 52-H2
Horse Stables Bldg, As Sammaliyyah Island — 46-D8
Hosn Medical Centre, Al, Markaziya West — 8-D3
Hosn University, Al, Al Karamah — 13-C6
Hot Plate Grills Hotel, Mohammed Bin Zayed City — 59-K1
Hotel Apartment, Tourist Club Area — 5-A1
Hoty Stanger Bldg, Al, Mussafah Industrial Area — 55-B5
Howard Johnson Diplomat Hotel, Markaziya East — 4-L3
HSBC Bank
...Madinat Zayed — 4-M6
...Mussafah Industrial Area — 55-G2
...Tourist Club Area — 5-F7
Humpty Dumpty Nursery
...Al Bateen — 17-E1
...Madinat Khalifa A — 52-D3
Hungary Embassy, Al Rowdah — 12-K8
Hunian School for Secondary Teaching, Officers City — 37-M3
Hurf Aluminium Company Bldg, Mussafah Industrial Area — 55-D3
Husain Supermarket, Al, Al Bateen — 21-L2
Husam Fire Production Systems Bldg, Al, Mussafah
 Industrial Area — 55-C7
Hussain Yousuf General Transport Bldg, Mussafah
 Industrial Area — 55-E3
HVAC Industries Bldg, Mussafah Industrial Area — 55-C5
Hyundai Elevator Company, Al Karamah — 18-C1
Hyundai Service Bldg, Mussafah Industrial Area — 55-D4

I

Iajan Computers, Al Manhal — 8-C8
IBC Scaffolding Bldg, Mussafah Industrial Area — 55-D6

Ibn Seena School, Al Shahama 2 — 44-L8
ICAD 1 Residential City, Industrial City of Abu Dhabi
...Al Madeena Supermarket — 55-B8
...Crystal Restaurant — 55-C8
...Emirates Al Madina Hypermarket — 55-C8
...Golden Spike Restaurant — 55-C8
...Millennium Supermarket — 55-B8
...New Alwafa Hypermarket — 55-C8
...Special Catering Service — 55-B8
...Topcare Medical Centre — 55-C8
ICAD Admin Office Bldg, Industrial City of Abu Dhabi — 59-H3
ICE Crystal Bldg, Mussafah Industrial Area — 54-M6
Ice Pack Cafe, Al Nahyan — 13-K8
Icon Bldg, Hadabat Al Zaafaran — 19-F8
Icon Cement Company Bldg, Al Meena — 40-K6
Icon Computers, Al Nahyan — 18-K4
Ideal Curtain, Tourist Club Area — 5-C3
Ideal Electro Mechanical Service Bldg, Mussafah
 Industrial Area — 55-E3
Idroesse Infrastructure, Al Mushrif — 23-D6
IKEA, Breakwater — 7-A6
Il Forno, (Abu Dhabi Mall), Tourist Club Area — 5-G3
Il Paradiso, (Sheraton Abu Dhabi Hotel & Resort),
 Tourist Club Area — 4-M1
Illusions, (Le Royal Méridien Abu Dhabi), Markaziya East — 4-L3
Iman Supermarket, Al, Al Manhal — 8-D7
IMECO Bldg, Mussafah Industrial Area — 55-B7
Immigration Office Bldg, Al Shahama 2 — 44-L3
Impact BBDO, Al Karamah — 18-E1
Imperial College London Diabetes Centre, Al Safarat — 27-D4
Imperial Enterprises, Hadabat Al Zaafaran — 19-B5
India Embassy, Al Safarat — 27-F2
India Social & Cultural Centre (ISC) Bldg, Al Meena — 2-E4
Indian Airline Building, Madinat Zayed — 8-K5
Indian Coffee House
...Al Rehhan — 24-G6
...Hadabat Al Zaafaran — 19-E7
Indian Islahi Islamic School, Hadabat Al Zaafaran — 23-J3
Indian Modern Science School, Madinat Zayed — 8-M1
Indigo, (Beach Rotana Hotel & Towers), Tourist Club Area — 5-G4
Indonesia Embassy, Al Bateen — 22-A4
Indonesian Restaurant, Tourist Club Area — 5-G6
Indoors Furniture Bldg, Mussafah Industrial Area — 55-D3
Industrial City of Abu Dhabi 1
...Industrial City of Abu Dhabi — 55-C7
...Abdul Monem Al Rashed Steel Industries Bldg — 59-A3
...Abu Dhabi National Cement Factory Bldg — 59-B3
...Abu Dhabi Precast Factory Phase 1 Bldg — 59-C2
...Abu Dhabi Precast Factory Phase 2 Bldg — 59-C2
...Abu Dhabi Scaffolding Factory Bldg — 59-E3
...Abu Dhabi Water & Electrical Authority Bldg — 59-A3
...Abudhabi National Carpet Bldg — 59-A2
...Al Jaber Aluminium Composite Panels Bldg — 59-A3
...Al Masaood Bergum Bldg — 59-B3
...CICON Bldg — 59-D2
...Ducab Dubai Cable Company Bldg — 59-B3
...Emarat Europe Bldg — 59-A3
...Exeed Aswar Bldg — 59-D3
...Foresight Cement Industries Bldg — 59-D3
...Ghuzlan Emirates Furniture & Decor Bldg — 59-E2
...GPCC Bldg — 59-E2
...Hafilat Industries Bldg — 59-D3
...Manazil Steel Framing Factory Bldg — 59-D3
...Micoda Oil & Field Processing System Bldg — 59-E3
...Middle East Industrial Factory Bldg — 58-M2
...National Paper Mill Bldg — 59-A2
...Ogasco Oil & Gas Construction Company Bldg — 59-B3
...Plaxit Dry Mix Company Bldg — 59-D2
...Reem United Industries Bldg — 59-E3
...Safe Water Chemical Bldg — 59-A3
...SCHMDLIN Bldg — 59-C2
...Star Cements Bldg — 59-E3
...Tayco Metal Industries Bldg — 59-E3
...TMI Steel Bldg — 59-A3
...Union Iron & Steel Bldg — 58-M3
...Union Rebar Factory Bldg — 59-C3
...White Aluminium Bldg — 59-A1
Industrial City of Abu Dhabi 2, Industrial City of Abu Dhabi — 58-G8
Industrial City of Abu Dhabi 3, Industrial City of Abu Dhabi — 59-B7
Inflight Catering Services Bldg, Abu Dhabi
 International Airport — 53-E1
Inmotion Media Rent A Car & Used Car Bldg, Bain Al Jessrain — 29-M7
Inova Airlines, Madinat Zayed — 8-K5
Insead Bldg, Al Karamah — 12-M2
Insead Bldg, Al Karamah — 12-M2
Institute of Training & Judicial Studies, Al Manhal — 8-F4
INSULCO Emirates Factory Bldg, Industrial City of Abu Dhabi — 59-G2
Inter AVH Rent A Car, Al Dhafrah — 8-L6
Inter Decor Bldg, Mussafah Industrial Area — 55-C3
InterContinental Hotel Abu Dhabi, Al Bateen
...Boccaccio — 11-D8
...Chamas Brazilian Churrascaria Restaurant & Bar — 11-E7
...Fishmarket — 11-E7
...The Yacht Club — 11-D8
International & Construction Company Bldg, Mussafah
 Industrial Area — 55-A1
International Academic School, Hadabat Al Zaafaran — 23-G3
International Capital Trading Bldg, Mussafah Industrial Area — 55-H5
International Community School
...Hadabat Al Zaafaran — 23-E3
...Markaziya East — 4-K7
International Fashion Factory Garments Bldg, Mussafah
 Industrial Area — 54-M6
International Gas Services Bldg, Mussafah Industrial Area — 55-A2
International Gym, Madinat Zayed — 8-L6
International Montessori Nursery, Al Zahra — 24-J4
International Rotana Inn Htl, Tourist Club Area — 5-B2

**International School of Choueifat, The**
...Al Mushrif ... 18-F1
...Madinat Khalifa A ... 52-C3
**International Shipping Agency Abu Dhabi Bldg**, Mussafah
Industrial Area ... 54-M7
**Invest Bank**, Markaziya East ... 4-M1
**Investment Bank**, Mussafah Industrial Area ... 55-G2
**Investone Financial Brokerage**, Al Khalidiya ... 7-M8
**Iqbal Used & Machinery Spare Parts Bldg**, Mussafah
Industrial Area ... 55-G5
**Iran Embassy**, Al Safarat ... 27-J4
**Iranian Private School**, Al Dhafrah ... 8-L6
**Iraq Embassy**
...Al Safarat ... 27-K3
...Markaziya West ... 8-C5
**Islamic Brokerage Financial Services**, Markaziya East ... 4-L3
**Islamic Cultural Centre**
...Hadabat Al Zaafaran ... 23-L1
...Mohammed Bin Zayed City ... 59-K3
**Islamic Facilities House**, Al Bateen ... 11-K4
**Islamic International School**, Al Dhafrah ... 9-C5
**Islamic Investment Company of the Gulf**, Markaziya East ... 4-M4
**Islamiya English School**, Al Dhafrah ... 9-D6
**Island City**, Al Madina Al Riyadiya ... 28-B3
**Istanbul Bakery**, Al Baladia ... 5-B7
**Italian Palace**, Al Nahyan ... 13-B2
**Italian Technical Company Bldg**, Mussafah Industrial Area ... 55-F2
**Italy Embassy**, Al Karamah ... 12-L8
**Itihad National Private School, Al**, Madinat Khalifa A ... 52-F5
**Ittihad Model School, Al**, Al Bateen ... 11-L5
**Ittihad Primary Health Care Centre**, Al Nahyan ... 13-G7
**Ivory Hotel Apartment**, Tourist Club Area ... 5-D4

### J

**J & H Emirates**, Madinat Zayed ... 9-A2
**Jabal Al Rahma Furniture**, Al Meena ... 40-H6
**Jaber Aluminium Composite Panels Bldg, Al**, Industrial
City of Abu Dhabi ... 59-A3
**Jaber Bin Hayyan Boys Primary School**, Hadabat Al Zaafaran ... 19-A7
**Jaber Bitumen Bldg, Al**, Mussafah Industrial Area ... 55-G1
**Jaber Bldg, Al**, Tourist Club Area ... 5-C3
**Jaber Group, Al**
...Al Jaber Energy Bldg ... 54-M3
...Mussafah Industrial Area ... 54-M2
**Jaber Industries Bldg**, Mussafah Industrial Area ... 55-A3
**Jaber Jewellery, Al**, Markaziya West ... 8-E4
**Jaber Khoory Bldg**, Al Meena ... 40-J8
**Jaber Lighting Bldg, Al**, Mussafah Industrial Area ... 55-A3
**Jabri Transport & General Contracting
  Establishment Bldg, Al**, Mussafah Industrial Area ... 55-D5
**Jadeed Bakery Bldg, Al**, Mussafah Industrial Area ... 55-H3
**Jafary Restaurant**, Markaziya East ... 8-H1
**Jamal Air Cargo, Al**, Madinat Zayed ... 8-L5
**Jamal Car Balance Bldg**, Mussafah Industrial Area ... 55-G2
**Jamal Supermarket**, Markaziya East ... 4-J6
**Jamea Trading Company Bldg, Al**, Mussafah Industrial Area ... 55-C3
**Jameela Supermarket**, Markaziya East ... 4-H7
**Janata Bank Limited**, Markaziya East ... 4-K8
**Japan Embassy**, Al Karamah ... 12-L8
**Japan Oil Company**
...ADOC Bldg ... 11-M2
...Al Bateen ... 11-M2
...W11 ... 11-L2
**Jasim Aluminium Bldg, Al**, Mussafah Industrial Area ... 55-E6
**Jawahr Property Management, Al**, Baniyas East ... 60-L7
**Jazeera Hospital, Al**, Al Manhal ... 12-L2
**Jazeera Medical Centre, Al**, Mohammed Bin Zayed City ... 59-K3
**Jazeera Printing Press, Al**, Al Manhal ... 8-C8
**Jazeera Tower Bldg, Al**, Markaziya East ... 4-H4
**Jazira Cultural & Sports Club Bldg, Al**, Al Nahyan ... 18-K3
**Jazira Jewellers, Al**, Markaziya East ... 4-H8
**Jazira Metal Industries Company Bldg**, Industrial
City of Abu Dhabi ... 59-F2
**Jazira Restaurant**, Tourist Club Area ... 5-H7
**Jazira Royal Hotel Apartment, Al**, Madinat Zayed ... 8-K3
**Jazz Bar & Dining, The**, (Hilton Abu Dhabi), Al Khubeirah ... 11-D5
**Jazz Supermarket**, Mussafah Industrial Area ... 54-M2
**Jearada Properties Bldg**, Markaziya West ... 8-D2
**Jessrain Medical Centre, Al**, Bain Al Jessrain ... 35-D4
**Jibreel Mosque**, Hadabat Al Zaafaran ... 19-K8
**Jocker Sport Club**, Al Manhal ... 8-F5
**Jordan Embassy**, Al Safarat ... 27-E1
**Jordan Stone**, Al Dhafrah ... 9-D2
**Jotun Abu Dhabi Bldg**, Mussafah Industrial Area ... 54-M6
**Jotun Paint Shop**
...Al Baladia ... 5-A7
...Al Nahyan ... 13-D5
**Jotun Paints**
...Al Dhafrah ... 9-C7
...Baniyas East ... 60-J6
...Madinat Zayed ... 5-A7
**Jubaili Bros Bldg**, Mussafah Industrial Area ... 55-D2
**Jubilee Private School**, Madinat Zayed ... 8-K4
**Judicial Authority Bldg**, Al Madina Al Riyadiya ... 27-M6
**Judicial Department Experts Section Bldg**, Hadabat
Al Zaafaran ... 23-H3
**Judicial Department of Commercial Court & Council Bldg**,
Al Nahyan ... 13-G2
**Juma Al Majid Complex Bldg**, Tourist Club Area ... 5-E4
**Juma Al Majid Establishment Bldg**, Mussafah Industrial Area ... 55-E2
**Juma Mohd Jamhoor Qubaisi Building**, Markaziya East ... 5-A5
**Juma Tower Bldg, Al**, Tourist Club Area ... 2-D8
**Jumaira Restaurant**, Markaziya West ... 4-F8
**Jumbo Electronics**
...Al Dhafrah ... 9-A4
...Al Nahyan ... 9-E6

...Markaziya West ... 8-D5
...Tourist Club Area ... 2-C8
**Jumbo Plastics Industry Company Bldg**, Mussafah
Industrial Area ... 55-A8
**Junana Bldg**, Markaziya West ... 8-E4
**Jundi Orthodontic & Dental Centre, Al**, Al Khalidiya ... 8-B7
**JW Marriott Grand Canal Abu Dhabi Htl**, Al Maqtaa ... 34-F2

### K

**K Mart Departmental Store**, Markaziya East ... 4-H8
**Kaddals Oilfield Service & Trading Company Bldg**,
Mussafah Industrial Area ... 54-L7
**Kalha Restaurant, Al**, Al Manhal ... 8-F4
**Kalispra Restaurant**, Al Nahyan ... 9-D7
**Kallor Medical Centre**, Madinat Zayed ... 8-L5
**Kamal General Transport Company Bldg, Al**, Mussafah
Industrial Area ... 55-E5
**Kamal Medical Centre, Al**, Markaziya West ... 8-C6
**Kanoo Group Machinery Bldg, The**, Mussafah Industrial Area ... 55-A3
**Karlstorz Endoscopy**, Al Mushrif ... 22-L6
**Kaseer Restaurant, Al**, Breakwater ... 7-E6
**Kashmir Carpentry Bldg**, Mussafah Industrial Area ... 55-G5
**Kasser Restaurant, Al**, Breakwater ... 7-D7
**Kawsar Rent A Car, Al**, Madinat Zayed ... 9-B2
**Kaya Skin Clinic**, Al Karamah ... 12-L4
**Kazakhstan Embassy**, Al Mushrif ... 23-C5
**Kenworth General Transport**, Mussafah Industrial Area ... 55-H2
**Kenya Embassy**, Al Bateen ... 12-E4
**Kerala Social Centre**, Madinat Zayed ... 9-A2
**KFC**
...Al Dhafrah ... 8-M7
...Al Khalidiya ... 7-M8
...Al Madina Al Riyadiya ... 28-E5
...Hadabat Al Zaafaran ... 19-D7
...Madinat Khalifa A ... 52-C2
...Markaziya East ... 4-L5
...Mussafah Industrial Area ... 55-H3
...Tourist Club Area ... 5-E3
**Khaleej Bitumen Company Bldg, Al**, Mussafah Industrial Area ... 54-K8
**Khaleej Enterprises, Al**, Mussafah Industrial Area ... 55-G2
**Khaleej Ready Mix Bldg, Al**, Mussafah Industrial Area ... 55-E8
**Khaleej Times**, Madinat Zayed ... 9-A2
**Khalid Bin Al Walid**, Al Bateen ... 17-F3
**Khalidia Centre Bldg**, Al Khalidiya ... 8-A6
**Khalidia Palace Reyhaan Htl**, Al Ras Al Akhdar ... 10-M8
**Khalidiya Co-operative Society**
...Al Dhafrah ... 9-B5
...Al Mushrif ... 18-A8
**Khalidiya Stationery, Al**, Al Manhal ... 12-A1
**Khalidiya Studio**, Al Manhal ... 8-D6
**Khalidiya Village**, Al Manhal ... 12-C1
**Khalidiyah Garden**, Al Manhal ... 12-A2
**Khalidiyah Mall**, Al Manhal ... 12-C1
**Khalidiyah Park**, Al Khubeirah ... 11-H2
**Khalidiyah Police Station** (Police Operations General Directorate),
Al Khubeirah ... 11-H4
**Khalif Compound, Al**, Al Safarat ... 27-K4
**Khalifa A Police Station**, Madinat Khalifa A ... 50-F8
**Khalifa Bin Zayed Secondary School for Boys**, Al Mushrif ... 23-F7
**Khalifa City Co-operative Society**, Madinat Khalifa A ... 52-C2
**Khalifa City Market**, Madinat Khalifa A ... 52-C2
**Khalifa Jewellery**, Markaziya East ... 4-G6
**Khalifa Medical Centre**, Madinat Zayed ... 9-B3
**Khalifa Park**
...Al Matar ... 28-J1
...Sheikh Khalifa Park ... 28-K1
...TDIC Bldg ... 28-K2
...Tourism Development & Investment Company (TDIC) Bldg ... 28-K2
**Khalifa University of Science, Technology & Research**,
Hadabat Al Zaafaran ... 18-M5
**Khalifa Urgent Care Centre**, Al Manhal ... 12-D2
**Khalil Al Sayegh General Maintenance Company Bldg**,
Mussafah Industrial Area ... 54-K7
**Khamis Ali Saeed Foodstuff**, Al Mushrif ... 24-C8
**Kharafi National Bldg**, Mussafah Industrial Area ... 55-B4
**Khatim Showroom Bldg, Al**, Mussafah Industrial Area ... 55-F1
**Khazna Insurance Company Store Bldg, Al**, Mussafah
Industrial Area ... 55-C6
**Khazna Insurance Tower Bldg, Al**, Al Baladia ... 5-B7
**Khazna Medical Clinic, Al**, Al Mushrif ... 18-H3
**Khoory Supermarket**, Tourist Club Area ... 5-C3
**Khubairah Palace Bldg, Al**, Al Bateen ... 11-B7
**Khubairah Tower Bldg, Al**, Al Khalidiya ... 11-L1
**Khunaiby Group Establishment, Al**, Al Manhal ... 8-G5
**Kia Motors**, Tourist Club Area ... 5-E4
**Kingsgate Hotel**, Tourist Club Area ... 5-E6
**Kish Travels**, Madinat Zayed ... 8-J2
**KKT International Spine Centre**, Al Bateen ... 11-K5
**KM Brothers National Company**, Al Meena ... 2-E3
**KM Trading**
...Al Manhal ... 8-C6
...Madinat Zayed ... 4-K8
...Markaziya East ... 5-B4
**Knowledge Sun Training & Language Center Bldg**,
Madinat Khalifa A ... 52-C2
**Kohinoor Automatic Bakery**, Mussafah Industrial Area ... 55-H3
**Korean Embassy**, Al Mushrif ... 18-H7
**Korean Stores Auto Parts Bldg**, Mussafah Industrial Area ... 55-F2
**Korfukan Restaurant**, Al Rehhan ... 24-E6
**KPK Quality Survey**, Al Mushrif ... 23-H6
**Kubaisi School, Al**, Al Dhafrah ... 9-E4
**Kunaiby Bldg, Al**, Markaziya West ... 8-E3
**Kuwaisi Bldg, Al**, Tourist Club Area ... 5-C3
**Kuwait Embassy**, Al Mushrif ... 23-C6
**Kuwaiti Danish Dairy Company (KCSC)**, Bain Al Jessrain ... 35-K5
**Kyeryong Construction Industrial Company**, Al Bateen ... 17-F3

### L

**L'Opera Brasserie**, (Le Royal Méridien Abu Dhabi),
Markaziya East ... 4-L3
**L.A.B. – Lounge At The Beach Bar**, (Beach Rotana Hotel
& Towers), Tourist Club Area ... 5-G4
**La Brasserie**, (Le Meridien Abu Dhabi), Tourist Club Area ... 5-F2
**La Mamma**, (Sheraton Abu Dhabi Hotel & Resort)
...Tourist Club Area ... 4-M1
...Tourist Club Area ... 4-M1
**La Terrazza**, (Hilton Abu Dhabi), Al Khubeirah ... 11-D5
**La Veranda**, (Sheraton Khalidiya Hotel), Markaziya West ... 8-C6
**Labour Camp Area**
...Fathima Supermarket ... 55-K5
...Gasos Staff Accommodation Bldg ... 55-K6
...ME6 ... 55-K6
...ME8 ... 55-K7
...Mohammed Bin Zayed City ... 55-K6
...Sigma Enterprises Staff Accommodation Bldg ... 55-K6
**Lacnor & Milco Company Bldg**, Sas Al Nakhl ... 29-K4
**Ladies Aesthetic Skin Care Centre**, Al Bateen ... 11-J6
**Lafzaeyya Tower Bldg**, Markaziya East ... 4-F7
**Lagoon Htl, The**, Al Khubeirah ... 11-F3
**Lake Park**, Markaziya East ... 4-E5
**Lamborghini Abu Dhabi (Motors)**, Al Dhafrah ... 9-C7
**Land Mark Plaza Bldg**, Tourist Club Area ... 5-C1
**Landmark Properties**, Al Karamah ... 13-B3
**Landmark Tower Bldg**, Markaziya West ... 8-C1
**Landscapping Gulf Nursery**, Madinat Khalifa A ... 52-C2
**Le Beaujolais**, (Novotel Centre Hotel), Markaziya East ... 4-J7
**Le Bistrot**, (Le Meridien Abu Dhabi), Tourist Club Area ... 5-F2
**Le Boulanger Beach Cafe**, Officers Club ... 33-H3
**Le Meridien Hotel**, Tourist Club Area
...Al Birkeh ... 5-F2
...Captain's Arms ... 5-F2
...G Club ... 5-F2
...La Brasserie ... 5-F2
...Le Bistrot ... 5-F2
...NRG Sports Café ... 5-F2
...Opus Bar ... 5-F2
...Pappagallo ... 5-F2
...Talay ... 5-F2
...Wakataua Terrace ... 5-F2
**Le Royal Meridien Hotel**, Markaziya East
...Al Fanar ... 4-L3
...Amalfi ... 4-L3
...Illusions ... 4-L3
...L'Opera Brasserie ... 4-L3
...Oceans ... 4-L3
...PJ O'Reilly's ... 4-L3
...SAX ... 4-L3
...Shuja Yacht ... 4-L3
...Soba ... 4-L3
**Le Vendôme Brasserie**, (Emirates Palace), Al Ras Al Akhdar ... 10-L5
**Leans Nursery**, Al Dhafrah ... 9-B5
**Lebanese Castre Restaurant**, Baniyas East ... 60-K7
**Lebanese Express Coffee Shop & Pastry**, Markaziya West ... 8-D4
**Lebanese Flower Restaurant**, Al Dhafrah ... 9-D6
**Lebanon Embassy**, Al Safarat ... 27-E2
**Leens School**, Al Dhafrah ... 9-B5
**Legal Affairs Department, Police Court Section Bldg**,
Al Rehhan ... 24-D6
**Liberty Abu Dhabi Automobiles**, Madinat Zayed ... 5-B8
**Liberty Abu Dhabi Service Centre Bldg**, Mussafah
Industrial Area ... 55-D5
**Liberty Rent A Car**, Al Manhal ... 8-G4
**Libya Embassy**, Al Bateen ... 22-A4
**Lifco Supermarket**, Tourist Club Area ... 2-C8
**Lifeline Hospital**
...Markaziya East ... 4-K7
...Mussafah Industrial Area ... 55-G2
**Linde Gas Middle East**, Al Mushrif ... 22-L6
**Lissaily, Al**
...Al Raha ... 31-H1
**Little Bird School**, Hadabat Al Zaafaran ... 19-G8
**Little Flower Private School**, Al Dhafrah ... 9-B5
**Liwa Car Exhibition**, Al Nahyan ... 18-H2
**Liwa Centre Bldg**, Markaziya East ... 4-H7
**Liwa ICE Factory Bldg**, Mussafah Industrial Area ... 55-A8
**Liwa Pure Drinking Water Bldg**, Industrial City of Abu Dhabi ... 59-F1
**Liwa Villas Bldg**, Madinat Khalifa B ... 57-B2
**London Center for Training & Consultancy**, Al Nahyan ... 13-H4
**Lonestar Technical & Industries Company Bldg**, Industrial
City of Abu Dhabi ... 59-H4
**Lounge & Cafe**, Al Khalidiya ... 7-K8
**Louvre Abu Dhabi**, Saadiyat Island ... 41-A5
**Louvre Abu Dhabi Bldg**, Saadiyat Island ... 41-A5
**Lovely Studio**, Tourist Club Area ... 5-E3
**Lulu Bldg**, Al Nahyan ... 9-D8
**Lulu Centre**, Markaziya East ... 4-J7
**Lulu City Watches**, Markaziya East ... 4-H8
**Lulu Fresh Chicken**, Baniyas East ... 60-K5
**Lulu Hypermarket**
...Al Manhal ... 12-D1
...Al Nahyan ... 13-B1
...Madinat Zayed ... 8-L1
**Luxury Cars**, Al Nahyan ... 9-G5
**Lycee Francais Theodore Monod School**, Al Bateen ... 11-L8
**Lycee Louis Massignon**, Al Rehhan ... 24-E7

### M

**Maazo Store Bldg**, Mussafah Industrial Area ... 55-G4
**Mac Burger**, Hadabat Al Zaafaran ... 19-E7
**Madani Travels, Al**, Al Nahyan ... 13-K8
**Madhrasathul Al Emaan Hasah**, Al Karamah ... 12-M2

| | | |
|---|---|---|
| Madina Printing, Tourist Club Area | 5-G5 | |
| Madina Restaurant, Mussafah Industrial Area | 55-C1 | |
| Madinat Zayed Fish & Vegetable Market Bldg, Madinat Zayed | 8-L3 | |
| Madinat Zayed Shopping Centre Bldg, Madinat Zayed | 8-K1 | |
| Madona Building, Tourist Club Area | 2-C7 | |
| Mafraq Dental Clinic, Mahawi | 60-M2 | |
| Mafraq Hospital Staff Accommodation, Mahawi | 60-L3 | |
| Mafraq Hospital, Al, Mahawi | 60-L3 | |
| Magic Tech, Tourist Club Area | 5-G6 | |
| Maha Arjaan Rotana Suites Htl, Al, Markaziya East | 4-L5 | |
| Maha Residential Complex, Al, Al Matar | 25-A8 | |
| Mahimat Tower Bldg, Markaziya East | 4-H7 | |
| MAI General Transport Bldg, Mussafah Industrial Area | 55-C5 | |
| Maihab Transport, Mussafah Industrial Area | 55-H3 | |
| Main Grandstand Bldg, Yas Island | 50-J1 | |
| Majestic Dental Centre, Al Bateen | 12-D4 | |
| Mal Investment & Development, Al, Al Manhal | 8-C7 | |
| Malabar Flower Restaurant, Mussafah Industrial Area | 55-H7 | |
| Malaysia Embassy, Hadabat Al Zaafaran | 19-D2 | |
| Mall Retail Centre Bldg, Al Safarat | 27-J7 | |
| Mamoura Building, Al | | |
| ...Al Nahyan | 13-J5 | |
| ...Mubadala HQ | 13-J5 | |
| Manaa Metal Construction Bldg, Al, Mussafah Industrial Area | 59-A1 | |
| Manara Jewellery, Al, Al Khalidiya | 11-M1 | |
| Manara Private School, Al, Al Zahra | 20-A8 | |
| Manaseer Police Station, Al, Al Bateen | 12-G6 | |
| Manazil Bldg, Al Matar | 25-J6 | |
| Manazil Steel Framing Factory Bldg, Industrial City of Abu Dhabi | 59-D3 | |
| Manbaa Drilling Company Bldg, Al, Mussafah Industrial Area | 55-H5 | |
| Mandi General Transport Bldg, Al, Mussafah Industrial Area | 55-G6 | |
| Mangrove Village | | |
| ...Officers City | 37-J5 | |
| ...Spinneys | 37-K4 | |
| Manhal Family Medical Centre, Al, Madinat Zayed | 9-A2 | |
| Manhal Palace Bldg, Al, Al Manhal | 8-F7 | |
| Manhal Private School, Al, Al Mushrif | 23-G8 | |
| Mansoor Plaza Bldg, Al, Markaziya East | 4-M4 | |
| Mansoori Tower Bldg, Al, Markaziya East | 4-M4 | |
| Manzel Hotel Apartment, Al, Tourist Club Area | 5-E3 | |
| Manzil Restaurant, Mussafah Industrial Area | 55-G6 | |
| Maqam Corner Restaurant, Al, Mussafah Industrial Area | 55-E7 | |
| Maqta Bldg, Al, Bain Al Jessrain | 35-D4 | |
| Maqta Fort Bldg, Al, Mangroves (Al Qurm) | 29-G4 | |
| Maria Jewellery, Al, Markaziya East | 4-M2 | |
| Marina | | |
| ...Al Bateen | 11-D8 | |
| ...Breakwater | 7-D5 | |
| ...Saadiyat Island | 41-D8 | |
| ...Tourist Club Area | 5-G2 | |
| ...Yas Island | 50-J4 | |
| Marina Al Bateen, Al Bateen | | |
| ...Dock Side Pool Bar | 16-H4 | |
| ...Riviera | 16-H4 | |
| Marina Cafe, Al Ras Al Akhdar | 11-B1 | |
| Marina Dental Centre, Markaziya East | 5-A2 | |
| Marina Hotel, Al Bateen | 16-H3 | |
| Marina Mall | | |
| ...Breakwater | 6-M5 | |
| ...Figaro's Pizza | 7-A6 | |
| ...Markaziya East | 4-L4 | |
| Marina Office Bldg | | |
| ...Al Bateen | 11-E8 | |
| ...Breakwater | 7-C5 | |
| ...Tourist Club Area | 5-G2 | |
| Marina Police, Al Meena | 40-G8 | |
| Marina Square, Al Reem Island | | |
| ...RAK Twrs Bldg | 5-M8 | |
| Marina Transport Bldg, Mussafah Industrial Area | 55-D7 | |
| Marina Villas, Breakwater | 6-J4 | |
| Marino Palace Restaurant, Mussafah Industrial Area | 55-G4 | |
| Maritime Museum, Saadiyat Island | 41-D8 | |
| Mariyah Community, Al | | |
| ...Madinat Khalifa A | 50-D8 | |
| Marjan Geo Services Bldg, Al, Mussafah Industrial Area | 55-E2 | |
| Marjan Plaza Bldg, Markaziya East | 4-J6 | |
| Markati Supermarket, Mussafah Industrial Area | 55-E5 | |
| Markaz Edawa Bldg, Mohammed Bin Zayed City | 55-J3 | |
| Markaziyah Garden, Al, Markaziya West | 8-A3 | |
| Market Control Section Bldg, Al Meena | 40-K8 | |
| Marks & Spencer, Markaziya East | 8-G1 | |
| Marlin Furniture, Al Nahyan | 13-A1 | |
| Marroush Restaurant, Tourist Club Area | 5-F7 | |
| Marthoma Church, Mussafah Industrial Area | 55-H4 | |
| Marwah Girls School for Basic, Al, Officers City | 38-A3 | |
| Masa Facility Services Bldg, Al, Madinat Khalifa A | 50-K6 | |
| Masala Magic Restaurant, Markaziya East | 4-M3 | |
| Masaood Automobiles Bldg, Al, Mussafah Industrial Area | 55-D4 | |
| Masaood Bergum Bldg, Al, Industrial City of Abu Dhabi | 59-B3 | |
| Masaood Oil Industry Supplies & Services Company Bldg, Al, Mussafah Industrial Area | 55-C1 | |
| Masaood Trucks Equipment Service Center Bldg, Al, Mussafah Industrial Area | 55-C2 | |
| Masaoud Tower Bldg, Al, Markaziya East | 4-K6 | |
| Masdar Institute of Science & Technology, Mohammed Bin Zayed City | 56-B6 | |
| Mashayil School (Arabic), Hadabat Al Zaafaran | 19-J7 | |
| Mashoor Foodstuff, Al, Al Bateen | 17-F3 | |
| Mashreq Bank | | |
| ...Al Baladia | 9-C1 | |
| ...Al Karamah | 13-C8 | |
| ...Al Nahyan | 13-D5 | |
| ...Hadabat Al Zaafaran | 19-C7 | |
| ...Madinat Zayed | 4-K8 | |
| ...Markaziya East | 4-H6 | |
| ...Mussafah Industrial Area | 55-H2 | |
| Masjid & Al Jazeer Garden, Al Mushrif | 23-B4 | |
| Masjid & Quran Study Center Bldg, Al Mushrif | 22-L5 | |
| Masjid Gubaishi, Bain Al Jessrain | 35-H6 | |
| Masood Automobiles, Al | | |
| ...Al Baladia | 5-B7 | |
| ...Al Khubeirah | 11-H4 | |
| Masood Motors Bldg, Al, Al Rehhan | 24-J8 | |
| Masood Travel & Services, Al, Markaziya West | 8-D2 | |
| Masood Tyres, Al, Al Nahyan | 9-E7 | |
| Masooma Supermarket, Al Bahia | 44-C5 | |
| Masraf Arab Bank Investment Foreign Trade, Al, Markaziya West | 8-D4 | |
| Massa Cinema, Al, Markaziya East | 4-J7 | |
| Massoud Bldg Bldg, Al Baladia | 5-B7 | |
| Master Field Mechanical Equipment Bldg, Mussafah Industrial Area | 55-F6 | |
| Matar, Al, Al Zahra | 20-G8 | |
| Materials Laboratory, Mussafah Industrial Area | 55-G7 | |
| Matrix Laboratory Geotechnical Service Bldg, Mussafah Industrial Area | 55-D7 | |
| Mawaheb Model School for Girls, Al, Al Bateen | 12-B5 | |
| Mawal, (Hilton Abu Dhabi), Al Khubeirah | 11-D5 | |
| Max Mart, Markaziya East | 5-B5 | |
| Max Mayer Eea Paul Auto Repair Bldg, Mussafah Industrial Area | 55-B4 | |
| Max Meyer Car Service Bldg, Mussafah Industrial Area | 55-G2 | |
| Maya Supermarket, Al, Tourist Club Area | 5-G6 | |
| Mazayed Village, Mohammed Bin Zayed City | | |
| ...Ittihad Bldg | 55-L3 | |
| ...L'Arabia Hotel Apartment | 55-L3 | |
| ...Lulu Express & Department Store | 55-L3 | |
| ...Mazyad Mall | 55-L3 | |
| Mazna Light Bldg Bldg, Tourist Club Area | 5-D1 | |
| Mazroui Company Engineering Bldg, Al, Mussafah Industrial Area | 55-B7 | |
| Mazroui Hospital, Al, Al Baladia | 9-C1 | |
| Mazrul & Hawi Painting Company Bldg, Mussafah Industrial Area | 55-D7 | |
| MBM Dallah Bldg, Mussafah Industrial Area | 55-D3 | |
| McDonalds, Al Manhal | 12-D1 | |
| Meat Co, The, (Souk Qaryat Al Beri), | 34-J3 | |
| Meca Quick Service Establishment, Al Manhal | 8-D7 | |
| Media Centre, Yas Island | 50-K2 | |
| Medical Laser Centre, Markaziya East | 4-G6 | |
| Mega Store Bldg, Mussafah Industrial Area | 55-G7 | |
| Megawatt Electrical Trading Company, Al Nahyan | 9-D8 | |
| Meher Medical Centre, Al Khalidiya | 8-A6 | |
| Mende Palace Restaurant, Baniyas East | 60-L7 | |
| Mercato, Al Nahyan | 18-K1 | |
| Metal Coating Industries Bldg, Mussafah Industrial Area | 54-M8 | |
| Mezin General Contracting, Al, Al Khubeirah | 11-H3 | |
| Mezzaluna, (Emirates Palace), Al Ras Al Akhdar | 10-L5 | |
| MGM Grand Htl, Al Meena | 2-B7 | |
| MI SWACO Company, Al Karamah | 12-K8 | |
| Micco Bldg, Al Baladia | 5-A6 | |
| Micoda Oil & Field Processing System Bldg, Industrial City of Abu Dhabi | 59-E3 | |
| Midco Industrial Equipment Bldg, Mussafah Industrial Area | 55-F3 | |
| Middle East Equipment Trading Bldg, Mussafah Industrial Area | 55-F1 | |
| Middle East Exhaust Manufacture Factory Bldg, Mussafah Industrial Area | 54-M7 | |
| Middle East Garments Manufacturing Bldg, Industrial City of Abu Dhabi | 59-E2 | |
| Middle East Industrial Factory Bldg, Industrial City of Abu Dhabi | 58-M2 | |
| Middle East Specialized Medical Centre, Al Nahyan | 13-G5 | |
| Middle East Travels, Al Dhafrah | 9-E4 | |
| Midel East Supermarket, Tourist Club Area | 5-G7 | |
| Milano Furniture, Al Nahyan | 13-C4 | |
| Military Physical Education Centre Bldg, Al Maqtaa | 34-D4 | |
| Millennium Hotel, Markaziya East | 4-K4 | |
| Millennium Supermarket, Al Nahyan | 13-B2 | |
| Milta, Madinat Zayed | 4-L7 | |
| Mina Bldg Bldg, Al Meena | 2-C6 | |
| Mina Fish Market Bldg, Al Meena | 2-C1 | |
| Mina Plaza Bldg, Al Meena | 40-J8 | |
| Mina Tower Bldg, Al Meena | 2-D5 | |
| Mina Vegetable Market Bldg, Al, Al Meena | 40-K8 | |
| Minhaj Interiors, Al, Al Karamah | 13-C4 | |
| Ministry of | | |
| ...Cultural Youth & Community Development, Al Nahyan | 13-J6 | |
| ...Economic & Insurance Authority, Markaziya East | 4-K6 | |
| ...Education, Al Khalidiya | 8-B6 | |
| ...Education, Baniyas East | 61 C8 | |
| ...Energy, Markaziya East | 4-G5 | |
| ...Environment & Water, Al Matar | 25-K7 | |
| ...Finance, Al Baladia | 9-D1 | |
| ...Foreign Affairs, Al Bateen | 16-F1 | |
| ...Foreign Affairs, Al Madina Al Riyadiya | 28-E4 | |
| ...Foreign Trade, Al Mushrif | 27-C1 | |
| ...Higher Education & Scientific Research, Al Dhafrah | 9-D3 | |
| ...Interior, Bain Al Jessrain | 29-J6 | |
| ...Interior, Al Maqtaa | 33-J2 | |
| ...Interior, Al Zahra | 24-D2 | |
| ...Judiciary, Al Khubeirah | 11-E5 | |
| ...Labour, Mussafah Industrial Area | 55-F3 | |
| ...Labour, Al Matar | 25-K8 | |
| ...Social Affairs, Al Nahyan | 9-G6 | |
| Mirage Marine Italiane Restaurant Il Porto, Breakwater | 6-L7 | |
| Mission Marine Bldg, Mussafah Industrial Area | 55-F1 | |
| Mithaq Aluminium Bldg, Al, Mussafah Industrial Area | 55-E3 | |
| Mitsubishi Bldg, Mussafah Industrial Area | 55-B3 | |
| Mitsubishi Motors, Al Baladia | 9-C2 | |
| Mobile Marine Materials Bldg, Mussafah Industrial Area | 55-C3 | |
| Moda Casa, Tourist Club Area | 5-D1 | |
| Model School Abu Dhabi, The, Hadabat Al Zaafaran | 19-K7 | |
| Modern A/C Factory System Bldg, Mussafah Industrial Area | 55-B2 | |
| Modern Bakery, Tourist Club Area | 5-C1 | |
| Modern Machinery Trading Bldg, Mussafah Industrial Area | 55-B4 | |
| Modern Plastic Company Bldg, Mussafah Industrial Area | 55-A6 | |
| Modern Star Bldg, Mussafah Industrial Area | 55-G6 | |
| Moghera Petroleum Chemical Industries Bldg, Al, Mussafah Industrial Area | 58-M1 | |
| Mohamed Abdul Rahman Al Bahar Bldg, Mussafah Industrial Area | 55-C1 | |
| Mohammed Bin Al Qasem School, Al Shawamekh | 57-F3 | |
| Mohd Bin Khalid Secondary School, Al Bateen | 12-G6 | |
| Mohd Bin Rashid Workshop Bldg, Mussafah Industrial Area | 55-G4 | |
| Mohd Irfan Kaltakji Medical Clinic, Markaziya West | 8-F1 | |
| Mohd Rafiq Used Spare Parts Bldg, Mussafah Industrial Area | 55-G4 | |
| Mohd Shahid Tools & Light Machines Repairing Bldg, Mussafah Industrial Area | 55-G3 | |
| Moherbie Transport Bldg, Al, Mussafah Industrial Area | 55-B3 | |
| Mohmood Ibrahim Steel & Turring Works Bldg, Mussafah Industrial Area | 55-F5 | |
| Mono Restaurant & Cafe, Al Dhafrah | 9-E5 | |
| Mood Indigo, (Novotel Centre Hotel), Markaziya East | 4-J7 | |
| Moopen's Medical Clinic, Mussafah Industrial Area | 55-F2 | |
| Moosa Industrial Company (MINCO ) Bldg, Mussafah Industrial Area | 55-B2 | |
| Moraik Bldg | | |
| ...Markaziya East | 4-L6 | |
| ...Mussafah Industrial Area | 55-F1 | |
| Morka Restaurant, Al Meena | 2-B2 | |
| Morocco Bank, Tourist Club Area | 5-C2 | |
| Morocco Embassy, Al Karamah | 12-L8 | |
| Mosart Marble & Mosaic Bldg, Mussafah Industrial Area | 55-C7 | |
| Mosart Morble Bldg, Mussafah Industrial Area | 55-D6 | |
| Mosque Gardens, Tourist Club Area | 5-C2 | |
| Moulin Rouge Cafeteria, Markaziya East | 4-K5 | |
| Mourouj Hotel Apartment, Al Dhafrah | 9-A5 | |
| Mr Clean Dry Cleaning, Al Karamah | 13-B3 | |
| Mr Jabir Jasem Al Maraiki Bldg, Tourist Club Area | 5-C3 | |
| Mr Shoe, Markaziya East | 4-J7 | |
| MTS Education Centre, Al Baladia | 5-C5 | |
| Muhairi General Transport Company Bldg, Al, Mussafah Industrial Area | 55-H5 | |
| Muhairy Centre Bldg, Al, Al Manhal | 8-F3 | |
| Muhandes Hydralic Engineering Equipment Bldg, Al, Mussafah Industrial Area | 58-M1 | |
| Muna Primary School, Al, Markaziya East | 4-J8 | |
| Municipal & Agricultural Department Bldg, Al Meena | 40-K8 | |
| Municipal Vegetable Market Bldg, Baniyas East | 61-G8 | |
| Municipality Airport Road Markets Bldg, Al Mushrif | 23-C4 | |
| Municipality Garden, Al Baladia | 5-D7 | |
| Municipality Market Bldg, Al Mushrif | 26-G1 | |
| Municipality Old Shopping Complex Bldg, Al Mushrif | 24-B8 | |
| Muqathara Restaurant, Al Meena | 2-E3 | |
| Muqudar Supermarket, Al, Tourist Club Area | 2-D7 | |
| Murray & Roberts, Al Maqtaa | 28-K8 | |
| Murree Trading Bldg, Mussafah Industrial Area | 55-G2 | |
| Museum, Saadiyat Island | 41-A4 | |
| Mushref Co-operative Society, Al, Al Mushrif | 26-F1 | |
| Mushrif Children's Garden, Al, Al Mushrif | 18-D2 | |
| Mushrif Inter Garden Bldg, Al, Al Mushrif | 18-K8 | |
| Mushrif Marriage Hall Bldg, Al, Al Mushrif | 23-A2 | |
| Mushrif Medical Centre, Al, Al Mushrif | 23-D4 | |
| Mushrif Palace Bldg, Al, Al Mushrif | 18-C4 | |
| Mushrif School, Al, Hadabat Al Zaafaran | 19-D8 | |
| Mussafa Health Care Centre, Mussafah Industrial Area | 55-H2 | |
| Mussafah City Supermarket, Mussafah Industrial Area | 55-B4 | |
| Mussafah Commercial Area | | |
| ...Abu Yusuf Restaurant | 59-K3 | |
| ...Al Ansari Exchange | 59-K3 | |
| ...Al Bashair Private School | 59-K4 | |
| ...Al Khan Dental Clinic | 59-K3 | |
| ...Al Muntaha School for Secondary Education | 59-K4 | |
| ...Al-Iman Muslim School | 59-K4 | |
| ...Arabian Exchange | 59-L3 | |
| ...Jazz Music Institute | 59-K4 | |
| ...ME12 | 59-K4 | |
| ...Mohammed Bin Zayed City | 59-K4 | |
| ...Mussafah Shabia Bus Station | 59-J4 | |
| ...New Sagar Restaurant | 59-L3 | |
| ...Tabarak Supermarket | 59-K4 | |
| ...Talat Medical Centre | 59-K3 | |
| ...The Indian Model School | 59-K4 | |
| ...UAE Exchange Bldg | 59-K3 | |
| ...Wide Vision Internet | 59-K3 | |
| ...Zia Medical Centre | 59-J3 | |
| Mussafah Gic Substation Bldg, Industrial City of Abu Dhabi | 59-F4 | |
| Mussafah Girls School for Basic Education/Cycle-1, Al, Mohammed Bin Zayed City | 59-L2 | |
| Mussafah Labour Clinic, Mohammed Bin Zayed City | 55-K4 | |
| Mussafah Police Station, Mussafah Industrial Area | 59-J1 | |
| Mussafah Port, Mussafah Industrial Area | 54-M1 | |
| Mussaffa General Transport Bldg, Mussafah Industrial Area | 55-F5 | |
| Mutawa Metal Establishment Bldg, Mussafah Industrial Area | 55-E2 | |
| Muzera Community, Madinat Khalifa A | | |
| ...District Cooling Bldg | 50-E8 | |
| ...Raha International School | 50-E8 | |
| My Campus Education Centre, Markaziya West | 8-E1 | |
| My Nursery School, Al Karamah | 18-D1 | |
| My Way Resturant, Markaziya East | 5-B4 | |

## N

| | | |
|---|---|---|
| Naboodah Labour Camp Bldg, Al, Mussafah Industrial Area | 55-F6 | |
| Naboodah Travels, Al, Al Nahyan | 9-G5 | |
| Nabordha Labour Camp Bldg, Al, Mussafah Industrial Area | 55-C4 | |
| Nadir School for Basics Education, Al, Al Baladia | 5-C8 | |
| Nadreen Beauty & Fitness, Bain Al Jessrain | 35-A4 | |
| Nadud Supermarket, Al, Al Bahia | 48-G2 | |

**Nael & Bin Harmal Hydro Export Establishment Bldg**,
Mussafah Industrial Area ... 55-H5
**Nahar Furniture, Al**, Al Nahyan ... 13-G5
**Nahda LPG Bldg, Al**, Mussafah Industrial Area ... 55-B6
**Nahda National School for Boys, Al**, Al Nahyan ... 13-H7
**Nahda National School, Al**, Al Mushrif ... 23-B3
**Nahel Tower Bldg** ... 5-B8
**Nails Secret Spa**, Hadabat Al Zaafaran ... 23-H1
**Najah Private School, Al**
...Al Mushrif ... 26-E1
...Mohammed Bin Zayed City ... 59-L1
**Nakheel Tower Bldg, Al**, Al Khalidiya ... 8-B7
**Nareel Island**, Al Bateen ... 11-A8
**Nasar Restaurant**, Tourist Club Area ... 5-E5
**NASCO Emirates**, Al Nahyan ... 9-J8
**Nasr Contracting Bldg, Al**, Mussafah Industrial Area ... 55-D3
**Nation Towers**, Al Khubeirah ... 11-E4
**National Bags Factory Bldg**, Industrial City of Abu Dhabi ... 59-G3
**National Bank of Abu Dhabi**
...Al Bateen ... 12-B7
...Al Khalidiya ... 7-L8
...Al Mushrif ... 26-F1
...Al Nahyan ... 13-J5
...Al Shahama 2 ... 44-J8
...Bain Al Jessrain (Academy) ... 35-D4
...Hadabat Al Zaafaran ... 19-C6
...Markaziya East ... 4-J5
...Mussafah Industrial Area ... 55-H2
...Tourist Club Area ... 2-B8
**National Bank of Bahrain**, Markaziya East ... 4-K6
**National Bank of Fujairah**, Mussafah Industrial Area ... 55-E2
**National Bank of Umm Al Quwain**, Mussafah Industrial Area ... 55-G3
**National Building Materials Bldg**, Mussafah Industrial Area ... 55-C5
**National Cadet Centre (NCC)**, Madinat Zayed ... 9-A2
**National Cement Factory Bldg**, Industrial City of Abu Dhabi ... 59-D5
**National Center of Metrology & Seismology Bldg**, Al Bateen ... 12-B6
**National Cinema**, Markaziya East ... 4-M5
**National Corporation for Tourism & Hotels (NCT & H) Bldg**,
Al Madina Al Riyadiya ... 27-L5
**National Dewatering & Land Draining Establishment Bldg**,
Mussafah Industrial Area ... 55-E5
**National Drilling Company Bldg**
...Al Baladia ... 5-C5
...Mussafah Industrial Area ... 55-B1
**National Electronic Wheel Balance Bldg**, Mussafah
Industrial Area ... 55-G1
**National Exchange Company**, Markaziya East ... 4-G7
**National Food Products Company Bldg**, Sas Al Nakhl ... 29-K5
**National Gulf Timber Factory Bldg**, Mussafah Industrial Area ... 55-B4
**National Hospital**, Al Baladia ... 5-B6
**National Industrial Company**, Al Baladia ... 5-B5
**National Investment Corporation Villa**
...Arab Administrative Association ... 6-L6
...Arab German International Broker ... 7-A7
...Arab Italia Investment Company ... 6-L6
...Breakwater ... 6-M6
...ICT International Capital Trading ... 6-M7
...Ocean View Abu Dhabi Real Estate ... 6-M7
...Orascom Construction Industries ... 6-L7
...Patton Boggs ... 6-M7
...Shaw Stone & Webster International ... 6-M5
**National Marine Trading Company Bldg**, Mussafah
Industrial Area ... 58-L5
**National Media Council Bldg**, Al Nahyan ... 13-K6
**National Paint**, Madinat Zayed ... 8-L1
**National Paint Bldg**, Mussafah Industrial Area ... 55-G2
**National Paint Shop**
...Al Baladia ... 5-C6
...Al Nahyan ... 13-H6
**National Paper Mill Bldg**, Industrial City of Abu Dhabi ... 59-A2
**National Petroleum Construction Company**
...Abu Dhabi Precast Bldg ... 54-L8
...Mussafah Industrial Area ... 54-K8
**National Private School**, Hadabat Al Zaafaran ... 19-H7
**National Ready Mix Bldg**, Mussafah Industrial Area ... 55-F8
**National Refreshment Company**, Mussafah Industrial Area ... 55-H3
**National Rehabilitation Centre**, Al Nahyan ... 13-H6
**National Rent A Car**, Al Dhafrah ... 9-C2
**National Screening Center for Man & Child Health Bldg**,
Al Mushrif ... 26-G1
**National Security Bldg**, Al Mushrif ... 27-B3
**National Security Institute**, Madinat Khalifa A ... 52-A5
**National Shield**, Hadabat Al Zaafaran ... 23-K2
**National Silks Store**, Markaziya East ... 4-J7
**National Square**, Capital District ... 56-E2
**National Taxi Bldg**, Mussafah Industrial Area ... 55-C4
**National Theatre Bldg**, Al Nahyan ... 18-H2
**National Trading Developing Establishment Bldg**,
Mussafah Industrial Area ... 55-D2
**National Transport Authority**, Al Matar ... 25-K8
**National Transport Company Bldg**, Mussafah Industrial Area ... 55-F2
**National Veterinary Hospital**, Al Mushrif ... 18-H4
**Nayadi Bldg, Al**, Al Karamah ... 13-C5
**NBB Group Bldg**, Mussafah Industrial Area ... 55-F4
**NBB Travel & Tourism**, Al Nahyan ... 13-E4
**NCC**, Madinat Zayed ... 9-A2
**NCE Camp Bldg**, Mussafah Industrial Area ... 55-G6
**NCO & Soldier Accommodation Bldg**, Al Zahra ... 24-A1
**ND SatCom Middle East**, Al Karamah ... 13-A6
**Neb Engineering Control Corporation**, Al Karamah ... 13-B4
**Neda Ali Contracting Bldg, Al**, Mussafah Industrial Area ... 55-E3
**Neopharma Bldg**, Industrial City of Abu Dhabi ... 59-H3
**Netherlands Embassy**, Markaziya West ... 4-K6
**New Al Majid Foodstuff Bldg**, Mussafah Industrial Area ... 55-D7
**New Al Shahama General Transport**, Hadabat Al Zaafaran ... 19-D6
**New Bombay Workshop Bldg**, Mussafah Industrial Area ... 55-D3
**New Colours Cafe**, Al Mushrif ... 18-K4

**New England Centre For Childrens, The**, Al Nahyan ... 9-H7
**New Golden City Supermarket**, Mussafah Industrial Area ... 55-H3
**New Marine International Bldg**, Mussafah Industrial Area ... 55-D3
**New Mina Market Bldg**, Al Meena ... 40-H6
**New Mix Ready Mix Bldg**, Mussafah Industrial Area ... 55-F8
**New York University**, Markaziya West ... 8-E1
**Nibras Furniture Factory Bldg, Al**, Industrial City of Abu Dhabi ... 59-E3
**NICO & MSG Bldg**, Mussafah Industrial Area ... 55-C2
**Nigeria Embassy**, Al Karamah ... 12-L8
**Nile River Supermarket, Al**, Al Dhafrah ... 9-B8
**Nissan Diesel Bldg**, Mussafah Industrial Area ... 55-G2
**Nissan Services Al Masaood Automobiles Bldg**, Mussafah
Industrial Area ... 55-D2
**Nissan Showroom**
...Al Dhafrah ... 9-G2
...Al Khubeirah ... 11-H2
**NMC Hospital**
...Al Safarat ... 27-G3
...Madinat Zayed ... 8-H2
...Mohammed Bin Zayed City ... 59-K1
**Noble Medical Centre**, Markaziya East ... 4-L6
**Nomas, Al**, Al Bateen ... 17-F2
**Noodle House, The**
...(Al Wahda Mall), Al Nahyan ... 13-B1
...Souk Qaryat Al Beri ... 34-J3
...Al Nahyan ... 13-B1
**Noor Cards Private Real Estate Admin**, Al Manhal ... 8-A8
**Noor Center for Special Needs Bldg, Al**, Al Zahra ... 24-G1
**Noor Hospital Stores Bldg, Al**, Mussafah Industrial Area ... 55-E5
**Noor Hospital, Al**
...Al Madina Al Riyadiya ... 28-G6
...Markaziya East ... 4-H6
...Mohammed Bin Zayed City ... 59-K2
**Noor Indian Islamic School, Al**, Al Dhafrah ... 8-M7
**Noor Islamic Bank**, Markaziya East ... 4-J4
**Noor Trading Company Bldg**, Mussafah Industrial Area ... 55-C3
**Nord Anglia Education**, Al Mushrif ... 22-M2
**Nortel Communication & Information Technology**, Hadabat
Al Zaafaran ... 19-A5
**North Grandstand Bldg**, Yas Island ... 47-K8
**Northern Technical ISD Division Bldg**, Industrial City
of Abu Dhabi ... 59-F3
**Norton Rose Middle East**, Al Mushrif ... 23-J7
**Norway Embassy**, Markaziya East ... 4-K6
**Nova International Bldg**, Mussafah Industrial Area ... 55-E4
**Nova Plastic Industries Bldg**, Industrial City of Abu Dhabi ... 59-F4
**Novotel Centre Hotel**, Markaziya East
...Le Beaujolais ... 4-J7
...Mood Indigo ... 4-J7
...Restaurant China ... 4-J7
**Noy Quality Tubing Coil Service Bldg**, Industrial
City of Abu Dhabi ... 59-E3
**NPC Bldg**, Industrial City of Abu Dhabi ... 59-B4
**NRG Sports Café**, (Le Meridien Abu Dhabi), Tourist Club Area ... 5-F2
**NSCC International**, Al Karamah ... 18-D1

# O

**Oasis Car Wash Bldg**, Bain Al Jessrain ... 35-D1
**Oasis Chinese Restaurant**
...Al Nahyan ... 13-H6
...Madinat Zayed ... 8-K2
**Oasis Heavy Equipment**, Mussafah Industrial Area ... 55-C2
**Oassis Printing Press**, Tourist Club Area ... 5-F6
**Obagi Specialized Hospital**, Al Karamah ... 12-M2
**Obaidali Supermarket, Al**, Mussafah Industrial Area ... 55-E2
**Obaidly Ceramics, Al**, Al Nahyan ... 13-F4
**Obeid Al Zaabi Trading**, Madinat Zayed ... 9-C1
**Ocean Plastic Factory**, Mussafah Industrial Area ... 55-B1
**Ocean Travels**, Al Manhal ... 8-G5
**Oceans**, (Le Royal Méridien Abu Dhabi), Markaziya East ... 4-L3
**Ogasco Oil & Gas Construction Company Bldg**, Industrial
City of Abu Dhabi ... 59-B3
**Ohio Cafe**, Al Meena ... 2-C6
**Old Abu Dhabi Co-operative Society Bldg**, Tourist Club Area ... 5-F2
**Old Post Office**, Al Manhal ... 8-H4
**Oman Embassy**, Al Mushrif ... 18-J7
**Oman Insurance Company Bldg**, Mussafah Industrial Area ... 55-C4
**Omnix International**, Al Zahra ... 20-E8
**One School Rule Respect**, Al Bateen ... 12-A3
**One To One Hotel – The Village**, Al Nahyan
...18Oz ... 9-J6
...The Village Club ... 9-J6
**One, The**, Al Bateen ... 11-K3
**Only One**, Markaziya West ... 8-D4
**Onshore Affaire Al Dafra Development Bldg**, Sas Al Nakhl ... 30-D3
**Optical Centre**, Markaziya East ... 4-G6
**Opus Bar**, (Le Meridien Abu Dhabi), Tourist Club Area ... 5-F2
**Orient Federal Arabian Agency**, Markaziya East ... 4-H7
**Orient House Development & Construction**, Al Manhal ... 12-J1
**Orient House Travel & Tourism**, Al Nahyan ... 13-H6
**Orient Travels**, Madinat Zayed ... 9-A4
**Oryx Hotel**, Al Khalidiya ... 11-K1
**Osool Finance Company**, Tourist Club Area ... 5-D3
**Otaiba Bldg, Al**, Markaziya East ... 4-G8
**Otaiba Group of Establishments Bldg, Al**, Bain Al Jessrain ... 29-J5
**Otaiba Tower Bldg, Al**
...Madinat Zayed ... 4-K8
...Markaziya West ... 4-E7
**Overseas AST Company Bldg**, Mussafah Industrial Area ... 54-L6
**Oxford Medical Centre**, Hadabat Al Zaafaran ... 23-H1
**Oxford School**, Al Manhal ... 12-B1

# P

**Pakistan Embassy**, Al Safarat ... 27-E3
**Pal Group of Company**, Al Dhafrah ... 9-D4

**Palestine Embassy**, Al Safarat ... 27-D1
**Palestine School**, Al Karamah ... 13-A3
**Palm Oasis**, Al Manhal ... 8-B8
**Palm, The**, (Al Diar Capital Hotel), Tourist Club Area ... 2-C7
**Palms Osise Villas**, Al Mushrif ... 23-M8
**Palzilevi Showroom**, Markaziya East ... 4-L4
**PAN International Metal Company Bldg**, Mussafah
Industrial Area ... 55-G6
**Pan World Car Exhibition**, Al Nahyan ... 18-H1
**Panacea Beauty & Spa**, Al Bateen ... 11-M5
**Panda Industries Bldg, Al**, Mussafah Industrial Area ... 54-M7
**Pappagallo**, (Le Meridien Abu Dhabi), Tourist Club Area ... 5-F2
**Paris-Sorbonne University Abu Dhabi**, Sas Al Nakhl ... 29-L5
**Park Hyatt Saadiyat Island Hotel & Resort**, Saadiyat Island ... 41-G3
**Park Rotana Htl**, Al Matar ... 29-A3
**Parker Store Bldg**, Mussafah Industrial Area ... 54-M3
**Pasteur Central Laboratories**, Al Karamah ... 12-M2
**Pearl Primary School, The**, Al Dhafrah ... 9-C6
**Pearls & Caviar**, (Shangri-La Hotel, Qaryat Al Beri),
Bain Al Jessrain ... 34-J4
**Peavls & Cavier**, Bain Al Jessrain ... 34-J5
**Penguin Cooling System Bldg**, Mussafah Industrial Area ... 55-C7
**Peppino**, (Grand Continental Flamingo Hotel), Markaziya East ... 4-L5
**Pepsi Company Bldg**, Al Safarat ... 27-D1
**Perfect Aluminium & Glass Bldg**, Mussafah Industrial Area ... 55-G6
**Performing Arts Centre Bldg**, Saadiyat Island ... 41-B6
**Petro Middle East Bldg**, Mussafah Industrial Area ... 55-G6
**Petroleum Institute, The**, Sas Al Nakhl ... 29-M4
**Peugeot Auto Parts Bldg**, Mussafah Industrial Area ... 55-F2
**Peugeot Bldg**, Tourist Club Area ... 5-E6
**Peugeot Service Centre Bldg**, Al Madina Al Riyadiya ... 28-C3
**Phantom Steel Trading Bldg**, Mussafah Industrial Area ... 55-G6
**Philippines Embassy**, Al Dhafrah ... 9-B4
**Phoenix Timber Factory Bldg**, Mussafah Industrial Area ... 59-A4
**Pioneer Steel Work Bldg**, Mussafah Industrial Area ... 55-G4
**Pipeline Services Bldg**, Mussafah Industrial Area ... 55-C1
**Pit Bldg & Team Bldg**, Yas Island ... 50-J2
**Pizaa More**, Tourist Club Area ... 5-F4
**Pizza Hut**
...Al Karamah ... 13-E7
...Baniyas East ... 61-B8
...Hadabat Al Zaafaran ... 19-D7
...Markaziya East ... 4-G6
...Mussafah Industrial Area ... 55-H3
...Tourist Club Area ... 5-E2
**Pizza Way**
...Al Manhal ... 8-C7
...Bain Al Jessrain ... 35-D4
**PJ O'Reilly's**, (Le Royal Méridien Abu Dhabi), Markaziya East ... 4-L3
**Planet Cafe**, Tourist Club Area ... 5-C3
**Plant Irrigation for Agriculture Bldg**, Madinat Khalifa A ... 50-L6
**Platinum Hotel Apartment**, Markaziya West ... 8-E3
**Plaxit Dry Mix Company Bldg**, Industrial City of Abu Dhabi ... 59-D2
**Poland Embassy**, Al Karamah ... 13-B7
**Polaris Automobile**, Tourist Club Area ... 5-D4
**Police College**
...Al Zahra ... 23-M3
...E36 ... 24-A3
**Police Cultural Sports Club Bldg**, Al Karamah ... 13-A4
**Police Operations General Directorate Bldg**, Al Khubeirah ... 11-G4
**Police Station**
...Al Bateen ... 12-G6
...Al Dhafrah ... 9-D2
...Al Khubeirah (Police Operations General Directorate) ... 11-H4
...Al Meena ... 2-E1
...Al Nahyan (Abu Dhabi Police General Head Office) ... 18-L4
...Al Rehhan ... 24-D7
...Baniyas East ... 60-K5
...Madinat Khalifa A ... 50-F8
...Mussafah Industrial Area ... 59-J1
**Poltrona Frau Design Centre**, Al Khubeirah ... 11-G2
**Poly Emirates Plastic Industries Bldg**, Industrial
City of Abu Dhabi ... 59-G3
**Popeyes Chicken & Seafood**, Al Karamah ... 13-F7
**Popular Auto Parts Bldg**, Mussafah Industrial Area ... 55-G1
**Popular Leasing & Car Rental**, Tourist Club Area ... 5-C3
**Popular Typing Office**, Mussafah Industrial Area ... 55-F3
**Porcellan Ceramic Tile Factory Bldg**, Industrial
City of Abu Dhabi ... 58-J8
**Porsche Centre Abu Dhabi Bldg**, Tourist Club Area ... 5-A1
**Port Zayed**
...Abu Dhabi Customs & Immigration Department Bldg ... 2-F1
...Abu Dhabi Municipality Bldg ... 40-K8
...Abu Dhabi Vegetable Oil Company Bldg ... 40-L5
...Al Meena ... 2-E1
...Al Mina Vegetable Market Bldg ... 40-K8
...City Restaurant ... 40-K8
...Emirates of Abu Dhabi Finance & Customs Administration Department ... 40-K8
...Grand Mills Bldg ... 40-L5
...Icon Cement Company Bldg ... 40-K6
...Market Control Section Bldg ... 40-K8
...Municipal & Agricultural Department Bldg ... 40-K8
...Transport Maritime Sector ... 40-K8
...Unifruitti Cold Store Bldg ... 40-K7
**Posco Engineering & Construction Company**, Al Bateen ... 11-K4
**Power Distribution Bldg**, Industrial City of Abu Dhabi ... 59-F3
**Power Economy Middle East Company Bldg**, Industrial
City of Abu Dhabi ... 59-G2
**Power Garments**, Markaziya East ... 5-A2
**Power House Body Building**, Mohammed Bin Zayed City ... 59-K3
**Power Station**, Sas Al Nakhl Island ... 49-B7
**Pred Progresive Real Estate Development Company Bldg**,
Mussafah Industrial Area ... 59-A4
**Prego's**, (Beach Rotana Hotel & Towers), Tourist Club Area ... 5-G4
**Premier Motors**
...Al Khalidiya ... 11-L1
...Mussafah Industrial Area ... 55-F2

Premier Motors Bldg, Mussafah Industrial Area | 55-C4
Premier Motors Ferrari Bldg, Sas Al Nakhl | 30-A6
Premier Oilfield Rentals Bldg, Mussafah Industrial Area | 55-B1
Presidential Palace Bldg, Al Ras Al Akhdar | 15-H2
Prestige Cars, Al Khalidiya | 11-M1
Prestige Steel Work Bldg, Mussafah Industrial Area | 55-F4
Primary Health Care, Al Bateen | 12-E3
Primary Health Centre, Madinat Zayed | 8-J2
Primary Substation Bldg, Mohammed Bin Zayed City | 55-L4
Prince Medical Centre, Al Dhafrah | 9-E5
Princess Cars Bldg, Bain Al Jessrain | 29-M7
Prismo Gulf Establishment Bldg, Mussafah Industrial Area | 55-D2
Private & Governments Company Vehicle License Bldg,
  Mussafah Industrial Area | 55-B6
Private Department of Sheikh Mohamed Bin Kalid
  Al Nahyan, Al Khalidiya | 11-K1
Private Security Business Department, Al Zahra | 24-H4
Prompt Steel Building Contracting Bldg, Industrial
  City of Abu Dhabi | 59-C4
Protech Bldg, Mussafah Industrial Area | 55-F1
Protect Aesthetic Solution & Pharma Traders Bldg,
  Bain Al Jessrain | 29-L7
PRP Architects International, Al Manhal | 12-H5
Public Garden
  ...Al Bateen | 11-L3
  ...Al Khubeirah | 11-D5
  ...Al Rehhan | 24-H8
  ...Al Shahama 2 | 44-L5
Public Garden Directorate Bldg, Mussafah Industrial Area | 55-H1
Public Health Section, Al Meena | 2-G3
Public Prosecution of the State Security, Al Mushrif | 23-D8
Public Work Department (Abu Dhabi Food Control Authority (ADFCA)),
  Al Karamah | 13-B5
Putra Perdana Construction, Al Bateen | 17-E4

Q

Q Link Transport, Al Karamah | 18-E1
Qabas Institute, Al, Al Karamah | 12-L3
Qadisiyah School, Al, Al Zahra | 24-F4
Qasem Al Marzooqi Factory for Production of Auto Bakeries
  Equipment Bldg, Industrial City of Abu Dhabi | 59-F3
Qatar Airways Bldg, Markaziya West | 8-B5
Qatar Embassy, Al Safarat | 27-D3
Qathara Supermarket, Al, Mussafah Industrial Area | 55-F2
Qazi Heavy Equipment Trading Bldg, Al, Mussafah
  Industrial Area | 55-F5
Quadra Industries, Al, Hadabat Al Zaafaran | 23-F3
Qualification Frame Work, Al Mushrif | 23-H7
Quality Makers, Al Karamah | 12-M3
Quay, The, Tourist Club Area | 2-E8
Qud Modern Bakery, Al, Al Nahyan | 13-H6
Qudra Bldg, Al Matar | 25-K7
Quds Specialized Dental Centre, Al, Baniyas East | 61-B8
Queen Saba Trade, Al Manhal | 8-B8
Queenex Bldg, Mussafah Industrial Area | 54-M7
Quick Intervention Unit of Civil Defense Bldg, Al Dhafrah | 9-B7
Quick Mix Company Bldg, Mussafah Industrial Area | 55-B5
Quickstep Manufacture Bldg, Industrial City of Abu Dhabi | 59-F4
Qurm Bldg, Al, Al Matar | 25-K8
Qurm Residential Compound, Al, Al Matar | 25-E4
Qurm Resort Villas, Al
  ...Al Muzoon | 26-B2

R

Rabeeh School, Al, Hadabat Al Zaafaran | 19-B8
Rabeh General Maintenance, Al, Al Rowdah | 17-H2
Radiant Montessori Nursery, Al Nahyan | 13-D4
Radio Station Bldg, Al Khubeirah | 11-F3
Radisson Blu & Park Inn Hotels, Yas Island | 50-H2
Rafa Audio, Markaziya East | 5-A3
Raha Beach Hotel, Al, Al Raha
  ...Al Raha | 30-K2
  ...Black Pearl | 50-D7
  ...Sevilla | 50-D7
Raha Garden, Al
  ...Madinat Khalifa A | 31-B3
  ...Al Raha Gardens Management Office Bldg | 50-C8
Raha Mall, Al, Al Raha | 50-E7
Raha Mechanical Equipment Company (ARMEPCO)
  Bldg, Al, Mussafah Industrial Area | 55-C7
Raha Supermarket, Al, Mussafah Industrial Area | 55-C3
Rainbow Hotel Apartment, Markaziya East | 4-K7
Rainbow Monitor Coatings Bldg, Mussafah Industrial Area | 55-C3
Rak Trading for Building Materials, Mussafah Industrial Area | 55-G7
Rakha Bldg, Al, Mussafah Industrial Area | 55-E2
Ramada Abu Dhabi Htl, Mahawi | 60-M3
Ramee Garden Hotel Apartment, Markaziya East | 4-J5
Ramee Guestline Hotel Apartment I, Tourist Club Area | 5-C1
Ramla Coast Restaurant, Al, Al Manhal | 8-E5
Ramla Supermarket, Mohammed Bin Zayed City | 55-K8
Rapiscan Systems Bldg, Mussafah Industrial Area | 55-A6
Ras Al Khaimah Bank
  ...Al Manhal | 8-B7
  ...Mussafah Industrial Area | 55-F4
  ...Tourist Club Area | 5-F4
Rashid Transport & Clearing Bldg, Al, Mussafah Industrial Area | 55-C7
Rawafeed Private School, Al Bateen | 12-C6
Rawafi Supermarket, Al, Markaziya West | 8-D5
Rawdah German Medical Centre, Al, Al Karamah | 12-M5
Rawdhathul Al Jeel Nursery School, Al Shamkha | 53-M8
Rawza Zajirah School, Al, Hadabat Al Zaafaran | 19-J8
Raya Spare Parts, Al, Mussafah Industrial Area | 55-G2
Rayan Investment, Al, Al Bateen | 12-C5
Rayyan National Private School, Al, Al Karamah | 12-K7

Rayyan Printing Press, Al, Markaziya East | 4-M3
Razeen, Al, Al Raha | 49-K8
Razi Medical Diagnostic Centre, Al, Markaziya East | 4-K8
Razi Scientific Bookshop, Al, Al Manhal | 12-B1
Reach Group, Al Mushrif | 18-J8
Ready Mix Cement Bldg, Mussafah Industrial Area | 55-B2
Readyfix Middle East Bldg, Mussafah Industrial Area | 55-B5
Recreation Park, Markaziya East | 4-K1
Red Castle Restaurant, Madinat Zayed | 8-K3
Red Crescent, Al Nahyan | 9-J7
Red Valley Restaurant, Madinat Zayed | 9-B3
Redsea Aluminium Bldg, Mussafah Industrial Area | 55-D1
Reef Downtown, Al, Abu Dhabi International Airport | 51-H4
Reem Aluminium Bldg, Mussafah Industrial Area | 55-C3
Reem Emirates Aluminium Bldg, Industrial City of Abu Dhabi | 59-C4
Reem United Industries Bldg, Industrial City of Abu Dhabi | 59-B3
Regal Art Decor Bldg, Mussafah Industrial Area | 55-D5
Regent Emirates Pearl Abu Dhabi, The, Al Bateen | 11-A7
Rehan Spare Parts & Trading Bldg, Al, Mussafah
  Industrial Area | 55-G3
Rent Dispute Settlement Committee, Al Karamah | 13-C5
Residence Bldg, Al Khubeirah | 11-H4
Restaurant China, (Novotel Centre Hotel), Markaziya East | 4-J7
Reyada Medical Centre, Al, Al Karamah | 13-C6
Reyami Office Furniture, Al, Tourist Club Area | 5-F4
Rheem Air Condition Company Bldg, Mussafah
  Industrial Area | 55-A6
Rief Bldg, Al, Al Khubeirah | 11-H4
Riviera, (Marina Al Bateen Resort), Al Bateen | 16-H4
Rivoli, Al Manhal | 8-E5
Riyadh Centre Bldg, Al Maqtaa | 34-E4
Riyadh Plastic Industries Bldg, Al, Industrial City of Abu Dhabi | 59-G3
Riyami Hotel Apartment, Al Dhafrah | 9-B6
Rock Bottom Café, (Al Diar Capital Hotel), Tourist Club Area | 2-C7
Rock Cement Industry Bldg, Mussafah Industrial Area | 55-F8
Rock Refreshment, The, Markaziya East | 4-G5
Rodent & Pest Control Center, Hadabat Al Zaafaran | 19-C7
Rodeo Grill, (Beach Rotana Hotel & Towers), Tourist Club Area | 5-G4
Romania Embassy, Al Karamah | 13-A7
Romantic Rose Gifts, Al Nahyan | 13-G4
Rosary School, Al Nahyan | 13-G8
Rosebuds, (Beach Rotana Hotel & Towers), Tourist Club Area | 5-G4
Rostamani Exchange, Al, Markaziya East | 5-B5
Rotana & Rotana Centro Hotels, Yas Island | 50-J2
Rotana Resort Sadiyat Beach Hotel, Saadiyat Island | 41-F4
Rottana Mall Bldg, Al Khalidiya | 11-L1
Roua Supermarket, Al, Baniyas East | 61-B8
Rowdah Arjan Hotel Apartment, Al, Al Nahyan | 13-B2
Rowdah Bldg, Al, Al Khubeirah | 11-G3
Rowdah Clinic, Al, Al Karamah | 12-L5
Rowdat Al Reef Palace Bldg, Al Falah City | 51-K7
Rowdathul Hidaya School, Al Bateen | 11-G6
Royal Bank of Scotland, Tourist Club Area | 5-C3
Royal City Restaurant, Mussafah Industrial Area | 55-G6
Royal Classic Interiors Bldg, Industrial City of Abu Dhabi | 59-G2
Royal Emirates Supermarket, Mussafah Industrial Area | 55-F2
Royal Falcon Surveying General Construction Bldg,
  Mussafah Industrial Area | 54-L6
Royal Falcon Trading Bldg, Mussafah Industrial Area | 55-F2
Royal Guard Bldg, Al Bateen | 17-F5
Royal Heavy Equipment Bldg, Mussafah Industrial Area | 55-G6
Royal House Furnished Apartment, Tourist Club Area | 2-E8
Royal Jet Bldg, Madinat Khalifa A | 52-F1
Royal Joinery Al Hamid Group Atlas Construction Bldg,
  Mussafah Industrial Area | 58-K4
Royal Orchid, (Hilton Abu Dhabi), Al Khubeirah | 11-D5
Royal Place Furniture Manufacturing Bldg, Mussafah
  Industrial Area | 54-M6
Royal Printing Rork, Al Manhal | 8-C8
Royal Regency Hotel Apartment, Markaziya East | 4-H7
Royal Seasons Hotel, Markaziya East | 5-B4
Royal Specialist Medical Centre, Al Manhal | 8-C7
Royal Thai Embassy, Al Dhafrah | 9-A6
Royal Wing Mafraq Hospital, Mahawi | 60-L3
Ruku Al Sultan Restaurant & Grills, Al Karamah | 13-B3
Rumaila, Al, Al Raha
  ...Abu Dhabi Commercial Bank | 50-E7
  ...Al Raha | 50-C7
  ...Al Raha Beach Hotel | 50-D7
  ...Al Raha Mall Bldg | 50-D7
  ...Black Pearl | 50-D7
  ...Emirates Sailing School | 50-D7
  ...Lulu Express | 50-E7
  ...Sevilla | 50-D7
  ...Subway | 50-E7
  ...Zari Zardozi | 50-E7
Rumis Power Company, Al Mushrif | 23-G6
Russia Embassy, Markaziya East | 4-M3
Rwad Aluminium & Carpentry Works Bldg, Al,
  Mussafah Industrial Area | 54-M8

S

Saada Restaurant, Al, Tourist Club Area | 5-G6
Saadiyat Beach
  ...Park Hyatt Saadiyat Island Hotel & Resort | 41-G3
  ...Rotana Resort Sadiyat Beach Hotel | 41-F4
  ...Saadiyat Island | 41-D3
  ...Sadiyat Beach Golf Club | 41-H3
  ...St Regis Hotel | 41-E5
Saadiyat Cultural District
  ...Saadiyat Island | 40-M4
  ...Guggenheim Abu Dhabi Museum | 41-A4
  ...Louvre Abu Dhabi | 41-A5
  ...Performing Arts Centre Bldg | 41-B6
  ...Zayed National Museum | 41-B5
Saadiyat Marina, Saadiyat Island | 41-D8

Saba Hotel, Tourist Club Area | 5-F5
Sada Al Ayyam Restaurant, Al Karamah | 13-B3
Sada Vegetables, Al, Baniyas West | 60-L8
Sadaf Fashion Department Store, Al, Madinat Zayed | 8-J1
Sadaf Grill & Bakery, Al, Al Nahyan | 18-L1
Sadiat Co-operative Society, Al Meena | 2-J3
Sadiq Auto Electro Repairing Bldg, Al, Mussafah
  Industrial Area | 55-G4
Sadiyat Beach Golf Club, Saadiyat Island | 41-H3
Sadiyath Tower Bldg, Markaziya East | 5-B4
Saeed Institute of Photography, Al Khubeirah | 11-H3
Safa Marble Bldg, Al, Mussafah Industrial Area | 55-C7
Safa Supermarket, Al, Madinat Zayed | 8-J1
Safa Tower Bldg, Al, Al Khalidiya | 11-K1
Safari General Contracting Company Bldg, Mussafah
  Industrial Area | 55-D6
Safe Water Chemical Bldg, Industrial City of Abu Dhabi | 59-A3
Safeer Mall Bldg, Al, Mohammed Bin Zayed City | 55-J8
Safeer Style, Al Manhal | 8-B8
Safeer Supermarket, Mohammed Bin Zayed City | 55-J8
Safety Palace Bldg, Mussafah Industrial Area | 55-D3
Safina Dhow Restaurant, Al, Breakwater | 7-C7
Safran Company, Al Mushrif | 27-B1
Safsaf Restaurant, Al, Mohammed Bin Zayed City | 59-K2
Safwa Mechanical Equipment Bldg, Al, Mussafah
  Industrial Area | 55-C7
Sagar International Bldg, Mussafah Industrial Area | 55-G6
Sagar Tower Bldg, Markaziya East | 4-M5
Sahara Hotel Apartment
  ...Al Baladia | 5-B5
  ...Al Dhafrah | 8-M7
  ...Markaziya East | 4-M6
Sahara Metal Industries Bldg, Al, Industrial City of Abu Dhabi | 59-G2
Saif Bin Darwish Carpentry Bldg, Mussafah Industrial Area | 55-E8
Salah Riyadha Arabic School, Al Bateen | 11-L8
Salah Tower Bldg, Al, Madinat Zayed | 5-A7
Salahuddin School, Al Karamah | 12-M2
Salam Emirates Primary School, Al, Al Dhafrah | 9-F3
Salam Tower Bldg, Al, Tourist Club Area | 5-C3
Salam Tyres, Al, Al Dhafrah | 9-G2
Salamah Binbui Secondary School for Girls, Baniyas East | 61-B8
Salaries & Allowance Section Abu Dhabi Police, Al Nahyan | 18-L5
Salem Al Saman Bldg, Markaziya East | 4-K6
Salm Printing Press, Al, Madinat Zayed | 8-J3
Salmeen Gold Tower Bldg, Al, Tourist Club Area | 5-C3
Sama Abu Dhabi Home Health Care Centre, Madinat Khalifa A | 52-F5
Sama Gulf, Al Nahyan | 18-H1
Samaliya Basic School, Al, Baniyas West | 60-M8
Samawi Neon Bldg, Mussafah Industrial Area | 55-G6
Sameer Al Mahmood & Sons Furniture, Al Karamah | 13-D6
Samiya Supermarket, Al, Al Mushrif | 26-G1
Samsung Engineering Construction, Al Manhal | 12-J2
San Diego Villas Bldg, Madinat Khalifa B | 57-A7
Sana Fashion, Al Baladia | 5-B8
Sangeetha Restaurant, Tourist Club Area | 5-B2
Sanyo, Madinat Zayed | 4-L7
Saqia Trading, Al, Al Baladia | 5-C6
Saqoor Model School, Al, Al Dhafrah | 9-C4
Sara Institute of Science & Technology, Markaziya East | 5-B4
Sara Nursery, Al Dhafrah | 8-L7
Sara Trading Establishment Bldg, Mussafah Industrial Area | 55-B5
Sarah Plastic Bldg, Mussafah Industrial Area | 55-D2
Saraya
  ...Corniche Hospital | 2-A8
  ...E12 | 1-M8
  ...Tourist Club Area | 1-M7
Sarhad Medical Clinic, Mussafah Industrial Area | 55-G2
Sas Al Nakhl School, Madinat Khalifa A | 52-D3
Sas Al Nakhl Village
  ...Madinat Khalifa A | 35-J2
  ...Spinneys | 36-B4
Saudi Arabia Embassy, Al Safarat | 27-G2
Saudi Kitchen, Al Meena | 2-C2
Sawaeed Employment Camp Bldg, Al Zahra | 20-J8
Sawari Tower, Al
  ...A Bldg, Al Khalidiya | 8-A6
  ...B Bldg, Al Khalidiya | 8-A6
  ...C Bldg, Al Khalidiya | 8-A5
SAX, (Le Royal Méridien Abu Dhabi), Markaziya East | 4-L3
Sayad, (Emirates Palace), Al Ras Al Akhdar | 10-L5
Sayadi Key, Al, Al Nahyan | 9-E6
Sayed Anver Spare Parts Bldg, Mussafah Industrial Area | 55-G4
Sayed Anver Used Spare Parts Bldg, Mussafah Industrial Area | 55-G4
Sayegh Centre Bldg, Al, Markaziya East | 4-G8
Scadia / Parson Adia Office Bldg, Abu Dhabi
  International Airport | 50-M6
SCAFFCO Bldg, Industrial City of Abu Dhabi | 59-F2
Scania Bldg, Mussafah Industrial Area | 55-C1
Sceco for Steel Tank & Sections Factory Bldg, Industrial
  City of Abu Dhabi | 59-F3
Schlumberger Middle East & Asia Learning Centre,
  Al Shamkha | 57-K3
SCHMDLIN Bldg, Industrial City of Abu Dhabi | 59-C2
School Health Administration, Al Bateen | 12-E3
Sea Bird Supermarket, Baniyas East | 61-G8
Sea Safety Engineering Service Bldg, Mussafah
  Industrial Area | 55-G6
Sea Shell Restaurant
  ...Al Manhal | 8-E5
  ...Al Mushrif | 22-A1
  ...Hadabat Al Zaafaran | 19-C5
Seashore Villa, Officers City | 37-L5
SEBA Tower Bldg, Al Khalidiya | 11-K2
Sedana Bldg, Mussafah Industrial Area | 55-C1
Sedar, Al Manhal | 8-E4
Seedra Fashion, Al Manhal | 8-D7

**Seef, Al**
...Al Raha ... 50-F6
**Seer Marine Bldg, Al**, Mussafah Industrial Area ... 59-A5
**Seha Ambulatory Health Care Centre**, Madinat Khalifa A ... 52-C1
**Seidco Contracting Company Bldg**, Mussafah Industrial Area ... 58-L1
**Seidco General Contracting Company Bldg**, Mussafah Industrial Area ... 54-L7
**Selective Design Factory Bldg**, Industrial City of Abu Dhabi ... 59-F3
**Send Exchange Establishment**, Markaziya East ... 4-G7
**Senegal Embassy**, Madinat Zayed ... 8-L1
**Sesame Street Nursery**, Al Dhafrah ... 9-A7
**Seven Star Auto Garage Bldg**, Mussafah Industrial Area ... 55-C6
**Seven Star Filter Factory Bldg**, Mussafah Industrial Area ... 55-A8
**SGS Marine Services Bldg**, Mussafah Industrial Area ... 54-M3
**Shabiya Police Station**, Al Dhafrah ... 9-D2
**Shahama Bus Station**, Al Shahama 2 ... 44-L4
**Shahama General Maintenance & Decoration Bldg, Al**, Mussafah Industrial Area ... 55-E7
**Shahama I, Al**, Al Shahama 2 ... 44-L5
**Shahama II, Al**, Al Shahama 2 ... 48-K1
**Shahama Market Bldg**, Al Shahama 2 ... 44-L4
**Shahama New, Al**, Al Shahama 2 ... 44-L2
**Shahama Old, Al**, Al Shahama 2 ... 44-J4
**Shahama Park 1**, Al Shahama 2 ... 44-K2
**Shahama Park 2**, Al Shahama 2 ... 44-K3
**Shahama School**, Al Shahama 2 ... 44-J5
**Shahama Wedding Hall Bldg**, Al Shahama 2 ... 44-J6
**Shaheen Medical Centre**, Al Dhafrah ... 8-L6
**Shaheen Supermarket**, Baniyas East ... 60-K7
**Shaheen Tyers Company Bldg**, Mussafah Industrial Area ... 55-E6
**Shahiz Twrs Bldg, Al**, Al Khubeirah ... 11-G2
**Shaleela, Al**
...Al Raha ... 31-D1
...Al Raha Beach ... 31-E1
**Shalimar Company**, Al Manhal ... 12-A1
**Sham Vedio & Gifts, Al**, Al Manhal ... 8-E6
**Shams Abu Dhabi**, Tourist Club Area ... 5-F5
**Shamsi Metal Furniture Factory Bldg, Al**, Mussafah Industrial Area ... 55-A6
**Shamyat Bldg**, Tourist Club Area ... 5-A1
**Shang Palace**, (Shangri-La Hotel, Qaryat Al Beri), Bain Al Jessrain ... 34-J4
**Shangri-La Hotel**, Bain Al Jessrain
...Bord Eau ... 34-J4
...Hoi An ... 34-J4
...Pearls & Caviar ... 34-J4
...Shang Palace ... 34-J4
...Sofra Bld ... 34-J4
**Shangri-La Residences**, Bain Al Jessrain ... 34-J2
**Sharjah Islamic Bank**, Al Baladia ... 5-B5
**Sharq Car Wash ENOC Bldg, Al**, Mussafah Industrial Area ... 55-G2
**Shatie Palace Bldg**, Al Bateen ... 26-A3
**Shatry Trading Establishment Bldg**, Mussafah Industrial Area ... 55-G2
**Sheikh Ahmed Bin Tahnoon Complex**, Al Matar ... 25-D5
**Sheikh Hamdan Bin Mohd Al Nahyan Mosque**, Bain Al Jessrain ... 35-K5
**Sheikh Khalifa Bin Zayed Arab Pakistani School**, Hadabat Al Zaafaran ... 19-C7
**Sheikh Khalifa Bin Zayed Bangladesh Islamia School**, Al Matar ... 24-J4
**Sheikh Khalifa Energy Complex Bldg**, Markaziya East ... 4-L2
**Sheikh Khalifa Hospital**, Al Manhal ... 8-L8
**Sheikh Khalifa Medical City Blood Bank Abu Dhabi**, Al Manhal ... 12-D2
**Sheikh Khalifa Residential Complex A**, Tourist Club Area ... 
...E16_01 ... 5-G4
...Safeer Departmental Store ... 5-G4
**Sheikh Khalifa Residential Complex B**, Tourist Club Area ... 
...Al Fardan Exchange ... 5-F3
...Mandoos ... 5-F3
...Subway ... 5-F3
...United Emirates Aviation ... 5-F3
**Sheikh Mohd Bin Khalifa Mosque**, Mohammed Bin Zayed City ... 59-K2
**Sheikh Mohd Bin Zayed Masjid**, Al Mushrif ... 18-H4
**Sheikh Saif Mosque**, Hadabat Al Zaafaran ... 23-C1
**Sheikh Sultan Bin Zayed Al Nahyan Personal Affairs Bldg**, Mussafah Industrial Area ... 55-E1
**Sheikh Sultan Bin Zayed Stadium**, Al Karamah ... 13-C6
**Sheikh Zayed Bin Sultan Al Nahyan Terminal Bldg**, Al Matar ... 28-D1
**Sheikh Zayed Bin Sultan Mosque**, Al Manhal ... 8-G3
**Sheikh Zayed Grand Mosque**, Al Maqtaa ... 34-A1
**Sheikh Zayed Private Academy**, Al Karamah ... 18-A2
**Sheikh Zayed Stadium Bldg**, Al Madina Al Riyadiya ... 28-C7
**Sheraton Abu Dhabi Hotel & Resort**, Tourist Club Area ... 
...Bravo Tapas Bar ... 4-M1
...Cloud Nine – Cigar & Bottle Club ... 4-M1
...El Sombrero ... 4-M1
...Flavours ... 4-M1
...Il Paradiso ... 4-M1
...La Mamma ... 4-M1
...Tavern ... 4-M1
**Sheraton Khalidiya Hotel**
...La Veranda, Markaziya West ... 8-C6
**Shibl Al Feda Restaurant**, Al Manhal ... 8-G4
**Shobra**, Al Baladia ... 5-B8
**Shohub School for Girls, Al**, Al Karamah ... 18-C2
**Shomoo Private School, Al**, Al Meena ... 2-D3
**Shoumukh Industries Bldg, Al**, Industrial City of Abu Dhabi ... 59-E2
**Shuaa Paper & Plastic Products**, Mussafah Industrial Area ... 55-B3
**Shuja Yacht**, (Le Royal Méridien Abu Dhabi), Markaziya East ... 4-L3
**Shuja, The**, Breakwater ... 7-D5
**Shurooq Residence, Al**, Markaziya East ... 4-M2
**SICHEM Bldg**, Mussafah Industrial Area ... 55-B3
**Siddiq Gifts**, Markaziya East ... 5-B4
**Siemens Service Centre Bldg**, Mussafah Industrial Area ... 55-H7
**Sigma Engg Works Bldg**, Mussafah Industrial Area ... 54-M6
**Signature Hotel**, Yas Island ... 50-H4
**Silent Vally Restaurant**, Industrial City of Abu Dhabi ... 59-A4
**Silver Sign Bldg**, Mussafah Industrial Area ... 55-G5

**Silver Star Office Supplies**, Al Nahyan ... 13-G6
**Silver Tower Bldg**, Markaziya East ... 4-G5
**Sinan Book Shop**, Al Manhal ... 8-B8
**Sinan Supermarket**, Al Bateen ... 11-M8
**Singapore Embassy**, Hadabat Al Zaafaran ... 23-K4
**Sinyar Logistics Bldg**, Mussafah Industrial Area ... 55-E6
**Sir Baniyas Secondary School**, Mohammed Bin Zayed City ... 55-L1
**Sisco Properties Management**, Al Dhafrah ... 8-M8
**SKF Distributor**, Madinat Zayed ... 8-L5
**Skyline General Contracting Establishment Bldg**, Mussafah Industrial Area ... 55-G5
**Skyline Metal Trading Bldg**, Mussafah Industrial Area ... 55-G5
**Skyway Trading Company Bldg**, Mussafah Industrial Area ... 55-E2
**Slide Star Real Estate Bldg**, Tourist Club Area ... 5-E3
**Smart Computer**, Markaziya East ... 4-K6
**Smart Design Bldg**, Mussafah Industrial Area ... 55-F3
**Smith Bldg**, Mussafah Industrial Area ... 55-C2
**Smokers Centre**, Tourist Club Area ... 5-D2
**Snow White**
...Madinat Zayed ... 8-K1
...Markaziya East ... 5-A4
**Soba**, (Le Royal Méridien Abu Dhabi), Markaziya East ... 4-L3
**Social Support Center Bldg**, Madinat Khalifa A ... 52-E3
**Sodap Emirates**, Al Mushrif ... 26-J2
**Sofiya Refreshment**, Al Mushrif ... 18-K5
**Sofra Bld**, (Shangri-La Hotel, Qaryat Al Beri), Bain Al Jessrain ... 34-J4
**Somalia Embassy**, Al Bateen ... 12-A3
**Sonic Car Wash**, Sas Al Nakhl ... 29-M6
**Sony**, Markaziya East ... 4-L5
**Sorouh**, Al Mushrif ... 26-H2
**Sorouh Bldg**
...Markaziya East ... 4-L3
...Mussafah Industrial Area ... 55-C6
**Sorour Bakeries, Al**, Al Nahyan ... 13-E6
**Souk at Qaryat Al Beri Bldg, The**, Bain Al Jessrain ... 34-K3
**Soul Stars Supermarket**, Mussafah Industrial Area ... 55-F4
**South Grandstand Bldg**, Yas Island ... 50-K3
**South Korea Embassy**, Al Karamah ... 18-B2
**South Spine Precinct**
...Abu Dhabi University ... 56-C4
...Capital District ... 56-A2
...The British International School ... 56-C3
**Southern Aluminium & Glass Bldg**, Mussafah Industrial Area ... 55-D6
**Southern Fried Chicken**, Al Nahyan ... 13-B2
**Southern Gulf Marine Industries Bldg**, Mussafah Industrial Area ... 54-M3
**Southern Marina**, Yas Island ... 50-J4
**Southern Marina Village**, Yas Island ... 50-J4
**Space Age Electrical Switchgear Company Bldg**, Industrial City of Abu Dhabi ... 59-F3
**Spain Embassy**, Markaziya East ... 4-K6
**Spare Parts Liberty Abu Dhabi Automobiles Company Bldg**, Mussafah Industrial Area ... 55-D2
**Sparks**, Tourist Club Area ... 5-E5
**Special Care Centre**, Al Dhafrah ... 9-A8
**Special Forces Bldg**, Mangroves (Al Qurm) ... 25-K3
**Specialized Oil Well Maintenance Company (SOWMCO) Bldg**, Mussafah Industrial Area ... 55-E8
**Speed Parts**, Madinat Zayed ... 8-K5
**Spencer Interiors**, Mussafah Industrial Area ... 55-G7
**Spinneys**
...Al Baladia ... 5-A7
...Al Khubeirah ... 11-H3
...Al Nahyan ... 9-D8
...Madinat Khalifa A ... 36-B4
...Mohammed Bin Zayed City ... 59-K3
...Mussafah Industrial Area ... 55-F1
**Spinneys Bar**, Markaziya East ... 4-M5
**Splash**, Markaziya East ... 4-J6
**Sports Care Program**, Al Bateen ... 12-A4
**Sports Centre Bldg**, Al Madina Al Riyadiya ... 28-A5
**Sports Restaurant**, Baniyas East ... 60-K7
**Squar General Contracting Company Bldg**, Mussafah Industrial Area ... 54-L6
**SR Electrical Abu Dhabi Bldg**, Mussafah Industrial Area ... 54-M8
**Sri Lanka Embassy**, Madinat Zayed ... 4-M7
**St Andrews Centre**, Al Mushrif ... 18-H4
**St Antony Coptic Orthodox Church**, Al Mushrif ... 18-G4
**St George Orthodox Cathedral Church**, Al Mushrif ... 18-J5
**St Joseph's School**, Al Mushrif ... 18-G5
**St Regis Hotel**, Saadiyat Island ... 41-E5
**Standard Chartered Bank**
...Al Khalidiya ... 8-A8
...Markaziya West ... 4-D8
...Mussafah Industrial Area ... 55-H3
**Stanley Consultants**, Bain Al Jessrain ... 34-L2
**Star Cements Bldg**, Industrial City of Abu Dhabi ... 59-E3
**Star Light Building Material Bldg**, Mussafah Industrial Area ... 55-G2
**Star Rent A Car**, Markaziya East ... 4-K7
**Star Security Service Bldg**, Mussafah Industrial Area ... 55-D7
**Starbucks Coffee**, Al Dhafrah ... 9-A5
**Stars For Special Abilities**, Al Karamah ... 13-F8
**Statistics Center Abu Dhabi Bldg**, Bain Al Jessrain ... 34-M4
**Stepping Stones Nursery**
...Al Bateen ... 11-H7
...Al Karamah ... 12-M8
**Stepping Stones Nursery Child Development**, Bain Al Jessrain ... 35-C6
**Strawberry Cafe**, Markaziya West ... 8-C2
**Strawberry Nursery**, Madinat Khalifa B ... 57-E2
**Stylee**, Markaziya West ... 8-D4
**Styrene Insulation Industry Bldg**, Mussafah Industrial Area ... 59-A1
**Styropack for Plastic Factory Bldg**, Industrial City of Abu Dhabi ... 59-G3
**Substation Bldg**
...Mahawi ... 60-M2
...Mohammed Bin Zayed City ... 55-L6
...Tourist Club Area ... 2-A8

**Subway**
...Al Dhafrah ... 9-A5
...Al Khalidiya ... 11-L1
**Sudan Embassy**, Al Mushrif ... 23-L8
**Sudanese Social Club**, Al Dhafrah ... 9-C3
**Suhail Al Mazroui Bldg**, Mussafah Industrial Area ... 55-C1
**Suhaila Supermarket**, Markaziya East ... 4-M2
**Sulathan Bakery, Al**, Al Shahama 2 ... 44-M2
**Sultan Bin Zayed**, Al Bateen ... 17-B3
**Sun Flower Refreshment**, Markaziya East ... 4-L6
**Sun Tower Bldg**, Yas Island ... 50-K1
**Sunrise School**, Mohammed Bin Zayed City ... 59-J1
**Super Engineering Industries Bldg**, Industrial City of Abu Dhabi ... 59-F3
**Super Star Heavy Machinery Bldg**, Mussafah Industrial Area ... 55-F3
**Supermarket & Departmental Stores**, Al Bateen ... 12-B6
**Supper Supplies Oil Field & Marine Service Bldg**, Mussafah Industrial Area ... 55-D2
**Support Pit Bldg Grandstand Bldg**, Yas Island ... 50-J2
**Suzuki**, Al Baladia ... 5-C6
**Suzuki Auto Sports**, Mussafah Industrial Area ... 55-G3
**Sweden Embassy**, Madinat Zayed ... 4-K8
**Swedish Medical Centre**, Al Bateen ... 11-K4
**Sweet Palace**, Tourist Club Area ... 2-D7
**Switzerland Embassy**, Al Bateen ... 12-E6
**Sycoms College**, Al Baladia ... 5-C5
**Sylhet Supermarket**, Mussafah Industrial Area ... 55-E6
**Symbol Computers**, Markaziya East ... 5-A3
**Symex International Motors**, Al Dhafrah ... 9-B5
**Synaxis Ready Mix Bldg**, Mussafah Industrial Area ... 59-E1
**Syria Embassy**, Al Safarat ... 27-J3
**System Development Division,** Abu Dhabi Police General Head Office Information Technology & Communication Department Bldg, Al Nahyan ... 9-F7

# T

**Tafseer Contracting & General Main Company Bldg**, Mussafah Industrial Area ... 55-H7
**Taha Medical Centre**, Madinat Zayed ... 9-A3
**Taj Perfumes, Al**, Al Nahyan ... 9-D7
**Takaseem Haute Couture**, Al Rowdah ... 17-G2
**TAKREER**, Markaziya East ... 4-L2
**Takreer We Refine Right Bldg**, Industrial City of Abu Dhabi ... 59-F6
**Talay**, (Le Meridien Abu Dhabi), Tourist Club Area ... 5-F2
**Talent Medical Centre**, Al Dhafrah ... 9-A4
**Tamam Aluminium Bldg**, Mussafah Industrial Area ... 55-C2
**Tamayoz Cement Product Factory Bldg, Al**, Industrial City of Abu Dhabi ... 59-E4
**Tameer Twrs Bldg**, Al Khalidiya ... 7-K8
**Tamkin Industries Bldg**, Mussafah Industrial Area ... 55-B3
**Target Engineering Contracting Company Bldg**, Mussafah Industrial Area ... 55-D7
**Tasah El Bldg**, Al Matar ... 25-K8
**Tasameen Real Estate**, Al Nahyan ... 9-F8
**Tasameen STX Bldg**, Al Rowdah ... 17-L5
**Tasees Consultancy**, Al Mushrif ... 23-B8
**Taste of Thailand**, (Al Ain Palace Hotel), Markaziya East ... 4-K2
**Tasty Refreshment**, Al Mushrif ... 18-K6
**Tavern**, (Sheraton Abu Dhabi Hotel & Resort), Tourist Club Area ... 4-M1
**Tawah Private School, Al**, Al Mushrif ... 22-M4
**Tayco Metal Industries Bldg**, Industrial City of Abu Dhabi ... 59-E3
**Tayeb Cold Stores Bldg, Al**, Industrial City of Abu Dhabi ... 59-H1
**Technical Dot Bldg**, Mussafah Industrial Area ... 55-D3
**Technical Industries for Melamine Boards & Powder Coating Bldg**, Mussafah Industrial Area ... 55-A8
**Technical Metal Industries Bldg**
...Industrial City of Abu Dhabi ... 59-F3
...Mussafah Industrial Area ... 58-M1
**Technical Oilfield Supplies Centre Bldg**, Mussafah Industrial Area ... 55-G1
**Technical Plastic Industries Bldg**, Industrial City of Abu Dhabi ... 59-G3
**Technical Rescue & Quick Intervention Branch Bldg**, Mohammed Bin Zayed City ... 55-L5
**Technical Resources Establishment Bldg**, Mussafah Industrial Area ... 55-A7
**Technical Scissors Company**, Al Nahyan ... 13-J7
**Teddy Bear American Nursery**, Madinat Khalifa A ... 52-D5
**Telecommunications Regulatory Authority (TRA)**, Markaziya East ... 4-K6
**Thamanna Studio**, Markaziya East ... 4-H5
**Thameer Trading Establishment**, Al Nahyan ... 13-F2
**Tharwaniyah, Al**
...Madinat Khalifa A ... 50-G7
**Thrifty Rent A Car**, Al Nahyan ... 13-E6
**Thuraya School, Al**, Al Bateen ... 17-C1
**Thurayya, Al**
...Al Raha ... 30-L2
**Thuvana Nursery, Al**, Al Bateen ... 12-E5
**Tihama Distribution Bookshop**, Al Manhal ... 8-B8
**Tilusanz More**, Al Baladia ... 5-B8
**Tinkerer Research Centre Bldg**, Sas Al Nakhl ... 30-A6
**TMI Steel Bldg**, Industrial City of Abu Dhabi ... 59-A3
**Tokyo Marine Boat Maintenance Bldg**, Mussafah Industrial Area ... 55-G5
**Top Aluminium & Glass Company Bldg**, Mussafah Industrial Area ... 55-C3
**Top Cars Rent A Car**, Al Nahyan ... 13-G3
**Top Star Hotel**, Madinat Zayed ... 8-L4
**Tornado Sport Cafe**, Al Manhal ... 8-C8
**Total Auto Spare Parts Bldg**, Mussafah Industrial Area ... 55-G5
**Toufan Travel & Tourism Bldg, Al**, Mussafah Industrial Area ... 55-B4
**Toufeeque Supermarket, Al**, Markaziya West ... 8-C5
**Tourist Information**
...Al Ras Al Akhdar ... 10-L5
...Sas Al Nakhl ... 29-H5
...Tourist Club Area ... 5-G3

Towers at the Trade Centre Bldg, Tourist Club Area 5-G4
TRA, Markaziya East 4-K6
Trade License Section, Court & Copyright Section,
  Markaziya East 4-K6
Trader Vic's, (Beach Rotana Hotel & Towers), Tourist Club Area 5-G4
Traders Hotel, Bain Al Jessrain 34-K1
Trading Enterprises Bldg, Mussafah Industrial Area 55-C1
Trading Enterprises Company, Al Baladia 5-A6
Traffic & Patrols Directorate Bldg, Hadabat Al Zaafaran 19-E5
Traffic Department Accommodation Bldg, Hadabat
  Al Zaafaran 19-F7
Trans Abu Dhabi (Transportation of Abu Dhabi) Bldg,
  Al Nahyan 13-G2
Trans Gulf Ready Mix Concrete Company Bldg, Mussafah
  Industrial Area 59-F1
Trans World Property Management, Madinat Zayed 8-M2
Transco Bldg
...Al Dhafrah 9-E3
...Markaziya East 5-A2
...Mussafah Industrial Area 55-H1
Transco Mussafah Stores, Mussafah Industrial Area 55-F6
Transco Water Head Company Bldg, Al Bateen 17-F2
Transport & Workshop Administration, Abu Dhabi
  Police Head Office Bldg, Al Rehhan 23-K5
Tremix Cement Bldg, Mussafah Industrial Area 54-M2
Tripes Repairing Workshop Bldg, Mussafah Industrial Area 55-D3
Tunisia Embassy, Al Khubeirah 11-H2
Turkey Embassy
...Al Karamah 17-L1
...Al Safarat 27-H2
Turkmenistan Embassy, Al Safarat 27-E3
Twofour54, Al Matar
...1 Bldg 25-H8
...2 Bldg 25-H8
...3 Bldg 25-H8
...4 Bldg 25-H8
Tyco Fire & Security, Al Bateen 11-M5

U

UAE Academy, Al Bateen 11-M7
UAE AID Co-ordination Office, Al Manhal 12-B4
UAE Control Authority of Islamic Affairs &
  Endowments Bldg, Madinat Zayed 8-M4
UAE Enterprises Company Bldg, Mussafah Industrial Area 55-B4
UAE Exchange
...Al Bateen 12-B6
...Al Matar 24-J5
...Al Shahama 2 44-M2
...Markaziya East 4-G8
...Mohammed Bin Zayed City 59-K1
...Mussafah Industrial Area 55-F2
UAE General Authority of Islamic Affairs &
  Endowments Bldg, Baniyas East 61-A8
UAE General Civil Aviation Authority Bldg, Al Madina
  Al Riyadiya 28-B4
UAE General Secretariat of Municipality Bldg, Al Madina
  Al Riyadiya 28-A3
UAE Ministry of Bldg, Al Mushrif 18-J6
UAE Naval Force Naval School Security & Safety Wing,
  Industrial City of Abu Dhabi 59-E6
UAE Wresting & Judo Federation, Al Mushrif 18-G8
UK Embassy, Markaziya West 8-D2
Ukraine Embassy, Madinat Zayed 9-A2
Ultra Care Medical Centre, Al Karamah 12-M5
Umm Al Nar Archaeological Site, Sas Al Nakhl Island 49-G6
Umm Al Nar Supermarket, Mussafah Industrial Area 55-G6
Umm Ammar School, Al Mushrif 18-H6
Umm Habib School, Al Bateen 11-M8
Unesco Project School, Madinat Zayed 8-M2
Unibeton Ready Mix Bldg, Mussafah Industrial Area 55-C5
Unicorp Technology, Al Zahra 23-L2
Unifruitti Cold Store Bldg, Al Meena 40-K7
Union Bank of India, Markaziya East 4-F8
Union Iron & Steel Bldg, Industrial City of Abu Dhabi 58-M3
Union Marble Bldg, Mussafah Industrial Area 55-C5
Union National Bank
...Al Baladia 5-C5
...Al Dhafrah 13-A1
...Al Nahyan 13-F2
...Al Rehhan 24-E6
...Al Shahama 2 44-J7
...Baniyas East 61-A8
...Markaziya East 4-K6
...Markaziya West 8-E4
...Mussafah Industrial Area 55-E3
Union Pipe Industries Bldg, Industrial City of Abu Dhabi 59-F4
Union Rebar Factory Bldg, Industrial City of Abu Dhabi 59-C3
United Arab Bank, Markaziya East 4-H5
United Bank Limited
...Al Nahyan 13-B1
...Madinat Zayed 8-M4
...Markaziya East 4-J7
...Mussafah Industrial Area 55-E2
United Color Films, Tourist Club Area 5-D1
United Emirates Agencies, Markaziya West 4-E8
United Engineering Construction, Al Nahyan 9-J8
United Metal Works Factory Bldg,
  Mussafah Industrial Area 55-A5
United Precast Concrete Bldg, Mussafah Industrial Area 59-F1
United Supplies Building Establishment,
  Mussafah Industrial Area 55-G3
United Utilities International, Al Karamah 12-J6
Universal Abu Dhabi Lab Bldg, Madinat Khalifa A 52-J4
Universal Computers, Al Manhal 12-B1
Universal Fire Fighting System Bldg, Mussafah Industrial Area 55-H7
Universal Voltes Bldg, Mussafah Industrial Area 55-F1

Universal Weather Maker Factory Bldg, Industrial
  City of Abu Dhabi 59-F3
University Bookshop, The
...Al Dhafrah 9-B6
...Al Manhal 8-D5
Ups Express, Al Karamah 13-B2
Urban Park, Markaziya West 4-C7
USA Embassy, Al Safarat 27-F3
Utmost Gulf Metal & Steel Industries Bldg, Industrial
  City of Abu Dhabi 59-F3
UTS Store, Al Baladia 5-B5
Uzbekistan Embassy, Hadabat Al Zaafaran 19-K8

V

Van Oord Middle East Bldg, Mussafah Industrial Area 54-K6
Vasco's, (Hilton Abu Dhabi), Al Khubeirah 11-D5
Vegetable Market Bldg, Al Manhal 8-B8
Vehicle Test Bldg, Al Rehhan 23-K4
Venecia Beauty Centre, Markaziya West 8-D4
Venezuela Embassy, Al Karamah 18-B2
Venito Iranian Carpets, Al Khalidiya 7-L8
Vietnam Embassy, Al Mushrif 26-L1
Village Club, The, (One To One Hotel – The Village), Al Nahyan 9-J6
VIP General Transport Bldg, Mussafah Industrial Area 55-G3
VIP Kitchen Bldg, Al Bateen 16-H3
Vision Hotel Apartment, Tourist Club Area 2-D7
Vision Printing Publishing, Mussafah Industrial Area 55-G7
Vision Private School, Al Mushrif 23-D6
Vision Steel Industrial Factory Bldg, Industrial
  City of Abu Dhabi 59-F3
Vision Twin Tower
...1 Bldg, Al Baladia 5-B7
...2 Bldg, Al Baladia 5-B7
Volcano Fountain, Markaziya East 4-G3
Volvo Famco Al-Futtain Auto & Machinery Company
  Bldg, Mussafah Industrial Area 55-B6

W

Wahda Mall Bldg, Al
...Al Nahyan 13-A1
...The Noodle House 13-B1
Wahda Residential Complex, Al, Al Nahyan 13-C2
Wahda Stadium (Sports Cultural Club) Bldg, Al, Al Nahyan 13-C1
Wahl International Food Equipment Bldg, Al,
  Mussafah Industrial Area 55-H2
Wajdan General Main Establishment Bldg, Al,
  Mussafah Industrial Area 55-H7
Wakataua Terrace, (Le Meridien Abu Dhabi), Tourist Club Area 5-F2
Waleema Restaurant, Al, Mussafah Industrial Area 54-L7
Warehouses, Mussafah Industrial Area 55-H3
Warner Brothers Theme Park, Yas Island 47-J5
Wasabi, (Al Diar Mina Hotel), Tourist Club Area 5-A1
Watch Land Abu Dhabi, Markaziya West 8-D2
Water Oasis Warehouse, Sas Al Nakhl 29-L4
Water Park, Yas Island 47-H6
Wathaba Tower Bldg, Al, Al Baladia 5-B7
Wathba Company for General Services Bldg, Al,
  Mussafah Industrial Area 55-D4
Wathba Printing Press Bldg, Al, Mussafah Industrial Area 55-A5
Wear Mart, Al Manhal 8-F4
Weatherford Bin Hamoodah Company Bldg,
  Mussafah Industrial Area 55-B2
Weatherford Middle East & North Africa Bldg,
  Mussafah Industrial Area 55-E5
Wedding Celebration Ground Bldg, Al Mushrif 18-A6
Wedding Hall Bldg, Sas Al Nakhl 29-K3
Well Gate Scaffolding Trading Company Bldg,
  Mussafah Industrial Area 55-D7
West Grandstand Bldg, Yas Island 50-J1
Western Motors, Al Khalidiya 8-A6
Western Motors Bldg, Mussafah Industrial Area 55-B2
Western Region Development Council Bldg, Al Karamah 13-B8
Westin Hotel, Madinat Khalifa A 31-B5
White Aluminium Bldg, Industrial City of Abu Dhabi 59-A1
White Aluminium Enterprises Bldg, Mussafah Industrial Area 55-A2
White by & Bird Engineering Consultancy, Al Karamah 12-L3
Wifaq Finance Company Bldg, Al, Al Karamah 13-B3
William Hare UAE Bldg, Mussafah Industrial Area 55-A6
Wintech International Bldg, Mussafah Industrial Area 55-C7
Women's Association Bldg, Al Shahama 2 44-K2
Workers Residential City (u/c), Baniyas West 60-J8
World Gym, Mohammed Bin Zayed City 59-K3
World of Furniture Bldg, Al Madina Al Riyadiya 28-C3
World of Lights, Al Baladia 5-B8
Worood Academy School, Al, Al Rehhan 24-E6

X

Xerox Emirates, Markaziya East 5-A4

Y

Yacht Club Bldg, Yas Island 50-K2
Yacht Club, Bar & Gallery, The, Al Bateen 11-E8
Yacht Club, The, (InterContinental Abu Dhabi), Al Bateen 11-D8
Yamaha Medical Centre, Markaziya East 4-K7
Yamamah Heavy Equipment & Spare Parts Bldg, Al,
  Mussafah Industrial Area 55-B5
Yanah Bldg, Al Matar 25-K7
Yas Hotel, The, Yas Island 50-K2
Yas Links Golf Course, Yas Island 47-J7
Yas Mall, Yas Island 47-K6
Yas Marina, Yas Island 50-K2
Yas Marina Circuit
...Circuit Medical Centre Bldg 50-J2

...Driving School Bldg 47-K8
...Main Grandstand Bldg 50-J1
...Marina 50-K2
...Media Centre 50-K2
...North Grandstand Bldg 47-K8
...Pit Bldg & Team Bldg 50-J2
...South Grandstand Bldg 50-K3
...Sun Tower Bldg 50-K1
...Support Pit Bldg Grandstand Bldg 50-J2
...The Yas Hotel 50-K2
...West Grandstand Bldg 50-J1
...Yacht Club Bldg 50-K2
...Yas Island 47-J8
Yasat Private School, Al, Al Dhafrah 9-A6
Yasmin Sweets & Restaurant, Madinat Zayed 9-A4
Yasmina Community, Madinat Khalifa A
...Al Yasmina School 31-M2
Yemen Embassy, Al Safarat 27-E1
Younus Foodstuff Trading, Markaziya West 8-F1
Yousef Tower Bldg, Al, Markaziya East 4-L5
Yousuf Motors Bldg, Al, Sas Al Nakhl 29-M6

Z

Zaafarana School, Al, Hadabat Al Zaafaran 19-A5
Zaatar Wa Zeit, Al Baladia 5-C6
Zadco, Markaziya East 4-L2
Zadco Housing Bldg, Al Khalidiya 11-L1
Zaeem Refreshment, Al, Al Bateen 11-M8
Zafco Trading Bldg, Mussafah Industrial Area 55-C2
Zafrana Centre Bldg, Al, Hadabat Al Zaafaran 19-E4
Zafrana Health Centre, Al, Al Zahra 24-F5
Zagros Mountains Building Materials Bldg,
  Mussafah Industrial Area 55-G2
Zahiya, Al
...Al Raha 49-L8
Zahrat Ashkhanan Supermarket, Mussafah Industrial Area 55-H7
Zahrath Al Emirates Car Accessories, Al Nahyan 9-E6
Zakat Fund Bldg, Al Mushrif 26-E1
Zakher Hotel, Markaziya East 4-L4
Zakriya Al Bakri American Auto Spare Parts Bldg,
  Mussafah Industrial Area 55-G5
Zamil Company Bldg, Industrial City of Abu Dhabi 59-C6
Zarina Lingerie (Fashion), Al Manhal 8-D6
Zayed Bay
...Environmental Research Authority Bldg 29-F4
...Mangroves (Al Qurm) 29-B2
Zayed Bin Sultan Al Nahyan Charitable & Humanitarian
  Foundation Bldg, The, Al Madina Al Riyadiya 28-B5
Zayed Centre Bldg, Al Bateen 16-K3
Zayed Higher Organization for Humanitarian Care Bldg,
  Mahawi 60-K4
Zayed Military Hospital, Al Safarat 27-D4
Zayed National Museum, Saadiyat Island 41-B5
Zayed Second Primary School, Al Bateen 12-E2
Zayed University, Al Nahyan 13-E3
Zeina, Al, Al Raha 50-L4
Zen, (Al Ain Palace Hotel), Markaziya East 4-K2
Zia Restaurant, Al Dhafrah 9-B8
Zone Waste Paper Bldg, Mussafah Industrial Area 55-D7
ZTE Corporation Abu Dhabi, Al Mushrif 23-C8
Zuama Group Trading, Al Zahra 24-E4

## Live Work Explore Guides

## Mini Guides

## Lifestyle Guides

## Magazine

    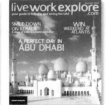

# Photography Books

# Maps

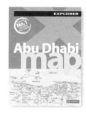       

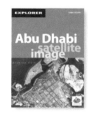    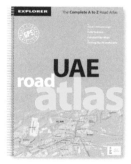  

# Mini Maps

Check out
www.**explorerpublishing**.com

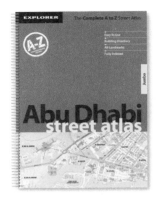

*Abu Dhabi Street Atlas Team*

**Project Manager** Alistair MacKenzie
**Cartography Manager** Zainudheen Madathil
**Cartography Team** Gayathri Cherukunnath, Noushad Madathil, Raghunath Melethil, Ramlath Kambravan, Ruksana P, Sameera Moorkath, Sudheer Mekkatu, Sunita Lakhiani
**Designers** Jayde Fernandes, Mansoor Ahmed, Shawn Zuzarte
**Sales** Pouneh Hafizi
**Digital Solutions Manager** Derrick Pereira

## Publishing
**Founder & CEO** Alistair MacKenzie
**Associate Publisher** Claire England

## Editorial
**Group Editor** Jane Roberts
**Lead Editor** Tom Jordan
**Deputy Editors** Pamela Afram, Siobhan Campbell
**Production Coordinator** Kathryn Calderon
**Senior Editorial Assistant** Mimi Stankova
**Editorial Assistant** Ingrid Cupido

## Design
**Creative Director** Pete Maloney
**Art Director** Ieyad Charaf
**Account Manager** Chris Goldstraw
**Junior Designer** Didith Hapiz
**Layout Manager** Jayde Fernandes
**Layout Designers** Mansoor Ahmed, Shawn Zuzarte
**Cartography Manager** Zainudheen Madathil
**Cartographers** Noushad Madathil, Sunita Lakhiani
**Traffic Manager** Maricar Ong
**Traffic Coordinator** Amapola Castillo

## Photography
**Photography Manager** Pamela Grist
**Photographer** Victor Romero
**Image Editor** Henry Hilos

## Sales & Marketing
**Group Media Sales Manager** Peter Saxby
**Media Sales Area Managers** Laura Zuffa, Pouneh Hafizi
**Marketing & PR Manager** Annabel Clough
**Marketing & PR Assistant** Shedan Ebona
**Group Retail Sales Manager** Ivan Rodrigues
**Retail Sales Area Manager** Mathew Samuel
**Senior Retail Sales Merchandisers** Ahmed Mainodin, Firos Khan
**Retail Sales Merchandisers** Johny Mathew, Shan Kumar
**Retail Sales Coordinator** Michelle Mascarenhas
**Retail Sales Drivers** Shabsir Madathil, Najumudeen K.I.
**Warehouse Assistant** Mohamed Riyas

## Finance & Administration
**Administration Manager** Shyrell Tamayo
**Accountant** Cherry Enriquez
**Accounts Assistants** Soumyah Rajesh, Sunil Suvarna
**Front Office Administrator** Janette Tamayo
**Public Relations Officer** Rafi Jamal
**Office Assistant** Shafeer Ahamed

## IT & Digital Solutions
**Digital Solutions Manager** Derrick Pereira
**Senior IT Administrator** R. Ajay
**Web Developer** Anas Abdul Latheef

## Contact Us
### Reader Response
If you have any comments and suggestions, fill out our online reader response form and you could win prizes. Log on to **www.explorerpublishing.com**

### General Enquiries
We'd love to hear your thoughts and answer any questions you have about this book or any other Explorer product. Contact us at **info@explorerpublishing.com**

### Careers
If you fancy yourself as an Explorer, send your CV (stating the position you're interested in) to **jobs@explorerpublishing.com**

### Designlab & Contract Publishing
For enquiries about Explorer's Contract Publishing arm and design services contact **designlab@explorerpublishing.com**

### PR & Marketing
For PR and marketing enquries contact **marketing@explorerpublishing.com** **pr@explorerpublishing.com**

### Corporate Sales
For bulk sales and customisation options, for this book or any Explorer product, contact **sales@explorerpublishing.com**

### Advertising & Sponsorship
For advertising and sponsorship, contact **media@explorerpublishing.com**

**Explorer Publishing & Distribution**
PO Box 34275, Dubai, United Arab Emirates
www.explorerpublishing.com

**Phone:** +971 (0)4 340 8805
**Fax:** +971 (0)4 340 8806